T0320862

Central Banks into the Breach

Central Banks into the Breach

FROM TRIUMPH TO CRISIS AND
THE ROAD AHEAD

Pierre L. Siklos

OXFORD
UNIVERSITY PRESS

OXFORD
UNIVERSITY PRESS

Oxford University Press is a department of the University of Oxford. It furthers
the University's objective of excellence in research, scholarship, and education
by publishing worldwide. Oxford is a registered trade mark of Oxford University
Press in the UK and certain other countries.

Published in the United States of America by Oxford University Press
198 Madison Avenue, New York, NY 10016, United States of America.

© Oxford University Press 2017

Library of Congress Cataloging-in-Publication Data
Names: Siklos, Pierre L., 1955– author.
Title: Central banks into the breach : from triumph to crisis and the road
ahead / Pierre L. Siklos.
Description: New York : Oxford University Press, 2017.
Identifiers: LCCN 2016047402| ISBN 9780190228835 (hardback) | ISBN 9780190228842 (updf) |
ISBN 9780190228859 (epub)
Subjects: LCSH: Banks and banking, Central. | Monetary policy. |
BISAC: BUSINESS & ECONOMICS / Banks & Banking. | BUSINESS & ECONOMICS /
Economics / Macroeconomics. | BUSINESS & ECONOMICS / Economics / Comparative.
Classification: LCC HG1811 .S363 2017 | DDC 332.1/1—dc23
LC record available at https://lccn.loc.gov/2016047402

9 8 7 6 5 4 3 2 1

Printed by Sheridan Books, Inc., United States of America

To Nancy, with whom I have had the good fortune of staying young with over these many years

CONTENTS

Note: Data and other ancillary materials are posted on
http://www.pierrelsiklos.com/into_the_breach.html.

PREFACE

The Great Recession of 2008–9 was preceded by the Great Moderation, a period thought to have lasted about twenty years. Yet, almost ten years since the Global Financial Crisis, there is impatience with and worry about the state of the global economy. Over two centuries ago Thomas Jefferson, in a letter to William Smith, argued that upheaval and rebellion are desirable as a demonstration of the need to set right an order that threatens a nation's liberty: "The people cannot be all and always well-informed. The part which is wrong will be discontented in proportion to the importance of the facts they misconceive. If they remain quiet under such misconceptions, it is lethargy, the forerunner of death to the public liberty."[1] And so it seems that the financial crisis has led to a resurfacing of misconceptions, the introduction of new myths, and a feeling that rebellion is brewing over the importance and authority of the central banks and the principles of good practice in the conduct of monetary policy.

This turn of events is perhaps made worse because central bankers especially became fond of repeating to the public that they were following a rule, albeit flexibly. Of course, flexibility taken to an extreme implies that rules are not followed. It is not surprising, perhaps, that a backlash against how central banks are conducting themselves emerged and has yet to dissipate. As the financial crisis deepened in 2007 and 2008, and then again as the 2010 sovereign debt crisis in Europe took hold, central banks were no longer seen as the forward-looking institutions that set the current stance of monetary policy with an eye to their short- to medium-term forecasts.

Central bankers insisted that the usual strategy had to be interrupted, owing to having to cope with the crisis and the Great Recession that, for a time, threatened to turn into the Great Depression. But we are still given to believe by the governors and presidents of major central banks, almost a decade later, that we continue to deal with the aftermath of events that are receding into memory. As a consequence, they argue, there is a need to continue delaying some semblance of a return to normal. But the rationale and methods used to justify their continued interventions in the financial system are becoming more difficult to defend, at the same time as the central bankers, with some justification, argue that accountability for performing the tasks that have been set for them by government leaves them with little choice but to keep trying.

---

[1] Thomas Jefferson (1787), "Letter to William Smith," Paris, November 13, available from the Library of Congress, https://www.loc.gov/exhibits/jefferson/105.html.

By the time I began writing this book, research was surfacing that told us that "normal" is not what we were led to believe it was—that is, the pre-2007 years of the Great Moderation. Instead, slower economic growth and permanently lower interest rates lay ahead, at least as far into the future as can be seen. I still recall participating in a panel session at a Bank of Canada Conference in September 2004 that was devoted to the measurement and usefulness of the "natural" rate of interest. This concept conveys the degree to which monetary policy is tight or loose, and it was long thought by central bankers as something to be avoided in public discourse because of the difficulties of explaining a rather arcane concept. The consensus was that, as critically important as the concept of a "natural" interest rate is, estimates of it are subject to a sufficient amount of uncertainty so as to be very imprecise. Yet, more than a decade later, new estimates are being debated in public as if the published point estimates, in their downward trend, are sufficiently precise as to confirm that a new era of secular stagnation is under way. If that is true, then it is clear that policies of the nonmonetary kind need to be considered. However, well over a decade since that conference, the lack of precision about an unobservable variable remains so large that it is far from clear where we stand.

But the same feeling of certainty that led the central banks to congratulate themselves as the financial storm was brewing is beginning to seep into the policy debate about the inevitability of slower future economic growth. As if all of this was not enough, the notion that simple rules can be followed flexibly, leaving aside a role for the stability of the financial sector, has now been replaced by difficult questions about how to simultaneously manage inflation control and mitigate the risks of another financial crisis through macroprudential means. Trade-offs between the two objectives must be considered, not to mention the domestic and international coordination problems arising from these developments. Domestically, the central banks need to confront new or reformed governance arrangements, while at the international level, officials debate minimum standards that are acceptable to all. Decades after the politics was largely taken out of monetary policy, the situation has been reversed. Central bankers are seen, rightly or wrongly, as interfering where previously doing no harm was their credo and, worse still, implementing policies that potentially impact the income distribution, a field that has always been the province of government policies.

This book concerns the positions taken by the central banks over the past decade or so, how the crisis has shaped the thinking of central bankers more generally, and what the future might hold for the place monetary authorities occupy as one of the institutions responsible for economic stabilization. All analyses of central banks and monetary policy require a retrospective view, but one that is, to be hoped, grounded in fact, with just enough speculation when, as is often the case, the data are contradictory or even murky. Personalities play a role, of course, especially in crisis conditions, but there are potentially so many to consider, and their fates are so intertwined with the events over which they responded to but could not control, that I instead prefer, and believe it more fruitful, to consider what the central banks as institutions have done, rather than try to second-guess the motives of the principal participants in a drama that continues to unfold. There are plenty of books on the subject of personalities, and no doubt many more to come.

My previous book on the evolution of central banking (Siklos 2002) ended on a hopeful note regarding the future ability of monetary policy to remain successful in the face of the political and economic pressures felt by the central banks. This book's conclusions are somewhat less optimistic about the future prospects for the central banks. Indeed, I hope the title hints as much.

ACKNOWLEDGMENTS

I have devoted a considerable amount of my career to studying central banks and their policies. The last time I wrote a book-length manuscript, little did I, or for that matter almost anyone else, know that the "science" of monetary policy would experience a major shock requiring a rethinking of the role of central banks and the conduct of monetary policy. Although I was careful enough, in 2002, to conclude that we cannot be certain that low and stable inflation was an adequate remit for any monetary authority, there were plenty of policymakers and academics who were considerably more optimistic than I was. The main portion of the title of this book derives, of course, from Shakespeare's *Henry V*, in Henry's speech that begins "Once more unto the breach, dear friends, once more" and seems to capture what central banks have been doing since 2008—namely, keep trying new ways to help their economies, with the hope that a return to some semblance of "normality" is just around the corner. Sadly, while the trying is not in doubt, the conclusion of all these efforts is very much in question.

I certainly did not intend to revisit the evolution of central banks or their policy strategies because we had reached the end of a history of sorts; indeed, half a decade after the 2002 publication of *The Changing Face of Central Banking* there seemed to be too little that was new or interesting to write about. Shortly after the global financial crisis hit the world economy, Scott Parris—who was then still at Cambridge University Press but would soon move to Oxford University Press—asked me whether it might be time to return to the topic. After some prodding, and the realization that the crisis was severe enough in size and duration to warrant a rethinking of the institution of central banking, I agreed in 2014 to prepare a new manuscript on the subject. I am immensely grateful to Scott, now retired, for nudging me to write this book.

Along the way, of course, there were many others who contributed to making it possible to complete this manuscript. Wilfrid Laurier University provided me with the time to devote to research and writing. Other institutions I am variously affiliated with, or who graciously allowed me to spend time with them, also helped intellectually and, occasionally, financially. They include the Centre for International Governance Innovation (CIGI), the many central banks around the world I visited over the past several years, the Bank for International Settlements (BIS), the C.D. Howe Institute, and the Hoover Institution, whose support through a W. Glen Campbell and Rita Ricardo Campbell National Fellowship is gratefully acknowledged.

Perhaps the most gratifying of all was the generosity of many of my colleagues who provided me with their comments on individual chapters. While I cannot claim to have dealt with all the criticisms I received, I want to assure all of the individuals mentioned below that I took every comment, minor or major, seriously. I know that the end product is much better for the comments received, and I only hope that I have been able to meet any disagreement at least half way. I would like to thank István Ábel, David Archer, Michael Bordo, Richard Burdekin, Menzie Chinn, Alex Cukierman, Stan DuPlessis, Michael Ehrmann, Barry Eichengreen, Andrew Filardo, Pierre Fortin, Andreas Freytag, Alicia Garia Herrero, Hans Genberg, Charles Goodhart, Eduard Hochreiter, Paul Jenkins, Evžen Kočenda, David Laidler, David Mayes, Donato Masciandaro, Rohinton Medhora, Matthias Neuenkirch, Michael Parkin, Monique Reid, Bill Robson, John Taylor, Dan Thornton, Sir Paul Tucker, Geoffrey Wood, and James Yetman.

David Pervin, Senior Editor at Oxford University Press; Emily Mackenzie, Assistant Editor; and David McBride, Editor-in-Chief, took over from Scott Parris and the transition was smooth and uneventful. I am also grateful to them.

Finally, and most important, I am grateful to my wife of 33 years and counting, Nancy. The dedication reflects the great good fortune of being able to grow older together. Since retiring she at least has been able to accompany me on many overseas trips while I was preparing the background research for the manuscript. This made travel far more enjoyable than otherwise. Although my children are grown and are beginning careers of their own, they too, on a few occasions, traveled with me. Needless to say, this also greatly enhanced my time on the road.

LIST OF ABBREVIATIONS

AUD	Australian dollar
BIS	Bank for International Settlements
BNP	Banque Nationale de Paris
BoC	Bank of Canada
BoE	Bank of England
BoJ	Bank of Japan
BRICS	Brazil-Russia-India-China-South Africa
CBOE	Chicago Board of Options Exchange
CHF	Swiss franc
CPI	Consumer price index
ECB	European Central Bank
ELB	Effective lower bound
EME	Emerging market economies
EMU	European Monetary Union/Economic and Monetary Union
EPU	Economic policy uncertainty
EU	European Union
Fed	U.S. Federal Reserve
FOMC	Federal Open Market Committee
FRFA	Fixed rate/full allotment
FSB	Financial Stability Board
G8, G7, G20, G4	Group of 8, 7, 20, 4 countries
GDP	Gross domestic product
GFC	Global Financial Crisis
IMF	International Monetary Fund
IT	Inflation targeting
JGB	Japanese government bonds
LTRO	Long-term refinancing operations
MAP	Mutual Assessment Program
MPC	Monetary policy committee
MRO	Main refinancing operation rate
NBER	National Bureau of Economic Research
NFCI	National Financial Conditions Index (Chicago Federal Reserve)
NIT	Non-inflation targeting

NZD	New Zealand dollar
OCR	Official cash rate
OECD	Organization for Economic Cooperation and Development
OMT	Outright monetary transactions
PBOC	People's Bank of China
PCE	Personal consumption expenditures
PTA	Policy target agreement
QE	Quantitative Easing
QQE	Quantitative and Qualitative Easing
RBNZ	Reserve Bank of New Zealand
RQ	Regulatory quality
S&P500	Standard and Poors 500 index
SGP	Stability and Growth Pact
SNB	Swiss National Bank
STLFSI	St. Louis Fed Financial Stress Index (FRED)
TFP	Total factor productivity
UMP	Unconventional monetary policy
USD	U.S. dollar
VA	Voice and accountability
VIX	Volatility Index
ZIRP	Zero interest rate policy
ZLB	Zero lower bound

Central Banks into the Breach

Moderation Before the Storm

The Backdrop

The term *The Great Moderation* was apparently coined in 2002 in an academic paper written by Stock and Watson.[1] The name was used to good effect two years later by Ben Bernanke, then Federal Reserve governor and chair of the Board of Governors of the U.S. Federal Reserve System (the Fed), who argued that the "[monetary] policy explanation for the Great Moderation deserves more credit than it has received in the literature" (Bernanke 2004). Nevertheless, the same 2002 study by Stock and Watson highlighted the role played by "good luck." Put simply, circumstances beyond the control of policymakers conspired to bring about years of small economic shocks that gave rise to lower inflation and real GDP growth variability. To this day, academics and policymakers debate the relative merits of the good luck versus good policies explanations for the turn of events between the mid-1980s and 2006.[2]

Less than a decade later, Fed Chair Ben Bernanke would express the view that monetary policy, especially in 2008 and 2009, had saved the U.S. economy—and by implication, the world economy—from "Great Depression 2.0" (Wessel 2009; also see Bernanke 2015a). It did not, however, prevent the Great Recession that followed the financial crisis, which began some time in 2007. Even if a second Great Depression in a hundred years was avoided, the subsequent slow economic growth, combined with low inflation, was indelibly

---

[1] The study in question was published in 2003. See Stock and Watson 2003.

[2] There is no widely accepted chronology that dates the beginning of The Great Moderation, but several studies point to 1984 as the approximate starting point. Stock and Watson were not the only ones investigating the apparent reduction in the amplitude of business cycle movements. Other well-known studies that explored the issues include Taylor 1999, McConnell and Perez-Quiros 2000, and Blanchard and Simon 2001. An early assessment of potential explanations for the emergence of The Great Moderation is found in Ahmed, Levin, and Wilson 2004, and Galí and Gambetti 2009.

linked to policymaking behavior. And central banks in particular could not avoid sharing at least part of the blame for the predicament the global economy found itself in.

In a BBC broadcast on December 29, 2014,[3] the former governor of the Bank of England (BoE), Mervyn King, would end an interview with Ben Bernanke, who left the Fed at the beginning of that year, by expressing the following sentiment: "It was great fun and fascinating to work with you during the crisis despite the fact that we were dealing with really serious problems. . . . I hope the experience was fun for you." The former Federal Open Market Committee (FOMC) chair, in reply, would temper King's enthusiasm by responding: "Well, fun would not be quite the right word."

To this day, we continue to live with the consequences of the dramatic events that came to be called the Global Financial Crisis (GFC). These include dramatic changes in the conduct of monetary policy and central banking stemming from a near breakdown of the global economy. Nor is a return to a semblance of normality in monetary policy apparent many years after the world economy hit rock-bottom in 2008. In a sense we have transitioned from an era of stability and then of crisis, fueled by an era that may be characterized as the period of the Great Deviation (Taylor 2011), at least when it comes to describing the stance of monetary policy, notably in the advanced economies. Discretion has come to replace predictable rules of behavior insofar as the conduct of monetary policy is concerned. These are some of the themes explored this book.

Coincidentally, in 2002, when economists began to take seriously the idea that business cycles had changed, my book *The Changing Face of Central Banking* was also published (Siklos 2002). At that time, I concluded that "it is always premature to declare that policy makers have found the Holy Grail in the current design of monetary policy." Little did anyone realize, myself included, how the script would be rewritten less than a decade after the new century had scarcely begun.

Indeed, the general impression was that central banks were smug, and that they had succeeded in running monetary policy smoothly in a manner that could tame, if not entirely do away with, the business cycle. In 2005, former Fed Chair Alan Greenspan, in a wide-ranging speech about the history and practice of economic policies in the United States, closed his remarks as follows: "[A]lthough the business cycle has not disappeared, flexibility has made the economy more resilient to shocks and more stable overall during the past couple of decades" (Greenspan 2005). He was by no means the only central banker to express such optimism in spite of the carefully calibrated words.

---

[3] See www.bbc.co.uk/programmes/po2g1zmb.

Not everyone, of course, was in the camp of the self-satisfied policymakers. In 2006, with little hint of the GFC still to come, William White, at the time economic adviser and head of the Monetary and Economic Department of the Bank for International Settlements (BIS), pointed out, "one senses a growing modesty in our assessment of what we really know" (White 2006). He was writing about the effects of financial globalization. Other policymakers were also apparently cognizant of the build-up of financial risks. Roger Ferguson, former vice-chair of the Board of Governors of the U.S. Federal Reserve, highlighted in early 2006 that "the outlook for real activity faces a number of significant risks, including the possibility that house prices and construction could retrench sharply and that energy prices could rise significantly further" (Ferguson 2006:3). In spite of warnings here and there, the march toward the GFC remained, as we now know, largely unopposed.

Equally important, perhaps, is that the events of the past few years have led academics to revisit the various forms that financial crises take, as well as their origins and scope. Whereas research has tended to focus on domestic sources of stress that lead to a full-blown financial crisis, there has been relatively less attention paid to the fundamental differences between local or regional crises and global financial crises. One of the complications that has emerged in investigating these crises is that the global variety can contain an element of contagion not easily reconciled with approaches seeking to associate economic fundamentals with the emergence of a subsequent crisis. As we shall see in chapter 3, a one-size-fits-all interpretation of the causes from financial crises is misleading.[4] Perhaps equally important is the reevaluation, at least in the economics profession, of whether policy coordination or cooperation is necessary, a question that had somewhat been put to rest in academic circles in the years leading up to the GFC.

On the eve of the turmoil that would culminate in the GFC, political leaders in the advanced economies were congratulating themselves on the calm state of affairs they presided over. The G8 Summit Declaration, published on June 7, 2007—a mere one month before Banque Nationale de Paris (BNP) Paribas halted redemption of some investment funds—declared that the "world economy is in good condition." Indeed, the leaders went on to highlight how "credit derivatives have contributed significantly to the efficiency of the financial system." Nevertheless, the Summit Declaration added: "the assessment of potential systematic and operational risks . . . has become more challenging." Clearly, the G8 participants recognized, arguably too late, that something was in the air. Even so, earlier that same year, on February 10, the

---

[4] Indeed, relying on a different set of explanations, Roubini and Mihm (2010: 116) make a similar point: "the contagion metaphor, so frequently involved, does not fully explain the crisis. . . . What seemed like a uniquely American ailment was in fact more widespread than anyone wanted to acknowledge."

G7 finance ministers noted that "challenges in this subprime mortgage market do not appear to pose a serious risk to the overall economy."[5]

Little did G8 leaders know or—for that matter, most of the public they represented—anticipate what lay ahead. Yet, there had been prominent expressions of concern leveled at the state of the financial sector years earlier; unfortunately, these voices were treated as doomsayers.[6] For example, in 2005, the BIS's 75th Annual Report concluded that the "financial sector faces significant macroeconomic risks." Interest rates and developments in housing prices were the main culprits, although the BIS also pointed out that "financial excesses linked to a generalized complacency toward risks" were also to blame (BIS 2005:120).[7] One can, of course, go back even further; for example, in the aftermath of the Asian Financial Crisis of 1997–98, Andrew Crockett, then general manager of the BIS, argued that "achieving financial stability is perhaps the most urgent task facing the world economy at the present time" (Crockett 1997).

The Way It Was

The arrival of the new century was accompanied by increased confidence that monetary policy followed a rule focusing on a single instrument—namely, an interest rate—driven by dual objectives of controlling inflation and ensuring the economy operates at capacity. However, in keeping with the rule—generally known as Tinbergen's Rule,[8] which matches the number of instruments with an equal number of objectives—many central banks placed relatively more weight on achieving the inflation objective. These ingredients constituted the crucial building blocks for best practice in monetary policy. Similarly, fiscal policy was ideal when it was not in conflict or at cross-purposes with monetary policy. To be sure, this is an old idea, but it is one that was frequently ignored, largely because it seemed politically expedient to do so.

---

[5] Unfortunately, dating the beginning of the GFC is, to a large extent, in the eye of the beholder. Different official sources (e.g., St. Louis Federal Reserve, New York Federal Reserve) begin and end their chronologies at different times. See www.stlouisfed.org/Financial-Crisis, www.newyorkfed.org/research/global_economy/policyresponses.html. The European Central Bank appears to have removed its crisis timeline, but the European Union's Economic and Financial Affairs has posted a chronology; see http://ec.europa.eu/economy_finance/crisis/index_en.htm.

[6] Eichengreen (2015:355) is one of several authors who reference a 2006 IMF report (IMF 2006:2) on the state of financial stability in Ireland that included the following commentary: "the financial system seems well placed to absorb the impact of a downturn in either house prices or growth more generally." Eichengreen added: "You can't make this up."

[7] There were other voices raising alarms of different kinds (e.g., see Shiller 2000; Roubini 2000), though the degree to which they put their fingers on the potential size of the shock that was to come is open to question.

[8] Named after Jan Tinbergen (1952), co-recipient of the first Nobel Prize in Economics.

The monetary policy rule, universally referred to as the Taylor Rule (Taylor 1993), was not intended as a device to be followed mechanically, or one that central bank governors and members of their policymaking committees were expected to be chained to. Instead, the rule was meant to provide guidance, especially outside central banking circles, about whether the current setting of monetary policy was consistent with "best practices." In other words, the Taylor strategy aimed at simultaneously minimizing the variability of inflation and that of real economic growth. Nevertheless, it is remarkable how, time and time again, observers of monetary policy conditions would focus on point estimates of the appropriate level for the policy rate, oblivious to the reality that mismeasurement and uncertainty rendered such precision questionable. At the very least, there ought to have been greater recognition that excessive precision in making economic predictions can be hazardous; indeed, it has never been the strong suit of economic analysis.[9] (I return, in chapter 4, to a more extensive discussion of the role of policy rules in the conduct of monetary policy.)

All these forces are partly reflected in the spread of inflation-targeting (IT) regimes of various types. Even when numerical targets were not adopted, there was worldwide consensus that placed primacy on price stability characterized by low and stable inflation.[10] Somewhat more contentious is the horizon policymakers should consider when evaluating their success at managing inflation (and inflation expectations, as we shall see).[11] In addition, there is the subtle but important distinction between indicators of inflation published by central banks or statistical agencies—called "headline inflation"—and various proxies for measures that exclude highly volatile prices, such as food and energy prices. The latter are called "core inflation" indicators. (I return briefly to the distinction later in this chapter. However, for the most part, the present study focuses on the behavior of headline inflation.[12])

---

[9] Instead, analysts and policymakers would tend to find comfort in the notion that there are always unknowable events that might throw the central bank off its Taylor Rule prediction. This is not the same thing, however, as granting that point estimates be accompanied by some recognition of a confidence interval surrounding some expected value.

[10] Inflation control and price stability are treated here as synonymous. Of course, strictly speaking, this is a simplification, since any inflation implies some drift in the price level. Whether biases in the measurement of inflation or the expectation that bygones ought to be bygones when it comes to price-level changes (to give two examples) prevent adoption of a price-level target is debatable. Nevertheless, I will follow the usual convention in this respect, but will return to the question of a price-level targeting strategy in chapter 7.

[11] This refers to the so-called transmission of monetary policy. The "long and variable lags" of around two years is often associated with Friedman 1972. Indeed, Havranek and Rusnak 2013 confirm that these lags do indeed vary widely across countries, but also that two years is about the correct horizon to consider.

[12] The distinction has a technical element to it (i.e., what to exclude, what is considered volatile), as well as a policy aspect (i.e., what the economic implications are of focusing on one indicator over another over time), that is best left for a more specialized analysis, if only because cross-country differences are likely to be substantial.

Of course, an inflation rate considered to be low in one part of the world might be deemed too high elsewhere, but there had been general agreement, at least among policymakers, that inflation rates that are too high and volatile are economically disruptive. Paralleling the consensus about the relative importance of adopting a price stability-oriented objective was the belief that central banks ought to be free from political pressures in deciding the appropriate monetary policy, though they must also be held to account for failing to meet any stated objective.

Monetary policy, in spite of the availability of greater quantities of data, remains an art. There was recognition that implementing policy rules and the attainment of low and stable inflation rates were goals to be achieved in a flexible manner. Therefore, the onus was placed on central banks to become more transparent and to communicate not only more frequently but also more clearly. Once again, this line of thought spread globally. However, as central banks emerged from the crisis, and as voices were raised about the slow and disappointing return to pre-crisis economic growth levels (if not growth in interest rates), forces were mobilizing to increase political pressure on the monetary policy authorities. Simultaneously, several of these same central banks were resorting to their old habit, supposedly long since discarded, of "surprising" the markets, or deliberately masking their intentions with opaque forms of guidance, at the same time as they were assuming even more responsibilities for economic stabilization.[13]

A Turn for the Worse

As the second decade of the twenty-first century comes nearer to a close, we still live with the fallout from the GFC. That crisis seamlessly turned into the euro crisis of 2010, whose end—if it has indeed ended as this is written—continues to be debated. Even as some central bankers, in light of the experience gained over the past several years, argue that the emphasis on price stability is not misplaced but, rather, needs reengineering, others are less sanguine about evincing too strong an attachment to low inflation lest we ignore the real economy or, perhaps more emphatically, the consequences of financial instability. As a result, unlike the first years of the new century that ushered in a globalization of sorts in the conduct of monetary policy, the years since 2007

---

[13] Certainly, fiscal policy also emerged from its passive state, but this would be short-lived. An initial return to favor active management of aggregate demand through government spending and taxes was soon overturned as worries about the prospect of low inflation, low economic growth, and rising debt levels—rightly or wrongly—dominated the policy debates soon after the worst of the GFC faded from view. In chapter 5, I again consider the influence of fiscal policy and public debt in regard to central bank policy during the last decade or so.

have given the impression of greater divisions regarding tactics and strategy in the conduct of monetary policy.

Strange as it seems, academics and policymakers in the United States had for many years previously given thought to the risks of a crisis in the aftermath of the stock market crash of 1987. This event cemented the reputation of then Fed Chair Alan Greenspan. As the following comments, from a volume edited in 1991 (Feldstein), suggest, we collectively overestimated the resilience and the ability of advanced economies to absorb economic shocks:

"[T]he financial stresses of recent years had relatively little effect of real economic activity" (Summers 1991:137). Even Minsky, the author whose name would be lent to the "Minsky moment" that financial markets apparently experienced beginning in 2007, declared: "I thought we might as well hear about the hypothesis from the horse's mouth. . . . [T]he financial instability hypothesis is addressed to this economy [i.e., the U.S.] rather than to an abstract economy" (Minsky 1991:158). He later goes on to credit the Fed for supporting financial entities that would otherwise engage in fire sales and credits this development with the result that "no generalized or long-lasting interactive process that led to a wide and deep decline of asset prices has taken place during the post-war period" (163). The Fed would be reminded of this again in 2008.

Equally telling are the remarks by former Fed Chair Paul Volcker, who would stress that: "We need to move to a stable financial system partly so that monetary policy itself can be free to act more in response to concerns about inflation and the stability of the currency instead of in defense of the financial system itself" (Volcker 1991:179).

Finally, for those who might argue that the GFC was the singular financial event since the Great Depression of 1929–1933, Paul Samuelson declared: "On every proper Richter scale, the 1987 crash rivaled that of the 1929 crash." He then warned: "Reacting and overreacting to each and every market crisis by macro policy can alter the historic pattern of GNP response to panics" (Samuelson 1991:169).

All the foregoing sentiments are worth keeping in mind when thinking about what central banks have done over the past decade.

Changes in the macroeconomy and finance since 2000 alone have been nothing short of wrenching. Yet, if the results of a survey of thirty-nine central banks, representing well over 90% of global gross domestic product (GDP), are to be believed, in some respects very little has changed in this decade (Siklos 2016a). A monetary policy that aims to deliver stable prices without actually ignoring the performance of the real economy, is still thought to be the best that a central bank can do. The difference today is that there is an almost knee-jerk acceptance of the idea that central banks also ought to concern themselves with stability of the financial system.

The difficulty begins, however, when they are asked how to define financial stability.[14] Matters become still more complicated when they are asked not only what instruments are required for the maintenance of financial system stability but also which institutions should be responsible and accountable for achieving such an objective. More often than not, policy analysts and other observers express their discomfort with the ability and efficacy of the broad range of policies labeled "macroprudential." These questions also raise the possibility that central banks have fallen into a kind of diversifier's fallacy by taking on responsibilities for which they are ill-suited or are at a competitive disadvantage relative to other existing institutions or new ones specifically designed to carry out a narrow set of objectives.[15] (The issues relevant to this matter are explored in greater detail in chapters 5 and 6.[16])

To provide background for the chapters that follow, this chapter offers a broad overview of macroeconomic and institutional developments that have a direct bearing on the conduct of monetary policy in particular and central banking more generally. As the events of the past decade or so were global in nature, it is useful to consider the record of the larger advanced economies, followed by the smaller open economies that led the way with adoption of policies geared toward inflation control. I also touch on the performance of other major regions of the globe, including emerging market economies.

It is useful to subdivide the period following 2000 into three phases. From 2000 to 2006, we see the Great Moderation reaching old age, with hints of the instabilities to come, in the bursting of the tech bubble in 2001 and the first wave of worries over possible deflation spreading beyond Japan, as well as rising asset prices.[17] By the mid-2000s, much of the world would experience the last time central banks, at least in advanced economies, would orchestrate a tightening cycle of monetary policy.

The years 2007 to 2010 are characterized by a financial crisis that originated in the United States but soon became global. Then, from 2011 to 2015, we have

---

[14] I return to this issue in the next chapter.

[15] The analogy to portfolio investment is instructive. While we are often told that diversification reduces risk, this is true only if the assets in the portfolio are largely uncorrelated. In the case of central banks, the additional responsibilities can create incentives that may well prevent one division's performing in society's best interests because doing so conflicts with another, more influential or powerful division.

[16] Also, see Lombardi and Siklos 2016.

[17] It is interesting how small was the impact of Japan's experience with failed banks and deflation in the early 1990s on policymaking elsewhere. Reactions ranged from "It can't happen here" to "How could they have allowed it to happen?" Of course, there were attempts to provide lessons for the rest of the world, however these discussions often got sidetracked, either because critics exaggerated the economic consequences of deflation (which continues to stalk Japan twenty years later) or because we overestimated our own ability to avoid Japan's policy mistakes. Like Japan, however, much of the Western industrial world began to experience an aging population, an unwillingness of governments to implement needed structural reforms, and a low inflation that often skirted with deflation.

the recovery phase as the global economy struggled to return either to normal or to a "new normal" of slow economic growth combined with continuance of ultra-loose monetary policies.

Needless to say, there is an element of arbitrariness in this subdivision of the 2000 to 2015 era. That much will soon become apparent. Nevertheless, the proposed demarcation points will be helpful in fixing ideas. Other than the difficulty of fitting in the eurozone debt crisis, which overlaps with the global recovery phase of 2011–15, these three periods represent the tectonic shifts that occurred not only in the macroeconomic environment but also in the thinking of policymakers about the role of central banks and the appropriate conduct of monetary policy.[18]

A Bird's Eye View of Global Macroeconomic Activity and Institutional Developments

To conserve space, only essential explanations are provided about the data summarized here.[19] Beyond the usual variables presented in reviews of the record of the central banks, I also offer less commonly mentioned aspects, in part to highlight the dramatic changes that have taken place in monetary policy since at least 2000.

CENTRAL BANK DEEDS AND WORDS

Perhaps unsurprisingly, considerable attention has been focused on the behavior of policy rates used by central banks around the world to guide market expectations concerning monetary policy. While most advanced economies have relied on an interest rate as the primary, if not sole, instrument of monetary policy for over a decade, the rest of the world transitioned to this form of policymaking only at around the turn of the century (e.g., Ho 2010). This development took place in conjunction with the global movement toward setting price stability as the principal goal of monetary policy. In several emerging markets, this prompted adoption of a numerical inflation objective.[20] While it is common in empirical studies that seek to evaluate the record of inflation targeting (IT) to assume that policymakers have a homogeneous view of what

---

[18] Where possible, data until 2015 are used. However, owing to data limitations when research for this book was completed (mainly in 2015), or other constraints that limited my ability to update the data, some samples end in 2014.

[19] An online appendix providing details about sources, definitions, and transformations is available; see www.pierrelsiklos.com/into_the_breach.html.

[20] The online appendix lists the countries that have adopted an inflation control objective, the adoption date, and the acceptable ranges where applicable; see www.pierrelsiklos.com/into_the_breach.html.

this kind of policy strategy entails, nothing is further from the truth. Once the observer moves beyond some concept of price stability, the manner in which the IT program is interpreted and implemented differs across countries.[21] (I return to this issue later.)

Figure 1.1a plots policy rates for the G4 economies—namely, the United States, the United Kingdom, Japan, and the eurozone since 2000. Figure 1.1b repeats the exercise for five emerging market economies that also happen to have adopted various forms of IT since 2000. In both groups of economies, the downward movement toward the zero lower bound (ZLB), generally viewed as the floor for nominal interest rates that central banks set,[22] is clearly visible. Of course, the advanced G4 economies reached the ZLB very quickly—soon after the GFC of 2008 occurred. Only the European Central Bank (ECB) was a laggard. It took a sovereign debt crisis and an economically weak eurozone, followed by a hesitant recovery, to finally push the central bank to reduce the policy rate to zero level.[23]

Turning to the IT economies in emerging markets shown in figure 1.1b, we find the story is a little more complicated. First, whereas the financial crisis clearly had an impact on the conduct of monetary policy in these economies, we also observe a reversal in the direction of policy rates soon after the crisis reached a peak in 2009 in almost every economy shown except Mexico. There are at least two major forces at play, with the globalization of finance assuming a role in the background. Several economies experienced an inflow of funds as investors reached for higher yields, since interest rates in the advanced economies became relatively less attractive (more on this later). Other economies experienced a surge in inflation, which prompted a few central banks to actually raise their policy rates. The combination of these developments also influenced the behavior of exchange rates, which appreciate in light of the inflow but depreciate in response to higher inflation rates. Regardless of the relative strengths of the respective factors at play, there are clear indications that monetary policies in the advanced economies spill over into other economies.

The foregoing developments also illustrate that something that *ought* to work in theory need not always work in practice. For example, it is commonly assumed that IT central banks allow the exchange rate to float freely. If, however, the central banks in question choose to intervene in foreign exchange markets, the ability of the exchange rate to act as a shock absorber is diminished. Nevertheless, the presumption made about the relationship between

---

[21] Also see Siklos 2008b, 2010a.

[22] That is, until some central banks introduced negative policy rates. I come back to this development in chapters 6 and 7.

[23] A great deal of attention was paid to the introduction of negative interest rates by the ECB. However, as this is written, these rates apply only to deposits at the central bank. The main refinancing operation (MRO) rate hit zero in 2016 and is usually considered to be the ECB's policy rate.

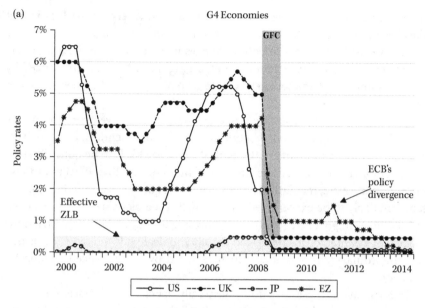

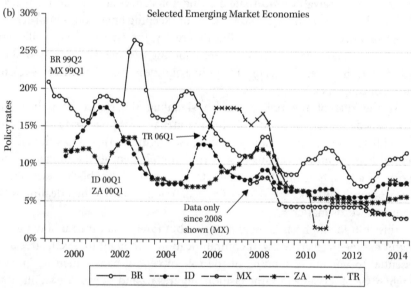

FIGURE 1.1 (a) Central Bank Policy Rates in the G4, 2000–2014

Note: The Fed funds rate is the policy rate of the Federal Reserve (U.S.); bank rate is the policy rate of the Bank of England (BoE); the rate on overnight collateral loans is used to proxy the Bank of Japan's (BoJ) policy rate; the interest rate on main refinancing operations (MRO) is used as the policy rate for the European Central Bank (ECB). Note that the mid-point of the target range of 0 to 0.25% is used since December 2008 for the Fed funds rate.
Source: IMF *International Financial Statistics* CD-ROM (February 2015).

(b) Central Bank Policy Rates in Selected Emerging Market Economies, 1999–2014

Note: For Brazil, the target SELIC (Sistema Especial de Liquidação e Custodia) rate is used; for Indonesia, the Bank Indonesia (BI) rate is used; for Mexico, the overnight rate is the one shown; for South Africa, the repo rate is employed; for Turkey, the overnight rate is plotted. The dates shown indicate when the countries in question adopted a form of inflation targeting (year and quarter). BR is Brazil, MX is Mexico, ID is Indonesia, ZA is South Africa, TR is Turkey.
Source: IMF *International Financial Statistics* CD-ROM (February 2015).

interest rates in advanced economies and those in emerging markets is that these economies operate as if they are on an equal footing. This is not the case, however. The impact of policy changes in advanced economies, notably the United States, on expectations in emerging markets is also influenced by other responses not immediately visible in plots such as the ones shown in figure 1.1a.

Financial systems across the globe are not equally developed, the policy credibility of the central banks in question is far from identical, and the institutional quality and fragility of the central banks are likely to be quite different across countries and over time. Indeed, if the response to spillovers of these kinds is inadequate, then imbalances in the global financial and economic systems are likely to be exacerbated. As we shall see, a global response has been to rely increasingly on regulatory measures or to impose additional frictions to stem or counteract the perceived inability to deal with spillover effects due to extraordinary circumstances, such as faced by the advanced economies after 2007.

Unfortunately, these reactions, generally labeled "macroprudential" in nature, can conceivably exacerbate existing imbalances and can arguably lead the world away from the age-old wisdom of "keeping one's house in order" as a best practice in policymaking. Put differently, the emergence of spillovers in policy debates risks decision makers' adopting treatments that may well be worse than the cure. (I consider the policy questions raised by these developments in chapters 5.)

As the role of the policy rate in signaling the stance of policy has diminished—clearly reinforced by the maintenance of policy rates at or near the ZLB for over six years and counting (see figure 1.1a)—so has the rise of central bank communications as a critical complement to the monetary authorities' attempts to influence markets, as well as the public's views about the economic outlook.[24] As Thaler (2013:329) points out, "When dealing with Humans, words matter."[25]

This shift in emphasis is often reported but rarely quantified in any meaningful manner. Nevertheless, if communication is thought to be effective and essential to our understanding of the role of central banks, then its impact ought to be observable in some fashion. Figures 1.2 and 1.3 provide an illustration of the U.S. case. Other examples will be introduced later (e.g., in chapter 4)

---

[24] The study of central bank communications has become a growth industry of sorts. There is a large literature that attempts to incorporate a role for what central banks say, not just what they do. See, for example, Blinder et al. (2008); Holmes 2014; and Schonhardt-Bailey 2013. In spite of the increased interest in the topic, there is considerable disagreement about how to quantify a role for communications alongside the other variables examined in this chapter.

[25] The "Humans" that Thaler is referring to are unlike the optimizing individuals at the center of macroeconomic models. They are, instead, rife with biases, including overconfidence.

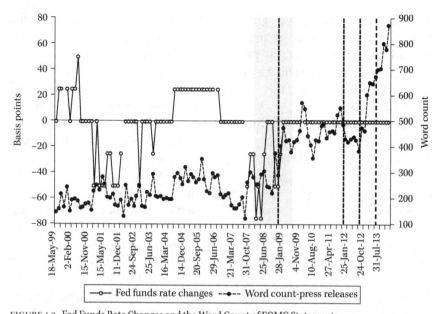

FIGURE 1.2 Fed Funds Rate Changes and the Word Count of FOMC Statements

Note: The shaded area and the vertical dashed lines highlight the period of the GFC and the implementation of unconventional monetary policies (i.e., QE1 to QE3). *Source:* Author's calculation based on statements from the Board of Governors of the Federal Reserve System (www.federalreserve.gov/monetarypolicy/fomccalendars. htm).

to marshal the potential significance of communication as one of the defining characteristics of the conduct of monetary policy in the 2000s.

Figure 1.2 plots changes in the Fed's funds rate—the policy rate of the U.S. Federal Reserve (left scale)—measured in basis point against the word count of the press release that accompanies decisions of the Fed's policymaking body, the Federal Open Market Committee (FOMC). The bottom axis indicates the dates when the FOMC meets. The shaded area highlights the recession that accompanied the financial crisis, often referred to as the Great Recession, while the vertical dashed lines indicate approximately when the Fed introduced the constellation of policies that have since been referred to as quantitative easing (QE). The QE name underscores the shift in emphasis by central banking away from changing prices (i.e., changing the policy interest rate) and toward changing quantities (viz., the composition of the central bank's balance sheet; see later discussion).

There are at least two salient features captured in figure 1.2. First, there was a long period following 2008 when the Fed funds rate remained unchanged. This was preceded, around the time of the GFC, by large reductions in the policy rate. Prior to that there were frequent, but gradual, rises and declines in the Fed funds rate. Indeed, the pattern of the Fed funds rate prior to 2008 had become one of the bones of contention concerning the performance of monetary policy during the dying days of the Great Moderation.[26] Until the GFC occurred, the length of press releases announcing FOMC decisions remained fairly stable. There was an upward movement during the period when the Fed slowly, but persistently, raised the Fed funds rate, and this mostly dissipated in the early phases of the GFC. As the financial crisis deepened, however, there was a sharp rise in the word count of the press releases, no doubt in part reflecting the unchanging Fed funds rate; but as 2013 ended, also there was a response to growing interest not only in what the Fed said but also about when the current policy was likely to change.

Markets often scrutinize every word in the FOMC's press releases. Many observers focus on parsing the Fed's announcements, hanging on certain words or expressions such as "exceptionally low" interest rates for "an extended period," "forward guidance," and "patience to normalize the stance of monetary policy," to give just a few examples. To be sure, this is understandable because key elements of the press releases are repeated over time. Nevertheless, the sentiment expressed in those press releases, or in other central bank documents, may change in subtle ways that a simple tracking of the number of words cannot grasp. Figures 1.3a and 1.3b illustrate this limited capacity.

Figure 1.3a plots the count for words in the press releases that communicate the FOMC's impression an economic recovery is under way.[27] Also shown in the figure are the National Bureau of Economic Research (NBER) recession periods and the unconventional policies introduced following the GFC (also see figure 1.2).[28] A good example is the recession of the early 2000s, which was brief and is thought to have been, at least partly, associated with the tech bubble burst and its aftermath. Shortly after the trough of the 2001 recession, the Fed's statements reflected a belief that a recovery was under way. This sentiment proved correct, as the economy entered the longest phase of economic expansion the NBER has ever recorded.[29] Indeed, there is effectively no recorded mention of words associated with (economic) recovery until the tail end of the Great Recession of 2008–9.

Notwithstanding the pros and cons of algorithms meant to quantify words and language, it is striking that the Fed began to include language indicating an incipient recovery in place. Unfortunately, this was overly optimistic (see later) and the FOMC began to backtrack, albeit briefly, in conveying the

---

[26] By historical standards these are large as well. Changes that equal or exceed 50bp are almost unheard of prior to the GFC and are generally reductions in the fed funds rate. Indeed, roughly two-thirds of the time in the United States the policy rate does not change at all. See Siklos 2002: table 4.3.

[27] The particular manner in which this sentiment is measured and evaluated is explained in chapter 6.

[28] The NBER is considered the arbiter for deciding when a recession begins and ends in the United States. Although based on observables, the precise dating of recessions and recoveries also involves judgment by members of the business cycle dating committee.

[29] NBER business cycle dates are available since the mid-nineteenth century. Expansion is defined from trough to peak in the business cycle; see www.nber.org/cycles.html.

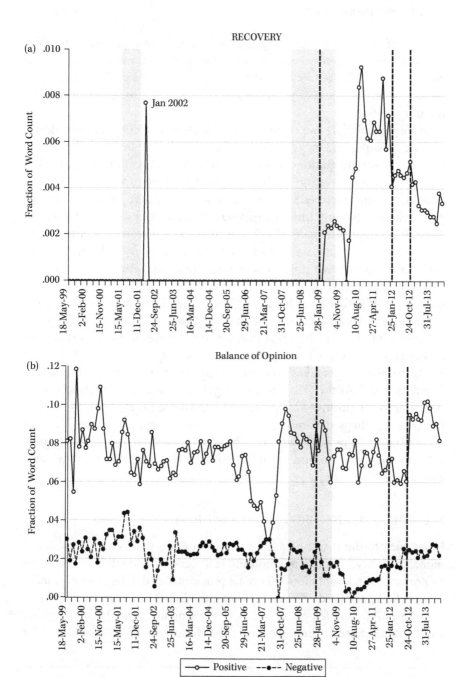

FIGURE 1.3 (a) Recovery Word Count in FOMC Statements, U.S.: 1999–2013

Note: The shaded areas are the recession periods as defined by the National Bureau of Economic Research (www. nber.org). *Source:* Author's calculation based on statements from the Board of Governors of the Federal Reserve System.

(b) Balance of Opinion in FOMC Statements

Note: See the online appendix for greater details concerning expressions deemed positive or negative. Also, see the notes to figure 1.2 for an explanation of the shaded area and the vertical dashed lines. *Source:* Author's calculation based on statements from the Board of Governors of the Federal Reserve System.

message of recovery. However, by 2010, a resurgence in sentiment about economic recovery was observed that remained persistent until the end of the period shown in figure 1.3a. Indeed, one may interpret the decline in language about recovery as a proxy for the slow but steady return to more normal economic conditions.

More generally, we can evaluate the extent to which FOMC press releases balance positive and negative sentiments about economic and financial conditions. An illustration aiming to deal with this question is provided in figure 1.3b. It is interesting to observe that, on balance over the full period, positive sentiment exceeded, by a wide margin, negative sentiment in each press release. The only time the gap was closed was in June 2007—that is, around the time the financial crisis erupted, which would soon prove far more damaging than anyone had expected at the time. Indeed, it is also worth highlighting that positive sentiment rose, paralleling Bernanke's retrospective view expressed in April 2008, that the bailout of Bear Stearns was necessary.[30] Whether he or his colleagues on the FOMC believed this action was sufficient is another matter. Soon after, positive sentiment declined and negative sentiment in the press releases rose. However, the gap remained high again, perhaps reflecting Bernanke's subsequent view that the Fed would do "whatever it takes" to extricate itself from the crisis environment it found itself in.[31] As the U.S. economy began to recover, and financial conditions improved, positive sentiment rose, but so did negative sentiment—an indication perhaps that the Fed did not want to give the impression that normalization of policy rates was at hand. Clearly, there is potentially great value in attempting to understand, if not quantify, central bank statements and not just their deeds.

MACROECONOMIC PERFORMANCE INDICATORS

I now turn to the two traditional variables used to evaluate the conduct of monetary policy—namely, inflation and real economic growth. Figures 1.4 and 1.5 provide the relevant plots. Figure 1.4 provides four different views of inflation performance (a–d). Graph (a) shows the inflation record in three large economies—the United States, the United Kingdom, and Japan—together with inflation rates in three regions of the world: advanced economies, East

---

[30] "[T]he damage caused by a default by Bear Stearns could have been severe and extremely difficult to contain. Moreover, the adverse effects would not have been confined to the financial system but would have been felt broadly in the real economy through its effects on asset values and credit availability" (Ben Bernanke, Testimony on the Economic Outlook, Joint Economic Committee of Congress, April 2008; www.federalreserve.gov/newsevents/testimony/bernanke20080402a.htm).

[31] "The Federal Reserve has done, and will continue to do, everything possible within the limits of its authority to assist in restoring our nation to financial stability," *New York Times*, February 19, 2009; www.nytimes.com/2009/02/19/business/worldbusiness/19iht-fed.1.20300659.html?_r=o).

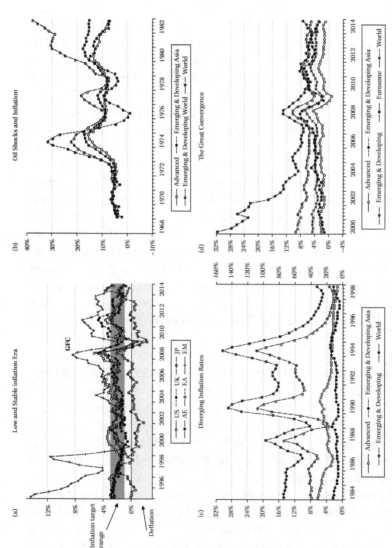

FIGURE 1.4 Evolution of Inflation Around the World, 1968–2014

(a) Low and Stable Inflation Era; (b) Oil Shocks and Inflation; (c) Diverging Inflation Rates; (d) The Great Convergence

Note: Inflation is measured as 100 times the year-over-year log change in a consumer price index. US is the United States, UK the United Kingdom, JP is Japan, AE are the advanced economies, EA are the economies of the European area, EM are emerging market economies. The definitions are ones used by the IMF (www.imf.org). *Source:* Author's calculations based on IMF *International Financial Statistics* CD-ROM (February 2015).

Asia, and emerging markets.[32] The darker shaded area represents the broad consensus that low and stable inflation, at least in advanced economies, consists of inflation rates between 1 and 3%. The lighter shaded area identifies deflation—that is, negative inflation rates.

Japan, of course, stands out because its inflation rate has been low to negative for well over a decade. At the other end of the spectrum are the emerging market economies (EME) whose inflation rates exceed, sometimes by a wide margin, the standard applied to advanced economies. Nevertheless, it is striking that, by the early 2000s, inflation rates even in EMEs did not look too far out of place when viewed against the rest of the world. Indeed, a large portion of the world experiences low and stable inflation rates that are broadly within the range considered consistent with standard definitions of price stability.

The remaining three graphs provide a visual reminder of how unusual the period since the late 1990s has been. Graphs (b) through (d) characterize the inflation process around the world as having passed through three phases during the past few decades. From the late 1960s, known as the start of the Great Inflation era (e.g., see Bordo and Orphanides 2013), rates of price change responded similarly in the face of the two oil price shocks of the 1970s, but inflation rates ran away from the rest of the world in emerging market and developing economies (figure 1.4c). The 1980s and early 1990s (figure 1.4c) saw inflation rates diverge to a much greater extent than was previously the case. This also captures differences in policy strategies to control inflation across the globe. Finally, we observe in figure 1.4d a different version of figure 1.4a, which makes clear how inflation rates in different parts of the world began to show signs of convergence.

Policy strategies remained diverse. However, the stagflation of the 1970s, and the costs of high inflation in the 1980s, convinced policymakers that lower, if not low, inflation rates, together with stability in inflation rates, represent best practice in the conduct of monetary policy. Of course, as pointed out at the beginning of the chapter, the extent to which these outcomes reflect deliberate attempts to achieve low and stable inflation rates, as opposed to a series of fortuitous and mild economic shocks outside the control of monetary (or fiscal) policy, remains unclear.

Figure 1.5 considers the history of real GDP growth. Repeating the exercise that was conducted for inflation, figure 1.5a highlights the global nature of the Great Recession of 2008–9. Certainly, the results were large and affected all parts of the globe, though some advanced economies such as the United Kingdom and Japan suffered comparatively greater loss than others, say the United States. (The role of the central banks in these developments is a topic

---

[32] Definitions for country groupings follow the International Monetary Fund's (IMF) classification as reported in its World Economic Outlook Database; see www.imf.org/external/pubs/ft/weo/2014/01/weodata/index.aspx.

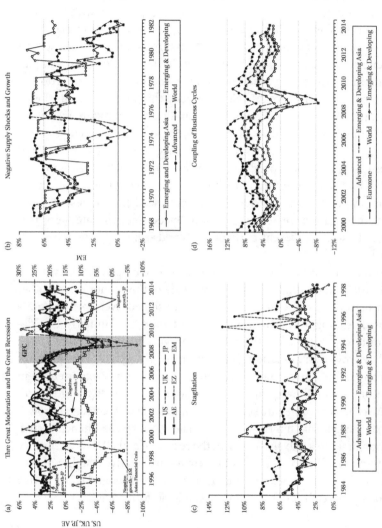

FIGURE 1.5 Coupling and Decoupling in Real GDP Growth, 1968–2014

(a) The Great Moderation and the Great Recession; (b) Negative Supply Shocks and Growth; (c) Stagflation;

(d) Coupling of Business Cycles

Note: Real GDP growth is 100 times the year-over-year log difference in real GDP. *Source:* Author's calculations based on IMF *International Financial Statistics* CD-ROM (February 2015).

I address throughout the remainder of this book.) Emerging markets, as a group, were not spared either, but the hit they took was mild compared to the earlier drop in output growth that occurred during the Asian financial crisis of 1997–98, which also spilled over into Japan. Hence, the Great Recession is perhaps more aptly named the Global Recession.

The remaining parts of figure 1.5 reveal that for real GDP, growth over the decades was an outcome reminiscent of the global experience with inflation. Hence, as seen in figure 1.5d, there was strong co-movement in economic growth across many regions of the globe. Not surprisingly, some observers began to refer to the "coupling" of business cycles to describe observed patterns in economic growth (e.g., see Kose, Otrok, and Prasad 2010; Bordo and Helbling 2010; and Siklos 2013b). Nevertheless, this interpretation glosses over the fact that there are clearly observable and persistent differences in the growth rates of emerging market and developing economies relative to the advanced and eurozone economies. In terms of the rise in *levels* of real GDP, this implies that the nonadvanced world has been effectively closing the gap in incomes with their counterparts in the advanced economies. Note, however, that as 2014 ended, the gap between the advanced and the rest of world has shrunk. These gaps have been more pronounced since the late 1960s (see figure 1.5b and 1.5c), as different parts of the world seemingly operate at different speeds.

The record of the 1970s is marred, of course, by two oil price shocks. These shocks, ostensibly stemming from the supply side of the economy, are rather different in nature from the financial shock that spilled over and became a demand shock leading to the Great Recession of 2008–9.[33] Similarly, the "decoupling" of business cycles in the 1980s (see figure 1.5c) took place in the context of low growth and inflation (see figure 1.4a), giving rise to the possibility of stagnation. Of course, this is a phenomenon previously experienced in advanced economies following the oil price shocks of the early to mid-1970s. Meanwhile, Asian economies are seen as entering an era of spectacular growth that was only temporarily interrupted in the late 1990s by the financial crisis. A comparison of figures 1.5b and 1.5c with the record of real GDP growth since the 2000s (figure 1.5d) also highlights the remarkable relative stability of economic growth rates over almost two decades of history. Therein lay the source of the notion of a Great Moderation in economic performance.[34]

---

[33] It should be noted that textbooks usually label the oil shocks of the 1970s as supply-side events. Of course, the inflation that resulted from these events may not have been exclusively driven by supply-side factors alone. Indeed, some (e.g., Parkin 1980) argue for a monetary explanation. The debate has not ended decades later, with other views not entirely in accord with the textbook story (e.g., Blinder and Rudd 2013).

[34] The connection between these developments and central bank policies and strategies was the focus of Siklos 2002.

THE FORWARD-LOOKING SIDE OF MONETARY POLICY

Retrospectives dealing with monetary and financial policies generally attempt to evaluate what went right or wrong. Nevertheless, a central element in the story of monetary policy since at least the mid-1990s is the increased emphasis on the forward-looking nature of policymaking. This turn of events was ushered in by adoption of inflation-targeting (IT) objectives that required central banks to commit themselves to inflation control. Indeed, as pointed out earlier, the commitment was sometimes expressed in terms of a specific numerical value or range of numerical objectives (also, see the online appendix). As a result, a central bank's reputation and credibility increasingly were linked to inflation performance.

Nevertheless, these same central banks understood that inflation performance would eventually depend on the markets' and households' expectations of inflation. This aspect of policymaking became the core of how monetary policy was delivered. As noted previously, the forward-looking nature of monetary policy placed a heavy burden on the monetary authority's ability to communicate its intentions, and when necessary, explain why outturns did not meet forecasts.[35] (This last part of the story is one I shall also return to frequently in later chapters.[36])

How was the movement portrayed to describe the conduct of monetary policy in terms of expectations in actual behavior? At this stage, only a very limited answer is provided. For example, the forward-looking nature of policy should have meant that central banks would be encouraged to release their own forecasts, as opposed to relying exclusively on market-based forecasts. With a few important exceptions, we have to wait until the mid-2000s for many central banks, even in the advanced economies, to publish their own forecasts. Moreover, even today, there are relatively few central banks that publish forecasts made by the actual policymaker or individual member of the policymaking committee. Instead, the forecasts tend to be produced by staff and based on econometric models, with the added touch of human

---

[35] "With an explicit target for inflation and the central bank accountable for achieving that target, there is a strong incentive to be as forthright as possible about any trends in the economy likely to influence inflation, the decisions policymakers may have to take to achieve the targets, the shocks that may temporarily push inflation outside the target range, and the pace at which inflation can be returned to the target" (Thiessen 2001: 78–79). Gordon Thiessen was governor of the Bank of Canada from 1994 to 2001.

[36] The increased emphasis on measures to hold central banks to account was also thought to be one way to deal with the time inconsistency problem, wherein policymakers would normally be tempted to boost the economy in an attempt to exploit the short-run trade-off between inflation and economic activity. Whether this trade-off operated as predicted in textbook descriptions is open to debate. Also debatable is whether the temptation to exploit any trade-off is unnatural to central bankers, who wish to be reappointed, as opposed to governments, which wish to remain popular and whose politicians hope to be reelected.

judgment.[37] Figure 1.6 illustrates some aspects of the forward-looking policies by plotting current calendar year and one-year-ahead private-sector forecasts.[38] And, for the time being, the forecasts examined have been produced by professional forecasters. Needless to say, other types of forecasts should also matter to a central bank. (I consider other forecasts, and their implications, in the context of a discussion that follows about forecast disagreement.)

The forecasts shown in figure 1.6 represent average inflation (a) and real GDP growth (b) across a fairly large number of forecasters.[39] There are several interesting features that carry over to the experience of many other economies, as we shall see later. In the case of inflation, current-year forecasts tend to be more volatile than one-year-ahead forecasts—a reflection of how current news is more likely to impact forecasters' very near-term outlook. Indeed, since a current calendar year and the following year's forecasts tend to follow each other, this suggests that economic shocks tend to have a temporary effect on forecasts. Given the availability of commodity and energy prices, not to mention the asset price volatility to be described later, this poses a problem for central banks that only temporarily shows up in headline inflation. Indeed, successfully communicating the distinction between headline and core inflation (see earlier definitions) remains one of the important challenges for central banks, despite the appeal of policy regimes that emphasize the importance of price stability.[40]

Next, fluctuations in inflation expectations take place within a fairly narrow range. Nevertheless, since the financial crisis, average inflation rates have tended to fluctuate around 2%, or slightly under this value. It is worth keeping in mind that the Fed adopted a 2% medium-term objective in 2012.[41]

Deflation is rarely forecast, though there was again a temporary overreaction at the height of the GFC. As we shall see, the range of inflation forecasts partly depends on institutional factors, some of which are discussed later, as well as external factors, such as the international spillover effects mentioned previously.

---

[37] One exception to the central banks' willingness to be held to account for their own forecasts is the U.S. Federal Reserve. I discuss Fed and FOMC forecasts in chapter 3.

[38] The forecasts, as shown in the figure, are a little problematic because they are fixed-event type forecasts—that is, they are an expectation covering a particular calendar year. It is often more natural to think of forecasts extending over a fixed horizon, such as a forecast for a year ahead or more. The distinction is one I return to it briefly in later chapters. For the time being, however, this complication need not detain us.

[39] These are known as consensus forecasts. The number and identity of the forecasters changes across countries and over time. Not surprisingly, there are many more available forecasts for the U.S. and advanced economies than for smaller economies.

[40] Of course, forecasts for core inflation do exist, but they are neither as frequently publicized nor as intensively studied as headline inflation forecasts. See, for example, Siklos 2017, forthcoming.

[41] The objective was set in terms of the index of personal consumption expenditures (PCE), which differs from the consumer price index (CPI) portrayed in the figure; see www.federalreserve.gov/newsevents/press/monetary/20120125c.htm. The differences are not especially critical for the arguments that will follow. Moreover, for a cross-country study of the kind done here, headline CPI data are more likely to be comparable across economies.

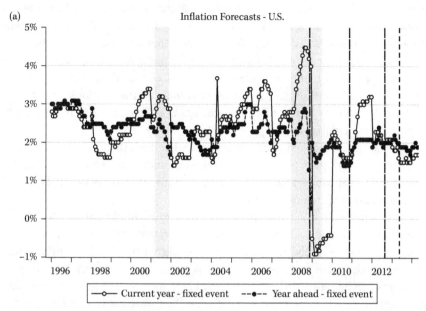

(a) Inflation Forecasts - U.S.

Current year - fixed event   Year ahead - fixed event

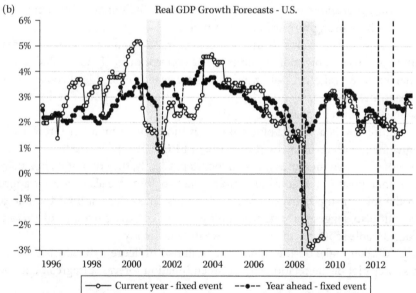

(b) Real GDP Growth Forecasts - U.S.

Current year - fixed event   Year ahead - fixed event

FIGURE 1.6   Private-Sector Inflation and Real GDP Growth Forecasts, 1996–2014

(a) U.S. Inflation Forecasts

(b) U.S. Real GDP Growth Forecasts

Note: Average of *Consensus Forecasts*, fixed horizon variety. *Source:* Consensus Economics.

The stability of inflation expectations is not necessarily replicated around the world. This gives rise to an element in the story of central banking over the past decade that has received relatively less attention, but may well represent a critical aspect of their search to earn and retain credibility—that is, the extent to which forecasters disagree. Indeed, the risk that forecasters might become lethargic or inattentive, and broadly accept the outlook of the central banks is a risk, especially when a large economic shock comes along. Otherwise, the response of expectations to current news events and the relationship between this year's and next year's inflation forecasts is a phenomenon that is largely replicated on a global scale.[42]

Several of the stylized facts described earlier for inflation forecasts carry over to real GDP growth forecasts. However, other than possibly during the era of the Great Moderation, there is no obvious trade-off between expected inflation and expected output growth.

At this juncture it is worth pausing briefly to highlight another feature of the macroeconomic and financial environment that continues to preoccupy policymakers— namely, economic policy uncertainty (EPU).[43] While it may be convenient to conflate, say, forecast disagreement with uncertainty, the two concepts can be rather different. *Disagreement*, in its purest form, reflects different interpretations by forecasters of what the future holds based on what is known. *Uncertainty*, in contrast, is a response to the unknown element once policies have been proposed or put into place.

In view of the events of the past few years, it comes as no surprise that there is considerably more interest in the concept of EPU. As we shall see in chapter 4, several other policy indicators are available for this purpose. In the meantime, figures 1.7a and 1.7b illustrate empirically the potential differences in the two concepts, based on U.S. data.

Figure 1.7a is a scatter plot linking an indicator of inflation forecast disagreement with a widely used measure of EPU.[44] The 45 degree line indicates whether the two measures move in lockstep. Clearly, they do not. While there is a small positive relationship between the two, there are also wide variations in the relationship between the two concepts. The ellipse around the line of best fit also suggests a statistical link between the two proxies, but there is considerable scope for the two to move independently.

A different take on the same issue is shown in figure 1.7b, which presents a scatter plot of the relationship between inflation forecast disagreement and

---

[42] Indeed, Morris and Shin 2002 raise the theoretical possibility that central bank forecasts effectively influence other forecasts. Hence, the transparency associated with the publication of forecasts can be counterproductive. Svensson 2006 refutes their analysis, which depends on the prior assumption that the central bank is completely credible. This need not, of course, always be the case.

[43] As the name implies, the index attempts to capture, relying on multiple news sources, references to uncertainty about the direction taken by economic policies; see Baker, Bloom, and Davis 2016.

[44] Ibid.

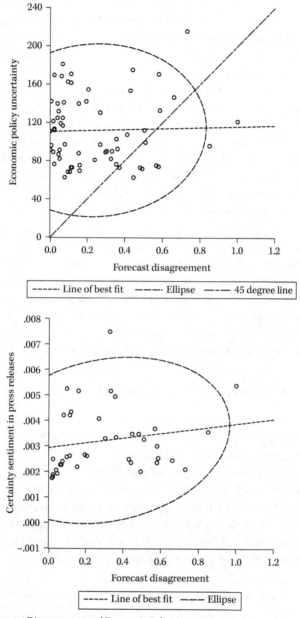

FIGURE 1.7 Forecast Disagreement and Economic Policy Uncertainty

(a) Economic Policy Uncertainty

(b) Certainty Sentiment in Press Releases

Note: The line of best fit is a linear regression on EPU. The ellipse represents a 95% confidence interval around the line of best fit. *Source:* Graph (b) is from Siklos 2017; (a) is from www.policyuncertainty.com/. *Source:* Data are from Baker, Bloom, and Davis 2016, figure 1.2, and author's calculations.

an indicator of the certainty communicated in Fed press releases.[45] We might expect a negative link between the two, since more certainty ought to translate into less disagreement, but the greater the sentiment of certainty expressed in Fed monetary policy press releases, the more forecasters seem to disagree. Note, however, there is considerable variability around the link, as seen from the ellipse around the line of best fit.

The bottom line is that forecasters might disagree because they interpret incoming economic and financial information differently. This need not be a reflection of poor monetary policy, although it does say something about the influence of central bank forecasts. In contrast, changing EPU can reflect unhappiness and unease with which policymakers, including central bankers, are perceived to deal with outstanding policy challenges. Obviously, rising levels of EPU ought to prompt policymakers to revisit their strategies.

Turning briefly to the record of real GDP growth forecasts, arguably the most interesting stylized fact is that, since the financial crisis, forecasters on the whole tend to be more optimistic about the future than before 2008. Before the Great Recession, forecasters were just as inclined to be pessimistic as be optimistic about the next calendar year's economic performance. Moreover, other than the temporary but sizable drop in real GDP growth, the mean forecast for real GDP growth during the most recent recession does not appear to show signs suggestive of secular stagnation.[46] Whether this is a reflection of wishful thinking or an outright rejection of the thesis is unclear.[47]

FINANCIAL ASSET PRICES COME INTO VIEW

Up until this point, the emphasis has been on macroeconomic developments, both past and expected, with a detour to deal with the increased emphasis on central bank communications. However, events since 2007 took place in response to a major financial crisis that would later be deemed one of the most serious in history, and one with global repercussions. Hence, it is vital to include an overview of global developments in a few asset prices. Figure 1.8a plots housing and stock market price indicators for a broad range of economies and regions of the globe. These two assets, perhaps more than any others, capture the forces that led up to and followed the financial crisis.

---

[45] This proxy is generated based on a particular algorithm that is explained in more detail in chapter 6.

[46] Secular stagnation is the revival of an idea that dates to the 1940s—namely, that an economy can be caught in a low economic growth trap (e.g., see Summers 2014; Eichengreen 2015). Escaping from this trap is made more difficult when interest rates are exceedingly low, as in the ZLB state many central banks find themselves in, when there is great emphasis on achieving financial system stability, and when governments are reluctant to resort to fiscal policy to stimulate aggregate demand. For a recent review of the debate, see Teulings and Baldwin 2014.

[47] Regrettably, a wide range of real GDP forecasts going back decades is unavailable. Some of the available forecasts for the United States only go back to the 1970s. It is doubtful whether the time series is sufficient long to adequately test for the presence of a permanent reduction in real economic growth.

Figure 1.8a shows the evolution of housing prices in selected economies around the world.[48] Rising housing prices are a feature of many emerging and advanced economies. Nevertheless, not all economies experienced the boom-and-bust pattern seen for the United States and the United Kingdom. Indeed, the "bubble" in housing prices burst long ago in Japan, which has seen housing prices fall steadily since the late 1990s. Similarly, while housing prices in the eurozone have also risen over time, the rate of increase has been modest and effectively dissipated once the financial crisis and then the eurozone's sovereign debt crisis are factored in. In any event, the eurozone example is not necessarily as informative if we examine the experience of housing prices in some of the member economies of the single-currency area (bottom of figure 1.8a). Spain is one example that largely mirrors the experiences of the United States and United Kingdom, as is Ireland (not shown), while housing prices have risen more consistently over time in France. Germany's experience is interesting since housing prices remained flat until the GFC. Since then, housing prices in Germany have risen more rapidly than in any of the other jurisdictions shown. Finally, there are the economies that, for the most part, have defied crises and threats of bursting bubbles, such as Hong Kong and Singapore.

Once the financial crisis is factored in, the picture around the globe becomes far more varied. In addition, the record of the eurozone highlights the sheer heterogeneity of member countries' experiences through the first decade and a half of the new millennium.

As yields on conventional financial assets, such as bonds and other similar instruments, declined, pulled down by central bank interventions in financial markets (notably in the G4 economies; see figure 1.1), the other financial asset that would be influenced by monetary policy actions was equities. Figure 1.8b plots developments in stock price indexes in the G4 economies. Japan, at least relatively speaking, is the oddity again, owing to the bursting of another bubble over a decade earlier. While stock indexes have displayed an upward trend since shortly after the depths of the GFC were reached, the clear standout is the United States. Stock prices in the United Kingdom recovered from their lows, but by the end of 2014, were only just above the peak reached in 2007, while equity prices in the eurozone had yet to fully recover during the period examined. Overall, the picture is a little more mixed than is sometimes portrayed.[49]

Indeed, it is worth noting that equity returns (not shown) began to drop in 2014 in much of the G4. The following year, 2015, would see more turmoil in equity markets as contagion from Chinese stock markets would further

---

[48] The data are shown using a normalized scale (rate of change deflated by the standard deviation of the series) so that the different economies' data are presented in a comparable manner.

[49] With asset returns low in response to low inflation expectations, aided by a sluggish global macroeconomic environment, households and companies are thought to gravitate to equities (and housing), pushing up their prices. See, for example, Filardo 2000; Gilchrist and Leahy 2002; Bordo and Jeanne 2002; Joyce et al. 2012; and Clarida 2012.

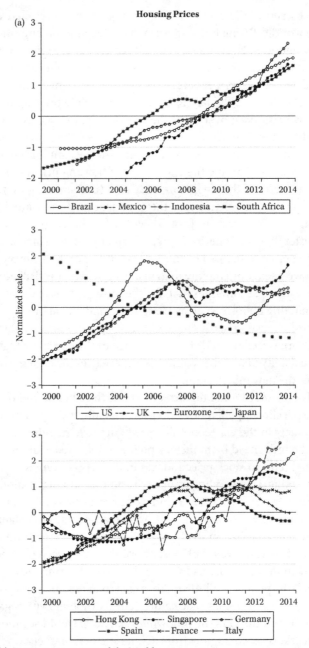

FIGURE 1.8 (a) Property Prices Around the World, 2000–2014

Note: Not all property prices are, strictly speaking, comparable across countries. See the online appendix for further details. *Source:* Bank for International Settlements.

(b) Stock Market Indices in the G4, 2000–2014

Note: Share price index levels are shown. For the US, it is the DJIA. For the UK, it is the FTSE All-Share index. For the eurozone (EZ), it is the mean of share index values for France (CAC), Germany (DAX), Italy (Milan), and Spain (Madrid). For Japan, the Tokyo Stock Exchange index is used. *Source:* IMF *International Financial Statistics* CD-ROM (February 2015).

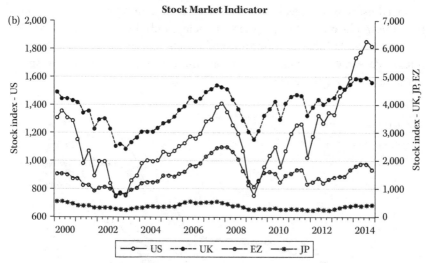

Stock Market Indicator

FIGURE 1.8 (*Continued*)

depress equity returns. These developments would begin to put to rest simplistic notions that a continuation of monetary policy easing would endlessly prop up equity markets because of investors' search for higher yields.

The foregoing merely highlights the emergence of a financial cycle to accompany the business cycles that has typically been the focus of stabilization policies.[50] Unfortunately, as we will discover in later chapters, even if there is little disagreement about its existence, there is considerably less agreement about how best to characterize or contain it. As with the parallel concept of financial stability, there is little movement toward a consensus definition. What we do know is that financial markets are subject to boom-and-bust cycles, and that financial asset price movements, especially large ones, have real economic consequences.[51] Finally, there is occasional grudging acknowledgment of an important role for credit. The latter can be illustrated in a variety of ways, but more often than not, the central bank is brought into the picture as a lender of last resort or via balance sheet operations, as we shall soon see.

GLOBAL INDICATORS

The phenomenon of globalization, financial or otherwise, suggests that the spillovers discussed previously may well have also played a role in international

---

[50] Borio (2012) and Koo (2015, 2008) are the two analysts often associated with raising the importance of the financial cycle in explaining macroeconomic outcomes.

[51] Laidler 2011 reminds us that the economist's habit of invoking stylized facts in the form of "cycles" is a longstanding one, going back at least to the nineteenth century when the notion of a trade cycle, wherein an economy goes through periods of stagnation and episodes of prosperity and excitement, was fashionable in policy circles. These descriptions are reminiscent of the boom-and-bust cycles we discuss nowadays.

financial asset price developments. There exist a number of ways to illustrate the implications, but for the time being, only two are mentioned here. Figure 1.9a plots the evolution of foreign exchange reserves in select economies. Figures 1.9b through d reveal something about the regulatory response to the rise of global financial flows.

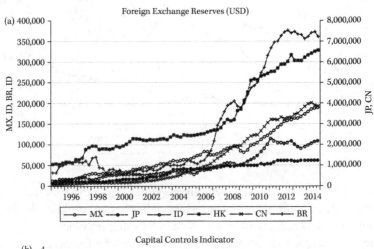

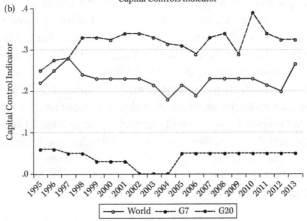

FIGURE 1.9 (a) Foreign Exchange Reserves in Selected Emerging Markets, 1995–2014

Note: Reserves are in millions of US dollars. MX is Mexico, JP is Japan, ID is Indonesia, HK is Hong Kong, CN is China, BR is Brazil. *Source:* IMF *International Financial Statistics* CD-ROM (February 2015).

(b) Capital Controls Around the World, 1995–2013

Source: Fernandez et al. 2015. The data used here is their aggregate indicator of capital controls. A lower value signifies greater capital market openness.

(c) Capital Controls in the G7, 1995–2013

Note: See notes to graph (b). CA is Canada, FR is France, DE is Germany, IT is Italy, JP is Japan, GB is the UK, and US is the USA.

(d) Capital Controls in the G20, 1995–2013

Note: See notes to graph (b). AR is Argentina, AU is Australia, IN is India, KR is Korea, RU is Russia, SA is Saudi Arabia, TR is Turkey.

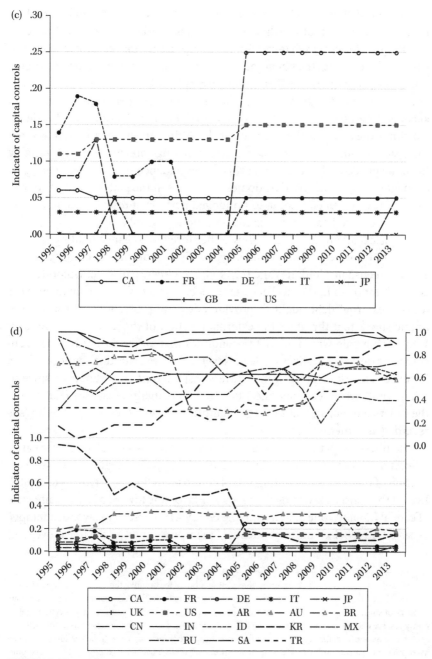

FIGURE 1.9 (*Continued*)

Figure 1.9a shows foreign exchange reserve levels, evaluated in U.S. dollars, for six economies, four of which are emerging market economies. The accumulation of foreign exchange reserves is especially noticeable in the case of China, of course, but the phenomenon is not completely restricted to emerging market economies, as is evident in the example of Hong Kong. Japan's experience with rising foreign reserves looks less impressive perhaps, but it is worth keeping in mind that the dollar amounts measured on the right-hand scale are ten times the ones on the left-hand scale. Although the extant literature has suggested a number of motives for accumulating foreign reserves,[52] ranging from the prudential to the mercantilist,[53] the evidence suggests that there is an element directly influenced by domestic policies in the patterns observed over the past several years, leading to prolonged periods of reserves accumulation that can be traced back to the conduct of monetary policy.

Empirical attempts to establish whether foreign exchange holdings are adequate, but not necessarily optimal, generally rely on the benchmark known as the Greenspan-Guidotti Rule (or G-G; see Greenspan 1999; Guidotti et al. 2004). A ratio of 1 in the level of external debt with a maturity of up to one year to total external debt ought to provide adequate protection against an economic shock that threatens the external position of the domestic economy.[54] Why such a rule would apply to economies that either do not borrow from abroad or do so modestly is unclear. Nevertheless, the rule does indicate a level of concern about insuring against adverse capital outflows. Moreover, since so many countries exceed this rule, often by a wide margin (e.g., see ECB 2008), the practice of accumulating large quantities of foreign exchange holdings is regarded as something of a puzzle.

The observed pattern of foreign currency reserve accumulation only partly reflects the choice of exchange rate and monetary policy regimes. It is also a reflection of the ability and willingness of countries to limit movements of capital. Even if the consensus during the 1990s was favorable toward a laissez-faire view of capital mobility, one fallout from the GFC was the return to favor of attempts, occasionally labeled "macroprudential," to impose limits on the free movement

---

[52] Filardo and Siklos 2016 briefly survey the existing motives for building the stock of foreign exchange reserves. That study was interested in investigating why countries in the Asia-Pacific region accumulate reserves in some cases over prolonged periods of time. First, it is found that the best protection against costly reserves accumulation is a more flexible exchange rate. Second, the necessity to accumulate reserves as a bulwark against goods price inflation is misplaced. Instead, a strong link is found between asset price movements and the likelihood of accumulating foreign exchange reserves. Hence, such policies may be costly and a consequence of divergent monetary policy strategies. That study also contains a brief survey of the extant literature. Also, see Bordo, Humpage, and Schwartz 2015 for the U.S. experience.

[53] There are different interpretations of mercantilism, but I am here referring to the policy that equates a favorable balance of trade with desirable economic outcomes.

[54] Jeanne and Rancière 2006 specify a model whose aim is to quantify the size of foreign exchange reserve holdings needed to satisfy precautionary motives. They conclude that the G-G Rule is plausible under certain circumstances and, hence, they provide a theoretical rationale for this type of rule.

of funds across borders. Nevertheless, it is difficult empirically to determine how restrictive countries are in their attempts to reduce capital mobility.[55]

An expression of how some economies responded to economic financial developments in the major advanced economies, especially the United States, has been to absorb the effects of trade surpluses, relatively higher economic growth, and interest rates through the accumulation of foreign exchange reserves.

Figures 1.9b through 1.9d provide annual data for an average overall indicator of the intensity of capital controls for various regions and select economies around the globe. The higher the value of the indicator, the greater are the restrictions on both inflows and outflows of capital. The index ranges from 0 to a maximum of 1. Other than for some G20 economies, there appears to be little permanent impact from the financial crisis. Even among the G20 economies, there is a shift back toward more liberal policies following what, in retrospect, appears to have been a knee-jerk reaction to the GFC.

Although it is not possible to assign a statistical interpretation to differences in the index values, there is a clear and persistent gulf between the G7 and the G20 economies. The latter group, of course, includes the G7, an indication that divisions remain concerning important areas of international financial and monetary policies. Nevertheless, even among the G7 economies, there is a slight reduction in capital mobility, although this takes place before the GFC. Figure 1.9b examines the changes in the intensity of capital controls among the G7 members. Other than Canada, Japan, and Italy, all other economies became less friendly toward capital mobility and, except for the United Kingdom, the changes that took place preceded the financial crisis.

Indeed, there is a broader decoupling of sorts between groups of economies and regions of the world when it comes to the imposition of capital controls. Figure 1.8d shows quite clearly that capital controls are more likely to prevail in emerging market economies than in the advanced economies, and that the movement to tighten, or not to loosen, is not directly associated with the crisis but, rather, preceded the events of 2008–9 in several cases (e.g., Argentina, Brazil, Turkey).[56]

The foregoing reactions of countries, particularly among EMEs, reflect the accusation leveled especially at the United States that it has alternatively engaged in a

---

[55] Fernandez et al. 2015 is one recent attempt to devise indicators of the intensity of capital controls. Among the many virtues of their indicators is that they attempt not only to capture limitations on inflows of capital, the traditional response, but also controls over outflows.

[56] It was only after the GFC that the IMF began to favor the use of capital controls as part of the macroprudential toolkit. While the theoretical rationale for resorting to capital controls under certain circumstances is reasonable (for example, see Ostry et al. 2012; and Korinek 2011) the same lack of comfort about the ability of macroprudential policies to deal with ongoing imbalances and policy divergences applies to these tools. Moreover, if policymakers cannot be trusted to do the fine-tuning necessary in other areas of regulation (e.g., financial supervision), then it is hardly convincing to expect

currency war and is implementing a beggar-thy-neighbor policy. What observers came to label "spillover effects" from monetary policy played a significant role in previous G20 meetings (e.g., in 2014). Put differently, the United States and, effectively all economies that introduced unconventional monetary policies (UMPs), were attempting to redistribute economic growth toward their own economies, an accusation that threatened cooperation and the cohesiveness within the G20.[57]

Needless to say, there is an inconsistency between nations adopting a rhetorical stance that amounts to defending their economic sovereignty and the fact, amplified by the GFC, that they are simultaneously helpless in the face of foreign economic shocks. A portion of the inconsistency is due to the adoption of different mechanisms to defend economic autonomy, such as capital control measures invoked by policymakers in some economies to a failure to allow the exchange rate to act as a shock absorber.

Of course, not all spillovers are benign or can be explained by differences in economic fundamentals. There are also contagion effects that transcend policies considered to be sound. Finally, even in economies that have demonstrated longstanding support of floating exchange rates, there is belated recognition that, for financial markets, a floating exchange rate can be a mixed blessing. For example, policies that keep interest rates low may be justified on economic grounds and have favorable exchange rate implications (i.e., currency depreciation)—unless, that is, there are countervailing policies to stem excessive domestic indebtedness. Hence, it is far from obvious that the combined effects will remain positive.

Ultimately, as many observers have repeated over several decades, keeping one's house in order is the best defense against having to face these dilemmas and the negative connotation given to spillover effects. (I return to this issue in the next chapter, where institutional and policy implications not given sufficient attention in the extant debate are discussed.)

CENTRAL BANK BALANCE SHEETS ENTER THE PICTURE

I complete the *tour d'horizon* of the global economy by focusing on some indicators that pertain more directly to the behavior of central banks. It was noted previously (see the discussion concerning figure 1.1) that the global fall

---

the same policymakers to successfully manage capital controls, let alone plan an exit strategy for their removal. Needless to say, the topic remains a contentious one. To be fair, there are likely instances where capital controls may well have succeeded, but any such examples are dwarfed by cases where capital control policies have failed and are difficult to introduce or remove with ease, especially in emerging market economies (e.g., Pasricha et al. 2015; Eichengreen and Rose 2014).

[57] Currency wars, or competitive devaluations, and beggar-thy-neighbor policies have a long history. See, for example, Eichengreen 1992. The latest complaint of a currency war apparently triggered by the United States was leveled in 2010. Subsequently, the U.S. dollar began to appreciate and complaints about U.S. monetary policy began to show up in the form of spillover effects. Also, see Lombardi, Siklos, and St. Amand 2017 forthcoming, and for a rebuttal of critics of U.S. monetary policy, see Bernanke 2015a.

in policy rates, together with the attainment of the ZLB in several advanced economies, has shifted the emphasis in our understanding of monetary policy from prices (i.e., interest rates) to quantities (i.e., central bank balance sheets).[58] Nowhere is this effect more visible than in the behavior of total assets on central banks' balance sheets. Figure 1.10 plots the size of central bank assets as a percentage of GDP in the G4. Arguably, these are the economies most directly implicated in the GFC; hence, the shift to the balance sheet to provide additional monetary easing is most evident in these economies. Even before the crisis, the Bank of Japan's (BoJ) balance sheet was elevated, a legacy of the first "lost decade," as successive bouts of easing of various kinds were introduced. In the years leading up to the crisis, the BoJ was already showing signs of attempting to shrink its balance sheet, only to return to a more aggressive stance once the financial crisis was under way.

The return of Shinzo Abe as prime minister, and the appointment of Haruhiko Kuroda to succeed for Masaaki Shirakawa as governor of the central

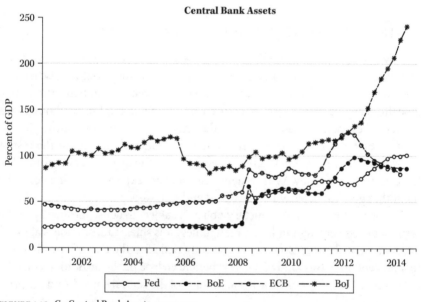

FIGURE 1.10 G4 Central Bank Assets, 2001–2014

Note: The raw data are in billions of domestic currency units (month end, not seasonally adjusted data). Data are normalized as deviations from the mean scaled by the standard deviation. *Source:* Bank for International Settlements.

---

[58] Not long after the influential work of Gurley and Shaw 1960 the profession ceased to show much interest in the degree of substitutability between inside (i.e., private debt) and outside (i.e., fiat) money. Also pertinent in the debate is McKinnon's work (1973). According to Mehrling 1997, McKinnon saw money as a form of wealth, the standard orthodoxy, while for Gurley and Shaw 1960, money is, at least partially, a form of debt. A useful summary of the debate is found in Lagos 2006.

bank in 2013, resulted in a massive expansion of the BoJ's balance sheet that easily dwarfs levels achieved by the other economies shown in the figure.

Only the ECB and the Bank of England (BoE) reversed course as early as 2012. The ECB's move would eventually be reversed in the winter of 2015 (not shown), when a eurozone version of QE was introduced. In the United Kingdom, evidence of a return to more normal economic conditions and the expiration of special programs contributed to a gentle reversal of the size of its balance sheet. What is absent from figure 1.10 are any imminent signs that balance-sheet values will return to normal any time soon.[59] Indeed, the distance between current policy rate levels in the economies shown in figure 1.10 and what passes for "normal" (see figure 1.1) is large enough that inflated balance sheets will remain for the foreseeable future. Indeed, the pre-crisis consensus of one policy instrument (namely, an interest rate) and one policy objective (a range of acceptable inflation rates) is likely one of the casualties of the events of 2008–9. What figure 1.10 does not reveal is that the twin concerns of maintaining economic stability and maintaining financial stability are driving the current monetary policy strategy, and may well be seen as incompatible.

CENTRAL BANK INDEPENDENCE AND TRANSPARENCY

Clearly, the current state of affairs facing the central banks derives partly from two other developments alluded to earlier but that may well be reversed in the not too distant future. First, the autonomy of the central banks became a globally accepted phenomenon. Figure 1.11 provides a graphic breakdown of a numerical estimate of central bank independence up to the eve of the GFC in 2008. Whether the economies are grouped into advanced, G20, or the rest of the world,[60] there is a remarkable convergence in the degree of autonomy that the central banks enjoy. With independence come expectations of a commitment that good policies will be adopted and followed.

Of course, the fear that monetary policy is subject to abuse, ordinarily in the form of excessively high inflation rates, unless it is shielded from political influence is a very old one. However, it was only well after the end of World War II that prevention of this kind of abuse experienced by a public institution could be obtained via laws that enshrine the autonomy of the central bank.[61] And the price

---

[59] Assuming a return to pre-crisis conditions balance sheet levels is deemed desirable. The "new normal" view argues against a return to pre-2008 values. As we shall see (especially in chapter 7), there are good reasons to argue both that central bank balance sheets will remain inflated for the foreseeable future and that allowing unlimited freedom to change the composition of the balance sheet is not desirable.

[60] Other combinations produced comparable results (not shown).

[61] For at least a century and a half, best practice in central banking consisted of a significant private involvement. For example, this was considered integral to Alexander Hamilton's vision of a central bank for the United States shortly after it declared independence. "To attach full confidence to an institution of this nature, it appears to be an essential ingredient in its structure that it shall be under a private not a public direction" (as quoted in Chernow 2004:349).

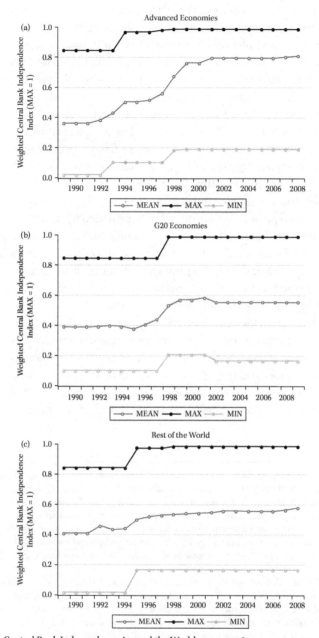

FIGURE 1.11 Central Bank Independence Around the World, 1990–2008

(a) Advanced Economies

(b) G20 Economies

(c) Rest of the World

Note: A higher value indicates a more autonomous central bank. Mean is the average value of the index for the group of economies in question; MAX is the highest value obtained; MIN is the lowest value obtained.

Source: Calculated from data in Dincer and Eichengreen 2014.

for granting unfettered control over short- to medium-term monetary policy is greater public accountability facilitated via transparency.

Perhaps the most obvious indicator of the influence of central bank autonomy is the transparency of the central banks. Just as quantitative measures of central bank autonomy can be somewhat arbitrary,[62] the process of deciding the degree of central bank transparency is based on an evaluation of observed practices.[63] Figures 1.12a to 1.12c indicate how far the central banks listed are from some ideal that could be characterized as complete transparency. This is evaluated in terms of an indicator that ranges from 0 to 15. Hence, maximum distance to complete transparency is 15, indicative of a central bank that is entirely closed to public scrutiny. Complete transparency implies a distance of 0. The indicator is a simple aggregation of fifteen characteristics that capture the nature and type of information publicly provided by central banks.

As with central bank autonomy, the distance measure considered here assumes that all the essential features equated with complete transparency have been properly captured. Yet, the provision of information is not enough. The information also has to be clear to audiences representing a wide spectrum of understanding of economic and financial issues.

Figure 1.12 subdivides the indicators by region. On balance, the monetary authorities in advanced economies are more transparent than elsewhere, especially when contrasted with central banks in selected economies outside the advanced countries and the BRICS (figures 1.12b and 1.12c).[64] Yet, even in the advanced economies, there is considerable variation in central bank transparency. Of course, it is also possible that our indicators of transparency fail to

---

[62] Moreover, there is the difficulty of making the distinction between de jure and de facto forms of independence. The former refers to a numerical indicator of central bank independence based on an economist's interpretation of the law defining and constraining central bank behavior. The latter is occasionally based on the impact that, for example, elections might have on the stance of monetary policy. De jure indicators have, on the whole, proved relatively more popular over time. The distinction matters, since the rule of law is not held in the same esteem everywhere and laws are, in any event, subject to different interpretations. See Siklos 2008a; Forder 2000; and Posen 1995 for an array of opinions on the subject.

[63] The BIS has conducted a series of surveys in recent years intended to evaluate how central banks communicate. See BIS 2009 and Filardo and Guinigundo 2008. The index of central bank transparency used here (see Siklos 2011) has been constructed on an annual basis since 1998, and was originally developed by Dincer and Eichengreen 2014, and was updated to 2013. The index aggregates fifteen attributes that describe the type and content of information released by central banks. The fifteen attributes are aggregated into five broad categories: political transparency, which measures how open the central bank is about its policy objectives; economic transparency, an indicator of the type of information used in the conduct of monetary policy; procedural transparency, which provides information about how monetary policy decisions are made; policy transparency, a measure of the content and how promptly decisions are made public by the central bank; and operational transparency, which summarizes how the central bank evaluates its own performance (see the online appendix for details).

[64] BRICS stands for Brazil, Russia, India, China, and South Africa.

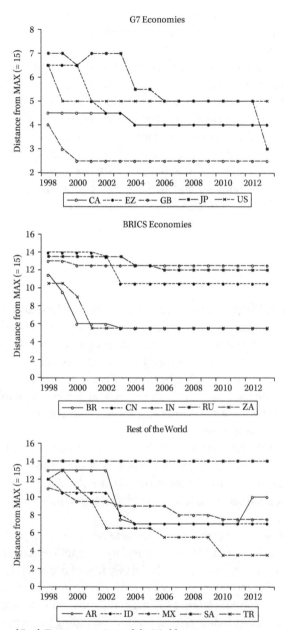

FIGURE 1.12 Central Bank Transparency Around the World, 1998–2013

(a) G7 Economies

(b) BRICS Economies

(c) Rest of the World

Note: A higher value indicates a more transparent central bank. See figure 1.8 for country labels. For the G7, the mean values for France, Germany, and Italy were used. *Source:* Siklos 2016a, 2011.

capture elements not well established before the GFC. Forward guidance and the management of expectations in a QE environment are two examples of factors difficult to incorporate into existing proxies for transparency. (I return to these examples in chapter 4.)

In any case, even more striking is how, by the early to mid-2000s, improvements in transparency stalled in most countries and regions of the world. This may be surprising if one believes that the crisis ought to have raised levels of transparency. Alternatively, the central banks may believe that greater transparency can contribute to more instability. As noted earlier, crucially, transparency need not be equated with clarity. Of course, I am assuming that transparency is properly measured. Since the crisis, the manner in which central banks "speak" has changed, and their overall communications strategy has been evolving. More generally, the degree of perceived transparency is always, to some extent, in the eye of the beholder.

Conclusions

The overview of the principal forces affecting the performance of economies and the potential role played by monetary policy and the central banks as institutions hints at the issues that require fleshing out in subsequent chapters. Nevertheless, a few broad conclusions emerge at this point. The past decade and a half in economic terms has been eventful, to say the least. Central banks appear to have stepped in to close the breach, as it were, arguably ending up doing some of the work that other institutions and governments were incapable of doing or were unwilling to do.

However, unlike the claim made by several authors (e.g., El-Arian 2016), central banks were the "only game in town" well before the GFC. It is simply that, after 2008, the failure to recognize this as not a durable strategy became obvious. As we shall see, this, too, is an old lesson that policymakers are having to learn again.

Academics, and policymakers more generally, were lulled into believing that monetary policy ought to focus primarily on stabilizing the real economy. Financial markets were assumed to be largely free of frictions. Even the analysis of the theory of monetary policy (Woodford 2003), which remains seminal to this day, has only one reference to financial markets and none to the concept of lender of last resort that is critical for understanding the origins and evolution of central banking.

If this is indeed the case, then the issues that need to be addressed include the implications of the monetary policy choices that were made, whether there were better ways of dealing with the events that transpired at the time of and following the GFC, and perhaps just as important, whether central banks will choose or be forced to step back from their outsized role in stabilization policies.[65] After all, it is doubtful that all indemnification agreements can anticipate every future state of the world.

The state of play in central banking at the beginning of the millennium appeared to suggest that there was no gain in requiring the monetary authority to meet a complex set of objectives relying on a vast array of policy instruments. Instead, a clear objective, not necessarily but preferably legislated in some fashion, with an easy-to-follow and equally clear instrument, ought to be all we can ask the central bank to be accountable for. Additionally, the public expects the fiscal and monetary authorities to operate in tandem, supporting each other when required but not to set the respective stances of their individual policies to give the impression they are in conflict with each other.

The financial crisis led to emergency measures of a dizzying variety as central banks, even if they shared part of the blame for the conditions that threatened a Great Depression 2.0, responded as they saw fit during the unfolding events.

The response of governments and central banks was nothing short of a repetition of an age-old principle that governments, when pressed, will do whatever it takes. As James Madison is said to have written over two centuries ago in one of the Federalist Papers: "No axiom is more clearly established in law or in reason than wherever the end is required, the measures are authorized; wherever a general power to do a thing is given, every particular power for doing it is included."[66] To be sure, there would be resistance to these principles from several quarters, as we shall see. However, short-term expediency would be the order of the day for years to come.

More than seven years after the global economy hit rock-bottom, there is an impression that policy thinking has moved away from the truths frequently repeated, especially by central bankers. Complexity can no longer be avoided, rules of conduct have been modified, transparency need not always be beneficial, and the meaning of central bank independence has been redefined in ways that have not been adequately debated in public.

To be sure, there continue to be prominent voices advocating a return to the pre-GFC consensus that monetary policy should have a singular focus—namely, maintaining price stability. Arguments leading to this conclusion have

---

[65] Central bank forays into wider areas deemed part of stabilization policy have led to accusations that fiscal and monetary policies are becoming intertwined. Directives and indemnification agreements are essential, as we shall see, for the two principal arms of stabilization policies to keep a comfortable distance from each other. Another implication of the narrowing of the gap between central banks and government is the worry that the former are being dragged into using monetary policy as well as, presumably, macroprudential policies, for redistributive purposes. Since interest rate and inflation changes always redistribute wealth, from borrowers to lenders and savers, or vice-versa, a certain amount of passive redistribution is always a by-product of monetary policy. See, for example, Brunnermeier and Sannikov 2012.

[66] From the Federalist Papers, no. 44A; see http://avalon.yale.edu/18th_century/fed44.asp.

sometimes been referred to as "divine coincidence."[67] Strong forces are suggestive of the lesser evil of more inflation,[68] although monetary history has not
been kind to the record of central banks in reducing inflation levels deemed
excessive without the attendant significant economic costs. Finally, policymakers' ability to rein in the financial sector's tendency to generate crisis after crisis
is questionable, though there is, for the time being, what appears to be a concerted attempt to at least try to address the problem on an international scale.

The last crisis appears to have exhausted much of the public's trust and
policymakers' capacity to respond to another GFC. We now face the dilemma
of how far back the pendulum can swing before creating conditions that are
even more hazardous than those encountered on the eve of the GFC. It remains to be seen whether, to paraphrase Lenin, "sometimes history needs a
push" becomes germane if we end up going too far in the wrong direction.
Approaching a decade of living in a crisis-like environment, we sense there are
plenty of reasons to be apprehensive, only somewhat mitigated by some signs
of hope.

The remainder of this book explores whether the foregoing impressions are
defensible. A more hopeful interpretation is that the road ahead, following a
triumph in policymaking as this century began by dealing with a global financial crisis, may well lead to a new triumph or, in the case of monetary policy,
a return to the central bank as once again subservient to an excessive politici-
zation of monetary policy, which would be a relic of an earlier era of central
banking (Siklos 2002).

---

[67] The concept is a theoretical one and it equates price stability with the stabilization of output.
However, this result only holds if fairly strict, and likely unrealistic, assumptions are correct. See, for
example, Blanchard and Galí 2007.

[68] One prominent supporter of this position is Ken Rogoff, at Harvard. See, for example, Rogoff 2008.

2 }

When Finance and the Real Economy Collide

Policymaking, Fast and Slow

Pre-crisis, when monetary policy and financial stability could be neatly separated, certainly in theory if not in practice, seemingly there was an obvious reason to do so. Economic shocks were small and apparently benign, and financial markets operated behind a veil that facilitated economic activity, but where frictions were sufficiently minor as to be largely ignored. It is not for want of trying that the possibility of experiencing the real effects of financial instability was largely suppressed. Some indications were given in chapter 1. Even trying to define the term "financial stability" was a matter that preoccupied some policymakers many years ago. Indeed, Andrew Crockett in 1997, at the Jackson Hole Symposium, began his plea to take financial stability seriously as a policy goal by defining it as follows:

> I will take financial stability to apply to both institutions and markets. In other words, stability requires (1) that the key institutions in the financial system are stable, in that there is a high degree of confidence that they can continue to meet their contractual obligations without interruption or outside assistance; and (2) that these key markets are stable, in that participants can confidently transact in them at prices that reflect fundamental forces and that do not vary substantially over short periods of time when there have been no changes in fundamentals. (Crockett 1997: 9)

Post-crisis, it is not surprising that so much effort is devoted to modeling financial markets as networks, since this is a means for understanding the precise linkages between participants in the financial sector. Nevertheless, we continue to grapple with an array of terms for what undermines financial stability. Crockett's definition is a fine one, but implicitly at least, it abstracts from the planning horizon of investors versus central banks, among other inherent biases we have come to learn can plague the financial system.

43

While some observers point to globalization or to the role of the financial cycle[1] as the primary candidate for the development of financial instability, the proximate explanation is more likely to include the speed and ease with which information spreads. What bedevils policymakers to this day is their inability to predict which event is likely to be the tipping point that renews financial crisis conditions.

Economists are fond of referring to "fundamentals" as the driving force for real and financial activity. These are the economic variables that theory and accumulated empirical evidence suggest drive changes in the indicators, such as inflation levels, real economic growth, or the state of the financial sector. Yet, one person's fundamental variable may be someone else's less critical piece of information. Sometimes this is due to disagreement about the source of the problem, which tends to be exacerbated in crisis conditions. Though it is only a few years after the events that began in 2007, one can fill a library with books on various facets of the GFC, reflecting wide opinion on the subject. Alternatively, the source of instability could be inattention, or simply complacency, about a problem widely thought to be brewing. An obvious example of the latter is the ongoing sovereign debt crisis in the eurozone, where it appears that serial disagreements have delayed the day of reckoning for dealing with Greece's inability to operate within the single currency and for following unchanged policies. (We return to the example of the eurozone in the next chapter.)

Suffice it to say that inattention is rife among market participants. It is unclear, of course, whether instability is the result of a natural tendency to underestimate the probability of a unique event or it is a belief that moral hazard is a pervasive condition that will always prompt policymakers to adopt a bail-out solution. In both cases, decisions take on the appearance of gambling. For example, if we completely dismiss the possibility of a financial crisis with global repercussions because it is thought to be inconceivable, then when such an event does materialize, it calls to mind the black swan metaphor[2]—even if we see that, after the fact, there may well have been signs pointing toward a major shock. Similarly, the moral hazard phenomenon is quite pervasive; in a world where information is typically asymmetric, there is incentive to shift risks if someone else, such as taxpayers, can bear the costs. Regardless, there is always an unavoidable conflict between the needs of monetary policy that, under normal circumstances, requires "slow"

---

[1] A difficulty in making the link is partly the result of a lack of consensus on measures of the scope of globalization and the meaning of financial stability (see later in chapter). See, inter alia, Berger et al. 2000; Obstfeld, Shambaugh, and Taylor 2005, as well as references to the financial cycle in chapter 1 this volume.

[2] The black swan metaphor was made popular by Taleb 2007, who uses this it to describe the characteristics of rare financial events.

thinking and the behavior of financial markets where, more often than not, "fast" thinking is the rule.[3]

The search for greater arbitrage opportunities, facilitated by technological innovations, allows central banks to monitor and potentially react daily, if not even more quickly, especially to events that influence the financial markets. Of course, this assumes that all the necessary data are indeed available. Unfortunately, as even central bankers have discovered (sometimes to their dismay), there continue to be important gaps in what is knowable about the functioning of financial markets. This information gap is occasionally facilitated by the institutional environment and sometimes by restrictions on the activities of the central banks.

The monetary authority in most industrialized countries is typically responsible for maintaining price stability. Monetary policy focuses on information available at infrequent intervals, usually monthly or quarterly (e.g., CPI inflation, GDP growth). Of course, some observers believe that macroeconomic data can be extracted more quickly. Indeed, there is a growing literature that seeks to exploit disaggregated information to generate new forms of aggregate data. Now-casting is one such example, intended to provide policymakers with more timely information about the state of the economy and the financial system.[4]

Alternatively, technological improvements have raised significantly the volume of available information on a global scale. As a result, there is greater scope to determine the sources of influence and changes occurring at both financial and macroeconomic levels. Analysts refer to "Big Data" as the product of this growth in available information, and they have developed new techniques to extract meaning that can illuminate the economic outlook or explain past sources of stress in the financial system. Curiously, or perhaps because the ability to exploit all available information remains at an early stage of development, little of this data has yet to filter down to a level where the monetary authorities are comfortable with it, or are able to communicate relevant findings, or can demonstrate the success of these information-gathering methodologies. Instead, a parallel effort aims to reduce the complexity created by the accumulation of vast amounts of information by seeking to reduce the potential number of explanatory variables to more manageable levels. In other words,

---

[3] The intellectual debt to Kahneman and his colleagues for some of the ideas in this chapter is obvious. See, for example, Kahneman 2011. Bernanke's (2015a) memoirs are also instructive in this regard. The former chair of the FOMC admits that focus on monetary policy and choosing the words to be uttered on behalf of the FOMC, which require patience and extensive and time-consuming deliberation, were difficult when serial crises in various parts of the financial system required quick, occasionally ad hoc solutions.

[4] Now-casting essentially seeks to forecast the current state of the economy based on a combination of large amounts of data from a variety of sources measured at different times, sampled at different frequencies, and with varying levels of accuracy. See, for example, Giannone, Reichlin, and Small 2008.

rather than attempt to distill vast amounts of data, an alternative strategy sets out to avoid being caught in the trap of not seeing the forest for the trees.

Even if, as is likely, vast amounts of disparate information can improve the accuracy of macroeconomic information, one must still ask: to what end? After all, the availability of more information means policymakers must confront both practical and intellectual constraints that have yet to influence the *strategy* of monetary policy.

What are some of the issues involved? For example, lags in the effects of monetary policy are generally believed to be long and variable, while the impact of other forms of central bank interventions in the financial markets (e.g., changing the central bank policy interest rate) potentially have a far more immediate impact. Since the GFC, the added twist is that interventions in the financial markets have real economic implications we are only now beginning to comprehend. As a result, there is a potential conflict between being overly concerned about minute-by-minute developments in financial markets and attaining a specific monetary policy objective whose horizon extends to the medium term. The risk is that monetary authorities become myopic or suffer from tunnel vision, overreacting to what appear to be random or inexplicable events from the perspective of meeting the overall objectives of monetary policy.

History offers many examples of policymakers who have displayed short-sighted behavior in one form or another, triggered by the misinterpretation or ignorance of available evidence. Milton Friedman (1992) reminded us some time ago that innocuous acts of policymakers whose full implications are not considered can have disastrous economic consequences. Several incidents of this kind were recounted in a collection of articles he called *Money Mischief*. [5] Taylor (1998) suggests that frequent monetary policy regime changes during the last century in the United States reflected a failure to accept that a set of rules consistent with "good" monetary policy is ultimately the most desirable form of policymaking. (The role and function of such rules is developed in greater detail in chapter 4.)

Other examples of myopia or tunnel vision include coordination failures throughout the 1970s among the central banks and governments in the industrial countries,[6] and the failure to anticipate the magnitude of the financial crises in both the more recent and the distant past (e.g., GAO 1996 and Fischer 1998). Of course, it should be noted that focus on a specific event need not

---

[5] Friedman was also fond of simple policy rules like the k-percent for growth in the money supply. Concerns over how much discretion policymakers, particularly in the area of monetary policy, ought to apply and remain consistent with best practice have been an academic preoccupation for some time. An early summary of the relevant issues is found in McCallum 1999, but of course, Kydland and Prescott 1977 remains the classic reference.

[6] Volcker and Gyohten 1992 is an authoritative and entertaining account.

always be a symptom of bad policymaking or shortsightedness. Hence, the U.S. Federal Reserve Board's reaction to the stock market crash of 1987 is generally regarded as having sent the right signals, even if the event was a singular one for which any long-term consequences for monetary policy were unclear (see chapter 1). The Fed's responses to the failures of Lehman Brothers and AIG in 2008, arguably, are examples that appeared to be the correct responses in theory at the time, but proved almost disastrous in practice. So, what may seem like a myopic response to some may not look that way when viewed from the broad macroeconomic perspective.[7]

It seems worthwhile, then, to debate the pros and cons of shortsightedness by the monetary authorities when events are constantly bombarding those policymakers. It is also critical to understand the inevitable collisions that occur between the needs of monetary policy and the quest for financial stability. The conflicts between these objectives can lead to an overreliance on attempts to limit all forms of behavior deemed "excessive." The resulting reactions exaggerate the appearance of financial stability through a form of financial repression, but they do so at the risk of limiting monetary policy's ability to meet its stated objectives. Unfortunately, there is as yet no comprehensive theoretical or policy solution to, let alone consensus on handling, the trade-off implicit in simultaneously conducting fast and slow policymaking. However, there is a need to better understand the strategy of monetary policy and what can be done to reform it, so that at least we can develop a way forward to mitigate future problems.

Monetary Policy Meets the Financial Stability Motive

Until the GFC, the usual narrative from the central banks was that the best way to maintain financial stability was to adopt a price stability objective. Economic historians were, of course, well aware that while price stability can assist with the maintenance of financial stability, it is no guarantee of it. However, the myth served to conveniently permit separating monetary policy from financial system stability.[8] For the time being, I will dispense with the question whether this strategy was best accomplished via a formal inflation target; even academics are careful not to make too strong a causal link between the two.

---

[7] I have essentially left out the role played by individuals or groups who deliberately exploit gaps in the regulatory and supervisory system, as well as those who are able to inveigle investors into believing that relatively high returns can be earned while simultaneously keeping risks in check. Unethical behavior is also a facet of most financial crises, as Sorkin 2009, Lewis 2010, and Morgenson and Rosner 2011, among others, remind us. Unfortunately, even as the worst of the crisis has passed, elements of bad behavior in the financial sector apparently persist. See, for example, Tenbrunsel and Thomas 2015.

[8] See, for example, Laidler 2011.

Indeed, as the crisis wore on, a debate took center stage over whether conventional monetary policy—namely, changes in central bank policy rates—was too blunt an instrument to tame financial imbalances. Central bankers were often left arguing that shaping expectations and warning of the consequences of excessive borrowing and debt ought to be sufficient to prevent monetary policy from creating crisis-like conditions. Macroprudential policies, also sometimes discussed, were not widely known, understood, or thought to be vital supplementary weapons in the monetary policy arsenal.[9]

Post-crisis, central bankers have been far more vocal about the differences between monetary policy and financial stability. Strategies for the former, it was thought, were well understood, while the latter was a work in progress. Conflict between the two was always resolved by notions that macroprudential policies would be available to deal with threats to financial system stability. Nevertheless, just as monetary policy strategies in retrospect look incomplete, this was even more pertinent in the case of macroprudential policies. The reaction in most instances, often independent of whether the central bank was believed to be at fault or not for the crisis, was to heap greater responsibilities onto the monetary authorities. As we shall see, this can be viewed as an odd response that raises serious questions about the future role of the central banks.

What else can we say about the links between monetary policy and financial stability? Since the epicenter of the global financial crisis was the United States, the focus here is naturally on developments there. To be sure, the experiences of other regions and countries are likely to have been somewhat different; however, even if what is true is largely applicable to the United States, the spillover of Fed decisions mattered greatly for the rest of the world. In any case, the arguments that follow are likely applicable also to the eurozone, Japan, and the United Kingdom. That is, what happens in the G4 cannot help but have a global impact.

The Chicago Board Options Exchange (CBOE) has its Volatility Index (VIX), which has become a popular indicator of choice for the state of financial stability. The VIX is an indicator we shall encounter repeatedly in this book, as academic research has seized on it as a gauge of "fear" in the financial markets. The VIX measures the implied volatility of S&P 500 index options (to buy or sell at some specified future price), thereby reflecting the short-term view of investors who hedge their bets against future behavior of the stock market. And since the stock market is often thought to be the harbinger of

---

[9] A brief definition was provided in the first chapter. Unlike pre-crisis monetary policy that, at the risk of some exaggeration, consisted of one instrument (interest rate) and one objective (preserving price stability), macroprudential instruments that permit the central bank, or some other agency, to intervene in financial markets via regulations, taxation, or other means of introducing frictions. We return to these issues in chapter 6.

things to come in the economy, any sudden shifts in the VIX are seen as point-ing to the risk of future changes in stock market performance.[10]

Since the crisis, other indicators have been proposed and created, but it is unclear how many additional insights are possible concerning the potential trade-offs between monetary policy and financial stability of the kind exam-ined here and incorporated into alternative measures.[11] Skepticism about the nature of any trade-off can be readily illustrated. Consider figure 2.1, which illustrates the dilemma faced by many central banks. As noted earlier, any theoretical trade-off between financial stability and monetary policy is hypo-thetical, but it is likely nonlinear or at least subject to some threshold effect. One can well imagine a range wherein the central bank is hesitant to react to changes in the link between financial stability and monetary policy for reasons already alluded to—namely, the incompatibility between the normal planning horizon of the monetary policy objective and the shorter horizon that finan-cial market participants likely maintain.

Figure 2.1 plots the VIX against either U.S. headline inflation[12] (the top two graphs) or core inflation (the bottom two graphs). The range of 2 to 3% infla-tion is considered desirable, certainly among central banks in the advanced world. It is less clear what constitutes normal financial stability conditions based on the VIX, though the range of 10 to 20 on the VIX is certainly within the "long-run" historical norm. The straight lines represent the linear regres-sion estimates to give a general idea of the potential trade-off between the two factors. Of course, there is no reason to expect any such relationship to be linear. (I briefly return to this issue later.)

For the figure, I assume that the monetary authority remains at least neutral in the square defined by "normal" conditions for the two variables.[13] "Neutral" here is interpreted as the condition whereby inflation is at an acceptable level given the prevailing stance of monetary policy (i.e., at current central bank policy rate levels) while the historical evidence would also suggest no alarm

---

[10] There is an enormous literature that finds an empirical link between macroeconomic fundamen-tals and risk; see, for example, Bloom 2009.

[11] There are plenty of other indicators, including the St. Louis Federal Reserve's Financial Stress Index (STLFSI) and the Chicago Federal Reserve's National Financial Conditions Index (NFCI). Relying on a variety of methodologies, all seek to combine the information from a large number of financial time series. When plotted together (not shown here, but see the online appendix), they behave in similar ways, particularly when market conditions are under severe stress or in crisis.

[12] U.S. policymakers favor the PCE index. Equivalent measures beyond a few economies are difficult to find, whereas there is greater comparability in CPI inflation across the globe. In any case, the results are broadly similar if we use the Fed's preferred measure.

[13] Clearly, to the extent that there are factors external to either the VIX or inflation, the monetary authority can reserve the right or deem itself to be responsible for a response even if inflation and the VIX happen to be in the neutral zone. We leave out this possibility at present, but return to such an eventuality in the final chapter.

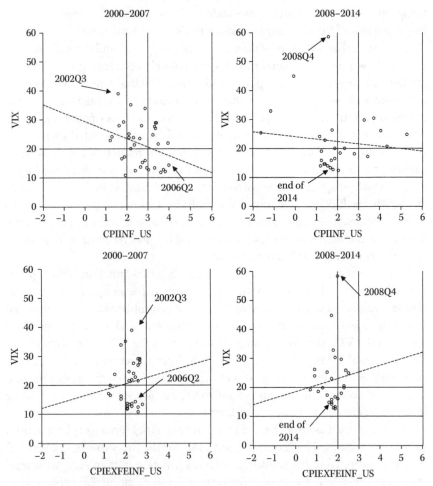

FIGURE 2.1 The VIX and Inflation, Pre- and Post-Crisis

Note: CPIINF_US is U.S. CPI inflation; CPIEXEINF_US is U.S. core inflation (excludes food and energy prices). VIX represents an indicator of the volatility of equity prices and the resulting index is derived from or implied by options on the S&P 500 index as calculated by the Chicago Board Options Exchange (CBOE).

bells sounding from the financial markets that would prompt policymakers to issue warnings of imminent financial instability.

If we think of the period from 2000 to 2007 as the high-water mark for the Great Moderation, then the VIX–headline inflation combinations hover relatively close to or well within the neutral zone, and even more so when core inflation is considered. Core inflation, after all, is the preferred measure of inflation to guide the conduct of monetary policy because it strips away volatile prices (i.e., food and energy) that should not trigger a monetary policy response, at least in the short run. Although there is the appearance of a negative relationship between the VIX and inflation, it is relatively weak. It is weaker still when the sample consists of the crisis and post-crisis samples. Moreover, there is a clear departure from the neutral zone whether inflation is measured in headline or in core terms. Outliers abound, unlike the comparatively smaller cloud of data that characterizes the pre-crisis sample. Indeed, the rise in financial stability (i.e., the drop in the VIX) from the height of the financial crisis, arguably starting in late 2008 and extending to the end of 2014, is dramatic.

Notice, however, that the negative trade-off apparently turns positive when we consider core inflation. Moreover, there is much more variation, both pre- and post-crisis, in the financial stability proxy than in inflation. Nevertheless, between the third quarter of 2002 (2002Q3)—that is, near the end of the Fed's sharp easing of monetary policy in the aftermath of the dot.com bubble burst—and the second quarter of 2006 (2002Q2), when the Fed neared the end of a tightening cycle, there was hardly any change in core inflation while headline inflation more than doubled. Financial stability actually rose during the tightening cycle. Therefore, if policy rate increases represent a blunt instrument for maintaining financial stability, that effect is not apparent in this episode of U.S. monetary history. In contrast, the continued easing of monetary policy after 2008 has brought about a dramatic rise in financial stability.

Finally, the crucial years 2007 and 2008, when monetary policy began a dramatic easing last seen only a few years before, in 2001–2, display signals coming first from the link between the VIX and inflation in neutral territory, followed by a bias, if anything, toward a need to tighten policy, as both indicators of inflation rose as did the risk of financial instability. The Fed, of course, adopted the opposite course of action and failed to openly tighten the stance of monetary policy.[14] All these stylized facts serve to complicate the narrative that links financial stability to monetary policy.

This discussion highlights the lack of confidence one should have in the kind of trade-off that has been suggested in some quarters; rather, the link may be episode- or event-specific and not a regular feature of the data.[15] Inflation ultimately reacts to changes in monetary policy. Figure 2.2, therefore, shows the Fed funds rate—the Fed's policy rate—over the same period. Beginning in December 2008, the Fed funds rate reached the zero lower bound (ZLB) as the U.S. central bank resorted to its balance sheet to further ease policy. In lieu of showing the swelling of the Fed's balance (see, however, chapter 3), the figure shows a "shadow" rate—that is, what the policy rate might have been had it turned negative once it reached the ZLB. There is a large reduction in financial

---

[14] Arguably, the reduction in long-term Treasury bonds purchases by the Fed, coupled with an appreciating U.S. dollar, is tantamount to an end of the loosening phase of monetary policy. Since the Fed, by design, kept all eyes focused on the fed funds rate, any hint of policy tightening was out of direct view.

[15] Whether central bankers believe in the existence of this trade-off is subject to subtle interpretation of their views on the subject. See, for example, Issing 2003 and Poloz 2014.

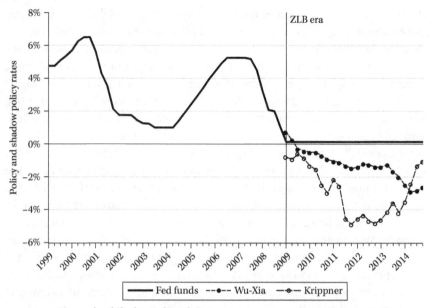

FIGURE 2.2 Observed and Shadow Fed Funds Rate, 2000–2014

Note: The thick solid line is the observed Fed funds rate; Wu-Xia is a shadow Fed funds rate proposed by Wu and Xia 2016. Krippner, from Krippner 2015, is an alternative measure of the same shadow rate. *Source:* Data can be downloaded from www.frbatlanta.org/cquer/research/shadow-rate.aspx?panel=1.

instability between the peak of the financial crisis and the end of 2014, while there is hardly any movement in either headline or core inflation rates.

In spite of the Fed's stronger emphasis on inflation performance, consistent with the profession's view that both economic and financial stability are best served by a policy geared toward ensuring low and stable inflation, its dual mandate explicitly requires a concern for real economic performance. A difficulty is that links between financial stability and real economic performance are even more opaque than those between financial stability and inflation performance. Therefore, I consider next how economic policy uncertainty (EPU), combined with a changing monetary policy stance, may be linked to real economic performance.

Figure 2.3 reveals several notable features of U.S. macroeconomic performance since the start of the new century. First, there has been a clear drop in economic growth across the two samples examined, 2000–7 and 2008–14. It is this kind of performance that has contributed to the notion that the U.S. economy and others have slipped into secular stagnation. While more policy certainty (i.e., a lower value for the indicator) appears to be associated with improved economic performance, the post-crisis link was driven almost entirely by several quarters of negative economic growth. Otherwise, there seems to be nothing that connects economic performance to EPU, at least over a relatively short period. Since the bulk of the combinations depicted in

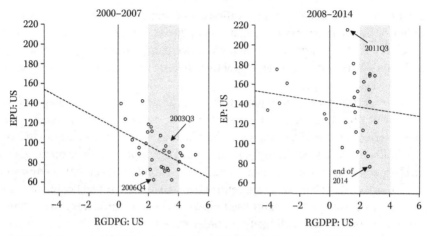

FIGURE 2.3 Economic Policy Uncertainty and Real GDP Growth, Pre- and Post-Crisis

Note: EPU: US is the measure of economic policy uncertainty, from Baker, Bloom, and Davis 2016. RGDP: US is US real GDP growth. The downward sloping lines represent lines of best fit (i.e., estimated via least squares). The shaded areas define a possible range of "normal" economic growth rates. *Source:* EPU data can be obtained from www.policyuncertainty.com/index.html.

the figure occurred well past the height of the crisis (i.e., after 2010), it does not appear to be the case that easing the monetary policy, or an unchanged Fed funds rate, has improved economic performance, even if EPU decreased dramatically. Even if a less accommodating monetary policy would likely have produced a worse outcome, it is unclear how continued policy easing could contribute to a return to economic performance of the kind experienced before the crisis.

Patience Meets the Need for Action

The availability of data at very high sampling frequencies may well lead central bankers to display a lack of understanding of or foresight about the consequences of their pronouncements and decisions; this would be evidence of myopic behavior. Alternatively, central bankers may be subject to tunnel vision, as when they focus on a particular problem, leaving aside the possible spillover effects of their actions. Both conditions are examples of shortsighted behavior that manifests itself in a number of ways.

A set of clear monetary policy objectives ought to limit the incentive of the policymaker to react too frequently to shocks whose effects are likely to be transitory, assuming the public sees it the same way and does not change its behavior. Indeed, it is sometimes forgotten that the spread of inflation targeting (IT) is explained, in part, by policymakers' acceptance that having less discretion can improve the focus of policy. Having limited options can also constrain central bank communications. Consequently, framing a monetary policy objective in terms of an inflation target—and if day-to-day news events have at most a transitory effect on price movements—ought to prevent a central bank's from becoming overly reactive, thereby reducing the chances that it will be viewed as myopic.

Alternatively, for a central bank with no explicit objective or, rather, a multiplicity of objectives, it is not obvious that *any* central bank reaction can be characterized as myopic. In this case, the cost may well be measured as a loss of credibility or trust, since both the markets and the public can develop exaggerated expectations about a monetary authority's ability to deal with a constant stream of events. Alternatively, a central bank that does not feel compelled to respond to events or to explain itself vis-à-vis specific objectives risks feeling political pressures and will likely shoulder excessive blame or become overly defensive when those expectations are not met.

It is clear from many central bank publications that policymakers' vision— and here I include the fiscal authorities also—of what constitutes "best practice" in monetary policy has narrowed considerably in the last few years, in the sense that inflation control is viewed as the mainstay of monetary policy. As we shall see, while this represents a sign of progress and must be given some credit for the world economy's ability to avoid a Great Depression 2.0, it still constitutes an incomplete monetary policy strategy.

Clearly, ignoring the potential informational content of all events may result in a central bank that is excessively shortsighted.[16] Similarly, when institutions such as the IMF or the BIS, partly as a result of their historical or perceived mandates, pressure policymakers to focus a disproportionate amount of attention on a specific aspect of economic performance, such as the current account balance, the budget deficit, or the capital adequacy of banks, this also raises the potential for tunnel vision in conducting policy.

An alternative form of tunnel vision or myopia emerges when, for example, a central bank reacts too quickly to some news events, as opposed to too often, without allowing time to pass for more sober economic analysis to confirm whether the impact on some stated policy objective is likely to be sufficiently large to breach an inflation or other policy target.[17] The ECB's decision to raise the policy rate twice during 2011 is sometimes seen in this light.

---

[16] As also claimed, for example, by Söderlind and Svensson 1997.

[17] In this connection, the analysis by Orphanides 1997 is interesting since he argues that more reasonable assumptions about data availability lead to policy recommendations quite different from ones that are obtained using final estimates. Adherence to a Taylor-type rule underpins Orphanides's analysis, whereby a central bank sets a benchmark interest rate according to the output gap and changes in the inflation rate. I consider the Taylor Rule policy prescription in greater detail in chapter 4.

There is little doubt that central banks are more forward looking than some of the empirical literature on central bank reaction functions gives them credit for. Nevertheless, it is also the case, cognizant of the inaccuracies and measurement biases inherent in several macroeconomic aggregates, that central bankers rely on a number of proxies for leading economic indicators and do not mechanically apply simple rules. Typically, central banks rely on a "portfolio" of models to generate inflation forecasts, as well as other informal information-gathering techniques in their conduct of monetary policy.[18] The reason is that myopic behavior can be less stabilizing than pure foresight.[19]

One can also conceive of myopic behavior as the outcome of a misunderstanding of, say, sources of price changes in a market economy. For example, some (e.g., Johnson and Keleher 1996) have argued that central banks should focus their attention almost exclusively on the behavior of commodity prices as a reliable guide to inflationary pressures. While central banks certainly do not ignore such information, it is doubtful that they are solely guided by movements in these prices, whose relationship with the overall objectives of monetary policy are still not well understood, since there are potentially several other, equally useful signals of future inflation performance.[20] Hence, a form of myopia emerges when the central bank chooses to restrict information it considers when facing policy decisions.

Since policy objectives, formal or not, are stated in terms of the *levels* of some aggregate, there is also the possibility that the *volatility* of time series— more apparent in data sampled at a higher frequency—may not be fully taken into account by policymakers.[21] Part of the reason might be the difficulty of distinguishing between the phenomena called "meteor showers" and those called "heat waves." A meteor shower gives the impression of events that originate from one source—namely, the domestic economy. In contrast, a heat wave implies that volatility spreads across economies. This resort to metaphors is only partly the result of incomplete knowledge about how volatility can influence economic and financial activity.

The foregoing suggests that there are good reasons for the central bank to be patient. Or, as Blinder wrote almost twenty years ago, "good policy

---

[18] Judgment is often also applied, though exactly how this is understood or translated into action is almost always unclear.

[19] Also, see Siklos 1999. Some of the ideas in this chapter are drawn from that article.

[20] In the sense that shocks arising from such markets are accommodated unless it is felt that there have permanent inflationary consequences. In IT countries, this shows up in the focus on inflation performance net of certain caveats as an indicator of policy success. These caveats, as discussed in chapter 1, include indirect taxes and food and energy price shocks.

[21] There is an implicit presumption here that volatility somehow has a negative connotation for economic performance. There is a large literature dealing with the connection between inflation levels and inflation volatility. The economic significance of that link is debatable, at least for advanced economies but less so for EME.

decisions require patience and a long time horizon" (Blinder 1999:118). But how does patience manifest itself? Is patience a sign of caution, informed by the need to carefully identify the transitory from longer-term or more permanent shocks?[22] Does patience contribute to fostering a policy of gradualism or inertia in policy decisions? There are certainly plenty of reasons to favor patience in policymaking. It has been known since at least Brainard (1967) that uncertainty ought to temper the incentive of policymakers to react to every wiggle in the data.[23] This is especially true for monetary policy, a point highlighted by Sack (1998) thirty years after Brainard's contribution. Gradualism is also behind Woodford's (2003) analysis, since it provides the central bank with a mechanism to influence longer-term yields and, hence, permits monetary policy to be potentially effective across the term structure.[24]

Part of the difficulty is that caution and patience also represent opportunities for financial markets to influence a central bank's decision making—a point made cogently by former policymakers, including Blinder (1999) and Stein (2014), based on their first-hand experience sitting on the U.S. Federal Reserve's policymaking committee. It is likely that their counterparts at other major central banks can tell similar stories. Much of the emphasis has been on how changes in policy rate *levels* can be influenced by market perceptions. This is understandable. As revealed in figure 2.4, for a selection of economies where policy rates serve as the principal instrument of monetary policy, other than during crisis periods, one is hard-pressed to find policy rate changes that depart from the 25bp (or .25%) model for a period of over sixteen years. Even for Brazil, where the macroeconomic and financial challenges are arguably greater than in the other economies shown, large policy rate changes took place only approximately 40% of the time.[25] There are other ways of

---

[22] Or, for that matter, demand-side versus supply-side shocks that require different types of policy responses. A demand shock—say, of the positive variety—is expected to be inflationary and stimulate economic activity. Hence, a tightening of monetary (or fiscal) policy is appropriate. In contrast, a positive supply-side shock (e.g., a fall in oil prices) should stimulate aggregate output and reduce inflation. Unless the central bank responds by reducing interest rates, monetary policy will be seen as being tightened. In both cases, expectations, as well as the size and persistence, of shocks are critical ingredients in the policy response. Moreover, policymakers must successfully identify one type of shock versus the other.

[23] Economic models on which this conclusion is based assume that uncertainty is multiplicative. Since the economic variables of interest are related to each other, possibly in a nonlinear fashion, multiplicative uncertainty is a plausible assumption. Otherwise, one could assume that uncertainty was additive.

[24] Still others (e.g., Rudebusch 2002) are skeptical of the gradualism argument because interest rates are not as predictable as they should be when interest rates are thought to change smoothly over time. This argument presumes, of course, that we have a clear idea of how interest rates across the term structure are related to each other.

[25] Since the central bank of Brazil meets monthly, there were over 190 meetings during the period shown in figure 2.4.

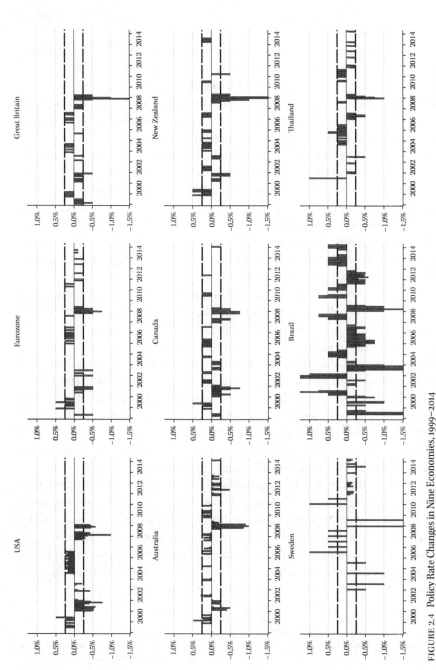

FIGURE 2.4 Policy Rate Changes in Nine Economies, 1999–2014

Note: Policy rate changes are measured in ±25bp increments. *Source:* International Monetary Fund, International Financial Statistics CD-ROM, June 2015.

quantifying gradualism, including measuring inertia based on estimates of a policy rule, such as the Taylor Rule (which I consider in chapter 4). In any event, all these approaches suggest a considerable amount of gradualism in policy rate changes.

Because of the tension between tunnel vision and myopia in policymaking, and the desirability of patience in conducting monetary policy, together with the difficulty of identifying a link between financial stability and monetary policy discussed in the previous section, one can ask whether policymakers ought to incorporate some indicator of volatility in influencing the degree to which they can afford inertia in meeting monetary policy objectives.[26] The "tapering" episode of 2013 (see later) is one illustration of how policy can influence or be affected by bond market developments. Similarly, the on-and-off sovereign debt crisis in the eurozone highlights the response and volatility of long-term government bond yields in that part of the world. Of course, there are plenty of other examples that underscore the need to consider not only level effects but also the impact of financial asset price volatility, including the series of decisions taken by central banks referred to as quantitative easing (QE) policies (which I will explore in chapter 6).

Figure 2.5 illustrates some of the challenges facing the monetary authorities in fast and slow policymaking environments. The plot, for U.S. data, shows futures prices for U.S. sovereign bonds (Treasuries) for maturities ranging from two to thirty years. The vertical lines highlight selected events during the period shown. The sensitivity of bond prices is roughly inversely related to the term of maturity, with longer-term bonds more volatile than short-term ones. The three episodes of QE in the United States, introduced once the Fed reached the ZLB, are identified, along with the taper comment in the wake of Bernanke's testimony, and speeches in May and June 2013.

Notice, however, that there were apparently several other episodes when bond price volatility surged or fell. In particular, the ECB's decision to raise the policy rate in the summer of 2011, followed by a decision the following month to enhance liquidity in the eurozone via the long-term refinancing operations (LTRO), appears to have played as much havoc, if not more, than some of the domestic actions taken by the Fed. What, then, is a central bank to do? Caught between the need for sober second thinking and pressures to respond to a fast-paced financial world, there seem to be few options other than to be selective when and/or whether or not to react to day-to-day shocks.

---

[26] A series of technical issues with Taylor Rules led Siklos and Wohar 2005 to propose that the interest-rate-setting behavior of the Fed ought also to be conditional on volatility, largely because inflation rates were originally found to have such effects. Hamilton 2010 also highlights volatility clustering and persistence in the Fed funds rate, with implications about views held concerning macroeconomic phenomena. Stein and Sunderam 2016 explicitly allow for bond market volatility to influence the Fed's desired policy rate setting behavior.

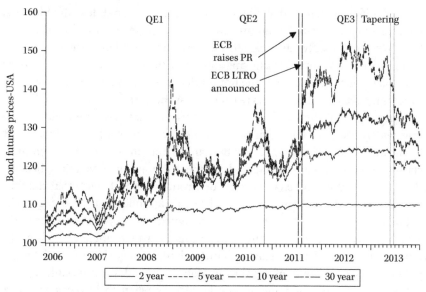

FIGURE 2.5   The Evolution of Sovereign Bond Yields, 2006–2013

Source: Datastream for bond futures; Federal Reserve Bank of St. Louis Financial Crisis timeline, www.stlouisfed.org/Financial-Crisis; and the ECB.

Yet, the crisis has taught us a few principles. One principle has to do with the overall policy strategy of the central banks. More important, central banks must be more forthcoming about the types of events that are likely to impinge on financial stability versus events that threaten monetary policy objectives. Too often the two are confused; yet, as we have seen, any trade-offs between these functions are ephemeral and poorly understood. Another is the belief that forward guidance, or some variant that shall be addressed in more detail in chapter 5, is the vehicle for helping smooth over market overreactions.[27] Since its introduction, forward guidance has lost a lot of its appeal, and rightly so. Its power and usefulness are a myth, except under particular circumstances. The reason for this is not the conditionality of any forward-guidance strategy. Most sensible individuals understand that central banks, not to mention other public officials more generally, cannot commit without taking into account as yet unknowable future economic conditions. To do so would not only be unrealistic but also be irresponsible, since such behavior flies in the face of the duty of central bankers to meet a policy objective and to explain their actions in a credible manner.

---

[27] Forward guidance is just one of a set of policies that central banks have used for years to convince the financial markets and the public of likely future changes in the stance of policy conditional on its outlook or some other metric. Markets, at least in theory, are supposed to be guided by these announcements, and the central bank is presumed to have the credibility for delivering on any threats or promises made to act in the future.

One difficulty here is that economists continue to hold dear the idea that the monetary authority has an information advantage over the financial markets. In truth, the only advantage that central bankers might have is their ability to process vast amounts information, draw the correct inferences, and set monetary policy accordingly. The notion that a central bank knows best when to act is far-fetched. It is for this reason, just as the correct policy was to launch QE1 in 2008, that the ECB's decision in 2011 to twice raise the policy rate is now widely seen as a bad decision.[28] Both resulted in volatile reactions in the financial markets. Similarly, Chair Bernanke's announcement that bond purchases would eventually be tapered off affected bond price volatility because the markets did not yet share, rightly or wrongly, the Fed's view that the time was right to reduce the amount of policy easing. Indeed, the Fed eventually delayed the start of that tapering off from September 2013 to December of the same year. Notice that, once the policy began, hardly a ripple was felt in the financial markets. Hence, rising or falling volatility per se should not to trigger policy changes or bouts of forward guidance. Instead, central banks appear better at communicating and sounding decisive when their views are more closely aligned with those of the financial markets. To be sure, there is the risk that the central banks will follow the markets. However, it is worth keeping in mind that the issue concerns financial stability, not monetary policy objectives. There continues to be plenty of scope for monetary authorities to preempt on those grounds. It is precisely for these reasons that communicating monetary policy concerns is vastly different from communicating worries about financial stability.

The Inevitable Collision?

As suggested in the previous section, policymakers who suffer either from myopia or tunnel vision can effectively be seen to conduct monetary policy as if they are rationally inattentive.[29] Even if both forms of behavior are not present, there exists a less obvious source of potential policy errors—namely, model misspecification. While central bankers are fond of repeating that they look at "everything," it is also the case that the conduct of monetary policy in recent years has relied more heavily on models and forecasts. This is not

---

[28] Other central banks also raised their policy rates. For example, the BoC raised the overnight rate three times beginning in 2010, before and after the scheduled end of its forward guidance policy. A retrospective analysis does not appear to give rise to the same complaints as the harsh ones leveled at the ECB, however (*inter alia*, Sandbu 2015).

[29] That is, policymakers make the best possible decisions, but as their time is constrained or their concern is for multiple issues simultaneously, they cannot be attentive to all forms of available information. See, for example, Wiederholt 2010 and Sims 2015 for a general summary of the extant literature on the subject.

only because of the central banks' success in taming and controlling inflation over two decades but also because financial and economic globalization have helped raise the potential complexity of economic relationships. Paralleling these developments has been the tremendous growth in the capacity of staff in the central banks to process vast amounts of information using their models and forecasts.

Yet, if models are misspecified, or if they omit important determinants in the transmission of monetary policy, or if they simply misinterpret the underlying forces at work in influencing economic outcomes, then no amount of comparative advantage by the monetary authority in the realm of data collection and analysis will spare the institution from bad decision making. Central bankers, of course, respond by claiming that judgment is applied when decisions are rendered. No doubt this is true, but the role of judgment is difficult to identify based on the decisions taken, particularly when these same central bankers are "data dependent" without ever specifying whether some types of data matter more than others. Moreover, explanations in press releases or the minutes of policy meetings are often insufficient to reveal the extent to which judgment was applied in reaching a decision. Finally, as discussed earlier, the mere persistence of policy rate changes suggests that an important contributor to gradualism or inertia is, in fact, caution. It is also the case, since considerable weight is attached to the forward-looking nature of policy, and the central bankers themselves have in recent years opted to publicize more the role of economic forecasts, that the technical aspects of policymaking have played a considerably larger role than ever as recently as ten or fifteen years ago.

Although several examples could not doubt be marshaled to substantiate some of these claims, I present two examples here. These could also be characterized as indicative of the fast and slow forces that impinge on the conduct of monetary policy.

One of the many developments that have occurred in the conduct of monetary policy during the past decade has been the proliferation of techniques to provide forward guidance or to reduce the surprise element in monetary policy. I return again to the question of forward guidance as practiced during and after the GFC in chapter 5. For the time being, I focus on one important element of forward guidance—namely, the introduction of a forward interest-rate track of some kind. That is, some central banks began to publish indicators of anticipated movement in future short-term interest rates—notably, future expectations of the central bank's policy rate. Typically, the central banks that had adopted a numerical inflation target were at the forefront of this development, as it provided a further signal of guidance, as well as a reaffirmation of the importance of transparency and the need for policy to be forward looking.

Another characteristic of several central banks that adopted this approach to policymaking is that they operate in small, open economies where changes in interest rates weigh on the exchange rate, and vice versa. Nevertheless, even when markets are ostensibly well prepared for a policy rate change, the central bank's views about the outlook for inflation and output, and by implication interest rates, will also be partly conditioned by its views about exchange-rate developments. However, if the release of this kind of information creates collateral damage via unexpected changes in the exchange rate, is such an approach a step too far? Does this introduce a needless potential for collision between markets that think fast and central banks that are generally mandated to think slow?

For example, on July 26, 2007, the Reserve Bank of New Zealand (RBNZ) increased the official cash rate (the RBNZ's policy rate, or OCR) by 25 basis points, a move that was believed to have been broadly expected by financial markets.[30] Nevertheless, by the end of the day, the New Zealand dollar (NZD) depreciated slightly below half a percent against both the Australian (AUD) and the U.S. currencies. Was there anything possibly newsworthy in the RBNZ's announcement? The RBNZ explained that "we think the four successive OCR increases we have delivered will be sufficient to contain inflation." Was "negative" news about inflation (i.e., higher imminent inflation), which prompted the RBNZ to tighten, have been "good" news for the exchange rate (i.e., a depreciation of the NZD)? If so, was the effect temporary enough that it could safely be ignored by the RBNZ as part of its strategy to look past transitory shocks? Even if a move of the RBNZ's policy rate was widely anticipated, the forward-looking sentiment in the wording of the RBNZ's statement may have independently influenced market expectations about the direction of change in the exchange rate.

Indeed, in a study of the NZD,[31] it was found that, contrary to expectations, the NZD appreciated in the face of a favorable monetary policy surprise.[32] If the latter is considered "bad news" about inflation, this translates into "good news" for nominal exchange-rate movements. For example, a monetary policy shock equivalent to a 100 basis point policy rate decrease explains a 3.3% appreciation of the NZD–AUD exchange rates.[33] More generally, monetary policy surprises were found to have large effects on the exchange rate.

Figure 2.6 plots the size of monetary policy surprises for New Zealand during the early 2000s, as estimated from the RBNZ's forward interest-rate track. The surprises, measured in basis points, can be quite large. However,

---

[30] This view is supported by reports on newswires immediately before the policy rate announcement.

[31] See Karagedikli and Siklos 2013, which serves as the basis for portions of this section. The connection between news about exchange rate changes and inflation was originally made by Clarida and Waldman 2009.

[32] A favorable surprise is one that allows the central bank not to act when otherwise conditions might favor a tightening of monetary policy. The size of the response is sensitive to the time span during which the exchange rate change is evaluated. Nevertheless, the direction of the change is unambiguous.

[33] Readers are reminded that the vertical axes in figure 2.6 are measured in basis points. Hence, it is appropriate to refer to 50bp changes as being large.

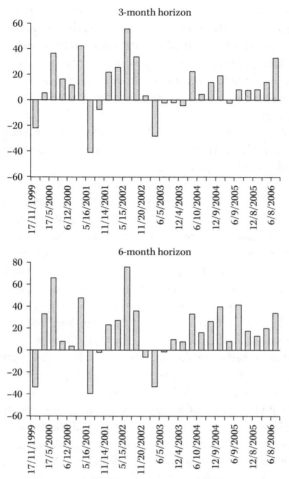

FIGURE 2.6 Market versus RBNZ Forward Interest Rate Track Differential

Note: The difference between the implied 3-month and 6-month horizon interest rates for 90-day bank bills, less the observed 90-day rate published by the RBNZ. Dates on the bottom axis are day/month/year when MPS statements and interest rate forward tracks are released. *Source:* Karagedikli and Siklos 2013.

what is especially noteworthy is that markets consistently overestimated the direction of future interest rates.[34] This is a good illustration of the collision between fast and slow thinking concerning future interest-rate developments. Another implication of these results is that, apparently, markets clearly interpreted the projections as conditional on the RBNZ's views concerning the existing macroeconomic environment. Otherwise, there would be little reason for surprises of the magnitude shown in the figure to be observed. Of course,

---

[34] A possibility is that inflation outturns are below expectations as long as they remain inside the central bank's inflation target range.

to the extent that there are persistent differences between the market's views of the future and the RBNZ's view, the results could also signal a lack of credibility in the projections contained in the forward track. It seems odd, then, as some critics have pointed out, to suggest that central banks that publish this kind of information have gone too far. Instead, a case such as this should be seen as indicative of a central bank that, rightly or wrongly, has not explained itself convincingly enough.[35] Alternatively, New Zealand's experience is more likely a reflection of the inevitable, if (it is hoped) only occasional collision between the financial markets and the policymakers concerning the different horizons involved in their planning.

A second example of forward guidance comes from an exploration of the effects of globalization, more recently of the financial kind. Even before the events of the past few years, economists and policymakers had been debating the apparent contradictions between globalization and the seemingly divergent paths in overall economic performance taken by the emerging and the more mature economies of the world. We have already seen (in chapter 1) how economic performance across various regions of the world diverged pre-crisis, only to briefly converge once the GFC was under way. Divergences would return once the world economy emerged from the depths of crisis conditions, but at different speeds. This resulted in a flurry of academic and policy papers, pre-GFC, asking whether business cycles, globally, were decoupling or not. Missing somewhat from this discussion was the apparent coupling of monetary policy strategies, to which I return later.

So, is it helpful to think of business cycle correlations as reflecting some form of coupling or decoupling? Or, is it more realistic to view international business cycle co-movements as reflecting a mutual dependence that is susceptible to short-run interruptions or is affected by changing economic factors? The latter interpretation has the virtue of focusing attention on some of the main sources of change in business cycle co-movements, as opposed to the more contentious explanation—that of the impact of "globalization." More important, one is able, then, to focus attention on the role of the policy strategy—notably the chosen monetary policy strategy and, consequently, on the role of institutions.

The choice of monetary policy strategy is an important factor in the mix explaining the degree of synchronicity in business cycles. The increased emphasis of a monetary policy focused on price stability, reflected in the rise of central bank transparency and the adoption of inflation targets around the globe, has also proved to be an ingredient in explaining the greater coherence

---

[35] The Swedish experience—when the financial markets and the Riksbank, the country's central bank, held opposite views about the interest rate outlook—is also reminiscent of the RBNZ's experience, although in the Swedish case the travails of the eurozone and a domestic asset price boom figured prominently. See, for example, Svensson 2013 and Milne 2014.

in business cycles. Rather than this development's being seen as capturing the "globalization" phenomenon, it is preferable to think of it as reflecting a shared belief in the desirability of inflation control. Nevertheless, this view has not survived the events of 2007–10 unscathed. Indeed, the future patterns of business cycle co-movements may well be influenced by the addition of a financial stability objective in ways that are still not well understood. This suggests that there is something left to be desired in our belief that currently popular monetary policy frameworks focusing on inflation control represent coherent or completely well-defined policy strategies.

Whither Monetary Policy Strategies?

Notions of strategic thinking in the realm of policymaking are a relatively recent occurrence (Freedman 2014). When applied to monetary policy, strategic thinking is more recent still, as policymakers, academics, and other observers have long argued that "rules" of some kind need to characterize, if not define, the conduct of monetary policy. But rules alone do not a strategy make, since unexpected events and large shocks—such the ones that occur in the midst of a financial crisis—also demand a flexible response.

Monetary policy has long struggled with these tensions, and this is partly reflected in the observation that central bank credibility has, over long periods of time, swung like a pendulum from when credibility was high under the classical gold standard before 1914, followed by the high inflation and stagflation of the 1970s and early 1980s, and not regained until the late 1990s.[36] The introduction of IT enhanced central bank credibility because it appeared to offer rules of conduct while retaining the flexibility to set those rules aside when needed. It is largely for this reason that Bernanke et al. (1999) referred to IT as a framework, since this put to rest the notion that monetary policy could be carried out by rigidly: "*By imposing a conceptual structure and inherent discipline on the central bank, but without eliminating all flexibility, inflation targeting combines some of the advantages traditionally ascribed to rules with those ascribed to discretion*" (Bernanke et al. 1999:6, italics in original).

The fact that credibility waxes and wanes over time also suggests that a policy strategy cannot be considered timeless. Indeed, "a strategy cannot be considered a settled product. . . .[There will be] important moments of decision" (Freedman 2014:541). IT also has the virtue of lulling the markets, the policymakers, and the public more generally into believing that, regardless of complexity, there are valid rules of thumb for evaluating how well monetary policy is conducted, at least in "normal" times. However, these beliefs,

---

[36] This is the essence of the argument in Bordo and Siklos 2016a, 2016b.

especially when they become well anchored, not only raise the likelihood of severe and systematic errors, as Kahneman (2011) observed, but also increase the determination of central banks to defend a framework or a strategy even when the evidence suggests the existing strategy needs a rethink. As a result, the relentless concern with what is measured—say, inflation and inflation expectations, as opposed to improving our understanding of threats to the economy from a loss of financial stability—is another risk to the viability of following an existing strategy. Perhaps unsurprisingly, then, instead of asking how the current monetary policy framework could be improved, too many central banks fell into the trap of overconfidence in exclusively an IT strategy to reverse a loss of credibility and trust in the monetary authorities.

Perhaps this is a natural reaction to the rhetoric used by critics for years, who have argued that if a central bank targets inflation, it must be ignoring everything else. This has been said, despite the increased emphasis on adopting a policy rule (see chapter 4) that parallels the spread of IT and that ought to have made clear how to balance inflation with real economic concerns in the delivery of monetary policy. In view of what central banks have said, and usually done—or even how legislators framed in legal terms their understanding of an inflation objective—the critics suffer from a form of confirmation bias. As Kahneman (2011:81) points out: "Contrary to the rules of philosophers of science, who advise testing hypotheses by trying to refute them, people (and scientists quite often) seek data that are likely to be compatible with the beliefs the currently hold."[37]

The list of speeches made by central bankers, who repeatedly have tried to assure audiences that they are not "inflation nutters," as Mervyn King, former governor of the Bank of England, put it,[38] is partial evidence of the challenge here. A look at what central bankers say about their IT regimes, together with the legislation that governs central bank authority in IT economies, ought to make clear that any inflation objective must be pursued in tandem with a concern for the general welfare of the population.[39] Indeed, one difference between IT in advanced economies and that in emerging markets and other economies is that the target is more likely to be clearly defined numerically in the former group than in the latter.

A second difference is the propensity for central banks outside the group of advanced economies to more explicitly link their mission either to the constitutional position of the monetary authority or to the legislation that defines their mission. This is partly a reflection of the relative youth of the central banks in

---

[37] Otherwise known as the confirmation bias phenomenon.

[38] See King 1997.

[39] See table 2.1 in the online appendix, which shows what IT and quasi-IT central banks around the world state as their aims and objectives, together with a separate column indicating the relevant wording of the legislation that defines the remit of these same central banks.

this part of the world and the comparatively recent acceptance that monetary policy should be conducted autonomously, free from political pressure.

The focus here on IT economies is deliberate. As others have already pointed out, adoption of IT spread quickly, beginning in the 1990s. However, less frequently discussed is why IT did *not* spread quickly beyond small, open economies in the advanced world. Indeed, only seven countries formally adopted this kind of framework.[40] I could be more generous and add the three large, globally important economies of the United States, the eurozone, and Japan, as well as Switzerland, even though central banks in these economies categorically deny having adopted this framework. At best, they might be treated as quasi-IT central banks.

In contrast, twenty-three countries in the emerging world to date have adopted what they call IT.[41] Details about how IT is practiced in each of these countries reveal that IT to one central bank is rather different from how it is in another. This suggests a gap between the impression given by policymakers about the strategy and the actual practice. "Strategy" has become vaguely defined to mean whatever policymakers decide it means. As Freedman (2014) points out, the challenge in defining a strategy, as well as the weakness of any such undertaking, is in finding the right words to characterize it. "Not only does strategy need to be put into words so that others can follow, but it works through affecting the behavior of others" (2013:614). Somewhat more charitably, it would appear that the space between rules and discretion is wide enough to incorporate a large variety of strategies that several central banks refer to as IT.

Yet, if a monetary policy strategy or framework is intended to communicate how economies behave in a more predictable way, that strategy as it is currently understood is clearly incomplete. That failing emerges in two observations. First, while the focus of monetary policy has been on inflation control, and by the 1990s there was plenty of evidence suggesting that price stability was the surest way to mitigate the amplitude of the business cycle, this objective was too narrowly defined. In particular, there was the presumption that the financial system would not interfere too much with the attainment of such objectives. Even Bernanke and Gertler's (1989) financial accelerator concept,[42] developed to explain how adverse financial shocks can amplify business cycle downturns, is predicated on the assumption of efficient markets. Second, there has too often been insufficient attention paid to what the medium- or long-term goals of monetary policy should be, and there's been too much emphasis on short-term objectives. Supporters of this kind of strategy are then left emphasizing or overweighting the flexibility of the framework at the expense of

---

[40] The United Kingdom is not considered to belong to this group.

[41] Again, see the online appendix.

[42] Also, see Kiyotaki and Moore 1997.

providing a menu of actions that might be required to meet longer-term goals that also ought to be incorporated into a monetary policy strategy. As a consequence, there is limited scope for action in extraordinary times, as well as inadequately defining the boundary between central bank action and governmental responsibility to communicate what society deems are the long-term objectives the central bank ought to aspire to.

No one expects, nor is it reasonable to suppose, that any legislation governing a central bank's responsibilities can anticipate all contingencies, particularly ones that involve a financial crisis whose severity and virulence are often unpredictable. Central bank laws that incorporate a directive when there is disagreement over the overall direction of policy have proved critical to understanding the democratic accountability of a central bank (Siklos 2002). Indeed, the GFC brought out the need for thinking about incorporating a directive when none exists, or contemplating additional directives in the event of extreme financial stress. Unfortunately, matters are considerably more complicated in this case because, in addition to government, other institutions (e.g., financial supervisory agencies, deposit insurance agencies) must be incorporated into the mix.

The challenge here is that, in an attempt to incorporate or, rather, remind governments and the public that central banks often came into existence to manage financial instability concerns, their relationship with monetary policy remains a work in progress. In policy circles, this refers to the role of macroprudential policies intended to supplement existing ones, so as to manage risks to the financial system. Consequently, the neat separation—in theory if not in practice—that existed pre-crisis between monetary policy and financial system stability was no longer valid and necessitated revisiting.

Instead of fashioning new directives, policymakers have instead embarked on creating new institutional structures that superficially give the appearance of letting everyone know who does what in the event of a crisis. Hence, we have the single-peak arrangement (e.g., the BoE), where the central bank sits atop the pyramid but responsibility is spread downward via multiple committees responsible for monetary policy and financial stability. Alternatively, we have organizations with multiple peaks, with various entities having responsibility for financial stability, with the central bank remaining accountable for meeting monetary policy objectives (e.g., the Fed, the ECB). To be sure, there is no single arrangement that is suitable for all countries and all times. However, the lines of accountability and responsibility for meeting as yet unclear financial stability objectives remain poorly defined.[43]

---

[43] As evidenced by the debate about the governance of central banks in a world where financial stability has become a separate objective of policy in several economies. See, for example, Lombardi and Siklos 2016.

As in the realm of monetary policy, there needs to be a directive in central bank legislation to cover the financial stability motive. That directive should specify that the ultimate strategy for maintaining financial stability be defined and designed by government, in consultation with the agencies responsible in this area. The consequences of disagreements or conflicts between agencies also need to be defined. In principle, this arrangement requires greater oversight by the legislature and transforms the central bank–government relationship from a largely bilateral one to a multilateral one. Finally, accountability for failures need to be clearly defined. Perhaps the overarching concern should be the recognition that failures will happen, that scapegoating in these circumstances is not desirable, and that mechanisms are in place for when crises happen.

Clearly, this is a more complex endeavor than the one that defined the pre-crisis environment, but it is not so complex that it cannot be tackled. Moreover, the importance of such an arrangement is enhanced by the fact that financial stability likely means different things to different institutions.[44] (I return to the issue raised by the foregoing discussion in the final chapter.)

Strategy is of little value if it cannot be properly communicated. A policy strategy needs to be expressed in language that the financial markets and the public can follow. Hence, lessons in good central bank communications represent an essential ingredient in mitigating the inevitable collisions that will occur between the real economy and the financial sector, to which I now turn.

Lessons in Communications

Even as the financial crisis was brewing and about to erupt, the major central banks that would eventually become ensnared in the GFC emphasized the need to keep a watchful eye on inflation. Among the hardest-hit economies, the BoE was officially in the camp of IT, while the Fed had adopted a medium-term inflation objective and the ECB also defined price stability in numerical terms. Only the BoJ would take longer to put a firm number on a definition of price stability that exceeded zero. For all intents and purposes, as pointed out in the previous section, these central banks had adopted all the principal elements of IT we have observed elsewhere—typically, small, open economies that pioneered the implementation of this type of monetary policy strategy.

However, it quickly became apparent that the financial crisis either did not fit the price stability strategy or was viewed as a phenomenon to be dealt with separately from any threat to an inflation objective. Explaining to the public the

---

[44] See Tucker 2014, 2006 for interesting and even broader views on the relationship between trust in a central bank and how such institutions should act in emergency situations.

course of action necessary to maintain some "medium-term" objective was lost, and the strategy of monetary policy did not fit well with the looming difficulties to be faced by the financial system. Even less obvious was where the threat to price stability would originate, as trade and then output began to shrink rapidly while commodity prices continued to rise (at least until late 2014). Indeed, the ECB engineered two ill-advised policy rate increases, seemingly oblivious to the economic storm within and the continuing slowdown of the U.S. economy. The mantra of price stability was frequently repeated, and action was taken fairly quickly to stem the loss of liquidity. However, the financial markets and the public could not understand how separate policies to deal with the financial crisis fit with the overall monetary policy strategy or framework.

Conditions would deteriorate even further as the global economy emerged from the financial crisis, with economies rebounding slowly and the problem turning from fears of too high inflation to fears of deflation. Even though the United States had faced an earlier episode of very low inflation in the early 2000s, and Japan had been mired in a mild deflation for two decades, once again the central bankers began to shift the emphasis of their communications toward the prevention of deflation. The presumption was that all deflations were bad, even though the evidence on that score was weak.[45] Precisely as suggested earlier, the major central banks began to take on additional risks to preserve the status quo. Once again, there was little clarity about how the various policies intended to ease conditions in the credit market—that is, QE—would support the existing framework of policy. Instead, almost before the worst phases of the crisis had passed, the monetary authority in the United States especially began to talk about "exit strategies." In Japan, where QE originated, there were complaints that the BoJ's earlier attempts to deal with the country's bursting real estate bubble in the 1990s were given insufficient credit for paving the way for other major central banks to adopt this kind of policy.[46] Of course, observers, including Bernanke, would point out that the BoJ did not follow a price stability strategy, among other failures to enact an effective version of QE.[47] Hence, there was no strategy in Japan's case, but since central banks in the advanced economies also chose to return to the ways of obfuscation, any preexisting strategy became lost in the confusion about how existing actions taken by various monetary authorities could contribute to a return to the principal objectives that central banks either set themselves or agreed to be accountable for in agreements with their political masters. As exit became an increasingly distant

---

[45] See the collection of papers in Burdekin and Siklos 2004. More recent evidence that casts doubt on the doom and gloom associated with most episodes of deflation is found in Borio et al. 2015.

[46] Former Governor Masaaki Shirakawa's 2010 speech about central banks is one example; see Shirakawa 2010.

[47] Bernanke (2015a: 418) rightly complains of his frustration with the failure to convince the public that the Fed was for a time engaged in credit easing, not QE. He interpreted the latter as attempting to increase the money supply while credit easing was meant to ease credit market frictions.

objective, the central banks were put in a position such that they defended the existing policy framework, though none of the obvious indicators supported their ability to achieve numerically stated goals for almost a decade.[48]

Next, for several central banks ostensibly of systemic importance, the ZLB in interest rates came into view as an additional constraint that would test their communications skills. Attention, therefore, turned to their balance sheets. Here, the assumption was that, just as policy rates can be compared across countries, so can balance sheet policies. This turns out to be incorrect.

An international study of the balance sheets for the central banks has considered the similarities and differences in financial position.[49] As the authors point out, the financial demands on the monetary authority increase in stressful or crisis conditions; hence, the size of their balance sheet reflects the underlying economic environment. Moreover, it is hardly helpful to state that the central bank can always "print money" and, hence cannot go bankrupt, with the mere size of its balance sheet raising questions of trust and credibility. This was certainly the case for the Fed in the aftermath of the GFC, as it sought to placate critics of its expanded balance sheet even as the crisis was showing no signs of abating. Nevertheless, it is curious that, unlike developments in the private sector where there is a concerted attempt to develop and enforce internationally accepted accounting standards, there is no such pressure to do so in the central banking community.

Even if a central bank cannot go bankrupt, there may well be instances where central bank cooperation, as was intensified at the height of the GFC, requires transactions that potentially affect the balance sheets of several central banks. An example is the swap arrangements the Fed entered into with several other central banks.[50] While the risks of doing so may be minimal, they need not be zero. The need for such arrangements is fairly clear, though, since the U.S. dollar (USD) is the world's primary reserve currency used in many international transactions, and key commodities (e.g., oil) are priced and traded in USD.

Another risk emerged in the experience of the GFC, wherein many central banks began to hold assets whose values could fluctuate and, hence, expose the monetary authority to unintended losses. Although several central banks (e.g., the Fed, the BoE, the BoC) were careful to negotiate indemnification agreements with their governments to shift any losses to the fiscal authorities, it is not obvious that all the parties to such transactions could anticipate the size and scope of losses arising in an environment where unconventional monetary policies are practiced. Even if the unforeseen losses that emerge are small, there is no telling how or when the appearance of those losses might

---

[48] Koo 2008, 2015 raises a similar concern.

[49] See Archer and Moser-Boehm 2013.

[50] Hence, the Fed has been careful to limit the number of central banks that can take advantage of this program. For the details, see www.federalreserve.gov/monetarypolicy/bst_liquidityswaps.htm.

impact the credibility of the central bank. All the more reason to ensure, in directives defining the responsibility and scope of allowable actions aimed at maintaining financial stability, that central banks obtain broad indemnification from activities taking place under emergency or crisis conditions.

There are additional considerations or risks associated with central bank policies that focus on altering the balance sheet that go beyond the scope of this book, but they are nonetheless worth pointing out. First, and perhaps most obvious, these policies potentially have important redistributive effects (e.g., between financial institutions and households). This is not a matter readily handled by central bank legislation; rather, it belongs in the realm of fiscal policy. Second, by altering the balance between long- and short-term assets in its portfolio, the central bank also alters the maturity structure of the outstanding debt, and this can affect the bank's balance sheet even if it is fully indemnified, because no indemnification agreement is likely to be foolproof. To be sure, even in purely theoretical terms, there are limits to the expansion of a central bank's balance sheet without risks having some fiscal implications.[51]

Surprising Lessons

One area where central banking arguably experienced a revolution during the past two decades concerns the role played by monetary policy "surprises." Consider Brunner's (1981:66) view about the conduct of monetary policy: "The esoteric nature of the art is moreover revealed by an inherent impossibility to articulate its insights in explicit and intelligible words and sentences. Communication with the uninitiated breaks down." It is, therefore, only a short step to the conclusion that monetary policy is implemented via surprise announcements. Fast-forward a couple of decades and the dominant view about how monetary policy changes should be explained changed dramatically. Bernanke (2004a), writing before he became chair of the Board of Governors of the U.S. Federal Reserve, argued that "clear communication helps increase the near term predictability of FOMC rate decisions." Hence, a premium is nowadays placed on avoiding surprises. Yet, as Blinder (2004:ch. 4), himself a former FOMC vice-chair, pointed out, "a new danger is emerging: that monetary policy might be tempted to . . . deliver . . . the monetary policy that the markets expect or demand."

The role of policy surprises is presented in figure 2.7, where once again the data from a survey (mentioned in chapter 1)[52] are subdivided into inflation-targeting (IT) and non-inflation-targeting (NIT) central banks. The bars

---

[51] See, for example, Reis 2015.

[52] The survey defined a monetary policy "surprise" as a change in monetary policy settings that market participants did not expect. No distinction was made, however, between changes that were expected but did not happen and policy rate changes that did not take place but that surprised the markets.

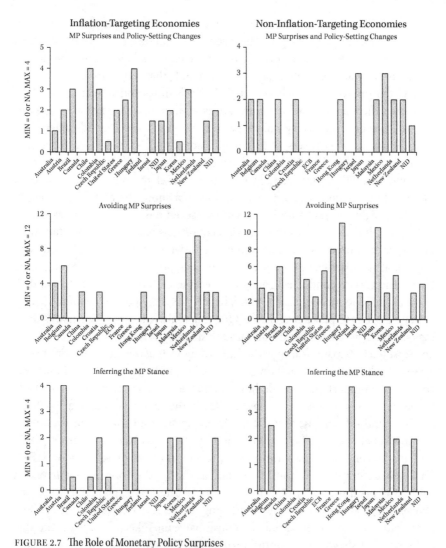

FIGURE 2.7 The Role of Monetary Policy Surprises

Notes: NID indicates central banks that did not want to be identified. If the central bank identified any of the above characteristics as "not important," it received a value of 0; "somewhat important," a value of 2; "important," a value of 3; "very important," a value of 4; and "other," a value of 1. *Source:* Siklos 2016a.

attempt to reflect the importance that central banks, by their own admission, place on avoiding monetary policy surprises. The responses to the survey were on a scale from "not important" to "very important." In addition, the survey asked the central banks to distinguish between crisis and non-crisis conditions, leaving it to them to define what was meant by the term "crisis."[53]

---

[53] The contents of the survey conducted together with the BIS, in 2013, are available in the online appendix.

In both IT and NIT economies, many central banks argue there is a difference in the role of policy surprises between crisis and non-crisis conditions. This is to be expected. While central bankers[54] generally support a systematic (or rules-based) monetary policy, flexibility demands that monetary policy be able to deviate from this approach, especially in crisis times and at least temporarily. Moreover, there are no doubt circumstances when policy surprises are necessary in the conduct of monetary policy, even if they are to be avoided under most circumstances. Nevertheless, in several NIT economies, surprises are not seen as playing an important role because there is little scope a priori to resort to this type of action. Hong Kong, for example, with its fixed exchange rate regime, comes to mind. A breakdown of the survey responses (not shown here) indicates that, of the thirty-eight central banks in the sample (seven did not provide a response), only four felt that surprises during crisis conditions were more important than during normal times, while nine of the respondents felt that normal conditions imply that surprises can play a relatively more important role than during crisis times. The survey, conducted only a few years after "normal" times had ended, may have bred more complacency and, hence, raises the possibility for monetary policy surprises to play a bigger role. One might also interpret the survey's findings as a reflection that central banks underestimate the length of time policy rates are expected to remain near or at the ZLB. Roughly half the monetary authorities surveyed felt that the distinction between crisis and non-crisis conditions was effectively unimportant. Overall, however, IT central banks are more amenable to the view that policy surprises have a place in the conduct of monetary policy.

That central banks have not completely abandoned surprising the financial markets is perhaps best exemplified by the Swiss National Bank's (SNB) decision to remove its peg limiting appreciation of the Swiss franc (CHF).[55] Variously described as a "bombshell" and a "shock," the floor in the currency's value was portrayed as a decision without a cause or explanation (e.g., see Davies 2015), as well as severely damaging to the SNB's credibility (Bernholz 2015). However, as noted earlier, a central bank must keep an eye on the size of its balance sheet, lest it suffer an irreparable loss of reputation. The currency floor led to a spectacular expansion of the SNB's balance sheet. In addition, the ECB was, for several weeks if not months, widely known to be on the verge of announcing entry into the QE realm. Even if the precise timing of the "surprise" ECB announcement was unknown, continued pressure on the CHF surely meant that the policy strategy would not continue indefinitely. As Herbert Stein, head of the U.S. Council of Economic Advisors, once put it: "If something cannot go forever, it will stop." In such circumstances, one could add that if there are political pressures to surprise the financial markets, likely

---

[54] For example, see Weidmann 2014 and Plosser 2014.

[55] The floor was 1.20 CHF to the USD, and was set on September 6, 2011. It was formally abandoned on January 15, 2015.

enhanced when a promise is hollow, the central bank needs to avoid policies that are not backed up with political support, even if temporarily justified. Again, with a suitable directive in place, such conditions can be avoided.

Next, the survey turned to the question of the predictability of monetary policy actions. Presumably, this is the corollary of avoiding policy surprises. The survey's findings are shown in figure 2.8. I was interested in obtaining information not only about the importance of predictability per se but also about whether a meaningful distinction exists between signs of changes in monetary policy and the magnitude of any changes in the policy stance. In every case, the focus was on policy rate changes. The height of the bars in the figure indicates the importance attached to the two types of changes in monetary policy. The survey showed that very few central banks believe that the sign and magnitude of policy rate changes is always anticipated (the maximum score was 4). Instead, almost all central banks, whether they targeted inflation or not, viewed the size and direction of policy rate changes as "usually anticipated." Only five central banks reported that financial markets were better at anticipating there would be a policy rate change than at judging its magnitude of change, with twenty-four central banks arguing that the distinction made no difference (six central banks did not respond). Moreover, there appeared to be no change in their views on this question since UMPs were introduced, as shown in the bar chart on the right side. Therefore, there appear to be no obvious differences between IT and NIT central banks concerning their views on the public's ability to predict the direction of changes in monetary policy stance.[56]

Of course, divining the direction of change in monetary policy is far easier both to observe and to communicate when it involves only a change in interest rate. In a world where interest rates have been near or at the ZLB for almost a decade—or longer in the case of Japan—and there is little prospect of anything more than a lift-off with very slow and deliberate rises for the foreseeable future, one must instead communicate the link between the stance of monetary policy and unconventional policy instruments. The communications challenges are more daunting, fraught with difficulties. In the case of the Fed, possibly the clearest illustration is the May 2013 testimony by then FOMC Chair Ben Bernanke, which produced the "taper tantrum" mentioned earlier. Bernanke stated on May 22, 2013, that "the committee currently anticipates that it would be appropriate to moderate the appropriate pace of [bond] purchases later this year." This statement was not intended to signal an upcoming tightening of

---

[56] Interestingly, this finding suggests that central banks have overcome a problem noted by Blinder 2004: "when they respond to news, the markets normally get the direction right but exaggerate the magnitude by a factor of between three and ten" (68). To the extent that current perceptions of policy predictability by central banks are due to improvements in central bank communications or are a consequence of recent financial crises is unclear. Moreover, the reaction of markets to the Fed's tapering (see later), at least initially, does suggest that some central banks at least are overly optimistic about how predictable monetary policy is.

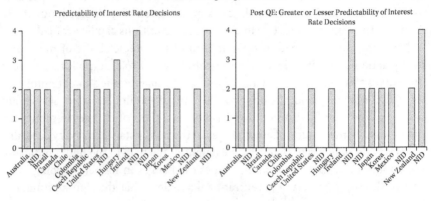

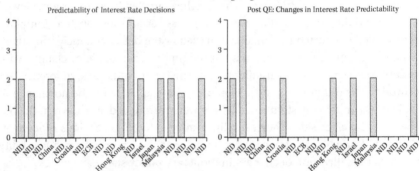

FIGURE 2.8 The Predictability of Monetary Policy

Note: The values on the vertical axis are determined in the same manner as the ones shown in figure 2.7.
Source: Siklos 2016a.

monetary policy but, rather, was meant to suggest that crisis conditions were easing and this permitted a reduction in the quantity of U.S. Treasuries purchased by the Fed.[57] The resulting effect on financial markets was unexpected, although the episode signaled that UMP do impact asset prices.[58]

A second example is the recent aggressive easing of monetary policy in Japan after Haruiko Kuroda became governor and launched, also in 2013, the policy of quantitative and qualitative easing (QQE). The intent of this policy was to assist in attaining a 2% inflation target that the BoJ set for itself via increases in the monetary base, as in the failed QE experiment of the early 2000s, coupled with aggressive buying of long-term Japanese government bonds (also known

---

[57] Bernanke's own recollection of the event (2015a, ch. 23), which involved changing messages "but sloppily," is worth reading.

[58] Long-term bond yields rose sharply. See, for example, Lombardi, Siklos, and St. Amand 2017 forthcoming.

as JGBs), which parallels some of the UMP adopted by the Fed. However, two years on, during which time oil prices dropped dramatically and fiscal policy was being tightened, in part because Japan's debt to its GDP ratio exceeded well over 200%, there are only passing signs that the BoJ's UMP are enough. The difficulty is that the BoJ's policy ostensibly also relies on the ability of the government to deliver the "third arrow" in its policy quiver.[59] Without the structural reforms that observers and politicians believe are essential, either more QQE will be necessary or the deadline for meeting the inflation objective will be delayed further.[60] Moreover, there is no indication, once achieved, that the 2% goal will be maintained.[61] Beyond these developments, however, one should not underestimate the accumulated cost to credibility and reputation from the failure of previous rounds of QE in Japan. Hence, even if a new policy is deemed to be correct, the legacies of past failures cannot be so easily dispensed with.[62]

A final illustration comes from Canada, a small, open economy that did not engage in UMP, but where the BoC's policy rate remained at the effective ZLB for almost a year in 2009–10 and near this level since shortly after the start of the GFC.[63] In January 2015, the BoC reduced the policy rate from 1% to 0.75% and the overnight target rate was reduced again the following summer to 0.50%. Governor Poloz admitted: "[W]e knew that financial markets would be surprised by the move" (Poloz 2015). Had the BoC's argument focused solely on the drop in oil prices, and the consequent drop in headline inflation, the surprise move might have been defensible. However, the BoC's decision also rested on the argument that such a move is akin to buying some insurance against future adverse economic effects from lower prices, whose impact and scope were never clearly spelled out: "[W]e took out some insurance in the

---

[59] The "third arrow" refers to structural reforms aimed at changing labor market regulations. When Prime Minister Shinzo Abe returned to power in 2012, he announced that aggressive monetary policy easing, fiscal policy, and structural reforms would constitute the three arrows intended to lift Japan from its decades-old deflationary cum slow growth slump. In spite of another election in 2014, the only effective arrow so far has been the one used to change monetary policy.

[60] By mid-2015, Governor Kuroda admitted that the inflation objective would be met later than the original two-year horizon envisioned by the BoJ's MPC. See, for example, Ito and Nakamichi 2015. Bernanke (2015a, pg. 519), reflecting on his earlier criticism of Japanese monetary policy, also pointed out that "raising people's inflation expectations substantially, using only talk, is easier in theory than in practice."

[61] See, for example, www.boj.or.jp/en/mopo/outline/qqe.htm. Inflation expectations data late in 2015 also reflected unease about the BoJ's commitment to the 2% objective beyond the short term. Also see, for example, Siklos 2017, forthcoming.

[62] Koo 2008, 2015 is testimony to the author's longstanding belief that, especially in Japan, monetary policy has been a string of failed attempts at generating a sustained recovery. Curiously, credibility and reputation play secondary roles in his analysis. One is therefore naturally led to ask: Even if his prescriptions are adopted to the letter, can Japan completely escape its past?

[63] The policy rate (overnight rate) fell to 0.25%, then considered the effective ZLB, in April 2009 from 3% in September 2008. The policy rate would reach 1% by September 2010, where it remained until January 2015, when the overnight rate once again began to fall back toward the ZLB.

form of a 25bp cut in interest rates. . . . [I]t would also help mitigate the rise in debt to income ratio" (2015).

Unfortunately, history suggests that attempts to cut interest rates often lead to more borrowing, thereby undoing the desire to ease household borrowing burdens. Financial institutions have demonstrated they possess other tools to fuel borrowing and, indeed, debt levels continued to rise, albeit more modestly, in the months following the BoC's policy rate cuts. Policy surprises, combined with ineffective moral suasion relying on inconsistent communication, can only reduce the effectiveness of monetary policy and the BoC's credibility. Moreover, if the 2014 oil shock, which was the trigger a change in the BoC's policy stance, was of sufficient magnitude, as the governor's speech cited seemed to indicate, then a 25bp cut would hardly seem to be enough.[64]

Finally, there was always looming tension between interest rates and exchange rates. A lower interest rate would, other things being equal, promote a currency depreciation as investors sold Canadian dollars to benefit from relatively higher yields elsewhere. Of course, a depreciating Canadian dollar could also promote inflation if, and when, pass-through effects from higher foreign prices impacted domestic prices and, eventually, headline inflation. This eased, of course, the BoC's task of remaining within its inflation target objective, particularly when inflation was below target and there was a further drag from lower oil prices. Yet, in spite of an earlier speech by Governor Poloz in 2014, emphatically supporting floating exchange rates (Poloz 2014),[65] BoC officials earlier expressed some dissatisfaction with the regime (e.g., see Murray 2013), and there are other indications that financial markets were skeptical about whether the central bank was more interested in a particular exchange rate level than in meeting its IT.[66]

Conclusions

Financial system stability, even if the concept is viewed as clearly defined and well understood, has usually been portrayed as an objective that can simply

---

[64] Indeed, as pointed out, the BoC would take out more insurance in July 2015 by reducing the policy rate once again by another 25bp. One has to wait almost a year until the governor, in a speech exploring monetary policy divergences around the globe (Poloz 2016), softened the view that the sharp decline in oil prices represented a negative shock overall while emphasizing the need for Canada's monetary policy to diverge from the one conducted in the United States. "We know that the overall effect on Canada is unambiguously negative. . . .. Nevertheless, at the global level, . . . [yields] a net positive impact on global growth." The speech is notable, however, because it largely ignored monetary policy spillovers into the financial cycle mentioned in chapter 1. In other words, the governor did not take a stand on interest rate policy's ability to get into "all the cracks" (Stein 2013).

[65] Also, see his speech in 2016 (Poloz 2016).

[66] One only needs to scan the media's interpretation of the BoC's public pronouncements, especially during 2015, to find evidence of the confusion that appears to reign among certain analysts. For example, see Palmer and Schnurr 2016.

be appended to an existing inflation-control mandate. Unfortunately, we only know financial stability when we experience it or, rather, we only agree that there is financial instability when it is typically too late. Moreover, the manner in which decisions are taken in financial markets, as well as the speed at which they function, can easily come into conflict with conventional monetary policy objectives driven by slow-moving macroeconomic aggregates. Reconciling the two should govern how central bank mandates and responsibilities are set out in the future. Current arrangements are inadequate.

A further implication is that the financial stability motive influences the degree of institutional complexity. In other words, whereas central banks aimed at narrow objectives prior to the crisis, reachable with a medium-term horizon and seemingly straightforward to communicate, post-crisis this will no longer do. Financial stability requires considerably more variable, and possibly flexible, policymaking horizons, ranging from the very short term that arise when financial markets are suddenly in turmoil, to the long term that defines how these markets will be regulated, supervised, and contribute to economic growth.

Even in the realm of monetary policy, the central banks have been forced to reconsider conditions under which it is appropriate to surprise markets. This implies some discretion in levels of transparency that the central banks can promote after having devoted over a decade or more to persuading the public that transparency was the *sine qua non* of good practice in monetary policy. However, there are as yet few indications that central banks fully understand the communications challenges of surprising financial markets in an effective manner. Even if policy surprises prove necessary, there is little understanding of the conditions under which these interventions are likely to be successful. Matters are even more complicated when the monetary policy is communicated via resort to non-interest rate or unconventional instruments.

Some of the ideas in this chapter relate to psychological elements that may influence the conduct and interpretation of monetary policy in a world where there is a belief in something akin to a trade-off with financial stability considerations. Nevertheless, some of the arguments made here are reminiscent of an idea, circa late 1970s, wherein separate departments of a central bank would be effectively responsible for short-run stabilization measures, a long-run inflation objective, and what we would today term macroprudential regulation.[67] Unfortunately, just as financial stability cannot be neatly separated from the search for and maintenance of price level stability, subdividing the tasks of a central bank along these lines is simply impractical.[68] Indeed, the potential

---

[67] See Niehans 1978, who devised the "three frequencies approach" alluding to the various horizons a central bank ought to consider in conducting monetary policy.

[68] Karni 1979 also makes this point in his review of Niehans's book.

for conflict between an inflation objective and a financial stability goal is inevitable, not only because of the state of our knowledge about how the two objectives are linked but also because it is easy to imagine that decision makers will, at various times, be swayed by a possibly exaggerated concern over one problem (e.g., whether and for how long to tolerate inflation target misses) at the expense of another (e.g., whether asset prices are excessively high). The Swedish experience[69] is one that is symptomatic of the challenges ahead for central banks.

---

[69] As ably told by Goodfriend and King 2015.

The Anatomy of Financial Crises and the Role of Monetary Policy

Varieties of Financial Crises

Financial crises come in a variety of forms. To paraphrase the often-quoted passage from Tolstoy's *Anna Karenina*, financial crises are all unhappy events in their own way, although even that remains very much debated. The fact that researchers have generally grouped financial crises into several categories suggests that some financial crises produce more unhappy outcomes than others, and for different reasons. Existing classifications include the following: currency crises, domestic and external or foreign sovereign debt crises, stock market crises, and banking crises.[1] Nevertheless, most authors agree that financial crises, regardless of their type, leave economic scars that last a considerable time.

Several attempts have been made to define individual financial crises and date their start and end dates. Differences in dating and in the severity of recorded financial crises partly reflect the fact that there needs to be reached a tipping point before an event can be declared a financial crisis. Similarly, the source of the crisis must be identified, and there will be some disagreement on that among analysts. As important as this consideration is, it will be set aside, as much of the data compiled to date, and employed by analysts to study the economic consequences of the financial crisis, tends to rely on common documentation. In what follows, then, data collected by Reinhart and Rogoff (2009), while Bordo et al. (2001), Caprio et al. (2005),

---

[1] Some also include inflation crises (e.g., annual inflation rates of more than 40% or some other threshold). To be sure, debt can be inflated away via inflation, while inflation may also represent the failure of governments to raise adequate tax revenues, leading them to debase the currency via excessive issuance of money. It seems, however, difficult to neatly distinguish between inflation and the other types of financial crises listed. And, as we have seen and will see again, some of the other forms of financial crises can be made worse when inflation is no longer seen as an exit strategy.

and Schularik and Taylor (2012) serve as the primary sources for some of the arguments that follow.[2]

Because financial crises emerge when domestic and international obligations are severely imbalanced, the result is often reflected in large exchange-rate depreciations. For example, depreciations of 15% or more on an annual basis are seen as evidence of a currency crisis.[3] Historically, financial crises are associated with debt crises. Hence, either the sovereign has issued too much debt in the domestic currency or it has borrowed excessively from abroad (i.e., debt denominated in an external currency). When the sovereign defaults on the principal, the interest, or both, it is reasonable to suppose that a financial crisis is under way. Of course, the conditions that led to that default may be years in the making or, conversely, delayed thanks to makeshift or temporary palliatives that push into the future what *ex post* is believed to be the inevitable outcome.

The stock market is sometimes seen as a harbinger of economic outcomes, both for inflation and real economic growth. Alternatively, stock market performance can be seen as representative of large downward movements, revealed in some index of equity prices. For example, if there is a stock market decline of 20% during some window of time,[4] followed by a "crash," this may also be indicative of underlying stress in the financial system.

Finally, and not surprisingly, a financial crisis is linked to the state of the banking system. Hence, if there is a run on the banks (e.g., as in the United Kingdom in 2008, when depositors lined up to withdraw their funds from the inaptly named Northern Rock), the banks are closed, nationalized, or otherwise taken over by government fiat or they fall under government management—all results are indicative of a failure of the banking system to operate normally.

All types of financial crises are pernicious in their own way, although, as Reinhart and Rogoff (2009:136) note, the lack of transparency concerning sovereign debt, unlike the other sources of financial crises that can be considered as "you know it when you see it," suggests that debt crises are in a class of their own. Banking crises receive special attention, however, not only because they regularly afflict both financially mature and less mature economies but also because they amplify the underlying weaknesses in the financial system.

Figure 3.1 illustrates the incidence of financial crises in ten economies considered advanced by today's metrics.[5] Graph (a) displays the mean and median

---

[2] More detailed definitions of the types of financial crises can be found in these sources. However, an extensive discussion is conveniently presented in Reinhart and Rogoff (2009, tables 1.1 and 1.2), along with commentary on the pros and cons of selecting a threshold or applying some arbitrariness to some of the definitions.

[3] Currency crises can also occur when there is monetary reform or a metallic currency is debased.

[4] The speed with which the index declines is also thought to be a symptom of the severity of the downturn.

[5] They are, in order of when the central banks were created, Sweden, the United Kingdom, Norway, France, Germany, Japan, Italy, Switzerland, United States, and Canada.

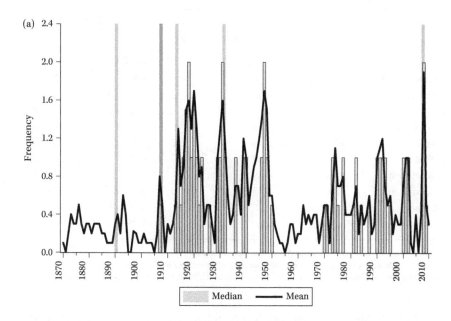

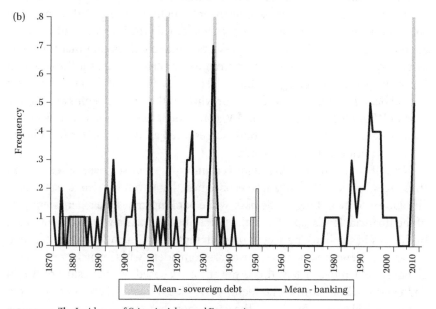

FIGURE 3.1 The Incidence of Crises in Advanced Economies

(a) All Types of Financial Crises

(b) Banking Crises

Note: The bars in (a) indicate the median number of all types of financial crises; the solid line is the mean number of crises. In (b), the mean number of sovereign debt crises is indicated by the bars; the solid line represents the mean number of banking crises, except inflation crises. *Source:* Data are from Reinhart and Rogoff 2009.

TABLE 3.1 } The Incidence of Financial Crises

Country	Year Central Bank Was Created	Crisis Incidence	
		Since 1945	Since 1915
Sweden	1668	0.36 (0.65)	0.42 (0.66)
United Kingdom	1694	0.47 (0.71)	0.57 (0.75)
Norway	1816	0.50 (0.69)	0.47 (0.71)
France	1800	0.61 (0.63)	0.71 (0.68)
Germany	1876	0.70 (0.88)	0.86 (0.84)
Japan	1882	0.71 (1.00)	0.70 (0.92)
Italy	1893	0.50 (0.71)	0.70 (0.80)
Switzerland	1907	0.35 (0.51)	0.32 (0.49)
United States	1913	0.61 (0.68)	0.76 (0.86)
Canada	1934	0.14 (0.39)	NA
45 Countries (1980–2011)		0.49 (0.72)	0.61 (0.77)

Note: Data are from Bordo and Landon-Lane 2010, based on the sum of domestic sovereign debt and external sovereign debt crises. The figures represent the annual average number of crises during the periods from 1945 or 1915 until 2008. The value for the 45 countries is based on Bordo and Landon-Lane's entire data set.

averages of financial crises (excluding inflation crises). Using either metric, the most recent financial crisis appears only slightly more global than earlier spikes in the number of crises that occurred during the interwar and immediate post-World War II eras.[6] This presents visual confirmation that this most recent crisis is indeed not different from earlier crises. Nor is it the case that the mean or median average for financial crises is directly linked to how long a central bank has been in existence, nor whether the sample begins around the start of World War I or after World War II ended; this is clearly seen from the data presented in table 3.1. On both scores, the Fed is not too far from being the worst performing central bank.

Next, if we attempt to highlight certain types of crises over others, graph (b) suggests, at least for advanced economies, that sovereign debt crises generally appear to be a thing of the past, while banking crises are a persistent part of the financial landscape. Since the latest financial crisis was also dominated by failures in the banking sector, one is tempted to conclude that higher than average incidences of banking crises are coincident with financial crises on a global scale. Unfortunately, this is not the case, based on the results of Bordo and Landon-Lane (2010), who identify five global financial crises as indicated by the vertical bars in figure 3.1. The good news, however, is that the frequency of global financial crises seems to have has declined, as central banks have gained experience—one reason given, among other proximate explanations.

---

[6] Bordo and Landon-Lane (2010) point out that three of the five global financial crises identified took place before World War I erupted.

In particular, it has not seriously been considered whether the monetary policy strategy adopted by central banks is a factor or, equally important, whether any cooperation, if not coordination, in their policy strategies played a role in this decline.[7]

Of course, the results we have seen so far are arguably based on a limited number of countries. Therefore, figure 3.2 largely repeats the exercise, but for a much wider set of countries (45) since 1980. To facilitate exposition, the individual countries in the data set are grouped into three categories: rest of the world, advanced economies, and the G20. The G20, which has taken a leading role in global governance particularly at the economic level, includes in its membership both advanced and emerging market economies. Both portions of the figure parallel, at least in some respects, the findings reported in figure 3.1. The incidence of financial crises is smaller in advanced economies; however, the time series behavior of the crises, whether in total or of the banking variety, broadly mirrors the experience of emerging and less developed economies in this sample.

Equally noticeable is the persistent gap between the incidence of all forms of financial crises and the banking crises during the Great Moderation (approximately mid-1980s to 2006) in advanced and other economies (rest of the world and G20 in part (a) and all other economies and the G20 in part (b) of Figure 3.2). It is only on the cusp of the financial crisis of 2007–8 that differences in the incidence of financial crises largely disappear. Once the latest global financial crisis emerges, the gap in the total number of crises surges worldwide, but the banking crisis in the advanced economies stands out as the most salient manifestation of financial crises in general.

What is absent from the foregoing descriptions is the cross-border element of a financial crisis. After all, if crises are largely confined to a domestic economy, then the policies needed to exit the crisis and prevent a recurrence are likely to be home-grown. If, however, there is a global element, even if only infrequently, then this factor needs to be explored more fully. It is also striking that Reinhart and Rogoff (2009) do not concern themselves with the exchange-rate regime as a conduit for either amplifying or diminishing the effects of financial crises.[8] Alternatively, it may be that financial crises morph from domestic to global events, for reasons that have little to do with economic fundamentals. In that case, some financial crises are contagious, while others are not.

These issues have implications for the design of central banks going forward and for the appropriateness of existing monetary policy strategies. A good

---

[7] See, however, Bordo and Siklos 2017.

[8] This is all the more surprising as these authors are also responsible for a comprehensive cataloguing of exchange rate regimes; see Reinhart and Rogoff 2004.

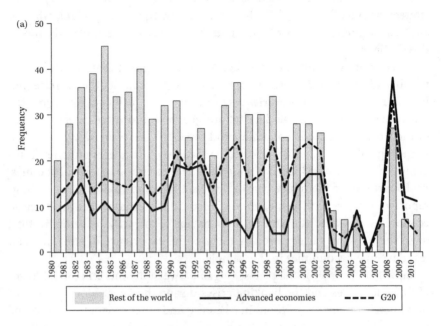

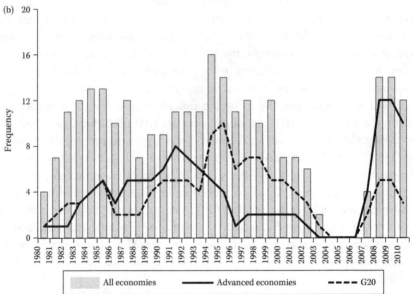

FIGURE 3.2 The Geographical Distribution of Banking Crises

(a) Rest of the World

(b) All Economies

Note: See note to figure 3.1. The bars indicate the frequency for all 45 countries in the sample. The solid line is for advanced economies (10 economies, identified in the text); the dashed line is for the G20 economies in the sample. *Source:* Data is from Bordo and Landon-Lane 2010.

place to start this examination is with the experience of the monetary union in Europe.

Does the European Monetary Union Serve as a Cautionary Tale?

While the degree to which economies are economically and financially open varies over time and across countries, the extent to which they are linked at the aggregate level is, at least partially, determined by their choice of exchange-rate regimes and the ease with which finances flow move across borders.[9] Europe's common currency is an extreme case of a fixed exchange regime that, legally at least, permits only internal and no external devaluations or revaluations. In this sense, it shares the essential features of the gold standard, with one important distinction. The gold standard was largely a voluntary arrangement, as in the European Union (EU), at least since the Lisbon Treaty of 2007,[10] while the European Monetary Union (EMU) is not intended as a voluntary system.[11] Nevertheless, as ongoing events make clear, the euro is not as irrevocable as the repeated references to Brexit suggested, nor is a reluctance to revisit the structure upon which the EMU was created; this is a cautionary tale about the incentives and limits of international cooperation, the drawbacks of tying one's hands, and the critical role played by monetary policy.

It is tempting to think we can write about the crisis in Europe using the past tense. However, the ongoing difficulties in the eurozone that erupted in 2010 continue to plague the EMU. Moreover, enough has been written recently about the origins of the common-currency project, how it came to fruition, how it is supposed to function, how it got into trouble, and how it is

---

[9] For purposes of what follows, the current debate about whether, in the pursuit of an independent monetary policy, a floating exchange rate remains essential, is not directly addressed. However, as will be seen later, even if one wishes to downgrade the importance of exchange rate regimes to achieve monetary independence, it has yet to be established whether the reduction of the trilemma to a dilemma is a passing phenomenon or a permanent feature of global monetary policy. The trilemma refers to the impossibility (hence, the alternative name for a trinity of choices) of simultaneously stabilizing the exchange rate, maintaining freedom of capital movement, and sustaining an autonomous monetary policy. In a globalized financial world, however, Rey 2014 argues that the trilemma becomes a dilemma only when an independent monetary policy is possible with restrictions on capital movements. Of course, not everyone is convinced by these arguments (e.g., see the general discussion surrounding Rey's paper in www.kansascityfed.org/publications/research/escp/symposiums/escp-2013.

[10] The Lisbon Treaty came into force after an earlier treaty was rejected by French and Dutch voters in 2005. Earlier, in 2003, Swedish voters decided against adopting the euro as its currency. Hence, even before Brexit (see epilogue), there were attempts to limit the extent to which members of the EU were potentially politically bound together.

[11] Joining the EU is, other than for reasons of geographic restrictions, voluntary. With only a couple of exceptions, however (the United Kingdom and Denmark), joining the EMU is not seen as voluntary. Some countries prefer to use the EMU acronym to mean Economic and Monetary Union, while others use it as employed here.

on its last legs, with only formal recognition that it is no longer an irrevocable arrangement.[12]

Among the forgotten legacies of the events that culminated in the introduction of the euro is the initial project for establishing a common currency, which involved only a small subset of the present EU. Nor is it immediately clear the extent to which the EMU—an economic arrangement—was foreseen as operating in parallel with or distinct from the EU, the latter being a political undertaking.

Ever since the Treaty of Rome (1957), the express wish of policymakers has been to lay "foundations of an ever closer union among the peoples of Europe," but the short-cut was that a single currency would be the rallying symbol that would encourage closer political union, desired by some. Indeed, by "pooling their resources to preserve and strengthen peace and liberty, and calling upon the other peoples of Europe to share their ideals to join in their efforts,"[13] what would eventually be called the European Union (EU)[14] was the vehicle that would finally support the wish for Europe expressed long ago by Norman Angell (1911) in *The Great Illusion* that peaceful coexistence is preferable to military conflict.

Unfortunately, conflict comes in many forms, and actual warfare has been replaced with economic warfare as the means of settling differences. Policymakers may well have been lulled into a new version of the great illusion. Just as in Angell's day the focus was on the relative importance and influence of Germany for Europe's well-being, the current impression is that the severity and duration of the crisis is directly attributable to the exercise of German economic power. However, Angell (1911:29) makes an observation that is equally true today: "The wealth, prosperity, and well-being of a nation depend in no way upon its political power; otherwise we should find the commercial prosperity and social well-being of the smaller nations, which exercise no political power, manifestly below that of the great nations which control Europe, whereas this is not the case."

Indeed, one has to wonder whether Germany, which along with other eurozone members has agreed to three bailouts for Greece in the space of around five years, actually behaves as a hegemon intent on imposing its political and economic power on smaller economies, notably Greece. Similarly, one has to ask how the population of Greece can persist with governments that have been unable or unwilling to adopt practices used for decades elsewhere in the

---

[12] A highly selective reading list would include de Haan 2000; de Haan, Eijffinger, and Waller 2005; de Grauwe 2009; Issing 2008; James 2012; Marsh 2009; Mayer 2012; Mourlon-Druol 2012; Münchau 2010; Padoa-Schioppa 2004; Piris 2012; Sinn 2014; and Sandbu 2015.

[13] The Treaty of Rome was signed by Belgium, Germany, France, Italy, Luxembourg, and the Netherlands.

[14] Consisting of 28 member states, as this is written.

common-currency area. Of course, the real error perhaps was to admit Greece in the first place, but this merely reflects the fact that, as in other stages on the road to monetary union, politics often trumps economics. Moreover, it is apparent there was an inability to create a structure that explicitly recognizes the difficulty of collective action even when a common interest exists, whether that common interest is to prevent wars or to develop a sizable market that could rival large economies elsewhere in the world. Finally, as membership in the EU and the eurozone have both grown, there continues to be a failure to acknowledge that the costs of maintaining any economic union will continue to grow while the collective benefits may rise more slowly.

This is not to say that striving for the common good needs to collapse when there are significant strains in a collective arrangement, such as in the example of a common currency. Instead, there is a need either to change existing incentives or to rethink some of the principles that encouraged the formation and growth of the group. Recent events in Europe are simply a reminder of Mancur Olson's (1965) *The Logic of Collective Action,* whereby just because a group has common interests, that does not imply it must act collectively whenever asymmetries emerge. Nowhere is this most keenly felt than in the case of Brexit in 2016, wherein the United Kingdom voted to leave the EU.

Two other examples illustrate this point. Since national central banks continue to exist inside the eurosystem, which consists of sovereign nations, there is the transfer of funds by banks to settle financial transactions.[15] Unless there are institutional or other constraints on the size and frequency of a payments system, there are likely times when some central banks in the eurozone—the gatekeepers, so to speak of the payments system—will be seen as "borrowing" relatively more funds than others. Sinn (2014: 181) argues that the dramatic changes in outstanding balances, seemingly to the detriment of Germany as the sovereign debt crisis wore on, are "of paramount importance to understanding what is going on in the Eurozone, much more than all of the rest." Indeed, he explains the problem as follows: "Target balances . . . actually reflect the amount if central bank credit that has been issued in excess of the liquidity needs for transactions within the NCB's [National Central Banks] national jurisdictions" (2014:180). While a debate over Sinn's remarks raged for some time,[16] the essential point is that in a currency union with unequal economic partners, there will be asymmetric outcomes of one kind or another. These asymmetries will be most visible in a crisis environment. The solution is not, as politicians and some policymakers have pretended, to find a way to treat everyone equally but, rather, to deal with the asymmetry in such a way

---

[15] The system is called TARGET, or Trans-European Automated Real-Time Gross Settlement Express Transfer System. See www.ecb.europa.eu/paym/t2/html/index.en.html.

[16] For example, Buiter et al. 2011, in a convincing piece, argue that some of Sinn's concerns are misplaced, but that the imbalances are not benign for the eurozone as a whole.

that the whole—that is, the entire eurozone—is better off, as opposed to reverting to national sovereignty as a means of rectifying a natural occurrence, thereby exacerbating the asymmetry.

A second illustration comes from monetary policy. The ECB introduced the policy of Outright Monetary Transactions (OMT) in 2012. This allows the ECB to effectively intervene, in a highly conditional manner, in eurozone member states' secondary bond markets[17] to stem a worsening crisis and prevent the risk of a breakdown in the eurozone's monetary transmission mechanism. Sinn (2014:118), quoting from ECB President Draghi's plea for support in the German Parliament, argued that OMT would offset the "greater risk to price stability is currently falling prices in some euro area countries. ... OMTs are essential for ensuring we can continue to achieve it." Sinn, however, rightly reminds his readers that "this concern is misplaced, since deflation in some countries would be useful and indispensable to restore their competitiveness" (2014:118). Other than the fact that Sinn does not mind some forms of asymmetry, the response by the ECB president does not properly explain the rationale for attempting to correct the asymmetry in question nor, more important, address why monetary policy should bear the responsibility for doing so. Again, asymmetries are the norm in all successful monetary unions (e.g., the United States or Canada), and policymakers would likely not be tempted to deal with relatively low inflation in part of the currency union via a policy stance applied to the entire currency area.[18]

Beyond Europe's borders, the development that tied the hands of policymakers is arguably the globalization of trade and finance. To the extent that this development overshadows the older role that exchange-rate arrangements had binds together the fortunes of the economies more so than in the past.[19] This has implications for the speed and amplitude of financial shocks and the extent to which they spread around the globe.

What is left unanswered, of course, is determining the point at which the cost–benefit calculus tips in favor of changing the makeup of any group that has common interests. It would seem apparent that the economic imbalances between member states render existing arrangements no longer sustainable. As will be shown shortly, these imbalances have both internal and external elements.

---

[17] Recall that each member state can issue its own debt even if it is denominated in euros. The conditions of the program are explained, for example, in www.ecb.europa.eu/press/pr/date/2012/html/pr120906_1.en.html.

[18] Canadians of a certain age have some experience with arguments that deal with apparent asymmetries in inflation performance inside a currency union; recall the early years following Canada's introduction of inflation targeting. See, for example, Siklos 1997 and references therein.

[19] The current era of financial globalization is not the first one, so explanations that center on the novelty of the present environment do not get us very far.

The Eurozone in the Global Context

Even before the global financial crisis, textbook notions linking exchange rates to the current account, or net exports, were questioned. Figure 3.3 displays three groups of economies, with current account balances as a percentage of GDP. I begin here with a selection of countries in the EU, since these economies, at least in principle, are eventually required to join the eurozone, but as this is written are unlikely to do so any time soon.[20] Hence, these countries effectively allow their exchange rate to move relatively freely against the euro.[21] It is also worth pointing out that while the eurozone member economies' exchange rates are pegged, the euro does float against other currencies in the world.

In principle, positive and negative net exports reflect a portion of the external disequilibrium in an economy. Indeed, the failed Bretton Woods system, born out of the devastation of World War II, was designed to place limits of sorts on both current account balances and, by implication, on exchange-rate movements. However, for reasons that would take us far afield, this global arrangement had a short and troubled history.[22] Nevertheless, the question of what a sustainable surplus or deficit is, in the current account, has preoccupied policymakers for decades, and the end of the Bretton Woods era has not diminished interest in that question.

Milesi-Ferretti and Razin (1996), for example, sought to come up with some guidelines for current account sustainability, but unsurprisingly, they concluded that the most important determinants are country-specific. This parallels Frankel's (1998) conclusion that the same currency regime is not suitable at all times for all countries. More recently, the EU began to report on current account balances inside the eurozone. The EU was careful, however, to avoid placing any numerical value on what is deemed excessive or unsustainable. Similarly, the G20 has periodically urged a "more balanced current account" since the 2009 Pittsburgh Summit, called in the midst of the GFC. Finally, the IMF has long sought to rely on current account balances as an indicator of a country's vulnerability when it comes to external debt especially (e.g., IMF 2002).

---

[20] The 27 governments that signed the Lisbon Treaty agreed, among other clauses, "RESOLVED to achieve the strengthening and convergence of their economies and to establish an economic and monetary union, . . . a single and stable currency." Even if some countries opt out, the treaty suggests that it could be perhaps not now but not never. The quote is from the preamble to the Lisbon Treaty; see www.lisbon-treaty.org/wcm/the-lisbon-treaty.html.

[21] Technically, non-EMU members who are part of the EU must be part of the Exchange Rate Mechanism II for at least two years. The exchange rate of the prospective member must remain within a ±15% fluctuation band against the euro. This hardly seems like a very strong or biding constraint on exchange rate movements.

[22] An excellent account if the various facets of the Bretton Woods system can be found in Bordo and Eichengreen 1993.

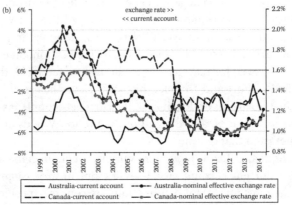

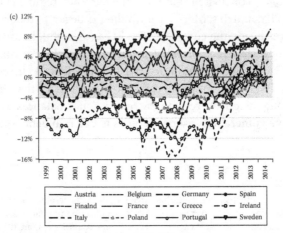

FIGURE 3.3 Current Account Imbalances Around the World

(a) Large economies

(b) Small Open Economies

(c) European Union Economies

Note: Current account to GDP ratios (in percent).). The shaded area in (c) highlights an estimate of the range of "sustainable" current account balances for the eurozone. *Source:* Data are from the IMF *International Financial Statistics* CD-ROM (June 2015).

The bottom graph (c) of figure 3.3 presumes that sustainable current accounts are within the range of +4% to -4% of GDP, which is also in the range of estimates referred to from time to time in the literature. On this score, only Portugal and Greece persistently exceed the zone of sustainability. However, it is especially notable that both economies deviated from a current account that has been in balance from the moment the monetary union came into force in 1999 (with Greece joining later in 2001). The GFC reversed the trend toward ever larger deficits, but only temporarily. It was only when the eurozone's sovereign debt crisis was in full swing in 2010 that both Portugal's and Greece's current accounts rapidly went into balance.

Nor is it especially the case that Germany stands out relative to, say, Sweden, the latter an EU member not likely to join the eurozone any time soon, but that has at least had the ability to rely on its exchange rate to maintain a surplus throughout the period shown. Notice also that Germany's surplus rose steadily but only once the set of structural reforms referred to as the Agenda 2010 (or Hartz) reforms[23] began to be discussed and implemented beginning in 2003. Nor can a floating exchange rate be used to argue that Poland, another EU member outside the eurozone, was employed to its advantage.[24]

The experience shown in graph (c) of figure 3.3 is not unique to the single-currency area. Graph (a) of figure 3.3 shows the current account to GDP ratio for the eurozone, China, and the United States. While the eurozone's net exports have generally been in balance since its creation, the surplus for China is often mirrored as a deficit for the United States. Notice, however, that China's current account declines precipitously beginning with the global financial crisis, and it is cemented with the Chinese authorities' decision to relax the peg of the renminbi against the U.S. dollar.

Finally, graph (b) of figure 3.3 illustrates the case for two archetypical small, open economies—namely, Australia and Canada. Here, to underscore the sometimes tenuous relationship between current account performance and the exchange rate, I also show the evolution of the nominal exchange rate vis-à-vis the U.S. dollar. Until 2001, when the United States experienced a brief recession, both currencies depreciated rather substantially and showed an almost simultaneous improvement in the current account balance.[25] Also, both currencies exhibited a steady appreciation until around 2013. The current

---

[23] Named after Peter Hartz, an executive of Volkswagen, who headed a commission looking into reforming how the German labor market operates. It was created by Chancellor Gerhard Schröder in 2002.

[24] Many of the arguments made here can also be made using charts that several other analysts have used—namely, showing the real exchange rate or unit labor costs in the eurozone. These reveal the rapid loss in the competitiveness of labor in Greece not only relative to German but all also other major single-currency member states. Ireland is the other outlier even more noticeable than Greece.

[25] Canada did not experience a recession in 2001, at least according to the business cycle analysis by Cross and Bergevin 2012.

account does not display a tendency to deteriorate in Canada, and does so only temporarily in Australia until the GFC, when Canada experienced a sharp deterioration while Australia experienced an improvement, albeit of the volatile variety. Of course, Australia did not record a recession, unlike Canada's brief downturn,[26] and continued economic growth clearly benefited Australia. The recent depreciation of both currencies, as the U.S. economy has improved while China's growth rate has slowed, has not yet shown up in the current account performance of either country.[27]

The current account is only half, as it were, of the forces that affect not only exchange rate movements but also monetary policy more generally. While economists have long known or worried about the flow of funds across borders, problems tended to be swept under the rug of capital controls or the inherent biases that favor domestic versus foreign investments.[28] However, since the 1980s, financial openness, at least according to some metrics, has risen substantially.[29] Four of the world's largest economies, in terms of both size and systemic importance—the United States, Japan, the United Kingdom, and the largest eurozone members (i.e., France and Germany)—are as open as can be, at least according to the indicators used by the IMF. China is the only other large economy that remains far from full capital account openness, although controls are being relaxed.[30]

It is now an article of faith that the financial sector is not the only proximate source for the global financial crisis. The forces unleashed by a combination of globalization in finance and monetary policy's unwillingness or inability to stem the rise in the flow of credit and other asset prices mark the fault lines in monetary policy strategies and highlight the difficulties in sustaining central bank cooperation since the crisis.

The Pivot Toward Financial Asset Prices

The next set of figures illustrates the role of the financial sector in the events of the past fifteen years, and along with the above observations about the importance of the current account, can help answer the question whether the EMU

---

[26] Ibid., who date Canada's recession as starting in 2008Q4, and ending in 2009Q2.

[27] The picture is not unique to small open economies of the advanced variety. Similar plots (not shown) for other BRIC economies (i.e., Brazil, India, Russia, and China), as well as for Turkey and other economies (e.g., Korea, Japan, the United Kingdom, and South Africa) reveal comparable patterns.

[28] The finding that domestic equities are preferred over foreign equities, for example, has a long history. Useful references on the subject include Coval and Moskowitz 1999; and Dalquist et al. 2003.

[29] See the Trilemma Indexes of Aizenman, Chinn, and Ito 2008, at (http://web.pdx.edu/~ito/trilemma_indexes.htm), sometimes called the Chinn-Ito Index.

[30] The indicator of financial openness cited earlier (see chapter 1 this volume) records a 0.2 for China in 2013.

indeed serves as the cautionary tale it is supposed to be. Figures 3.4 and 3.5 focuses on two asset classes, credit and property prices,[31] that have been the center of so much attention in the years running up the GFC and since.

Other than Japan, arguably a special case that reflects the effects of what has become referred to as the "lost decades," there is clearly very strong co-movement in the rise of credit over time (part (a) of Figure 3.4).[32] This pattern holds both for the economies of the eurozone represented in the figure (i.e., France, Germany, and Italy) and other large advanced economies and emerging market economies. The middle graph (b) shows a strikingly similar development for property prices. Once again, Japan stands out with an economy experiencing not only the collateral damage of a banking system that failed during the 1990s and could not fully recover[33] but also low deflation overall. The United States stands out because of the speed with which property prices rose by the mid-2000s, only to fall faster than anywhere else, as shown in the figure. As noted earlier, the rapid inflation in property prices took place while the Fed was tightening, albeit too slowly for some, suggesting either that monetary policy was not tight enough (a point first raised in chapter 1 but also see chapter 4) or that other mechanisms, currently known as macroprudential policies, were ill-prepared for the task. (I return to this question in chapter 6.) Finally, Germany's experience appears somewhat atypical, with flat property prices until around the time the GFC erupted. Since that time, property prices have risen rapidly and have overtaken others shown in the figure, a feature of the data also alluded to in chapter 1.

The rise in property prices, as is true for credit conditions, is apparently even more pronounced in the emerging markets, shown in graph (c) of figure 3.4. Therefore, both credit and property price conditions show signs of being a global phenomenon, excepting perhaps Japan. Accordingly, figure 3.5 plots a measure of global gaps for credit (a) and property prices (b). These were obtained by weighting the estimated gaps by the relative size of each economy as a percent of the world's GDP.[34] Not surprisingly, global

---

[31] I use the term "asset" only for convenience. Clearly, credit offered by financial institutions is an asset to these institutions and a liability to the holders of the credit. Similarly, property is an asset to the owners, but to the extent that borrowing has been used to finance its purchase, it is also a liability.

[32] A plot expressed in constant purchasing power, or real terms, would produce largely the same pattern (results not shown). A difficulty with real magnitudes is that it then is not immediately obvious, at least in a cross-country setting, that deflating the relevant nominal magnitudes by a CPI, GDP deflator, or some other proxy is appropriate in all cases.

[33] Arguably, because of very poor policy choices. See, for example, Cargill, Hutshison, and Ito 2003; and Kanaya and Woo 2000.

[34] The United States' share of the world's GDP has fallen steadily from 21.3% in 1999 to 16.5% in 2014. During the same period, China's share of the world's GDP has risen from 7.2% to 15.8%. The Eurozone is next among the large economies (17.6% of world GDP in 1999, falling to 12.3% in 2014). The United Kingdom and Japan are considerably smaller in size (ranging from 3% to 6.8% in the 1999 to 2014 sample). Indeed, the share of world GDP accounted for by these five economies has dropped from 55.9% in 1999 to 51.5% by 2014.

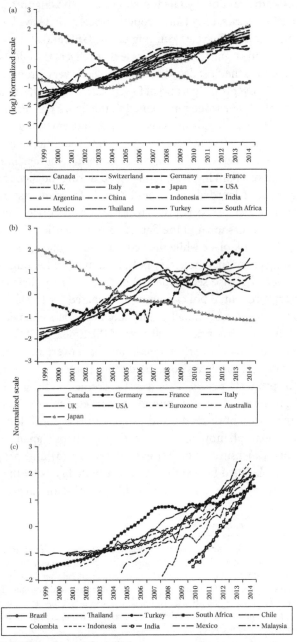

FIGURE 3.4 Property Prices Around the World

(a) Credit

(b) Property prices in Select Advanced Economies

(c) Property Prices in Select Emerging Market Economies

Note: The vertical axis is on a normalized scale (i.e., scaled by the standard deviation of the series). Further details concerning the property price series are available from the online appendix. *Source:* Data are from the BIS.

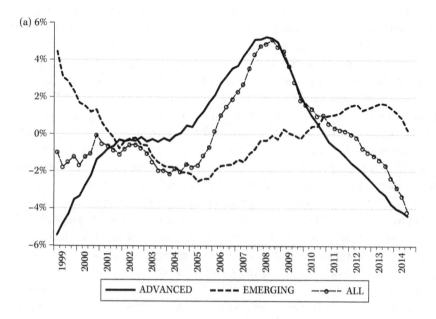

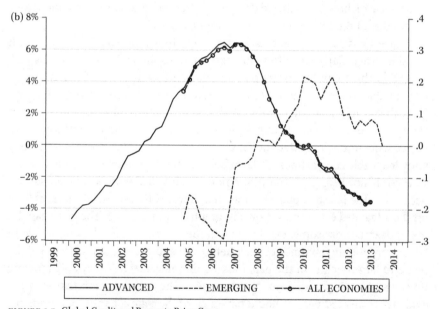

FIGURE 3.5 Global Credit and Property Price Gaps

(a) Credit

(b) Property Prices

Note: "All economies" are the sum of available advanced and emerging market economies; details are provided in the online appendix. The gap is the difference between a measure of potential credit or prices and observed values. Potential is estimated assuming we know the future level of observed credit or prices. *Source:* Data are from the BIS. Advanced economies and emerging economies are as defined by the BIS.

gaps are dominated by estimates from the advanced economies in the sample. Nevertheless, the calculations reveal some additional insights about subtle but important differences between advanced and emerging market economies. That is, credit gaps rise above zero in the emerging world shortly before ones in the advanced economies turn negative. However, it is important to note that while gaps remain sharply negative in the advanced world, they are largely eliminated in the emerging market economies. This suggests one potential source, with broader implications for the conduct of monetary policy, for the weak and unsatisfactory recovery in the world economy since 2010—namely, that the repeated easing of monetary policy has failed to be reflected in credit market conditions. (I return to this question again in Chapter 6.) A broadly similar path for global gaps in property prices is apparent in graph (c) of figure 3.5. For a time, between 2007 and 2009, emerging markets picked up the slack created by the sharp drop in property prices in the advanced economies. However, paralleling the credit aggregate, a persistent decline in property prices began in 2011 in emerging markets.

Before concluding the discussion of the role of the financial sector in recent economic history, it is worth pausing to ask how robust the results were in dealing with the evolution of credit and property price gaps. Figure 3.6 gives some idea of how solid the data are to alternative assumptions about our knowledge of the future course of economic events.

Figure 3.5 is based on calculations as if the future were known, if not with certainty, then fairly close to being extremely farsighted. Figure 3.6, instead, asks what the credit and property price gaps might look like if policymakers were unable to look ahead more than a few quarters.[35] The top graph (a) suggests that a less farsighted view of the pattern of credit creation does not change the overall picture, although the speed of the rise in credit gap and its subsequent decline after the GFC is faster than in the case of completely knowledgeable central banks. Alarm bells should have started ringing as early as 2005, if not before, as the BIS, among others, has pointed out on several occasions. The picture appears somewhat different for property prices, at least for the advanced economies shown in graph (b) of figure 3.6. The price gap did not appear as worrisome, say, in 2005 to the central banks who are unable to be forward looking, but notice that, before the end of 2005, there was a persistent and large decline in the gap, moving into negative territory and showing no signs of ending until 2010, at the earliest. The decline, combined with the evidence from credit gaps, should have alerted the central banks that problems were appearing in the financial markets.[36]

---

[35] The underlying data used in figures 3.3–3.6 on are at the quarterly sampling frequency.

[36] The evidence for property markets in the EME is not greatly affected by the factors considered here, but this is partly due to the much shorter sample.

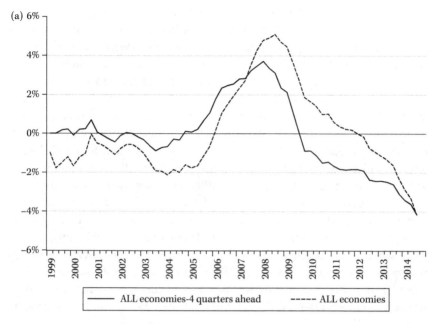

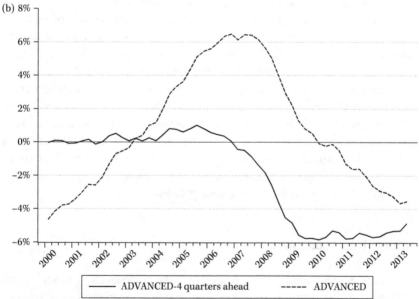

FIGURE 3.6 Global Property Price Gaps

(a) All Economies

(b) Advanced Economies

Note: See note to figure 3.5. The solid line is estimated gap, assuming we know only four quarters ahead what observed property prices will be. The dashed line assumes that the entire future is known. *Source:* Data are from the BIS. Advanced economies and emerging economies are as defined by the BIS.

The appearance of co-movements in financial developments across the major advanced and emerging market economies since the 2000s suggests a common element was driving these variables. Earlier, it was suggested that the stance of the monetary policy might be a culprit. However, other explanations are also possible. As shown in figure 3.7, gross capital flow movements—which can be large and volatile, as found by Broner et al. (2013)—rose strongly until 2007 in three of the four large economies shown in graph (a). Again, confirming the earlier interpretation of recent Japanese economic history, Japan is noticeable as a small participant in these flows. The collapse is clearly evident for the United States beginning in 2007 and in the United Kingdom beginning in mid-2008; even before the events of 2009–10, the reduction in flows to the eurozone is also apparent. Thereafter, however, there is no recovery in the single-currency area or the United Kingdom, while Japan continued to remain immune to international developments. Assuming that these flows are pro-cyclical, only the United States showed signs of a recovery by 2013, though levels were no higher than before the U.S. Federal Reserve began gradually raising its policy rate in 2004. Graph (b) of figure 3.7 suggests that some of the effects in the advanced economies spilled over into some emerging markets which had not experienced the full brunt of the GFC. Gross capital flows in Turkey and Thailand rise modestly but steadily over time.

All the foregoing results combine to suggest that the absence of exchange rate flexibility, while important, cannot fully explain the predicament that the eurozone found itself in. To be sure, there are well-known institutional flaws that must be added, but there is too little appreciation of the divide between economics and politics in attempting to answer the question of whether the EMU serves as a cautionary tale.[37] As argued briefly next, the current leaders of the eurozone system have turned the European project on its head. In addition, an overview of current account and financial conditions in the advanced and emerging market economies suggests that discussion about "exit strategies" conflate two types of problems that call for different policy prescriptions. The next two sections elaborate on these points.

Politics Meets Economics

If the recent experience of the eurozone does not provide a model of the consequences that result from tying one's hands regarding monetary policy, then in what sense does the EMU project serve as a cautionary tale? To be sure, factors that many observers have raised, such as an aging population,

---

[37] After this section was originally drafted, Aizenman, Chinn, and Ito 2016 reached a conclusion that is not dissimilar to mine. However, they rely on different data and do not consider implications of the gap between economic policy and political imperatives that influence policymaking.

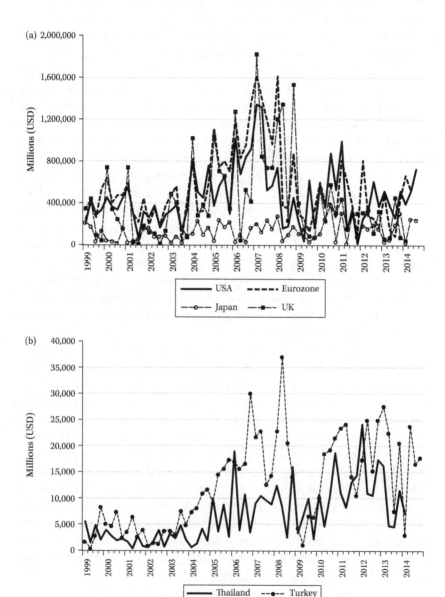

FIGURE 3.7   Global Capital Flows in Selected Economies

(a) Large Economies

(b) Select Emerging Market Economies

Note: Graph shows gross capital flows. *Source:* Data are from Broner et al. 2013.

the difficulty of implementing structural reforms, the complexity of managing differences in a diverse group of countries by size, culture, and fiscal capacity, and the constraints of a single monetary policy applied to divergent economic circumstances, all play roles in the ongoing drama of EU and EMU survival.

More important, however, and less evident from the data and not easily replicable elsewhere, is the gulf between good practices in economic policymaking (and monetary policy especially) and the political motives of the members of the single-currency area. To explain, I begin with a short review of what I refer to as "truths" about the current structure of the eurozone zone.[38] In doing so, I note how incomplete these truths are for the European project, as conceived by generations of policymakers and academics.

Stability, broadly speaking, is a primary objective on a continent that has been beset by disorder and war for centuries. To achieve this end, a political arrangement was necessary. Nevertheless, the Maastricht Treaty that underpins the structure of the European Central Bank (ECB) largely aims at an economic end, with the political framework taking a back seat. While the treaty boldly declared that "it opens the way to political integration," the desire to establish an economic and monetary union represent its primary objectives. Unfortunately, there has never been an understanding of what economic stability is supposed to represent; it was simply assumed to follow, once the convergence requirements were met.

The monetary union was designed by central bankers with the imperative that the institution be immune, as much as possible, to political pressures. The fear was excessive, but it reflected worry on the part of the German partners that other Europeans were more receptive to a central bank's bending in the face of political pressure than would be the Bundesbank, even though the Maastricht Treaty was signed while reverberations of the German government's pressure on the Bundesbank in the aftermath of reunification were still vivid. Perhaps more damaging was that the treaty did not provide for a mechanism that existed in the legislation governing the Bundesbank to manage such government–central bank conflicts. Since such conflicts are inevitable, the imposition of irrevocable exchange rates and the absence of any exit strategy from the eurozone under exceptional circumstances were major flaws in the design of the ECB. Requiring the ECB to report to a European Parliament incapable of real authority only added to the inherent inability of the central bank to hold a proper place among the existing political institutions of Europe.[39]

---

[38] Some of these truths apply more generally to the EU, but since this book focuses on monetary policy and central banking issues, I consider only the single-currency area.

[39] It is also worth remembering that the often-mentioned flaws inherent in the EMU, which intensified as the eurozone's sovereign debt crisis worsened (and even after ECB President Mario Draghi vowed to prevent the break-up of the EMU by adopting the "whatever it takes" strategy that had served

The foregoing arguably are technical truths about the EMU. While the ultimate objective was political union, the central bankers especially were more interested in the narrower objectives of forming a monetary union. They clearly understood that even a proper economic union, however defined but based on experiences from elsewhere in the world, works best when there it is held together with the glue of a political union of some kind. Interpreted slightly differently, the monetary union was a practical, symbolic, and achievable goal to be met along a longer road to political union that, likely, would never result in a loss of sovereignty by member states as great as that experienced in most other federations.[40] The oddity of the current situation is that, by neglecting the inherent weaknesses of the eventual monetary union formed, all of which are well known and have been widely discussed for years, if not decades, successive generations of policymakers have felt it more expedient to avoid jointly pursuing a political and economic union. Hence, the Stability and Growth Pact (SGP) was demoted to an agreement that would not have the force of a treaty obligation. Instead, it was watered down and neglected, especially by the very countries that would later insist on fiscal rectitude from the economically weaker members of the EMU. Indeed, when a new SGP was negotiated in 2012, it could not even be supported by all EU members.

As a result, the politics of the current eurozone have meant abandonment of the original and lofty goals of the EU. Instead of using its success at creating a single currency for sovereign states—a novel arrangement by historical standards—to build a structure that might lead to an as yet unknown form of political union, successive politicians kept the focus narrowly on the rules of macroeconomic conduct that were enshrined in the Maastricht Treaty. As the sovereign debt crisis wore on, policymakers, especially in government, were left with short-term palliatives to solve design flaws of their own making. Meanwhile, the ECB, time and time again, stepped in to close the breach created by those narrow objectives set by the politicians. This supra-national institution tested the boundaries of its remit by becoming more closely identified as a central bank like all the others—that is, a quasi-lender of last resort—instead of being the pure guardian of price stability it was designed to be. As a result, the ECB came to be seen as the only eurozone-wide institution capable of responding to the stresses created by the single-currency arena.

---

the Fed well), were all well-known. This is true not only of today's policymakers but also of those who helped conceive the single currency project; see, for example, James 2012.

[40] Many, of course, would point to the Swiss Federation as the kind of loose political union that Europe might adopt. Its size, however, does contribute to its success, and this is something that cannot easily be replicated at the Europe-wide level. On the other hand, the linguistic and cultural diversity of the Swiss nation do offer some possibility that such an arrangement can be replicated elsewhere. Finally, one must also consider that the Swiss Confederation is several centuries old. Therefore, one should not view the likelihood of replicating its success at the European level based on its current state.

Nevertheless, the ECB was largely reacting to outside political events and not behaving like a forward-looking institution trying to forestall negative economic shocks coming its way. Hence, unlike other central banks, monetary policy seemed to be too narrowly defined for the ECB, only because other institutions were not yet in place to deal with conditions that pitted the sovereign economies against each other within the single currency. If there ever was a central bank that behaved like the "only game in town," it was the ECB—and likely not because it chose to. As mentioned, the institution filled a yawning gap created by the political environment that surrounded it. In this sense, the ECB faced a different set of circumstances than those that affected other central banks, especially in the systemically important advanced economies. An incomplete banking union, an SGP that stretched credulity, bail-outs that left no one happy and did not solve the underlying problems, and lack of a clear roadmap to a return to normal economic growth left the eurozone beleaguered.

The parlous state of affairs, late in 2015, was heightened by the twin constraints of an absence of fiscal space in the weaker parts of the eurozone and the extreme reluctance of stronger members to provide additional transfers that might alleviate the economic difficulties of fellow EMU members, complicated even more in an era of low inflation.[41] This last point made it impossible to resort to the tried-and-true method of dealing with a debt overhang; to do so would have undermined the years it took to persuade the public of the obvious advantages and desirability of low and stable inflation rates. Indeed, to reverse course in this manner would expose the central banks, fearful of losing their credibility, to large and possibly permanent damage to their reputation. Bordo and Siklos (2016a, 2016b), who explore central bank credibility during the past century, quote Benjamin Franklin: "It takes many good deeds to build a good reputation, and only one bad one to lose it," a statement that captures a sentiment equally apt to the eurozone predicament. Moreover, it has never been clear why this form of debt relief, unlike other available mechanisms, is less costly. Since inflation affects all groups of society differently, and it is certainly less transparent than other solutions to the debt problem, such an approach ought to be the least desirable one.

The cautionary tale, then, to be seen in the EMU experience is not so much the incomplete structure and institutional mechanisms that underpin the single-currency area. Rather, the EU and EMU are illustrative of what happens when policymakers, especially politicians, chose to reverse the order of

---

[41] It is difficult to ignore the role played by fiscal policy (briefly discussed in chapter 1), but space limitations prevent a fuller treatment. Needless to say, some of the monetary policy actions taken by the ECB may well have been prompted by key EU member countries' preference for not relying on fiscal policy to assist in the eurozone's economic recovery. Nevertheless, the desire to create eurozone-wide fiscal rules that parallel the orthodox constraints imposed on the ECB predates the sovereign debt crisis. For discussions of related questions, see, for example, Sinn 2014 and Sandbu 2015.

causation from seeking a political objective to relying on a political project based on narrow economic and largely monetary goals.

Exiting Is Hard to Do

Crises inevitably require policymakers to seek an exit strategy. The crisis of 2007–9 was only a few months old when the Fed, arguably then at the center of the financial crisis, faced early political pressure to provide an exit strategy. Debate focused on the combination of extraordinarily loose monetary policy and a greatly expanded balance sheet. In the eurozone crisis that immediately followed what came to be called the GFC, the yearning for an exit strategy was also a reflection of two forces. The first was to seek relief from eventual levels of debt deemed excessive, but the second stemmed from an existing arrangement that statutorily prevented exit from the common-currency zone. In this case, political pressure came from the association of debt levels with the implementation of bad policies, together with the realization that single-currency arrangements perhaps should not be held together at all costs.

I have already discussed the second form of exit from a crisis. Here, I examine the matters facing central banks that also concern the first form of crisis exit. In what follows, I address four issues that must be addressed if we are to answer with the main question posed earlier.

An obvious challenge for central banks at the ZLB[42] is to decide how much and how quickly to raise the policy rate. Recall that criticism of the Fed in particular during the mid-2000s was that the FOMC tightened the money supply too gradually, illustrated in figure 3.8. There has been a noticeable drop in FOMC members' views about what constitutes the "new normal" in the Fed funds rate, from February 2012, when data were first made public, to July 2015 when the "long-term" Fed funds rate was set at 3.75%.[43] Instead, the number of FOMC members at the high end of the long-term Fed funds rate range has dropped substantially over time, while those advocating the lowest rates changed only marginally.

After seven years at the ZLB, the challenge might well have been to tighten more gradually than might otherwise be the case. However, while the Fed routinely signaled the need to exit in 2015, the members of the board have also substantially changed their view of what "normal" looks like for the Fed funds rate. Not only does this render normality a moving target, but it also substantially changes the use of instrument rules relative to pre-crisis days, when, for example, the neutral real rate was assumed to be constant.

---

[42] Or, if one prefers, at the effective lower bound (ELB) in recognition of the push by some central banks to introduce negative policy rates. In what follows, however, the distinction is not crucial.

[43] Not much changed in the year following, as the return to "normal" continues to be delayed.

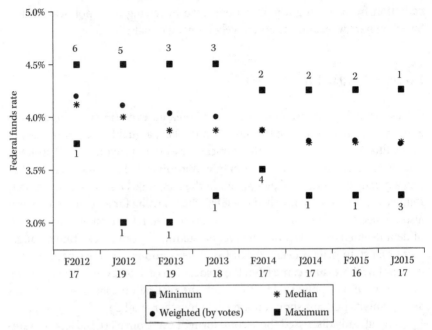

FIGURE 3.8 The FOMC's Dot Plot

Note: The numbers above the symbols show the number of FOMC members who set the "long-run" Fed funds rate at levels, in percentages, measured on the vertical axis. The solid dot and asterisks are, respectively, the weighted (by votes) and median values for the long-run Fed funds rate. The month/year of release of the Fed's report and the total number of FOMC voting members is shown below the dates: F = February, J = July (or June). *Source:* Data are from the Monetary Policy Reports of the U.S. Federal Reserve.

Indeed, the second challenge, then, is to define the new normal. This is rendered more difficult because, even if central banks would prefer to return to the days when the interest rate instrument was the only one that mattered, they will have to operate in a world where they will be tempted to avail themselves of multiple instruments while simultaneously ensuring the primacy of low and stable inflation.

When the BIS published its 85th Annual Report in June 2015, the title of the chapter dealing with monetary policy was "Another Year of Monetary Policy Accommodation." The BIS complained about a "risk of competitive easing," which amounts to a financial version of beggar-thy-neighbor policies. While this suggests that the global stance of monetary policy is going in the same direction, the facts suggest the return of an older phenomenon in a new guise—namely, the emergence of divergences in monetary policy, especially among the major economies.

All these developments raise the possibility that existing monetary policy strategies may not be well suited to dealing with exit or with the desire to manage financial imbalances. In particular, if it is deemed appropriate to keep interest rates lower for longer, is it also sensible to allow inflation to be higher for longer, either to limit the possibility of a return to the ZLB or to deal with the debt overhang via an inflation tax? Of course, the risk is that expectations will no longer be anchored, and the public may well lose its trust in the central banks as guarantors of economic stability.

Finally, an exit from UMP must confront the possibility that shrinking a central bank's balance sheet is not as easy as reversing policies that led to the expansion in the first place. We may find out that, in an ironic twist on the remarks made by former FOMC Chair Ben Bernanke, when he commented that "the problem with QE is it works in practice, but it doesn't work in theory," shrinking the central bank's balance sheet may work in theory but not in practice. Even if central banks retain a larger balance sheet for macroprudential reasons, several central bankers have publicly acknowledged that some reductions will eventually become necessary. If this is the case, then there will have to be some explanation of what the new normal entails for the financial position of the central banks.

Recall that to address the consequences of the GFC, key central banks in the advanced economies quickly lowered their policy rates to levels approaching or at the ZLB. The situation then was ripe at some central banks for switching to unconventional tools that considerably expanded their balance sheets, as well as devoting more effort to communicating their stance via explicit guidance of market expectations. This included expressing a desire to maintain policy rates at the ZLB for an extended period of time. The major central banks, such as the Fed, the BoE, the BoJ, and the ECB, also introduced asset purchase programs that expanded the size of their balance sheets, primarily through the acquisition of government securities or by effectively underwriting certain forms of private debt. This had the effect of lowering debt servicing costs, as well as allowing fiscal authorities to rely on the accommodative monetary policy stance to manage a sustainable debt position, for example, through an extension of the maturity of the debt. In other words, central banks shifted their policies toward influencing other interest rates along with the term structure.

As shown in figure 3.9, the diversity of balance sheet positions is striking, with the non-crisis economies of Australia, Canada, and New Zealand in graph (a) only modestly away from pre-crisis conditions. The situation is vastly different for the other economies shown in graph (b), including the crisis-stricken economies of the United States, the United Kingdom, and the eurozone, with Japan reversing its earlier QE experience in spectacular fashion following the introduction of QQE.

Unconventional monetary policies (UMPs) were intended as vehicles for "borrowing time" for much-needed structural reforms, private-sector balance sheet repair, and fiscal consolidation, particularly in the economies most impacted by the crisis. These arguments have been noted by some observers for some time now.[44] Such policies were also intended to boost aggregate demand

---

[44] See, for example, BIS 2013a.

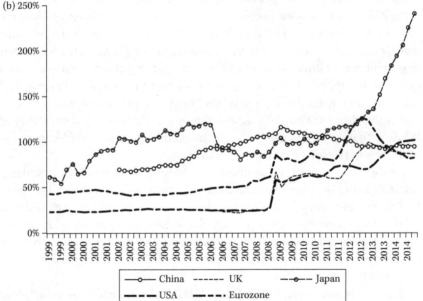

FIGURE 3.9 Central Bank Assets to GDP Ratio in Selected Economies, 1999–2014

(a) Central Bank Assets to GDP in Select Inflation Targeting Economies

(b) Central Bank Assets in Select Large Economies

Source: Data are from BIS.

as a way of reducing the economic costs of reforms. In contrast, economic growth in emerging markets remained healthy while that in the advanced economies in particular entered a sharp, but brief slump that has been followed by persistent sluggish and disappointing growth. None of this is terribly surprising, since much academic research, including the much-cited work by Reinhart and Rogoff (2009), demonstrates that recovery is especially slow in the aftermath of a financial crisis of the kind experienced in 2008–9.

While the GFC effectively resulted in a global loosening of monetary policy to an unprecedented extent, the impact of the crisis was not evenly distributed. Accordingly, thinking about the role of monetary policy changed, and the crisis highlighted the importance of having a resilient and well-regulated banking system. Emerging markets complained about the negative spillover effects from the prospective withdrawal of what were previously ultra-loose policies in the advanced economies. These arguments were countered by pointing out that several emerging market economies failed to use the opportunity to reform their own economies or to correct persistent current account imbalances. Casting blame on the emerging markets seemed like a repeat of the complaint leveled at these economies by Fed Chair Bernanke in 2005, when he suggested that the "global savings glut" reflected inappropriate policies outside the United States. Moreover, the central banks in the economies most affected by the crisis argued that their attempts to boost aggregate demand would make their way through the global economy. These conflicts heightened tensions between the central banks, while the will to cooperate explicitly dissipated. By their actions, some central banks revealed what was a largely unspoken rule: that domestic priorities come first, and the international consequences of their actions take second place. However, this comes as no surprise. After all, a central bank is governed by the laws of its sovereign state, and not by international agreements or treaties.

Against this backdrop, a withdrawal of monetary stimulus too early could halt or even reverse the recovery. It is only recently that Fed transcripts from the GFC period reveal explicit acknowledgment that the U.S. central bank was "behind the curve" (e.g., see Appelbaum 2014). Accordingly, there is little reason a priori to believe that the exit from an ultra-loose monetary policy would be managed any better. Recall how markets became turbulent during the summer of 2013 at the mere mention of "tapering," as discussed in chapter 2. This episode did not represent a tightening of monetary policy but, rather, a slowing down of the rate at which the Fed intended to provide monetary stimulus to the economy.

Combine the difficulties of exiting with benign neglect of the global consequences of their actions and the major central banks could be creating favorable conditions for a new crisis. Hence, by failing to tackle the external dimension of their policies, the central banks may well contribute to a further reduction in the likelihood of a successful exit from unconventional monetary policies. The challenge for the central banks in managing the exit is to clearly define their objective(s) and their decision-making process; in so doing, they would express an understanding that their policies have global consequences, as they assist the global economy in a return to more normal conditions. Indeed, the complaints emanating from some large emerging market economies (e.g., India, Brazil, and Indonesia, to name but three) suggest that there remains considerable room for central bank cooperation, if not improved communications.

As pointed out earlier in this book, the marginal gains from international cooperation may be small if each house is kept in order. The implication, however, is not that monetary policies will as a result cease to be divergent. Quite the opposite is true. As this is written, it is clear that the United States and the United Kingdom are emerging from the fallout of the GFC faster than are the countries of the eurozone, which are now mired in QE,[45] while other advanced economies (e.g., Australia, Canada, New Zealand) that did not resort to UMP to date may now be preparing to enter the field and some emerging market economies are slowing, albeit at different rates (e.g., China, India, and Brazil). Hence, there is little reason to expect policy coordination. Nevertheless, the well-established presence of significant monetary policy spillovers does demand greater interaction between the central banks, precisely because the next GFC, if and when it comes, is likely to be dealt with more effectively if some form of international cooperation is employed.

It has been known for several decades that, so long as there is a mechanism to resolve conflicts, institutions can operate independently of each other.[46] Central banks, for the many reasons already alluded to, are well placed to meet this requirement. Indeed, this may partly explain why inflation targets in the advanced economies have not changed since the crisis, while a similar reluctance to redefine price stability is also seen in emerging markets.[47]

However, these same central banks, by virtue of the fact that they operate within their respective governments, cannot resolve conflicts or economic imbalances alone. Unfortunately, as I discuss more fully later, collective action by

---

[45] In most instances this means that a bond purchase (e.g., sovereigns issued by a European member state) is offset by a reduction in another interest earning financial instrument. Once the ECB ceased its sterilization policy in 2014 it was effectively engaging in QE.

[46] While Olson's work, cited previously, is clearly pertinent, so is the research by the Nobel Laureate Elinor Ostrom; see, for example, Ostrom 2009.

[47] This development has taken place without any formal attempt by, for example, the IT central banks to collectively defend their respective inflation objectives. These same central banks have, independently, pushed back against suggestions that inflation targets be raised, either because the costs of doing so are small or because of the need to insure against more frequent occurrences of the hitting the ZLB or the ELB. Indeed, by conflating so-called structural reforms and fiscal policy considerations with the need for more inflation, as well as how these would spill over into emerging markets, critics of IT in the advanced economies (e.g., see Blanchard et al. 2010; Ball 2014; and Krugman 2014) have effectively weakened their case to raise inflation as a solution to what ails the global economy.

governments at the global level have disappointed, except when conditions are most dire. This suggests, in particular, that current institutional structures at the political level lack effective mechanisms to build trust. Central bankers are more apt to understand this point than the politicians they report to.

The desire to engage in greater cooperation is not new. Indeed, central bankers are fond of repeating that they have done so for years, and nowhere as closely as during the GFC.[48] However, what is less appreciated is that, even if more joint initiatives are seen as advantageous, these cannot take place in the vacuum created by politicians who shy away from demonstrably adopting such a strategy. Central banks are limited, by statute, to represent domestic concerns. It is up to their governments to define the space in which the monetary authorities can act cooperatively. To date, there is little interest in exploring the details and enforcement of collective action.

The Consequences of Staying Too Easy for Too Long, Without Empathy for Others

What are the costs of balance sheet policies? And, have the major central banks already gone too far? First, it is broadly acknowledged that UMP were effective at preventing the collapse of certain market segments, forestalling widespread financial instability, and stimulating a recovery in the real economy.[49] But it equally seems true that these same policies became less effective at the margins while the risks continued to grow.

There are three economic risks and an institutional one associated with keeping monetary policy too easy for too long. The first economic risk is the potential for distorting the functioning of the financial markets, especially when the central bank becomes the dominant active trader. Markets for government securities are important for the transmission of monetary policy. Therefore, market distortions could render the use of the policy rate ineffective during the exit process. The second economic risk is the potential build-up of financial instability. With negative real yields, investors may engage in imprudent practices in searching for higher yields. In addition, financial institutions might undertake irresponsible lending practices by giving loans to private individuals who will not be able to manage their debt once the interest rates rise.[50] A third economic risk operates through global spillover effects. In

---

[48] See, for example, Bernanke 2015a.

[49] See, for example, IMF 2013a; Williams 2013.

[50] Both of the preceding fallouts from ultra-loose monetary policy may well produce real economic distortions that go beyond the financial consequences mentioned so far. These real effects are not easy to identify and are not, so far, conclusive. However, see Borio et al. 2015 for some evidence that these additional real distortions are empirically meaningful. Whether, as a result, financial crises worsen an incipient episode of secular stagnation is unclear, because it is notoriously difficult to identify short-run

particular, exchange rate and capital flow volatility in emerging markets and developing countries have the potential to spark financial and macroeconomic instability abroad. In general, the more accommodative the monetary policy stance, and the longer central banks delay tightening their policies, the larger are these risks.

The foregoing risks are based on well-known fundamentals of how financial markets operate. Beyond them, the ever present risk of contagion has resurfaced, this time in emerging markets, and this risks a further delay in exiting to more normal monetary conditions. Alternatively, benign neglect in the advanced economies where the last GFC originated risks even lower global growth and a deflationary trap. One reason the global economy did not suffer a larger drop in output in 2008–9 noted earlier (see chapter 1) is due to the economic performance of emerging markets.

The institutional risk threatens the de facto independence and credibility of the central banks. The more accustomed fiscal authorities and financial institutions become to an (excessively) accommodative policy stance, the longer they may draw out the process of debt consolidation and balance sheet restructuring. This may lead the government or the financial sector to put pressure on the central bank to buy more time by keeping its policy easy for longer. If the monetary policy objectives or the decision-making process is influenced by these forces, central banks effectively lose their de facto independence and, along with it, their credibility.[51] Central banks can protect themselves by following the adage expressed long ago by Bundesbank President Karl Blessing, who argued that "[a] central bank which never fights, which at times of economic tension never raises its voice, . . . that central bank will be viewed with mistrust" (as quoted in Marsh 1993:256–57). If history is any guide, the risks are considerably greater in the emerging market economies. Once again, these developments underscore the importance of what the central banks communicate. The old paradigm wherein central banks are not expected to comment on matters outside their remit no longer applies when fiscal and monetary policies clearly share a common interest and are no longer as neatly separated as was the case pre-GFC.

Although the potency of these risks varies by country, they are not negligible in the United States, the United Kingdom, Japan, or the euro area. The risk of distorting the securities markets is larger for the BoE, the BoJ, and the Fed, who hold a sizable fraction of the total amount of their outstanding government securities, while at least in 2015, holdings by the ECB were comparatively modest (less than 5%). The risk of financial instability from reaching for

---

from longer-run forces that impinge on economic activity. How these combine to influence the depth of a downturn in a financial crisis and the strength of a subsequent recovery are far from straightforward to estimate. In this connection see, for example, Cukierman 2015 and Cukierman and Izhakian 2015.

[51] Hannoun 2012 expresses a similar sentiment.

higher yields and abrupt asset re-pricing is also higher in the United States, the United Kingdom, and Japan because yields on government securities are at an all-time low and equity and corporate bond prices could begin to bubble if easy monetary policy encourages a higher risk appetite.[52]

The risk of financial instability is even stronger in the United Kingdom in the face of substantial increases in housing prices. The bodies who set monetary policy at the Fed and the BoE are monitoring potential build-up of financial risks through searches for higher yield or imprudent lending practices. Those at the Fed generally view these risks as moderate, but they continue to play a key role in the short-term monetary policy decision-making process. Those at the BoE believe that monetary policy does not pose a significant threat to financial stability and that it could be contained by the macro- and microprudential supervisors and regulators. We have heard this story before. Unfortunately, so long as the effectiveness of macroprudential regimes remains in question, we should stay hopeful but skeptical about the promise of macroprudential regulations. In Canada, for example, the impact of successive tightening of mortgage lending rules has been undercut by the BoC's low policy rate for the foreseeable future. The BoC believes that its policies, which include a form of moral suasion intended to temper banks' ability to freely lend credit, work well in tandem with the stand taken by the Department of Finance. However, it is also the case that, internationally, policy rates close to the ZLB encourage a search for higher yields and, as a consequence, heighten the incentive for risk-taking by investors, both domestic and foreign. On the domestic front, the mere fact that private debt to GDP in Canada is higher than it was in the United States on the eve of the crisis, with the gap having risen over time, lends ammunition to critics of the macroprudential solution for avoiding bouts of financial instability.

International markets are particularly sensitive to the Fed's monetary policy because of the dominance of U.S. Treasury securities in the global markets. Fed tapering has contributed to an outflow of funds from emerging markets, particularly in Brazil, India, Indonesia, Turkey, and South Africa, weakening currencies that are needed to fund foreign-denominated debt.[53] In response, some central banks in these countries have been tightening monetary policy, but this does not encourage more economic activity. The Fed's current attitude toward the international effects of its monetary policy appears to be that it will clearly communicate the expected path of its policies, so that emerging markets can adjust their respective policy stances using domestic policy instruments. Janet Yellen, the Fed's FOMC Chair, solidified this view during her testimony to Congress, when she stated, "We have been watching closely the recent volatility in global financial markets. Our sense is that at this stage these

---

[52] Also, see Rawdanowicz, Bouis, and Watanabe 2013 on these points.

[53] A positive note is that recent events may well reinforce emerging markets' desire to issue debt denominated in their own currencies.

developments do not pose a substantial risk to the U.S. economic outlook" (Yellen 2014b).

Outside the United States, views are different. Even if the feedback loop to the United States is negligible, this seems to assume that emerging markets will adopt the correct policies in return. It is hard to imagine that a slump in the BRICS countries will not reverberate back to the United States. Taken at face value, reactions such as these ought to increase the challenge of coordinating monetary policies around the globe. Effective communication is not a science, however, and as argued earlier in this chapter, pleas by some central bankers (e.g., Raghuram Rajan, former governor of the Reserve Bank of India) for more cooperation should not be ignored.

To illustrate the potential importance of spillover effects, I consider a straightforward example of how some economists at least have tried to quantify the question. Suppose that we can describe the macroeconomic environment that two large economies live within—say, the United States and China— with only a few business cycle and financial cycle variables. Typically, such a model would include real GDP growth, inflation, an indicator of commodity price movements, a measure of credit growth, and a proxy indicator of the stance of monetary policy.[54] If we are interested in understanding the link between real and financial factors in either economy alone, our model would not concern itself with spillovers. But with the possibility of spillover effects, there are additional challenges, partly because we have a relatively short sample to work with and partly because the size and complexity of the model increases greatly when we merge the models for both economies.

Omitting the technical details, a simple way of ascertaining the significance and size of spillovers is to examine each economy separately, but also allow for two additional variables that influence real economic and financial activity in each of the two economies. Once we label these factors real and financial, we can ask whether China's economy is affected by the U.S. economy, or vice versa. Equally important, we can ask whether our interpretation of economic activity in either economy is greatly influenced whether we ignore spillover effects or not. If the answer is that spillovers matter, and especially of the financial kind, then policymakers need to not only recognize the link between the real and financial sides of their economy but also understand that what happens in financial systems abroad also plays a role.[55]

---

[54] More precise details are given in the online appendix. Commodity prices will be represented, as they often are, by oil price inflation; inflation will be measured, in this case, by using PCE inflation for the United States. With China, data-quality-related issues are always brought up; see Burdekin and Siklos 2008, Pang and Siklos 2016, and references therein, for a brief discussion and additional references. The issue, while far from trivial, is outside the scope of the present example.

[55] To be sure, it is a factor that in China's exchange rate system the currency does not float freely. However, as discussed in chapter 2, in a world where real and financial factors interact, the "shock absorber" properties of the exchange rate are far from perfect.

Figure 3.10 illustrates how China's economy responded to a "shock" (i.e., an unexpected movement) in the variables listed at the bottom of each graph. For each, the shock happened in the first quarter only and the lines trace the effects on the variables over a ten-quarter period. Four potential variables are considered for their impact on real economic growth, inflation, and monetary policy. They are investigated for two cases in China: no spillovers (a) and spillovers from the United States (b). When the spillovers are ignored (a), we see what appear to be results that would have obtained independently, whether there was a crisis or not.[56] For example, real economic growth responded positively to inflation, credit growth also fueled real economic growth, and when the People's Bank of China tightened its monetary policy, there is a temporary (about two-year) drop in growth, which then resumed. The tightening of monetary policy also resulted in some disinflation, and the PBOC tends to tighten monetary policy when there is a rise in inflation. In these respects, China's economy behaves not very differently from that of so-called advanced economies.

If we now allow spillovers from both real and financial elements of the U.S. economy, we obtain the second set of results (b). We now see that inflation in China actually stimulated economic growth for longer and remained positive for at least ten quarters into the future. Credit growth in China was even more inflationary than when we ignored the U.S. spillovers. Indeed, we can see that a tighter monetary policy by the PBOC, once a disinflation phase passes, actually becomes inflationary after several quarters. This likely reflects the temporary nature of the tightening of policy and the offsetting effects from more credit growth.[57] Indeed, when spillovers from the United States are factored in, higher credit growth actually led to an even greater loosening of policy than in the no-spillovers case. Clearly, one gets the impression that the Chinese authorities are well aware of such spillover effects and that they cannot be ignored.

What about spillovers in the other direction? Table 3.2 provides some of the findings. What is especially notable is that real economic effects from China (i.e., real GDP growth, commodity prices, and other variables combined to create the "real" factor have significant effects on real U.S. indicators such as U.S. real GDP growth and PCE inflation, while financial factors (e.g., credit

---

[56] There is no separate attempt to "model" the crisis, even in an ad hoc manner. It should be kept in mind, however, that economic performance across most of the variables would clearly pick up the impact of the financial crisis of 2007–9. The estimates presented in figure 3.10a and 3.10b (and table 3.2) are based on quarterly data covering the 1999–2014 period.

[57] The inflationary impact of a tighter monetary policy seems counterintuitive, although such a result is also the finding reported by other authors. It has been called the "price puzzle" and is likely due to the omission of some intermediate variables (most notably, inflation and growth expectations). Complicating matters in China's case is that it is not necessarily so that the inflationary effect of a tightening comes from a higher interest rate, as is the case in, say, U.S. studies. For a more in-depth analysis of these issues, see Pang and Siklos 2016.

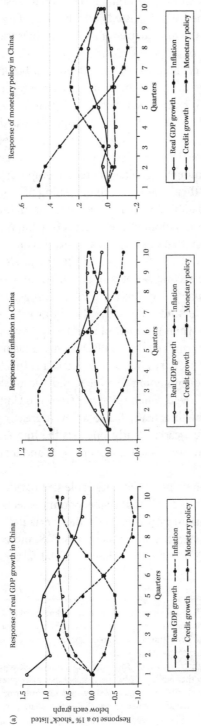

FIGURE 3.10 Macroeconomic and Financial Interactions between China and the U.S.

(a) Assuming No U.S. Spillovers: real GDP growth, inflation, monetary policy

(b) Allowing for U.S. Spillovers: real GDP growth, inflation, monetary policy

Note: Estimates show the impulse responses—that is, the response of the series labeled at the top of each graph to a shock equivalent to 1 standard deviation in the residual of the equation describing the endogenous variable listed at the bottom of each graph. The shock occurs in period 1 only, and the effects are traced for over 10 quarters. Additional technical details are in the online appendix. *Source:* Author's calculations.

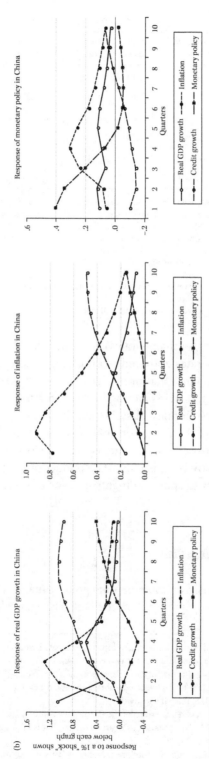

FIGURE 3.10 (*Continued*)

TABLE 3.2 } Chinese Spillovers onto the U.S. Economy

	U.S. Output Gap*	U.S. PCE Inflation†	U.S. Oil Prices**	U.S. Fed Funds††	U.S. SLOS***	U.S. Loans†††
Real factor from China lagged 1 quarter	−0.25	0.18	5.9	−0.018	−0.68	-30
	(0.13)	(0.11)	(3.7)	(0.096)	(1.8)	(35)
	[−1.93916]	[1.66195]	[1.61809]	[−0.19198]	[−0.37129]	[−0.87774]
China Monetary Policy lagged 1 quarter	−0.29	−0.044	−2.9	−0.17	4.8	69
	(0.13)	(0.11)	(3.8)	(0.1)	(1.9)	(36)
	[−2.19536]	[−0.38061]	[−0.76307]	[−1.71427]	[2.53716]	[1.92183]

Note: The estimates (coefficients, followed by standard errors in parenthesis, and t-ratio in brackets) are derived from the model described in the chapter text for U.S. data, with the addition of the two estimated factors based on Chinese data. (Additional technical details are provided in the online appendix.)
*The output gap is the difference between observed and estimated potential output (based on the H-P filter).
† PCE is the personal consumption expenditures deflator.
** Oil prices are West Texas intermediate crude prices.
†† Fed funds is the Fed's policy rate.
***SLOS is the Senior Loan Office Survey conducted by the Fed (a higher number means tighter standards, a lower number signals looser standards).
††† Loans are commercial bank loans deflated by the PCE index.

growth, interest rates, exchange rates) influence the U.S. financial system—that is, U.S. interest rates and credit conditions—more generally.[58] Perhaps it is findings such as these that prompted the Fed, in early 2015, to highlight the role of global factors in explaining its delay in raising the Fed funds rate.[59]

Clearly, if these economies' business and financial cycles are linked, then that linkage hampers the ability of policymakers to neatly differentiate elements in the respective financial systems that threaten real economic performance, thereby greatly complicating the conduct of monetary policy. At the very least, this ought to spur arguments in favor of greater, not lesser, global cooperation.

Together Apart: *Plus ca Change*?

The challenges and risks of implementing policies that will ensure healthy economic growth remain significant, as the IMF has acknowledged (IMF 2013b).

[58] The factors estimated here are essentially linear combinations of several variables that capture real economic and financial conditions in the two economies. Unfortunately, it is not straightforward to interpret the economic significance of the estimates in table 3.2. We would also need to isolate from the various variables that make up each factor to obtain an idea, for example, of how much a slowdown in China would influence U.S. real GDP growth.

[59] The October FOMC press release states: "The Committee continues to see the risks to the outlook for economic activity and the labor market as nearly balanced but is monitoring global economic and financial developments."

See www.federalreserve.gov/newsevents/press/monetary/20151028a.htm.

In this environment there is seemingly more that divides groups, such as the G20, than that unites them in restoring faith in international cooperation. However, before one reaches the conclusion that only bad outcomes are likely in the foreseeable future, it is useful to look back to 1971 when the Bretton Woods system was abandoned and policymakers were debating the kind of monetary system that would replace it. In a speech by Arthur Burns, former FOMC chair during the 1970s, he pointed out that "[a] major weakness of the old system was its failure to treat in a symmetrical manner the responsibilities of surplus and deficit countries. With deficits equated to sin and surpluses to virtue, moral as well as financial pressures were very much greater on deficit countries to reduce their deficits that on surplus countries to reduce surpluses" (Burns 1972).

Those words were uttered over forty years ago. Yet, a look at the global economy today suggests that the weaknesses present then are still there. Unlike then, however, it is no longer possible to envisage the G3 (United States, Japan, and Germany) agreeing on a realignment of exchange rates (e.g., as in the Smithsonian Agreement of 1971), even if one believes that it can put an end to a "dangerous trend toward competitive and even antagonistic national economic policies" (Burns 1972). When it comes to international trade, the current environment has led to a curious state of affairs whereby the threat of a currency war is ever present, whereas in a common-currency area like the eurozone, the war is one of attrition with the governments of member states determined to rely on internal devaluations and fiscal restraint, because the alternative of an exit from the eurozone cannot be contemplated. In the meantime, financial globalization has ensured that even if gains in competitiveness are sought via more favorable exchange rates, the resulting advantage can be offset by the reaction of the financial markets and their ability to move vast amounts of funds with little delay.

It is equally curious that those who warn about looming currency wars[60] choose to focus mainly on China, exaggerate the degree to which currencies are being manipulated, and fail to acknowledge that exchange-rate depreciation simply no longer delivers the same benefits that it used to. In addition, it is difficult to see how exchange-rate movements alone can be expected to help return advanced economies to pre-crisis growth levels. China's exchange rate appreciated considerably until the summer of 2015, when it reversed course.[61] Also, while it is true that some central banks (e.g., Switzerland, New Zealand) have shown more enthusiasm for intervening in foreign exchange markets, the amount of forex intervention pales in comparison with what used to be the

---

[60] A prominent exposition of this view is Bergsten 2013.

[61] China, as have other economies, used this device to boost its domestic economy. The timing may have been influenced by a looming IMF decision, finally taken in November 2015, to effectively declare the yuan (or renminbi) a reserve currency.

norm decades ago. Finally, there is considerable evidence that exchange-rate pass-through effects have diminished substantially in recent years, largely because low and stable inflation has become an accepted strategy for delivering good monetary policy. [62]

Of course, to the extent that destructive currency manipulation poses real economic effects, one course of action would be to sanction or fine countries that resort to beggar-thy-neighbor policies. Even if this were a feasible policy, there are simply no successful historical examples of a "system" of sanctions of this kind to serve as a model. If member states of the eurozone can negotiate delays in the resolution of excessive budget deficits[63] that are, in principle, subject to sanctions, it is even less likely that the international community can agree on dealing with currency manipulators. The bottom line is that the current international monetary system has not improved much since the GFC.

All is not as bleak as might at first appear. Gone are the days when a few large economic powers made decisions having global repercussions, with little dialogue with those affected by their decisions. In spite of its flaws, the G20 does represent a start toward developing a mechanism to deliver good global governance.[64] Paralleling this development is the recognition that low and stable inflation continues to represent an essential ingredient of good practice in monetary policy.

There remain, however, two large gaps of a "technical" nature and one of a "cultural" nature that must be filled in order to lay the groundwork for renewed economic growth. The "cultural" gap is likely the most intractable. While some[65] have noted that China is uncomfortable with the notion of "global governance," the same sentiment applies to the United States, not to mention the United Kingdom. Whether it is in the areas of banking and financial reform, debt restructuring, or fiscal policy, the U.S. Congress has routinely shown hostility toward global governance strategies. An obvious illustration, noted earlier, is when U.S. monetary policy is carried out without much care given to potential global spillover effects, in spite of a growing body of research

---

[62] For example, see Bailliu, Dong, and Murray 2010. More recently, Forbes, Hjortsoe, and Nenova 2015 find that the source of the shock (viz., monetary versus demand) plays a decisive role in dictating the size of exchange-rate pass-through effects.

[63] At least members of the EU have agreed on a definition of what "excessive" means, even if they resort to accounting and other devices to escape their agreed-upon fiscal restrictions. There is even less agreement on what "excessive" means when it comes to exchange-rate movements.

[64] Nevertheless, as will be discussed in the final chapter, it is worth asking whether the current structure or organization of the G20 is conducive to creating a more cooperative environment. It is ironic that supposedly like-minded politicians, at least when the term is applied to economic policy strategies, and unlike their counterparts in the central banks, are unlikely to be accused of groupthink when they deliberate the economic fate of the globe. Indeed, if anything, groups such as the G20 are more likely to reach rancor and dysfunction. The secret, if the lessons from Tetlock and Gardner 2015: 74 are to be believed, is to aggregate "the judgments of an equal number of people who know lots about different things . . . because the collective pool of information becomes much bigger."

[65] For example, see Shambaugh 2013: ch. 4.

suggesting that spillovers are significant.[66] Of course, it helps that the resulting spillovers are believed to be *positive*, or at least not negative (Bernanke 2012b), even though agreements such as the G20's Mutual Assessment Program (MAP) commits its members "to monitor and minimize the *negative spillovers* of policies implemented for domestic purposes" (IMF 2013a:1).

Agreements of this sort emphasize the asymmetric implications of domestic choices made, in part, because the pursuit of a reasonable set of objectives is all they can agree to—namely, solid economic growth together with low and stable inflation. There is the presumption that negative spillovers must be avoided at all costs; positive spillovers, on the other hand, are to be encouraged and available to everyone. Even if these spillovers can be precisely identified—at best a daunting task—there is no enforcement mechanism in place nor a recognition that spillovers reflect policy divergences in a world where business cycles are not synchronized.

Groups such as the IMF or the G20 should devote more effort to persuading their largest and most influential members that there is more to gain from a coherent international policy regime than is lost in the costs of monitoring and enforcing a policy broadly seen as ineffective in promoting cooperation. Policymakers may wish to heed Woodrow Wilson's advice of long ago, during the dying days of World War I, about how to ensure the peace: "There must be, not a balance of power, but a community of power" (Wilson 1917).

A related issue is whether the size and diversity of the G20 or the IMF give rise to problems endemic to large groups of the kind Mancur Olson (1965) discusses in his seminal contribution on the challenges of collective action. Rather than being viewed as an organization where all its members are treated equally, at least in principle, it ought to act more like a federation where certain blocks more affected by some policy questions than others are permitted to opt out, so long as some minimum established standards are maintained. An escape clause that is transparent and that sets limits on international cooperation would represent a step forward.[67] Ironically, the escape clauses that permit the United Kingdom and Denmark to stay out of EMU or, rather, voluntarily join the common-currency area, are positive examples from EU history.

Another example comes from the implementation of the Basel III reforms (e.g., see BIS 2013b). In a sample of banks examined by the Basel Committee G20, several members have no internationally active banks (Argentina, Indonesia, Mexico). Similarly, the sample included several other member countries where banks are small and are not internationally active (Brazil,

---

[66] For example, see Bauer and Neely 2012; Lombardi, Siklos, and St. Amand 2017 forthcoming and references therein.

[67] Siklos 2013a makes a similar point.

China, Saudi Arabia, and the United States).[68] To suggest that a one-size-fits-all regime will work is neither helpful nor realistic.

Turning to the "technical" gaps that need to be filled, we find two are most glaring. One is greater acceptance that international standards for financial supervision and regulation are essential, and the other is rules for good conduct in fiscal policy. Failure to deal with the first gap will once again permit financial institutions to exploit new openings or, worse still, undo the very benefits of financial globalization—namely, the flow of credit to where it is most valuable. Forces leading in this direction are already under way (Economist 2014). As indicated earlier, a single regime will not "fit" a diverse group of economies. Since financial structure and the degree of maturity across countries varies considerably, there ought to be room for idiosyncratic arrangements while simultaneously minimizing the regulatory arbitrage that contributes to a build-up of financial imbalances, culminating in a crisis such as the GFC.

In the area of fiscal policy, just as central bankers learned the hard way that only a judicious mix of rules and discretion can lead to low and stable inflation, a similar effort needs to be undertaken to find that mix. To be sure, several such arrangements have been proposed and implemented, but there is as yet no common ground on the subject, possibly because existing rules are seen as too complex.[69] Unlike monetary policy, where technocratic answers to problems tend to predominate, politics can never be too far from fiscal considerations. Hence, organizations must balance the need to maintain effective policies while not bending to an excessive degree the need to preserve the democratic accountability of elected officials.

There is, however, an underappreciated additional constraint on international cooperation. It is typically assumed that a government's ability to engage with other governments is unfettered. This is an exaggeration. After all, in democracies, elected representatives must keep an eye on political inevitable differences of opinion.[70] In contrast, central banks, within their mandate, likely feel less constrained.[71] They are charged with doing what's best for the aggregate economy, as defined in the legislation that governs their mission or in their agreements with the government in power. In some countries, such as the United States, domestic considerations cast a larger shadow

---

[68] The banks referred to are the Group 1 banks (capital in excess of €3 billion and internationally active). All other banks are considered Group 2 banks.

[69] As argued also by Schaechter et al. 2012.

[70] In addition, depending on the type of international agreement, legislatures must be involved. Matters are less clear-cut in non-democratic countries. However, concerns over internal divisions are likely universal.

[71] Mario Draghi's often-repeated response to act more aggressively "within our mandate" is a perfect illustration. The less precisely defined the space in which a central bank acts, the greater its freedom to intervene when necessary. This explains, partly, why U.S. reforms to legislation governing the Fed have limited its freedom to respond in the next crisis.

than in parliamentary democracies, where majorities are freer to enter into international commitments.[72] Moreover, at certain moments when the push for reforms is greatest, such as during financial crises, tensions between the desire to cooperate and the concern for domestic disagreements are also most pronounced.[73]

Perhaps the best that can be expected is to ensure that avenues of cooperation are kept open, permitting policymakers to learn from each other. The forces that historically have led countries to adopt one another's monetary policy strategies represent a form of cooperation that is less explicit than others, but it can be equally effective.[74] I defer to the last chapter to suggest whether a forum such as the G7 or G20 is the best place to encourage such learning.

While this discussion presents a list of what international cooperation can accomplish, there is also one suggestion for what governments should avoid doing—namely, relying too heavily on the central banks to deal with the structural challenges they face. Not only does doing so violate any reasonable principle of good "global governance" by increasingly transferring the adoption of policies and decision making to unelected officials, but the recent course of events makes it plain that monetary policy has its limits. Unfortunately, this principle, like some of the others mentioned earlier, has also been violated time and time again. Paul Volcker, in the early 1980s, warned as much when he stated: "[I]ndustrial nations, . . . nowadays rely heavily—sometimes too heavily—on their central banks and on monetary policy to achieve our economic goals; to promote growth and employment, to blunt the forces of inflation, and to maintain financial stability" (Volcker 1984). Once again, it is a lesson that has yet to be learned.

Conclusions

There is a natural tendency to search for a one-size-fits-all solution to the consequences of financial crises. Yet, these crises come in a variety of forms. Complicating matters is that some financial crises propagate across borders, although historically very few have become global in scope.

---

[72] Recent events in the United States—notably the polarization of politics—is nothing new. As ably recounted in Lowenstein 2015, the fallout from the panic of 1907 that eventually led to the creation of the Fed was marked by a politically poisoned environment. Also, see Bruner and Carr 2007 and Timberlake 1993.

[73] How else can one explain the differences in the speed, scope, and content of financial reforms in the United States, the United Kingdom, and the eurozone after the events of 2007?

[74] The spread of inflation targeting is a good example of what constitutes good practice in monetary policy.

Clearly, the choice of exchange-rate regime potentially ought to play a critical role in our understanding of financial crises. This element also ought to be highlighted, in view of the lessons from EMU, as an example of the dangers of relying too much on the macroeconomic and financial fortunes of others. Nevertheless, once institutional factors and changing fashions in the desirability of international cooperation are factored in, the influence of exchange-rate choice is smaller than we were led to believe a decade ago or so.

More remarkable are the common developments in some financial asset prices. These seem to transcend the choice of exchange-rate arrangement and, to a degree, the choice of monetary policy strategy. This further contributes to an exaggeration of the role of the exchange rate in the events that transpired in the eurozone during the past decade. It also underscores the desirability of highlighting how political constraints can dictate economic policies.

The expectation that the advanced economies will emerge from a reliance on UMP presents an opportunity for greater prominence given to the global element that stems from sovereign monetary policy decisions. Beyond domestic decisions about the choice of appropriate monetary policy strategy, policymakers must also ask, as Sir John Hicks (1967) once did, whether central banks can be purely national—and if not, whether and how much international cooperation is desirable.

Cooperation—namely, a code of conduct that places primacy on domestic goals but is sensitive to international considerations—is always desirable. Yet, there is little indication that this cooperation can be successfully accomplished. Instead, policymakers jump to coordination when a crisis or an emergency is ongoing. Alternatively, it might be more desirable to work out cooperative agreements or solutions that reduce the size of the step needed for full-fledged coordination on those rare occasions when it is needed. The exit strategy, at different speeds and on different schedules, offers policymakers an opportunity to engage in this approach to global governance. Even if this recommendation is adopted, though, the sheer size and complexity of the economic problems we face suggests that policymakers should avoid singular solutions that limit too much the participants' options. Successful cooperation must always allow for escape clauses.

Equally troubling is putting off a return to more "normal" interest rates, even to maintain lower long-term economic growth and lower inflation, because of the perceived economic and financial risks that this might entail. Of course, these risks are unobservable and just as difficult to quantify as the risks of lower inflation for longer periods. Moreover, left unexplained is why the benefits of ultra-low interest rates exceed the potential costs of greater financial instability, identified so far in this and in earlier chapters. Finally, there is potentially a contradiction in policies aimed at keeping monetary policy loose for an extended period, when what stands out are memories of the severity of the crisis and an impression that normality has not yet returned, and not the duration of attempts to prevent a return to more normal financial conditions. If a "peak-end" type of rule operates at the macroeconomic level, then it is the failure to successfully and credibly set in motion a series of decisive steps to restore economic conditions that will remain salient in the minds of the public.[75] After all, policymakers have declared that the GFC is over, while simultaneously suggesting either that the "old normal" (ill-defined as it is) has not yet returned or that a "new normal" (yet to be fully articulated) is what the public ought to expect. The financial markets and the public will not look kindly on attempts to defer any economic costs stemming from the GFC via ultra-easy financial conditions if, having failed to produce a satisfactory recovery, the global economy is plunged into a recession that monetary policy is powerless to prevent. Another economic contraction is more likely to be remembered, as will the financial conditions alleged to have contributed to it, than will attempts to forestall a downturn over several years. As Gilovich and Ross (2015: 2755) conclude, in drawing lessons from "peak-end" type behavior, "it is cautious inaction rather than impulsive action that [people] most likely come to regret."

---

[75] This rule refers to the observation that an individual's memory tends to be selective, dominated by what was experienced at some peak or defining moment. A classic reference is Redelmeier and Kahneman 1996. Obviously, what is true for the individual need not be true in the aggregate. Moreover, if preventing Great Depression 2.0 is the peak goal for some (e.g., central bankers), others (e.g., politicians and the public) may well connect the central bank policies with the resulting distortions in financial asset prices, especially if financial instability returns on a global scale. The impression that all is far from well so many years after the GFC began and ended suggests that a "looser for longer" monetary policy may not be enough tonic to repair the more intractable problems affecting the global economy.

4 }

The Decline of Simplicity and the Rise of Unorthodoxy

Ambition Stymied

The Bank of England was still on a mission to tighten monetary policy in early 2007,[1] when Mervyn King, then governor of the Bank of England, uttered these words: "Long before I became Governor I said that my ambition was for monetary policy to be boring."[2] As noted in chapter 1, central banks had the mandate as well as the theoretical and empirical backing for the notion that stability in inflation, anchored by a numerically announced target as in the inflation-targeting (IT) economies or through policy, represents best practice for monetary policy. Indeed, in 2000, the former governor of the Bank of Canada, Gordon Thiessen, put it in the following terms: "Simpler and more straightforward approaches have generally turned out to be better. . . . What is needed to get the job done are one clear objective and one simple instrument."[3]

The simplicity of this approach to the conduct of monetary policy could not be denied. It was rooted in both economic theory and political economy. Economic theory long ago demonstrated that that the number of policy objectives cannot exceed the number of policy instruments. Hence, all that was needed to achieve an inflation target was a single instrument, and an interest rate became the preferred candidate. It was easily observable, its impact was largely understood by the public, and economic analysis had established explanations linking different debt instruments to their terms to maturity.[4]

---

[1] The bank's policy rate rose 75 basis points between August 2006 and January 2007.

[2] From a speech, "Monetary Policy Developments," at the Birmingham Chamber of Commerce Annual Banquet, January 23, 2007.

[3] From a lecture to the Faculty of Social Science, "Can a Bank Change? The Evolution of Monetary Policy at the bank of Canada 1935–2000," University of Western Ontario, October 17, 2000.

[4] This is the term structure of interest rates and expectations that were the dominant reason for establishing a predictable relationship between short- and medium-term interest rates. The "expectations hypothesis," once a preferred explanation linking yields across the term structure, did not always

This is the essence of Tinbergen's (1952) Rule.[5] Of course, this left open the issue of whether price stability was sufficient to achieve financial stability. The latter objective, as we have already seen, was deemed either to follow from the price stability goal or to be the concern of microprudential regulators and supervisors.

It is reasonable, of course, to assume that price stability is conducive to financial stability, however broadly one cares to define the latter term. After all, there is considerable theoretical and empirical evidence linking the level of inflation to financial volatility, and thence to economic performance and uncertainty.[6] What remains unclear is whether price stability is sufficient to meet a financial stability objective, even if we set aside the question, to be addressed later, of the extent to which the responsibility for achieving this financial stability ought to rest with the central bank.

Taken literally, the notion that one instrument—namely, an interest rate—is somehow able to achieve economic stability, including the smooth functioning of the financial markets, seems a stretch. Yet, writing in 2006, Anna Schwartz, Milton Friedman's co-author of A *Monetary History of the United States,* does hint at a link between the two objectives: "[I]f inflation and price instability prevail, so also will financial instability" (Schwartz 1995:21). Schwartz is careful enough to suggest that price stability is the "route" to financial stability, and not its *sine qua non.* Moreover, the idea was not conceived in 2006, but actually much earlier (Schwartz 1988) and later found support in empirical evidence (e.g., see Bordo and Wheelock 1998). Nevertheless, many observers, especially central bankers, were quick to draw attention to a seeming natural connection between the two forms of stability.

One difficulty is that, as is often said, the devil is in the details—that is, we must be clear about what form of inflation begets financial instability and whether all types of financial crises are more or less equally associated with poor inflation histories. In addition, as will be explained, we have little in the way of data for a reasonably long enough period to monitor and evaluate the likelihood of what is today referred to as "tail risks." Indeed, while we have reasonably good histories, data, and narratives for many of today's advanced economies, the available information dwindles quickly when we move beyond this group.

---

find strong empirical support and has lost even more favor as an explanation of the behavior of the term structure. This, in spite of the fact that its validity has been challenged for about thirty years (e.g., see Fama and Bliss 1987; Campbell and Shiller 1991) not least because there exists a term premium that is largely unobservable. Increased intervention by central banks beyond the market for short-term government debt instruments has also complicated explanations of the behavior in the spread between long and short rates.

[5] Named after the Dutch economist and recipient of the first Nobel Prize in Economics.

[6] Indeed, at the risk of oversimplification, this is the gist of Milton Friedman's (1977) Nobel Prize lecture.

Of Crises and Tail Risks

Economists have come up with a variety of definitions for financial crises, as we have seen in the previous chapter. Even if we can't agree on what kind of crisis has taken place, we typically know one when we see it. Yet, defining a crisis also requires taking a stand on *when* the current economic and policy environment is no longer sustainable.

Some have focused on currency crises, wherein the exchange rate, the balance of payments, or both is the proximate cause of the problem. Other forms of crises include banking crises, domestic or sovereign debt crises, and stock market crashes. Banking crises can originate from multiple sources, such as insufficient capital or a severe mismatch between assets and liabilities that leads to inadequate liquidity. Sovereign debt crises stem from a fiscal position that has been weakened to the point where holders of government debt no longer have confidence that the interest and/or principal will be repaid. As Reinhart and Rogoff (2009) discovered, no doubt to their dismay, beyond this straightforward observation we cannot draw firm conclusions about where the tipping point is—that point beyond which a full-blown sovereign debt crisis erupts. Greece and Japan readily come to mind.[7] The point at which debt becomes unsustainable in the eyes of the financial markets differs considerably for the two economies, and not only or even principally because exchange rates are more flexible in one than in the other. Clearly, the future capacity of the respective economies also matters, as does the source of its debt finance—that is, how much of it is raised domestically as opposed to being obtained from abroad.[8] In extreme cases, sovereigns themselves default. Finally, in the case of stock markets, since they are supposed to help predict inflation and output, a sharp decline may portend a bleak future and can contribute to a significant decline in economic outcome. The previous chapter considered some of the cross-border effects of financial crises that have implications for whether and how countries cooperate in the area of monetary policy.

---

[7] Reinhart and Rogoff 2010, 2012 argued that debt levels beyond 90% of GDP have a substantial negative effect on economic growth. Their finding was challenged by Herndon, Ash, and Pollin 2013 on the grounds that the data analysis was sloppy. Later, Pescatori, Sandri, and Simon 2014 also found evidence against the importance of a debt threshold. The controversy sparked a media frenzy, but the matter remains largely unresolved. It is equally unclear how much emphasis should be placed on a single numerical value that is imprecisely measured and likely to be highly variable across countries and over time.

[8] With a debt to GDP ratio exceeding 200%, one has to wonder whether Japan will soon reach the point beyond which it can no longer borrow. It is worth noting that one of Prime Minister Abe's three arrows involves rationalizing fiscal policy, and this includes reducing or at least stabilizing the debt to GDP ratio. In addition, Japanese policymakers have been reminded that former Finance Minister Takahashi Korekiyo, often referred to as Japan's Keynes, found it difficult to borrow from abroad. Nevertheless, he also felt that fiscal policy can give the economy a boost when the economy would otherwise face a depression; see Smethurst 2009.

While there may be some disagreement about whether certain events constitute a crisis, on the whole a backward-looking view yields a fair amount of consensus on the timing and frequency of such events. Figures 4.1 and 4.2 plot mean inflation and real GDP growth rates, respectively, for advanced and emerging market economies (right hand axis) against an indicator of the incidence of financial crises of all kinds (left hand axis). The data are annual and stretch back to 1940.[9] There appears to be relatively little connection between the two relationships for advanced economies, whereas inflation could well be a lagging indicator of financial crisis in the emerging markets. The possibility, and one that many other observers have made, is that advanced economies have both the institutions and the wherewithal to avoid a reliance on inflation levels as a means of exiting crisis conditions. This point is relevant for the most recent crisis and it is a question we return to from time to time throughout this book.

Turning to economic growth, there seems to be a more predictable global relationship between the incidence of financial crises and economic growth. In the case of the advanced economies, the most recent crisis saw a sharp decline in growth that was more or less coincident with the appearance of the financial crisis. Another case in point is the late 1940s, as the advanced economies were emerging from the end of World War II and its economic consequences, as well as struggling to put into place the postwar institutions intended to promote stability and growth. Also worth highlighting is the fact that over the six decades of data shown, only once did real GDP growth become, on average, negative and that was in the crises of 2008–10.[10]

The same negative relationship between financial crises and growth is evident at other times, even if the link may not be as strong as when the crises were most severe. The case of emerging markets is more blatant, although the link between the size of the crisis, measured in terms of the fall in real GDP growth, and the incidence of crises is less clear. Moreover, it is also worth noting that, unlike the experience of the advanced economies, economic growth never became negative in the emerging market economies.

The picture so far is incomplete, however, and it is worth asking whether the connection between overall economic performance, as illustrated in figures 4.1 and 4.2, can be ascribed to some types of financial crises and not to crises that emerge in other forms. Figures 4.3 and 4.4 provide partial answers to that question.

---

[9] Data exist going back to the middle of the nineteenth century. However, longer-run observations do not allow us to readily compare the experience of emerging and advanced economies. Historical comparisons are also complicated by the fact that economies that may have been emerging in one era might become advanced in a later era.

[10] A longer-term perspective would, of course, reveal other examples of negative growth in the wake of financial crises, such as the Great Depression. See, for example, Eichengreen 2015.

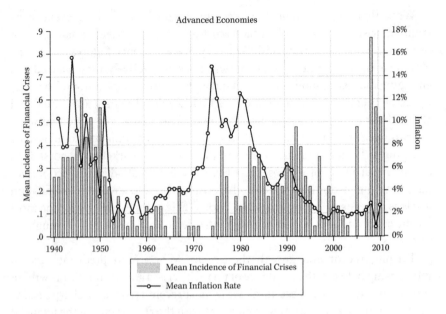

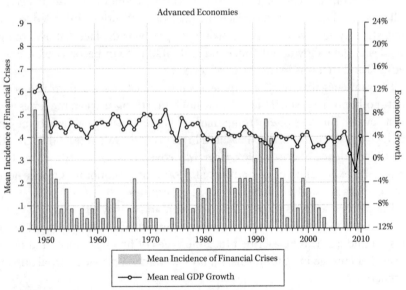

FIGURE 4.1 The Nexus Between Inflation, Real GDP Growth, and Financial Crises:
Advanced Economies

(a) Inflation

(b) Economic Growth

Note: All types of financial crises are considered. Inflation is defined in terms of CPI inflation. *Source:* Financial crises are from Reinhart and Rogoff (2009). Inflation and real GDP growth are based on author's calculations using data from January 2015 IMF International Financial Statistics CD-ROM (Washington, DC: International Monetary Fund).

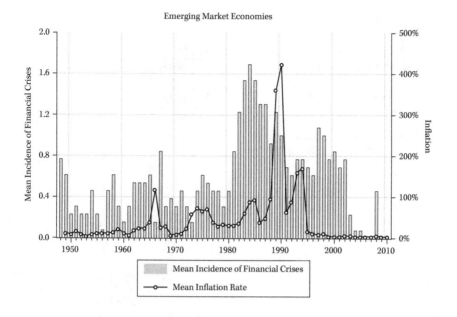

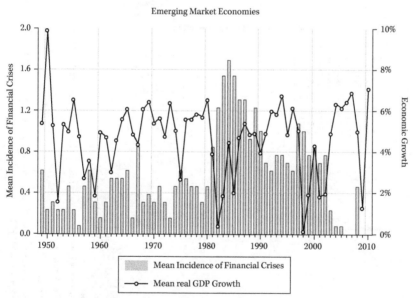

FIGURE 4.2 The Nexus Between Inflation, Real GDP Growth, and Financial Crises:
Emerging Market Economies
(a) Inflation
(b) Economic Growth

Note: All types of financial crises are considered. Inflation is defined in terms of CPI inflation. *Source:* Financial crises are from Reinhart and Rogoff (2009). Inflation and real GDP growth are based on author's calculations using data from January 2015 IMF International Financial Statistics CD-ROM (Washington, DC: International Monetary Fund).

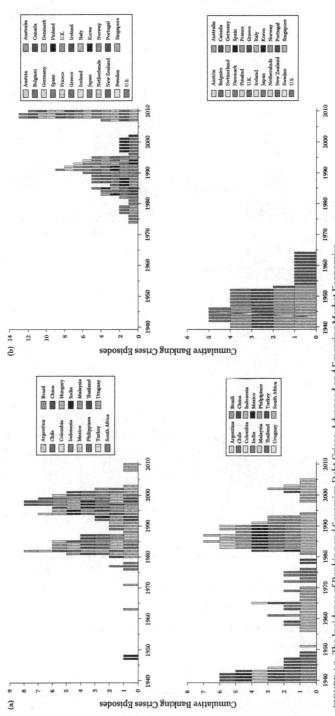

FIGURE 4.3 The Incidence of Banking and Sovereign Debt Crises: Advanced and Emerging Market Economies

(a) Emerging market economies

(b) Advanced Economies

Note: Episodes in the economies sampled are "stacked" one on top of the other; hence, the higher the bar, the greater the number of crises in a given year. *Source:* Author's calculations using data from Reinhart and Rogoff (2009).

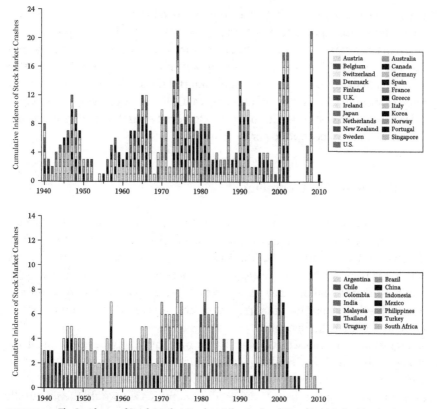

FIGURE 4.4 The Incidence of Stock Market Crashes: Advanced and Emerging Market Economies

(a) Stock market Crashes: Advanced Economies

(b) Stock market Crashes: Emerging Market Economies

Note: The data represent a count of episodes of stock market crashes in the countries labeled on the right. For each time period the higher the bar the greater the number of episodes in the country shown. *Source:* Author's calculations using data from Reinhart and Rogoff (2009).

Figure 4.3 plots the cumulative incidence of banking and external sovereign debt crises.[11] These two forms are, arguably, the most virulent types of financial crisis. The bars reflect the frequency of crises in both advanced and emerging market economies. Each portion of a bar records the occurrence of a crisis; hence, the higher the bars, the more economies in each group experienced either banking or sovereign debt crises. The left side of the bar charts display the results for emerging markets while the right side provides the record for the advanced economies in the sample.

Banking crises are not unique to emerging markets. Indeed, they can be characterized as a regular event on the global stage, at least since the 1970s. Nevertheless, while the crisis of 2008–10 did spill over into the emerging

---

[11] Other insights about these types of data were also considered in the previous chapter.

markets, it was largely a feature of the advanced economies. Moreover, external debt crises appear to be a thing of the past in the advanced economies. Stock market crashes, shown in figure 4.4, are both frequent and regular features of the global financial landscape, however. Indeed, stock market crashes are such a regular occurrence that it is doubtful these can have, at most, more than a temporary impact on inflation or real GDP growth. In contrast, visually at least, the strongest connection appears to be between the incidence of banking crises and real economic performance.

Why Did No One See It Coming?

The now famous reaction of Queen Elizabeth II,[12] on a visit to the London School of Economics, to the size and impact of the GFC suggests that policymakers (and academics) were blindsided by the onset of the financial crisis. Much has been written on this topic, and there is little new to add except to point out that the failure may have less to do with what we did not know and more with the assumption that regulators and supervisors were on the watch for looming financial instability.

Figure 4.5 illustrates this point. Based on a qualitative evaluation of the strength and quality of banking supervision and regulation in the advanced economies, the data reveal steadily rising levels of oversight of one kind or another in a growing number of advanced economies. One would then naturally be inclined to conclude that the likelihood of a "black swan" emerging should

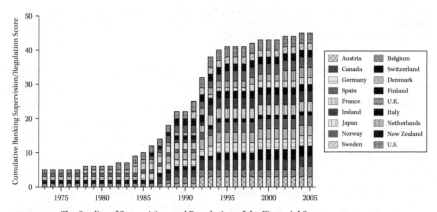

FIGURE 4.5　The Quality of Supervision and Regulation of the Financial Sector

Note: Index of official supervisory powers (with a higher number indicating greater power) and overall restrictions on banking (a higher score indicating more restrictions). *Source:* Data are from Barth, Caprio, and Levine 2013.

---

[12] See, for example, www.telegraph.co.uk/news/uknews/theroyalfamily/3386353/The-Queen-asks-why-no-one-saw-the-credit-crunch-coming.html. In response, U.K. academics sent a letter of apology.

have been lower. Instead, as we now know, there was a collective failure to prepare for what transpired beginning in 2007.

The allusion to the rare events implicit in the "black swan" hypothesis suggests that even if policymakers were asleep at the wheel, the financial markets might have given some indications that "tail risks" were rising. As described in chapter 2, the concept describes rare events in probabilistic terms and is suggestive of the possibility that extraordinary events, such as the collapse of inter-bank lending that took place in 2008, are the least likely of events that one can contemplate. Hence, these show up in the "tails" of a distribution of asset prices.

Yet, as discussed earlier, financial crises are not especially rare events. Their severity is another matter, and the extent to which events in one part of the world can spread to another is also in question. The contrast between the global impact of the Asian financial crisis of 1997–98 and the GFC of 2008–10 is a case in point. The former did not spread globally, even though it left a permanent mark in large parts of Asia. Of course, the latter emerged from a systemically important economy—namely, the United States. Put differently, we are once again led back to the distinction made earlier between systematic and contagious elements in the transmission of economic and financial shocks.

One way of illustrating the difficulty in identifying the two types of effects is considered in figures 4.6 and 4.7. The horizontal axis in figure 4.6 shows the growth rate in total credit, while the same axis in figure 4.7 measures the rate of change in housing prices. The vertical axis in both figures represents the probability that the rate of change in the series falls within the intervals represented by the vertical bars. The dashed line is also a smoothed estimate of the probabilities so that the overall shape of the distribution is easier to visualize. Booms in credit growth or large increases in housing prices would be captured by the right tail of the various distributions shown while the left tails would indicate busts.

A selection of evidence from both advanced and emerging market economies is shown in these figures. Beginning with credit growth, we immediately observe that rapid increases in credit are more likely than are large negative values in credit growth. In advanced economies, negative growth rates—an indication of severe credit crunches—are infrequent and, with the exception of Japan, essentially never exceed 5%. The situation is dramatically different in emerging markets, which see large swings in credit growth. Indeed, only Argentina, India, Indonesia, and Thailand experienced large negative growth rates in credit, although these too are comparatively infrequent. China did not experience any negative growth rates for the period considered.

The evidence is not much different for housing prices. However, large declines in housing prices are less unusual than they are for credit. For

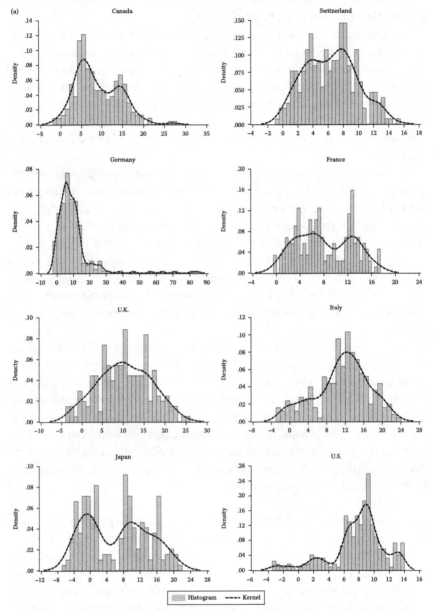

FIGURE 4.6 Tail Risks in Credit Growth

(a) Advanced Economies, 1987–2014 (8)

(b) Emerging Market Economies, 1987–2014 (8)

Note: Credit growth (see chapter 4) is expressed as a distribution that is subdivided into equal-sized "bins" or intervals. The vertical axis gives the number of observations that fall into each interval. Hence, the histogram is an estimate of the probability density function for each interval. The dashed line represents a smoothed estimate under the assumption of a normal distribution. *Source:* Data are from the BIS and estimates are based on author's calculations. A quarterly sampling frequency is used.

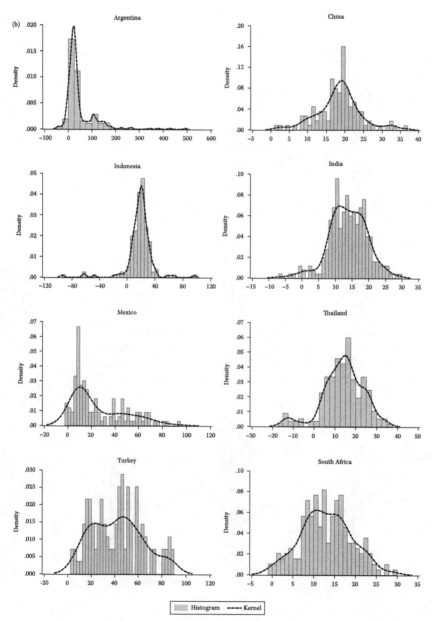

FIGURE 4.6 (*Continued*)

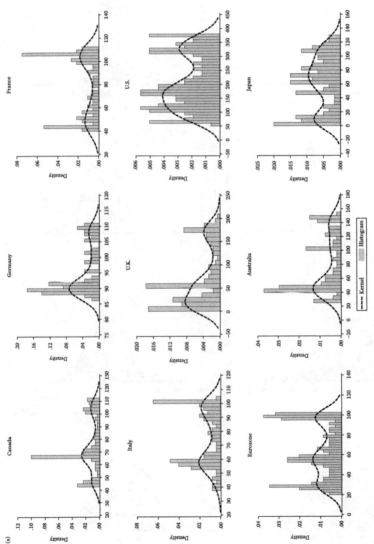

FIGURE 4.7 Tail Risks in Housing Prices

(a) Advanced Economies, 1987–2014 (9)

(b) Emerging Market Economies, 1987–2014 (10)

Note: Credit growth (see chapter 4) is expressed as a distribution that is subdivided into equal-sized "bins" or intervals. The vertical axis gives the number of observations that fall into each interval. Hence, the histogram is an estimate of the probability density function for each interval. The dashed line represents a smoothed estimate under the assumption of a normal distribution. *Source:* Data are from the BIS and estimates are based on author's calculations. A quarterly sampling frequency is used.

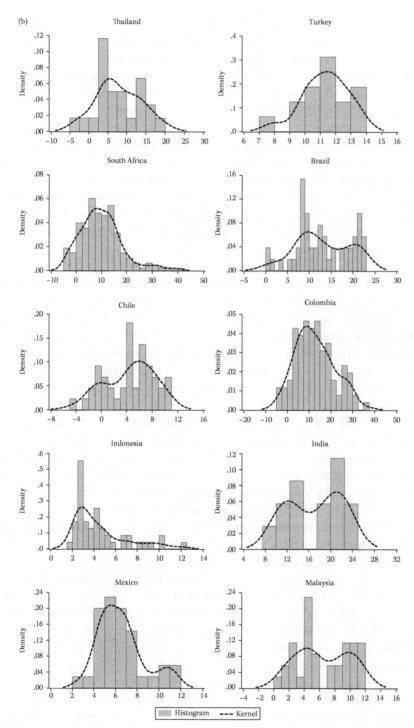

(b)

FIGURE 4.7 (*Continued*)

example, Germany experienced an average fall of around 3% for one-tenth of the sample. Similarly, cumulative declines in housing prices of over 4% in the United States cannot be said to have been rare events. Japan's record represents an outlier of sorts, with the peak in the distribution in negative territory. This was likely fallout from the cumulative impact of Japan's lost decades. In contrast, negative growth rates in housing prices in the emerging markets (figure 4.7[b]) are the exception rather than the rule. Of the ten countries shown, only Thailand, South Africa, Chile, and Colombia recorded negative growth rates. Finally, it is worth highlighting that there seems to be a strong idiosyncratic element to the experiences across the economies shown in figures 4.6 and 4.7. A visual examination of the smoothed estimates of the distributions makes this readily apparent. Overall, then, it is not too much of a stretch to think that the financial crisis of 2008–10 had a "black swan" aspect to it.

Nevertheless, one must be careful in drawing strong conclusions. In particular, the figures represent snapshots of history. Moreover, the figures do not allow an assessment of the evolution of tail risks over time, nor can they explain the role played by the monetary policy in place. Finally, to the extent that there are global spillovers in the behavior of credit or housing prices—a reflection of the extent to which the globalization of finance has proceeded— the data in figure 4.7 are not informative about the channels through which asset price movements, and their consequences for the real economy, can spread.

Accordingly, figure 4.8 presents a measure of the correlation in credit growth for three pairs of countries. The correlations vary over time and are constructed in a manner such that the interrelationships across economies are taken into account.[13] The shaded areas indicate when the United States was in recession. Correlations change frequently between the United States and Canada, though; with the exception of recessions, they tend to be well above 40%. The high and persistent level for the correlations is even more apparent in the comparisons of the United States and the United Kingdom, as of Japan and Mexico. Whereas one might expect, based on trading patterns, the correlations to be high in the first two cases there is little a priori economic reason to expect such correlations for Japan and Mexico. As with the U.S.–Canada example, correlations quickly become negative when the United States is in recession. The fact that correlations remain high most of the time, and only decline temporarily, is further evidence that signals of changes in financial conditions are ephemeral.

---

[13] In constructing the correlations, five economies were jointly considered. There are several caveats to consider when computing and reporting correlations of this kind. While these can affect the results, they do make the point that there is an important and systemic element to credit growth that extends across countries.

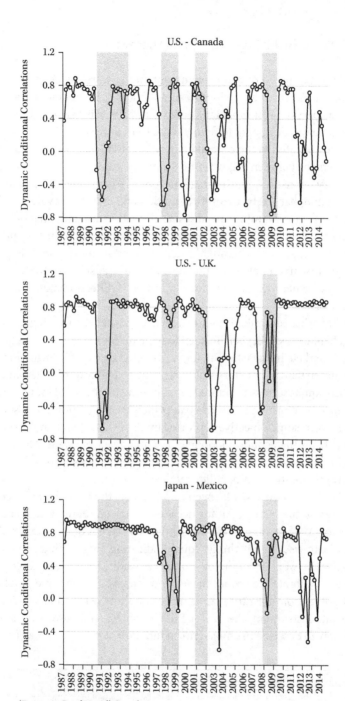

FIGURE 4.8 (Dynamic Conditional) Correlations

(a) U.S.–Canada; (b) U.S.–U.K.; (c) Japan–Mexico

Note: The shaded areas are the recession dates as published by the National Bureau of Economic Research. The solid line represents correlations that are conditioned on changes in the mean and volatility across the markets considered. The sample is 1987–2014 (quarterly data). *Source:* National Bureau of Economic Research (www.nber. org. The technique used here was originally developed by Engle 2002.

From Rules as Orthodoxy to the Great Digression

Paralleling the spread of central bank autonomy were the adoption of inflation control measures and widespread adoption of accountability and transparency as part of most monetary policy strategies. This signified recognition
that monetary policy ought to follow some rules of conduct. Whether the level
of authority granted to the central bank was legislated, arrived at via an informal agreement between a government and the central bank, or written into
the country's constitution, the stagflation of the 1970s and early 1980s led to
the realization, backed by theoretical models and empirical evidence, that the
best means for maintaining low and stable inflation and pursuing output near
the economy's potential lay in changing an instrument of monetary policy. As
discussed in chapter 1, a nominal interest rate was chosen for this purpose.
The single instrument also had the advantage of transmitting the appropriate
signals to all other interest rates for maturities of different lengths and by different issuers.

The links just described could indeed be reduced to a single equation.
Central bankers were especially keen to explain, frequently, to a public and to
financial markets hungry for the forward-looking type of information necessary to understand a monetary policy strategy geared toward inflation control,
that setting interest rates amounted to calibrating the stance of monetary policy
according to two principles. Those two principles are: (1) how far observed inflation is from some objective set for or by the central bank, and (2) how far
output is from the economy's potential at any given moment. Moreover, the
rule to be followed, universally known as the Taylor Rule,[14] would indicate at
what level the central bank's policy rate would be set.

Unlike most countries, advanced or otherwise, the United States had relied
on an interest rate instrument for decades.[15] The Fed funds rate, as the policy
rate is known, served as an indicator of the Fed's stance of monetary policy for
decades, with rises, other things equal, indicating a tightening of policy and
falls suggestive of a loosening of monetary conditions. Indeed, Taylor (1993)
was able to calibrate the proposed rule and thereby explain quite well how the
Fed set policy from 1987 to 1992. As more and more central banks adopted an
interest rate instrument, the Taylor Rule became a straightforward and fashionable way to describe the most critical function of a central bank. The device

---

[14] Named after John Taylor of Stanford University.

[15] The role of that instrument was subject to considerable variation over time. It was secondary in
importance during the 1960s through 1980, and largely abandoned during the early years when Paul
Volcker was FOMC chair, only to play center stage in the conduct of monetary policy beginning with
Alan Greenspan's tenure, until the Fed, now under Chairman Ben Bernanke, reduced the policy rate to
the ZLB by the end of 2008, where it remained unchanged until the end of 2015. With some exceptions
(e.g., Canada; see Siklos 2010a), using an interest rate instrument is a development of the late 1990s or
early 2000s.

also gave rise to commentary such as the one expressed by former Bank of Canada Governor Gordon Thiessen, noted at the beginning of this chapter. Indeed, by the mid-2000s, one would be hard pressed to find very many central bank governors who did not rely on some version of the Taylor Rule to describe their policymaking process.

Even if the rule can be explained rather straightforwardly, it is easy to be deceived by its simplicity. Since there is vast literature in this area, I will not devote too much space to all sides of the debate concerning the conduct of monetary policy via the Taylor Rule other than to highlight a few important complications that undermine its simplicity. First, even if everyone refers to Taylor's depiction of U.S monetary policy as a rule, it is not, strictly speaking, a rule. As Taylor himself later suggested (Taylor 1998), the manner in which a central bank responds to inflation and output shocks is best thought of as a guiding principle, not as a rigid or knee-jerk response to observed or expected economic outcomes.

The core purpose of best practice in monetary policy is to change the *real* interest rate when necessary, as this is the signal that communicates to markets, and to the public more generally, that monetary conditions are changing. The money tightens when the real interest rate rises and it falls when the real rate falls. Hence, the *constant term* in the Taylor Rule or equation plays a critical role.[16] Therein lies a second difficulty with a simplistic implementation of the Taylor Rule.

So long as the real interest rate is near its long-run average, the central bank can focus on how to respond to inflation and output shocks.[17] However, if changes in productivity that have originated from technical changes or demographic factors, such as an aging population, alter the economy's potential output, the *intercept term* in the Taylor Rule will change. Normally, these forces act slowly and can be ignored in the short-run.[18] However, it is also the case that the neutral real interest rate is not observed and must

---

[16] Indeed, the role of the real interest rate is one that many economists have highlighted as the source of policy errors over time. For example, Meltzer (2003, 2009a), in his exhaustive study of U.S. monetary history, reminds us frequently that policymakers at the Fed simply did not understand the real interest rate concept and were frequently deluding themselves into thinking that policy was loose or tight based on observation strictly of the nominal interest rate.

[17] As a result, the intercept or constant term in the Taylor rule is referred to as the "natural" or "neutral" real interest rate.

[18] Proxies of technological change are usually called total factor productivity (TFP). Not surprisingly, since the impact of technical change is not easily observed, there is considerable debate about how to come up with the best possible indicator. See, for example, Basu, Fernald, and Kimball 2006. Data from several OECD economies display considerable variation, with countries such as South Korea experiencing strong TFP growth at least since the mid-1990s. TFP growth in the United States tends to be more moderate and fluctuates considerably less than in many other economies. For the United States, where at least three TFP proxies are available, there is noticeable variation across estimates. (Additional information is relegated to the online appendix.)

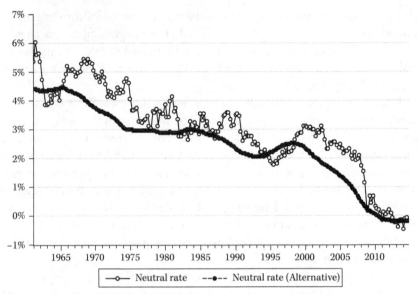

FIGURE 4.9 Neutral Real Policy Rate: US, 1960–2014

Note: The alternative rate is derived from the application of a "standard" Taylor Rule specification $i_t = r_t^* + \pi_t^* + 1.5(\pi_t - \pi_t^*) + 0.5\tilde{y}_t$, where the time-varying neutral rate is r*, π* is the Fed's inflation objective, π is CPI inflation, and is the time-varying output gap derived by applying a Hodrick-Prescott filter to the logarithm of real GDP with a smoothing factor of 1,440,000. *Source:* The raw data are from Laubach and Williams 2016.

be estimated.[19] Accordingly, there will always be some imprecision about its current level. Indeed, based on some estimates,[20] there are large variations in the neutral real interest rate.

Figure 4.9 plots estimates of the real interest rate,[21] revealing a steady decline in the United States since the early 1960s. Notice also the rapid decline in the real interest rate around the time of the global financial crisis. Some have interpreted this as evidence of "secular stagnation." Since the demographic and technological factors that affect the United States need not be replicated elsewhere, it is not always possible to generalize, although the phenomenon has been evident in countries such as Japan and appears to be spreading globally. Nevertheless, it is likely that a steady decline in the neutral real rate is a common occurrence in advanced economies but arguably less so in developing or emerging market economies.

Next, while the difference between observed and targeted inflation is at least in principle observable, the degree to which the economy experiences some slack is not. The amount of slack requires knowledge of the economy's

---

[19] The same, of course, is true of measures of an economy's potential output.

[20] Laubach and Williams 2003.

[21] The data are available in quarterly form from www.frbsf.org/economic-research/economists/john-williams/Laubach_Williams_updated_estimates.xlsx.

potential output. If the growth in potential output were reasonably predictable, then calculations of the gap between observed and potential output would be subject to some noise, and this would simplify the decision makers' problem. Unfortunately, this is not the case. An economy's output is subject to numerous revisions, sometimes many years into the future, while potential output can take surprising turns, largely because of "unknown unknowns." The latter were especially evident in the wake of the financial crisis of 2008–9 and is also reflected in discussions surrounding the behavior of the neutral real interest rate.

Revisions to GDP figures are especially problematic; if changes in potential output take place only slowly over time, these can give false signals to policymakers.[22] Once again, the events of recent years provide numerous examples of policymakers who have either acted in haste in attempting to set policy according to more "normal" economic conditions or delayed taking action and have risked accusations in the future of being too patient in tightening the stance of monetary policy. Real GDP data revisions imply that new estimates are published over time and, like wine, the earlier ones become "vintages."[23] Assuming that, as additional data arrive and subsequent estimates improve the picture, economic performance may be substantively different from that policymakers faced earlier, when a choice to change monetary conditions presented itself.

Figure 4.10 helps fix these ideas. Graphs making up (a) provide comparable estimates of GDP in constant prices for nine economies, all OECD members and two of whom are emerging market economies (Chile and Turkey). With the exception of Chile, five different "vintages" were selected for analysis. The earliest is dated December 2006, arguably during the time that that of the Great Moderation was nearing its end. Next, I chose real GDP performance at the end of December 2008, when the Fed lowered its policy rate to the ZLB, where it remained until December 2015. The Fed was also in the early stages of introducing various programs subsequently referred to as quantitative easing, or QE. The May 2010 revision shows GDP in constant prices just when the first indications of a financial crisis in the eurozone were beginning to emerge, with Greece on the receiving end of the first of several "rescue" packages combined with varying doses of fiscal austerity. May 2014 represents the one-year anniversary following Ben Bernanke's announcement of "tapering"—that is, the gradual elimination of QE. Finally, January 2015 is the latest available revision when this passage was written.

---

[22] Bernanke (2015:503) expressed very well the dilemma of policy makers that must take decisions in real time with imperfect and incomplete data. "Economists are criticized for not being able to predict the future, but, because the data are incomplete and subject to revision, we cannot even be sure what happened in the recent past."

[23] The OECD refers to this kind of data by calling them "editions".

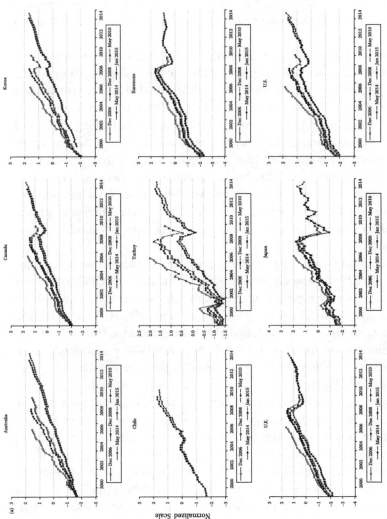

FIGURE 4.10 Selected "Vintages" in Real GDP

(a) Advanced Economies (9); (b) Eurozone Economies (4)

Note: The vintage concept is explained on page 145. The data in question were released in the month and year shown in the legend, and this dictates the length of the available sample. The precise vintage (month/year) used is listed below each figure. *Source:* The data are from the OECD.

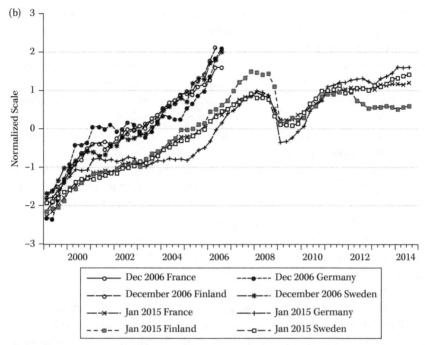

FIGURE 4.10 (*Continued*)

Several key features are apparent from figure 4.10a. First, not all the economies experienced a significant drop in real GDP after the 2008 crisis erupted; Australia is a case in point. Second, the consequences for the real economy from the financial crisis are heterogeneous.[24] That is particularly noticeable for Turkey, the United Kingdom, the eurozone, and the United States, but less so for Canada, Chile, and Korea. Lastly, and likely most critical for an assessment of the amount of economic slack, revisions in real GDP over time show a recovery but also what appears to have been an extended period of reduced levels of real GDP. By January 2015, real GDP levels reached approximately pre-crisis levels in Australia, Canada, Korea, the United Kingdom, and the United States, but not in Turkey, the eurozone, or Japan. It is important to keep in mind that the "lost" output—essentially an area under the levels of real GDP at the end of 2006—is sizable. It is also worth highlighting that the downward shift in the levels of real GDP has a permanent component: either the "curve" representing potential real GDP has bent backward, or there has been a shift in potential output. The latter appears consistent with the hypothesis of secular stagnation.[25]

---

[24] The manner in which the data are presented makes the results comparable across countries.

[25] The difficulty, as is often the case in economic analyses of this kind, is to know how much to attach history to an observed phenomenon, and therein lies the dilemma of how much importance to attach to the hypothesis of secular stagnation.

Figure 4.10b is useful in discussing the important role of output conditions in setting the correct stance of monetary policy. The "vintages" of real GDP for three eurozone members—France, Germany, and Finland—are shown together with the aggregate output measure for Sweden, an EU member. As in figure 4.10a, the effects of the financial crisis, the permanent drop in output levels, and the speed of the recovery are noticeable. However, the record is quite uneven, especially for the three eurozone members, with Germany well ahead of Finland especially, and with Sweden, which has the added flexibility of a floating exchange rate, also recovering nicely.[26] In spite of the additional freedom in economic policy afforded to Sweden, its performance is not especially superior to that of France. These findings point to additional complications for the ECB, which must conduct a single monetary policy for nineteen euro member economies, including the three shown here.

As noted, some of the measurement problems associated with estimates of slack in the aggregate economy, or the output gap, apply to inflation as well. Even if the central bank announces a numerical target for inflation, all such policy regimes have built-in flexibility to miss targets, at least in the short run;[27] hence, there is always some unobservable element in estimating a central bank's inflation objective. On the whole, the problems facing policymakers concerning the size of the inflation gap— namely, the difference between observed and targeted inflation—are less acute than in estimating the output gap.

Where to Go from Here?

Do the foregoing considerations undermine the simplicity or the usefulness of the Taylor Rule policy prescription? Perhaps surprisingly, the answer is no. What are the implications stemming from uncertainty about the factors that drive setting the appropriate stance of monetary policy? The challenge is to explain the flexible nature of the Taylor Rule while guarding against any loss of central bank credibility. As we shall see shortly, central banks have fallen into the trap of wanting it both ways—that is, to continue with the pretense that "rules" govern policy while insisting that they can suspend them for long periods of time without a loss of reputation. This strategy seems implausible.

It is useful at this point to recall that, in its most straightforward form, the Taylor Rule for best practice in the conduct of monetary policy is to persuade the public that an unwanted increase in expected inflation will be met by a

---

[26] Sweden is interesting for reasons other than the exchange rate. We saw some of this in chapter 3, and I return to the less than happy Swedish experience later in this chapter.

[27] The usual rule of thumb, associated with Milton Friedman's notion that monetary policy affects the economy with long and variable lags, is that the central bank expects on average to hit its target over a two-year time period.

rise in the *real* interest rate. Therefore, any rise in the *nominal* policy rate will not do. Instead, the real cost of borrowing, and by implication the real return to lending, must rise. This is the only way to turn back the rise in anticipated future inflation. It is also important to underscore the idea that the focus on inflation expectations does not, at least in theory, imply that real economic considerations are ignored, since the two are inextricably linked. (More on this issue later.) In any event, the Taylor Rule explicitly recognizes a role for the behavior of aggregate economic output.[28]

Figure 4.11 plots the one-year forecasts for real GDP growth and inflation for three regions of the globe—namely, the eurozone, advanced economies, and the economies of the Asia-Pacific.[29] For the eurozone and advanced economies, The Great Moderation is apparent in the real GDP growth (a), since real GDP growth forecasts were stable from the early 1990s right up to the GFC of 2008–9. The relatively strong growth in the Asia-Pacific region throughout this period is also apparent. There are only two brief exceptions to this description—the Asian financial crisis of 1997–98 and a temporary decline in real GDP forecasts in 2008. In the eurozone, and in the advanced economies more generally, one would be forgiven if, by 2007, when there was a surge in real GDP growth forecasts on the heels of almost two decades of steady economic growth, forecasters thought that the "trend" might continue into the future. Also, whereas the forecasted recovery from the Asian financial crisis was a slow and economically painful one, the return to strong growth in the aftermath of the events of 2008–9 was swift.

Turning to forecasts of consumer prices, we find there is a noticeable but gentle reduction in inflation forecasts for all the economies shown in the figure (b). However, while inflation forecasts returned to the 2% range, where they were in the early 2000s, forecasts for the Asia-Pacific rose sharply. There seems to be an approximate positive relationship between inflation and real GDP growth forecasts, reflecting forecasters' view that higher growth rates imply diminished economic capacity that is met through higher inflation. Generally speaking, this also reflects the thinking behind the Taylor Rule.[30]

---

[28] Traditionally, the Taylor Rule is expressed in terms of an output gap measure, although some (e.g., Stock and Watson 2001) prefer a version in terms of the unemployment rate. A variety of explanations are used to motivate this alternative for the U.S. case. In a cross-country study, the differences in how unemployment rates are measured makes it rather hazardous to think of the Taylor Rule in this form. Hence, in what follows, the standard strategy of relying on the output gap is followed. Linking output changes to the unemployment rate is Okun's Law, which apparently survives the GFC. See, for example, Ball, Leigh, and Loungani 2013.

[29] The countries included in each group are defined by the International Monetary Fund. (As earlier, details are relegated to the online appendix.) There is, of course, some overlap in the three regions, since eurozone economies are considered advanced while some Asia-Pacific economies (e.g., Australia, New Zealand, Hong Kong, Singapore) are also included in the group of advanced economies.

[30] As usual, care must be exercised when making these broad characterizations, since the relationship between the two may not only be different across the economies in each of the regions represented but also different over time.

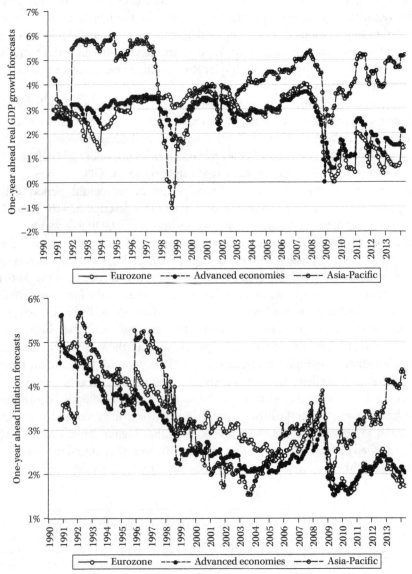

FIGURE 4.11 One-Year Ahead Real GDP Growth Forecasts in Various Regions of the World

(a) GDP Growth Forecasts

(b) Inflation Forecasts

Note: The eurozone, advanced, and Asia-Pacific economies are as defined by the IMF. Fixed horizon forecasts are shown; see chapter 1 for additional information. Also see Bordo and Siklos 2016b. *Source:* The data are from Consensus Economics.

Figure 4.12 illustrates, for a sample of eleven economies, many of which adopted a numerical inflation target objective, the message from the application of the Taylor Rule to our understanding concerning the evolution in the stance of monetary policy since the 2000s. All the figures, save for the United States, plot the observed policy rate used by the central banks in the G4 against the rate predicted if the Taylor Rule is strictly applied. As discussed earlier, while no one expects the two lines to be coincident at all times under normal circumstances, they should not be too far apart from each other.

Of course, if the two lines depart from each other, this could also suggest that the central banks care about more than just inflation and real economic performance. The question then is: At what point do "other" factors undermine the simplicity and desirability of policy rules? Moreover, if flexibility in the conduct of monetary policy is the proximate reason for deviating from rules, then how much of it undermines the credibility of a central bank whose primary mission is inflation control?

Two estimates of the policy rate using the Taylor Rule are shown as an illustration of how different views of the neutral real interest rate can affect the outcome.[31] Both estimates are reasonably similar, and all estimates compared with the actions taken by the Fed show that the policy rate was too low in the early 2000s. While the actual rate did catch up to the one implied by the Taylor Rule, this happened shortly before the 2008–9 GFC. Since that time, the calibrated and observed interest rates have diverged, though the divergence becomes especially noticeable after 2012. By then, as noted earlier, the economy had largely made up ground lost during the Great Recession.

The message is, broadly speaking, the same for the other G3 economies shown in the figure, but the gap between the calibrated and the observed policy rates is particularly noticeable for Japan and the eurozone. If we now turn to smaller and more open economies—namely, Australia, Canada, Korea, and Sweden, shown in (b)—the gap between the policy rate under a best-practice policy and the actual stance taken by these central banks is generally smaller than for the G4 economies, only one of which was held to account to for a numerically announced inflation objective (i.e., the United Kingdom), at least until the GFC.[32] Sweden is the only case where the gap between what was deemed a desirable monetary policy and what was actually in place is substantial and persistent. The gaps that do emerge in the figure are most apparent

---

[31] The line labeled calibrated (alternate) uses the estimates from Laubach and Williams 2016 instead of the ones generated using a procedure that is applied identically to all the economies considered.

[32] To the extent that the monetary policy strategy of IT gets the credit, the result reflects how policymakers in IT central banks view the credibility question. As Sir Paul Tucker, former deputy governor of the BoE, put it, "the monetary authority's ability to deliver, and its will to stick to its inflation target over the medium run[,] is never in doubt. . . .. [T]hat kind of credibility needs to be earned and re-earned, over and over again" Tucker 2006:9.

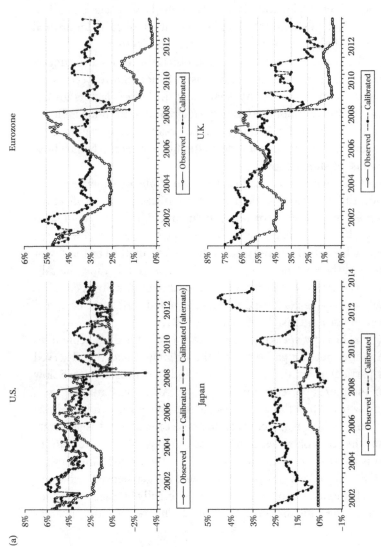

FIGURE 4.12 One-Year-Ahead Observed and Calibrated Inflation

(a) Select Large Economies

(b) Select Inflation Targeting Advanced Economies

(c) Select Inflation Targeting Emerging Market Economies

Note: The eurozone, advanced, and Asia-Pacific economies are as defined by the IMF. Fixed horizon forecasts are shown; see chapter 1 for additional information; also see Bordo and Siklos 2016b. Calibration is performed according to a Taylor Rule specification; see note for figure 4.9.

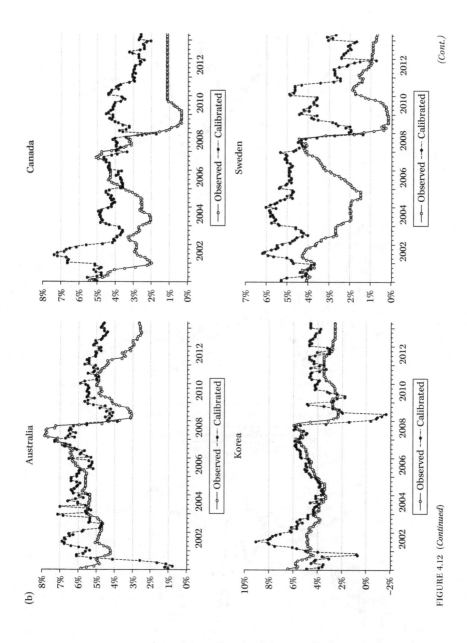

FIGURE 4.12 (Continued)

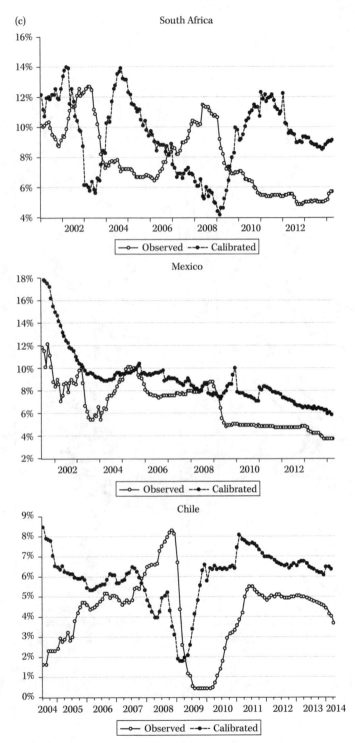

FIGURE 4.12 (Continued)

beginning late 2008. Indeed, the situation is repeated in the three emerging market economies shown in (c). South Africa, Mexico, and Chile were relatively early adopters of inflation targeting among the emerging market economies, and just as in the other cases examined, a persistent departure, since referred to as the "great deviation" (Taylor 2011), from the Taylor Rule is readily seen beginning in late 2008.

Perhaps unsurprisingly, retrospective analyses have taken two relatively polar positions. Other than during the height of the crisis, when virtually every observer agreed that monetary policy ought to support economic recovery through extremely low policy rates, some have argued that the stance of monetary policy, particularly in the advanced economies, was too low for too long. In contrast, others have argued that the combination of slow recovery, which is typical of large financial crises, and the resulting high levels of uncertainty that also accompanied the events of 2008 and 2009, followed by the continuing eurozone crisis, perhaps combined with a bout of secular stagnation, calls for the continued maintenance of ultra-low interest rates.

Moreover, since positive but slow growth returned to the global economy fairly quickly after the GFC, as we saw in chapter 1, one is also prompted to ask whether the passage of time implies that another recession, perhaps of the global variety, is near. This hints that expansions, however weak, can "die of old age," to borrow a phrase used by Zarnowitz (1992). While research suggests that the answer is in the negative, prominent and influential voices have raised the possibility that, even if interest rates rise, the room to reduce them will be largely nonexistent when the time comes.[33]

As shown in table 4.1, expansions and contractions do not last forever. Moreover, there does not appear to be a regular duration for business cycles. Since growth has been sluggish, at least in relation to that of recent decades, it is feasible that current growth rates can persist for some time. Notice also the obvious asymmetry in business-cycle movements, with expansions typically longer in duration than contractions, also confirmed by other evidence for the United States. Finally, since table 4.1 arbitrarily represents the last expansions and contractions, it is worth pointing out that, on this basis, one can only go back to the 1950s to find the first cycle for Australia, 1960 for the United States, followed 1969 for Sweden. On average, these are the economies with the longest average expansions.[34]

There are additional difficulties to living in a world with ultra-low interest rates, or ones that remain at the ZLB. First, the notion of the ZLB itself appears

---

[33] See, for example, Summers 2015; Krugman 2015a; and Economist 2014.

[34] Strictly speaking, one can go back much earlier for the United States and Canada if the NBER reference-cycle type chronologies are used. However, to ensure comparability in the face of different methodologies, older data are not examined.

TABLE 4.1 } Business Cycle Durations (from earliest to latest, December 2015)

Country/Economy (earliest recorded year)	Duration (months) of Contraction	Duration (months) of Expansion
United Kingdom (1973)	11,23,22,18,22	265,46,108,194,7
Canada (1974)	3,6,16,13,7	164,57,12,89,198
Mexico (1984)	13,12,8,36,13	27,71,13,61,56
Brazil (1904)	6,18,10,8,5	36,25,22,10,53
Germany (1973)	23,34,39,31,9	75,54,99,81,56
France (1981)	32,18,9,12,19	22,86,108,57,25
Italy (1969)[1]	10,12,36,20,19	67,32,61,105,166
Spain (1979)[2]	50,25,65	78,170,29,77,82
Switzerland (1981)	14,42,22,24,12	66,88,14,54,62
Sweden (1969)	13,28,40,37,11	44,27,84
Austria (1979)	35,14,10,11,16	56,111,23,58,75
Japan (2000)	32,13,8,8,17	13,58,17,13,14
Korea (1979)[3]	19,11,10,7	182,53,58,84
Australia (1953)	9,10,7,11,18	39,52,153,89,85
New Zealand (1984)	16,57,7,18,5	18,6,57,57,76,114
South Africa (1981)	14,20,42,19,12	48,17,36,56,113
Eurozone (1974)	6,15,15,12,12,17	59,113,173,26,33
United States (1960)[4]	[10, 11, 16] 6,16,8,8,16	[24,106,36] 58,12,92,120,73
Overall Mean[5]	11.1	58.4

Notes: [1] Peak recorded April 2011; no trough recorded yet.
[2] Only three peak to trough episodes recorded.
[3] Only four peak to trough episodes.
[4] Contraction is peak to trough; expansion is previous trough to peak. In brackets, 1960–1979.
[5] 1945 to 2009.
Sources: Data from NBER, Economic Cycle Research Institute, Cross and Bergevin 2012, and Centre for Economic Policy Research.

to be a moving target.[35] Table 4.2 shows the state of play at the end of 2015. The same table would have looked considerably different as recently as a year earlier, when the ECB and the Riksbank, for example, joined the ranks of central banks with negative interest rates. Negative interest rates change the incentive to hold the financial instrument in question, from a reward to a penalty rate. The objective is to persuade asset holders to shift to other assets, whether in the domestic currency or in another currency, and encourage the purchase of riskier assets or prompt more lending that earns a positive return. In spite of these developments, there continues to be both a willingness to hold assets with negative returns, largely of the riskless variety, and simultaneously a reluctance to pass on these costs to others.[36] Far from suggesting that a central

---

[35] In October 2015, ECB President Mario Draghi, at a press conference announcing the central bank's latest decision, stated: "Now we are at the zero lower bound." The rate on the ECB's deposit facility was then set at -0.20%. Evidently, by November of the same year, the ECB found a new ELB as the policy rate was set to -0.30%. As this is written, it stands at -0.40%.

[36] Some institutions began to charge some of their large depositors in Switzerland, which was the first central bank listed in table 4.2 to introduce negative interest rates.

TABLE 4.2 } **How the ELB Is Defined by Different Central Banks**

Economy	ZLB Rate	ZLB Period	Explanations
Canada	-0.50%, overnight rate	April 21, 2009, to May 31, 2010	Press release from the BoC judged the ZLB to be 0.25%; revised in December 2015 to -0.50%
Denmark	-0.75%, certificate of deposit	July 6, 2012, to April 24, 2014, and September 5, 2014, to present (December 2015)	The Danish central bank refers to negative interest rates as "business as usual." It also claims that pass-through effects to money markets have not been weakened.
Eurozone	0,00%, marginal refinancing operations rate	July 4, 2014, to present (December 2015)	In June 4, 2015, Draghi first indicated that "for all practical purposes, we have reached the zero lower bound." However, further adjustments were deemed possible.
Japan	0.1%, basic discount rate; 0.0% uncollateralized overnight rate	February 1999–August 2000; September 2001–June 2006; October 2010–present (December 2015)	ZIRP policy introduced in 1999, followed by QE in 2001 and QQE in 2013.
Switzerland	-1.25% to 0.25%, 3 month Libor	August 3, 2011, to present (December 2015)	Libor was set at 0.25% to 0% on August 3, 2011 (aiming for as close to zero as possible), until December 17, 2014. It was lowered again on December 18, 2014, and again January 14, 2015.
Sweden	-0.50%, repo rate	July 2, 2009, to June 30, 2010, and July 9 2014 to present (December 2015)	The policy rate was set at 0.25% from July 2, 2009, until June 30, 2010. Following increases, it was returned to 0.25% on July 9, 2014, and then cut until the present. The Riksbank did not state that 0.25% was the ZLB. Minutes of the MPC indicate its members believed that negative rates were, in fact, possible.
United Kingdom	0.5%, bank rate	March 5, 2009, to present (December 2015)	
United States	0.0% to 0.25%	December 16, 2008, to December 17, 2015	

Sources: Central banks and Shirai 2013.

bank's strategy is correct, these developments highlight how far markets are willing to go to avoid risk. Surely, this is indicative of a lack of confidence in what some central banks are attempting to accomplish.

The second challenge at the ZLB or the ELB is the portrayal of the stance of monetary policy when a central bank, such as the BoE and the Fed both chose to do, did not adopt negative interest rates.[37] Both central banks instead resorted to other unconventional instruments and attempted to convey policy easing via the expansion of their balance sheets.

It is a reflection of the influence of the Taylor Rule and the desire to translate UMP into an interest rate equivalent that researchers began to generate estimates of "shadow" policy rates.[38] Figure 4.13 plots the actual and available shadow policy rates until the end of 2014 for four economies that have hit the ZLB.[39] The U.S. case clearly reveals that shadow rate estimates are sensitive to assumptions about the factors that effectively drive interest rates below zero. Notice also that, by the end of 2014, other than perhaps for the United States, there were few indications of a return to anything approaching levels that had prevailed before the GFC.

The avoidance of zero interest rates suggests that central banks must have used other devices to maintain their credibility. Otherwise, in principle, faith in the central banks' ability to maintain low and stable inflation, while supportive of "normal" economic growth, would have been threatened. The foregoing discussion suggests the question of when policy rates should rise and how fast. Central banks most directly impacted by the crisis naturally have argued that patience is called for under the circumstances. If so, what arguments for patience and a continued delay in the return to normalcy in interest rates were marshalled and can we evaluate the effectiveness of this strategy? Equally important, does patience and continued financial repression not have other macroeconomic consequences that central banks, and policymakers more generally, ignore at their peril? In other words, at what point is the cure worse than the disease? We turn to these issues in the following section.

From Prices to Quantities: The Zero Lower Bound and the Central Bank Balance Sheet

Several authors have described how a seemingly innocuous series of small events in 2007 would culminate in the panic that eventually gripped the markets in 2008. Arguably, the tipping point came when the Fed was unable to find a buyer for Lehman Brothers. Once the determination not to bail out a large financial institution became counterproductive, the Fed and other

---

[37] The considerations that favor or not the resorting to negative interest rates is, to some extent, a function of the institutional environment that the financial markets operate within in each economy. See Burke et al. 2010 for the U.S. case, Bean 2013 for the United Kingdom, and Alsterlind et al. 2015 for Sweden.

[38] The concept, from Black 1995, is essentially based on the idea that there are latent factors that effectively turn an interest rate normally bounded from below at 0% into a negative rate.

[39] More recent data are available in a few cases, but not for all the available proxies.

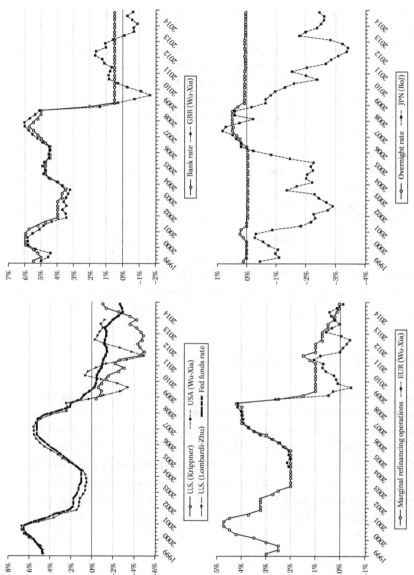

FIGURE 4.13 Policy Rates and Shadow Policy Rates

Note: Policy rate definitions and sources for shadow rates are given in chapter 4. USA is US data. GBR is data from the UK, EUR is eurozone data, and JPN is data from Japan. The sources of data are in parenthesis. *Source:* Wu and Xia 2016, Krippner 2015, Lombardi and Zhu 2014, and data obtained from the Bank of Japan.

policymakers quickly changed course and began to find creative ways to support various markets and institutions in need of financial assistance. The fear that moral hazard would undermine the reputation of policymakers initially blinded or paralyzed them. This changed quickly, however, and the determination not to allow a repeat of the Great Depression, captured in an earlier promise made by then Fed Governor Bernanke to Milton Friedman and Anna Schwarz on Friedman's ninetieth birthday, took over. This was so much so that, after over seven years following the events that produced the greatest financial crisis since the 1930s, there is the distinct impression that the central banks especially may have become overactive in their determination to prevent a repeat of their failure to see what was coming. Whether the possible over-reaction represents a "march of folly" remains to be seen. Nevertheless, in a short period of time, the financial system shifted from being seen as more decoupled than it has ever been from the strictures of proper oversight[40] to one that threatens to become sufficiently repressed as to create conditions ripe for the next crisis.

Ultimately, the central banks in the crisis-stricken economies shifted away from a monetary policy strategy centered on a price—that is, a policy interest rate—to changing the quantities captured in their balance sheets. Multiple sources of failure in various parts of the real and financial sectors made it impossible to rely on a single policy instrument. Several instruments would be needed to prevent an ongoing economic downturn from becoming even worse.[41]

This Time Is Different, at Least for Monetary Policy

It would be a mistake to think that the period covered in this study largely represents the story of one crisis. At least in the realm of monetary policy, it is the story of several crises, although four stand out. First, there is the ongoing period of mild deflation in Japan that produced the "lost decades." Then, there is the bursting of the tech bubble, soon followed by a fear of deflation during the first few years into the new millennium. Next, of course, are the events now labeled the Global Financial Crisis (GFC) of 2008–9, which would soon be followed by the continuing sovereign debt and economic crisis in the eurozone.

---

[40] As discussed previously, it is not correct to suggest that policymakers had fewer regulations, or less supervision in principle, in the years leading up to the crisis. Instead, there was a failure to properly carry out their responsibilities that lies at the core of the events that culminated in the GFC.

[41] Ironically, just as advanced economies were rediscovering the importance of their balance sheets, the world's largest emerging market—China—was attempting to shift away from a quantity-driven monetary policy to one increasingly dictated by price. See Pang and Siklos 2016, and references therein.

The distinctive element of the first half of the decade of 2000 to 2009 is that, for the most part, a large number of central banks relied on monetary policy tools that by then had become standard. These are in the main instruments that signaled changes in the stance of monetary policy via prices—most notably changes in some policy rate.[42] Of course, it may be that the severity of the earlier crises did not rise to the level of the one that eventually hit the global economy beginning in 2008; hence, there may not have been enough fear among policymakers to abandon the tools of monetary policy that were already in place and seemingly were functioning well. Alternatively, seen from the perspective of the early 2000s, there was no way of knowing what lay ahead. As discussed earlier, there is little—but not nothing—that is readily measurable in the macroeconomic or financial sphere that suggested to policymakers or other observers that a cataclysm was imminent.

The GFC led to a major, if not radical, change in how monetary policy is conducted. Prices no longer signaled the policy stance, and quantities became the *modus operandi* of monetary policy. Fear of a future crisis was to be banished at all costs, and it once again became fashionable to argue that restrictions of various kinds on financial markets were necessary to prevent a recurrence of a great recession or, worse still, a great depression.[43] As a result, for example, capital controls, long thought to be ineffective and inopportune, along with other restrictions on borrowing and lending referred to as macroprudential instruments, were revived and celebrated as the way forward to supplement conventional monetary policy actions. Unfortunately, this strategy created the myth that real and financial factors can be neatly separated, resting on as yet unproven policy instruments. Representative of such a view is the following quote: "If the monetary policy that stabilizes supply and demand in the real economy destabilizes the financial system, the problem is the latter" (Wolf 2015). Unfortunately, real and financial factors are not so easily segregated.

We have already seen (in chapter 1) that there are several indicators of the unprecedented nature of the current state of monetary policy. In particular, the reduction of policy rates to the ZLB, combined with the striking rise in the size of central bank balance sheets in a few key advanced economies, was highlighted. Omitted from that discussion is a bit more historical perspective. Accordingly, figure 4.14 plots long-term interest rates on government securities in eight economies. Three of the eight central banks

---

[42] An exception might be made in the case of Japan, but as we shall briefly see, this was a somewhat half-hearted and unconvincing explanation.

[43] Roubini and Mihm (2010:148) expressed the change using somewhat different, but not entirely incorrect, language: "The Federal Reserve and other central banks . . . had gone from being lenders of last resort to lenders of first, last, and only resort. In the process, they crossed the proverbial Rubicon not once or twice but many times."

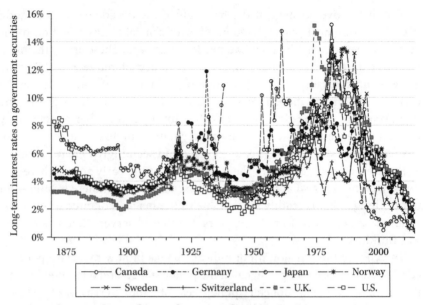

FIGURE 4.14 Long-term Interest Rates on Government Securities, 1875–2015
Source: Data are from Bordo and Siklos 2016a.

in the countries shown[44] were created early in the nineteenth century—or even earlier, as in the case of Sweden, generally considered the oldest central bank of all. Others, notably of Japan and Germany, have directly experienced the full disruptive effects of two World Wars.[45] Finally, the central banks of the United States, Canada, and Switzerland are comparatively young institutions.[46]

By the early 2000s, it was apparent that long-term interest rates had reached lows that were unprecedented since the second half of the nineteenth century in most of the countries plotted in the figure. By 2014, it is safe to say that all the economies in figure 4.14 experienced long-term yields that were not seen even during the depths of the Great Depression of the 1930s.

Long-term interest rates, at least in theory, incorporate three factors: (1) expectations of inflation over the medium term, (2) the neutral real interest rate previously described, and (3) a premium for holding a long-term security. Two of these three factors are within the purview of a central bank's mandate, since low and stable inflation rates are generally what a monetary authority

---

[44] In Germany's case, the Bundesbank was replaced in 1999 by the European Central Bank.

[45] Hence, some gaps in the data for the period of 1914 to 1919 and again for 1939 to 1945 are apparent from the figures.

[46] An exception is again Germany, whose central bank was called the Reichsbank until World War II ended, when it became the Bundesbank, which was followed after 1999 by the European Central Bank.

aims for, while its activities, which influence the size of its balance sheet, can impact the term premium on government bonds. It is only the neutral real interest rate that reflects the "deep" parameters (i.e., of the structural variety) influencing trends in the overall economy (i.e., demographic, labor force, and investment behavior). If the above explains a substantial portion of the variation in yields, then it is not a stretch to conclude that the central banks can take a considerable amount of credit for the remarkable state of affairs shown in figure 4.14.

How did the central banks manage to achieve such an outcome? At the risk of oversimplification, a combination of two strategies helped reduce long-term interest rates to near zero levels. QE is one explanation, and at least in some economies this policy would be combined with forward guidance. Unfortunately, both policies are concepts fraught with misunderstanding. In the early days of the 2008–9 financial crisis, former Fed Chair Ben Bernanke, in a speech,[47] referred to policies aimed at lending to financial institutions, easing of liquidity constraints in the financial markets, and the purchase of long-term government bonds, as methods of credit easing. Since then, most observers label such attempts as QE. Etymological considerations aside, the point is that all such interventions by a central bank have the effect of raising the price on long-term government bonds. As a consequence, the yields decline and remain low so long as the central bank continues to purchase those instruments.

The strategy adopted to intervene in the market for long-term bonds does vary across other jurisdictions where these policies were introduced, such as in the United Kingdom, Japan, and the eurozone. Accordingly, so have the names used to describe these actions, which were meant, it seems, to simultaneously signal to the financial markets the areas that the central bank felt needed support, while at the same time publicizing the activist nature of monetary policy once there was no room to maneuver on the policy rate front and the effective ZLB had been reached.

A challenge in understanding the role of these central bank purchases of government securities is to estimate how large the term premium is. After all, the premium itself is unobservable, as it can depend on the treasury's needs and policies, general market conditions, and the attitude of investors toward holding long-term government securities. Nevertheless, one can glean the likely impact of this factor on long-term yield developments by examining, in the U.S. case, two widely used indicators of financial conditions—the VIX and the National Financial Conditions Index (NFCI) published by the Federal Reserve Bank of Chicago. Figure 4.15 provides the evidence. The VIX is intended as a forward-looking indicator of stock market volatility, while the NFCI captures

---

[47] See www.federalreserve.gov/newsevents/speech/bernanke20090113a.htm.

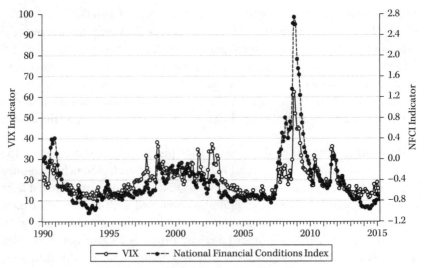

FIGURE 4.15 Economic Policy Uncertainty and Financial Conditions

Note: Both series are described in the text; the VIX is also discussed in chapter 2. *Source:*

risk, credit, and leverage conditions in the U.S. financial system. Increases in the values of both indicators signal tighter financial conditions or enhanced financial risks, while the opposite holds, of course, when the indicators experience a decline.

Although the indicators shown are for the U.S. situation, many other agencies and central banks have begun to create and publish broadly comparable indicators. The sharp rise in both indicators, beginning in 2008 and extending into 2009, is plain to see in the figure. It was not until 2013 or 2014 that levels of financial ease reached levels not seen since the mid-1990s. Notice also that there were secondary spikes in the index in 2010 and again in 2011, largely due to the onset of the eurozone financial crisis. Finally, in line with the earlier discussion, we see that there were rises in financial tightening in the early 2000s in the aftermath of the tech bubble and an earlier deflation scare, as well as a response to the early indications of a financial crisis in Japan, indicated at the beginning of the sample. The Asian financial crisis of 1997–98 is hardly noticeable compared to the other events highlighted here. If we focus attention on the last decade, then, as shown in figure 4.16, the fall in long-term yields parallels the fall in financial tightness, which is evident from the behavior of the two indicators shown.[48]

---

[48] It is likely that changes in long-term interest rates foreshadow changes in the VIX.

When Words Are the Only Game in Town

Even the actions leading to a fall in the term premium were not seen as enough for the central banks. Notice that, in 2011 and again in 2013, long-term interest rates began to rise, a reflection of a nascent economic recovery in much of the advanced world. However, long-term yields turned down again when central bankers argued that the return to a normal stance in monetary policy was an increasingly distant outcome. Even as the U.S. economy was recovering, weaknesses in the Japanese and eurozone economies became more apparent. On these two occasions, then, we saw central banks deploying new tools to once again drive down long-term interest rates. The downward movement in interest rates continued into 2014, even as the U.S. Fed reduced or tapered its support of the market for long-term government securities. Both the BoJ and, later, the ECB stepped in to replace the U.S. Fed in providing QE. Indeed, supporting these developments was the adoption of forward guidance.

Former BoC Governor Mark Carney once defined "forward guidance" as "[explaining] what central banks are trying to achieve and how they go about achieving it" (Carney 2013). Greater transparency can shed light on why the central bank acts the way it does. In contrast, forward guidance represents an explicit attempt to influence market and public expectations, especially of

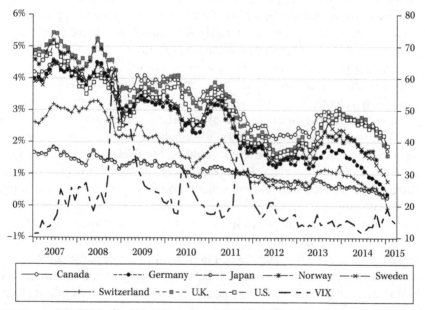

FIGURE 4.16   Post-GFC Decline in Long-Term Sovereign Yields, Advanced Economies

Note: Bond yields are long-term bonds (10 years or more to maturity) for the countries shown. Also, see note to figure 4.15. *Source:* Data are from FRED, Federal Reserve Bank of St. Louis database.

inflation, by providing insights about the possible *future* stance of monetary policy. This development reflects the premium central banks place on public communication. However, forward guidance is a sleight of hand and may also be interpreted as an indication of central banks' unwillingness or inability to clearly communicate the *limits* of monetary policy.

When it was implemented, was the forward guidance strategy effective? Might central banks have gone too far? The simple answer to both questions is yes. Originally, the promise of forward guidance was that it would be a natural extension of central banks' expressing a desire to be both more transparent and more accountable. Having exhausted the ability to use policy rates to clearly signal changes in the stance of monetary policy, the monetary authorities attempted to allay fears of an imminent interest rate rise by conditionally promising to maintain ultra-low interest rates for as long as necessary. Indeed, forward guidance is intended to put an explicit face on what it means for a central bank to be forward looking by providing the public with the circumstances under which the stance of monetary policy will change. Some might even say that its explicit aim is for central banks to "put their money where their mouth is."

Beginning in the 1990s, greater transparency led the central banks to rely on verbal signals to communicate any future bias in their stance of monetary policy. Usually, this was reflected in the precise language used to communicate policy rate decisions via press releases. Examples include statements by the U.S. Fed to communicate the outlook for their stance of monetary policy, such as "the Committee expects that a highly accommodative stance of monetary policy will remain appropriate for a considerable time."[49]

Earlier, a few central banks became more explicit about the direction of change in their future policy rates by publishing forward interest-rate paths. Until fairly recently, however, these forward paths provided only limited information about the future course of monetary policy, since interest rates going forward were either assumed to remain constant or they depended on what financial markets believed would be the likely future course of interest rates. The U.S. Federal Reserve, Norway's Norges Bank, and Sweden's Riksbank publish forward rate paths that are qualified with input from central bank staff forecasts or forecasts issued by members of the monetary policy decision-making committee. Unlike other devices to enhance transparency, the use of forward interest-rate path publications has not spread. Some have argued that the conditionality implicit in such forward rate paths cannot easily be communicated or, rather, that markets may be all too willing to treat the information as an indication of what the central bank believes future policy

---

[49] This quote is from the Fed's May 1, 2013, press release; see www.federalreserve.gov/newsevents/press/monetary/20130501a.htm.

rates are likely to be. More troublesome is the communication and credibility implications when the central banks and the financial markets see the future differently. An example from New Zealand was discussed earlier, but Sweden's Riksbank is a more dramatic illustration. Svensson (2015) describes how, in 2011, the Riksbank published an interest-rate path suggesting a future 75bp rise in the policy rate, while market expectations were that rates would fall by 75bp. As in the example of a few other central banks (e.g., the ECB), markets correctly guessed that the Riksbank would have to reverse its intended course for its stance of monetary policy. Perhaps more than anything else, it is the fear of policy reversals, poorly communicated or simply unexplained, that is the root of the problem, not the decision to be more transparent. The Canadian experience (e.g., Siklos and Spence 2010) suggests that avoiding the negative side effects of forward guidance is possible, as we shall see.

Of course, even as some central banks became more explicit in describing their future outlook for the economy—that is, the likely evolution of interest rates, inflation, and real economic activity—they were always careful to point out that, as facts change, so would their stance of monetary policy, which would be adjusted accordingly. This is the proverbial reliance on data to dictate when or how a central bank might react. However, as discussed in chapter 2, in an era of Big Data, it becomes increasingly easy to shift objectives and selectively decide what data would trigger a course correction.

The behavior of the FOMC in 2015 is a clear example of the confusion that can dominate central bank communications when that bank is unable to systematically inform the public in a credible manner. The Fed had long advertised a likely exit from the ZLB, only to delay the exit owing to concerns about the global economic environment. Although FOMC minutes have consistently provided a summary of international economic conditions, policymakers have equally been adamant that domestic economic conditions are the driving force for setting the stance of monetary policy. A more cynical illustration perhaps is the BoJ's attempt in 2015 to redefine how it measures inflation, in the vain hope of getting closer to meeting its commitment to reflate the Japanese economy.[50]

In 2009, the BoC took the conditionality of monetary policy one step further by explicitly committing to policy rates for a specified horizon—namely, up to one calendar year—but revisiting that commitment if the outlook changed and threatened the bank's remit of a 2% inflation target. In April 2010, the bank successfully convinced the financial markets that the outlook had changed sufficiently to remove that earlier commitment before it was due to expire in June 2010.[51]

---

[50] See, for example, Miller 2015.
[51] See Siklos and Spence 2010 and He 2010 for assessments and the precise details.

It is notable, however, that the Bank of Canada's conditional commitment was based on nominal variables—that is, interest rates and inflation rates—and not on real variables such as GDP growth or unemployment. Moreover, the policy was linked to a calendar. In the United States and the United Kingdom, policymakers would argue that the calendar should not dictate policy.[52] They were wrong, as I will argue next, because they viewed the calendar as divorced from economic performance. Yet, accountable policies should have a clearly attainable objective that can be met within a time frame that is based on expectations created by those policymakers in the first place. This involves taking a stand that is, in fact, linked to a calendar.

In 2013, the U.S. Fed adopted a form of conditional commitment when it agreed to maintain the current stance of monetary policy so long as the medium-term inflation target of 2% was not threatened and the unemployment rate remained above 6.5%. In so doing, the Fed strayed directly into making commitments that are driven by meeting a numerical target for real economic performance.

Forward guidance, like that introduced by the U.S. Fed, can lead to tension and confusion. Central banks became more confident in their ability to deliver stable and predictable inflation beginning in the mid-1990s. They were, in no small part, encouraged by the macroeconomic environment of the Great Moderation. However, as the financial crisis of 2008–9 deepened and recovery proved exceedingly slow, they faced pressure from politicians, markets, and the public not only to do more to help economies around the world but also to ensure that advanced economies especially reached "escape velocity," a concept that current BoE Governor Carney (2013), in an earlier speech, borrowed from physics to justify the continued need to persist with loose monetary policies. Commitments of this kind can be said to be consistent with the notion of "constrained discretion," which is viewed by most economists as compatible with good monetary policy and with the idea that, in times of crisis, central bank communications ought to differ from the strategy followed in normal times. There is, however, the danger that central banks are going too far and will end up confusing rather than clarifying what monetary policy can or cannot do.

The dangers of central banks' basing the conditionality of their policies on real economic outcomes are present on both theoretical and practical grounds.[53] When the Fed made its announcement, it did not specify whether the threshold of 6.5% for the unemployment rate was driven by a belief, shared by the members of the FOMC, that it was appropriate to aim for the percentage

---

[52] "Policy needs to be contingent on the economy, not the calendar" (Blinder 2013: 373). "Monetary policy should be contingent on the economic environment and not on the calendar" (Plosser 2014).

[53] Bullard 2013 provides a good summary of the theoretical objections raised by the Fed's recent changes in the forward guidance it provides.

that characterized the pre-crisis state of the U.S. economy. Indeed, if one believes that an aging population and the "low-hanging fruit" of productivity-enhancing technological change are conspiring to produce a future with lower economic growth,[54] then it is far from clear that the pre-crisis state of economic activity is what we should return to. And if the pre-crisis state is inappropriate for the future, then exactly what economic state should we aim for? Woodford (2012) demonstrates that these kinds of considerations affect both the credibility of and the net benefits from exiting a state in which monetary policy does not operate as usual.

Empirically, we know that economies can produce a wide range of unemployment rates consistent with price stability. Indeed, Staiger, Stock, and Watson (1997), among others, have shown how imprecise the estimates of a noninflationary rate of unemployment are over time. Moreover, there is the risk that any trade-offs between changes in inflation and in unemployment rates have changed over time, making it unclear precisely what conditional commitments—of the Fed variety—can actually achieve.

Next, as several authors have pointed out,[55] there is a long-held tradition that monetary policy is neutral in the *long run*—that is, it cannot influence the level of unemployment or output to be consistent with full-capacity utilization or full employment. However, promises of the kind the Fed has made, even if they are conditional and carefully articulated, raise the possibility that the "do no harm" principle of monetary policy is being violated. Indeed, when central banks stray into the territory of making commitments on real economic variables, no matter how they are conditioned, they risk feeling even greater political pressure and the consequent loss of autonomy when elected officials begin to question their chosen thresholds.

Even as the Fed was being criticized for the type of forward guidance it had adopted, the BoE would not only repeat the mistake the Fed made but also would eventually have to refine, and eventually retract, forward guidance altogether. A more limited conditional commitment such as the one the BoC pioneered in 2009 is not only appropriate, especially when the threat of deflation is looming, but also serves to strictly limit what a central bank can promise and over what period of time. This type of commitment makes clear that monetary policy can do only so much to help an economy recover. A conditional commitment of the kind made by the Fed raises a host of questions that may well push monetary policy into perilous territory.[56] However well-intentioned the policy is, as well as a signal that the central bank is adopting a

---

[54] See, for example, Gordon 2012.

[55] See, for example, Caruana 2013 and Masson 2013.

[56] Also, see Filardo and Hofmann 2014 who also highlight the potential risks and limitations of state-dependent forms of forward guidance.

"whatever it takes" attitude (which was essential during the height of the GFC of 2008–9), monetary policy cannot credibly make conditional commitments about real economic outcomes. In other words, forward guidance embodied a moment when some central banks revealed overconfidence in their ability to influence economic outcomes. Naturally, their response would be that the strategy reflects their determination to meet a stated monetary policy objective. However, when it is combined with the belief that their UMP will work, yet careful to repeat that forward guidance is always "data dependent," this leaves open the possibility that promises of this kind made by a central bank can be hollow if the basis of the commitment is not clearly spelled out or is vulnerable to new information.

One would also be remiss in not heeding the warnings of a strategy to undermine organizations that was articulated during World War II: "[M]ake speeches. Talk as frequently as possible and at great length. . . . Haggle over precise wordings of communication, minutes, resolutions. . . . Advocate 'caution'" (Office of Strategic Services 1944:28). Presumably, the central banks have no desire to sabotage their own institutions. Nevertheless, excessive reliance on forward guidance, or a stance that is inappropriately designed, helps erode the central bank's credibility.

Conclusions

It has been remarked by some that the central banks had a "good crisis." A second economic depression was averted, and the abandonment of rules-like and transparent monetary policies, supported by more effective communication, does not appear to have produced lasting damage. We can praise the central banks for how they implemented policy in the midst of the crisis, but this does not free them from criticism about the aftermath of the crisis.[57] Going forward, there are more profound and less favorable implications for the central banks. Chapter 3 discussed the potential negative consequences of central bank autonomy. I conclude this chapter by highlighting one of these negative implications. Others, such as inflating the responsibilities governments burden their central banks with heralds a return to a form of central banking not seen for decades, are the subject of the next chapter.

Arguably, the years spent convincing the financial markets and the public that monetary policy ought to be predictable and based on straightforward principles were wasted when the central banks deemed it necessary to adopt a new playbook. Yet, in three economies at the center of the economic storm that began in 2008, the consequence of this move was a seemingly

---

[57] Nor, for that matter, from creating conditions conducive to creating a crisis.

permanent rise in policy uncertainty.[58] Figure 4.17 plots the Baker, Bloom, and Davis (2016) indicator of economic policy uncertainty for the United States, the United Kingdom, and Europe. Notice the gradual rise in uncertainty beginning in 2007; it reaches a peak well after the central bankers had congratulated themselves on handling the worst of the global financial crisis. Even as policy uncertainty began to recede in 2013, levels have remained higher than at any other time plotted in the figure, except for the tech bubble and deflation scares of the early 2000s. It is also plain to see that volatility in the monthly indicators remained high and apparently showed no signs of declining as 2015 began. Presumably, the success of the central banks in preventing another crisis, as well as their delaying the start of a return to more normal monetary conditions, has been one of the contributors—perhaps even the main explanation—for this rise in economic policy uncertainty. After all, as noted in this chapter and detailed in the next, the central banks took on more responsibility for economic management after the crisis. Hence, they bear considerable blame for the greater uncertainty, even if they take some of the credit for preventing a Great Recession from becoming a Great Depression.

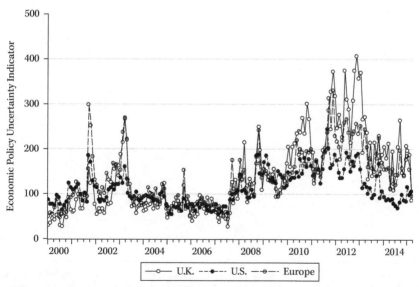

FIGURE 4.17 Economic Policy Uncertainty in the G3, 2000–2014

Source: Data are from Baker, Bloom, and Davis 2015.

---

[58] See Baker, Bloom, and Davis 2016 and chapter 1. There is, needless to say, no unique way of measuring policy uncertainty. After all, uncertainty reflects our ignorance of how the future will unfold. The notion of economic policy uncertainty relies on data collected from the media, uncertainty in fiscal matters, and the level of disagreement among forecasters.

Stated differently, the central banks were able to put out the fire they had helped stoke, and they compounded what some might term the "institutional hubris" they had demonstrated both before and after 2008.[59] Nevertheless, it is difficult to believe, a decade after the shock of the GFC, that the central banks have learned all the necessary lessons. Rather than reach for some modesty and engage their political masters in effectively placing their economies on a sounder footing, they have become all too enamored with policy innovations that at best represent only a transition to a "new normal."[60] That "new normal" continues to be undefined, and the central banks themselves appear incapable of explaining what it should look like.

---

[59] A well-intentioned example of this comes from the BoC's April 2009 Monetary Policy Report, in which Mark Carney, then governor, writes: "There is a plan to restore confidence and growth, we are implementing it, and it will work. The impact of these policies will build over time and will be significant. . . . Citizens must be able to hold policy-makers accountable. Policy-makers must rise to the occasion." Viewed more than seven years later, Carney's ambitions have gone largely unfilled. As Kahneman (2011:212) points out, "declarations of high confidence mainly tell you that an individual has a coherent story in his mind, not necessarily that the story is true."

[60] As several observers (e.g., Cowen 2013; Gordon 2012; and Dotsey 2016) have pointed out, to a considerable degree the "new normal" will rest on our belief about whether future productivity improvements can replicate those that influenced economic outcomes in the past.

The Over-Burdened Central Bank and the Shift Away from Autonomy

Overwhelmed and Overreaching?

Even before the GFC erupted in 2008, fiscal policy had retreated as a stabilization tool of first resort in an economic slump. To be sure, politicians still relied on changing taxes and spending to stimulate economic activity, but the notion that a separate fiscal stimulus program offered a solution to a major economic problem had faded from view. In several countries, such as Canada, the experience of the late 1980s and early 1990s led to a sea change in views about the role and effectiveness of fiscal policy. Instead of being seen as an effective stabilization tool, fiscal policy was thought to be best delivered in a manner that promised the least disruption as possible to the macroeconomy. The parallel with the theory and practice of monetary policy—namely, that it was thought to be neutral in the "long run"—is notable.[1]

While not all jurisdictions adopted this attitude literally, there was at least some consensus that a fiscal stimulus might be useful if necessary, but that it was not necessarily as useful when monetary policy might be able to deliver low and stable inflation while also supporting satisfactory economic growth (also see chapter 1). Arguably, one of the least publicized characteristics of the Great Moderation is the absence of a noticeable or permanent shift in the

---

[1] The negative attitude toward the effectiveness of fiscal policy, at least in some parts of the world, contributes perhaps to the continuing debate about some earlier experiences with fiscal policy as a tool to generate economic growth. For example, whether a tighter fiscal policy in the late 1930s plunged the United States back into a recession is still debated. As far back as Brown 1956, if not even earlier (Hansen 1941), there have been doubts about the significance of fiscal policy during the years shortly after the Great Depression. In contrast, monetary explanations for the U.S. recession of the late 1930s have become more prominent; see, for example, Velde 2009.

share of government spending (or consumption) as a fraction of economic activity in the advanced economies.[2]

Therefore, in 2007, even as the first hints that a serious financial crisis were looming, the immediate reactions of policymakers did not include resorting to a major fiscal stimulus. Instead, news stories about disruptions in the financial sector focused on how and whether the central banks should respond. Governments were effectively left using "open mouth" operations to give the impression that the crisis was under control and that the monetary authorities would be appropriately responsive to any financial collapse. In other words, verbal announcements were believed to be sufficiently credible to influence people's expectations about the true state of the economy.

As criticism of the central banks began to mount in early 2008, especially in the United States, and there were comparisons made to another apparently unsuccessful central bank, namely the BoJ, expectations and responsibilities were heaped on the monetary authorities to manage the problem.

Remarkably, at the apex of the financial crisis, around April 2009, leaders of the G20 communicated their determination to reform financial systems, restore confidence, and usher in plans to revive global economic growth. Not a word was said about the future role of the central banks, nor indeed was there even a call for reflection on the role of the monetary authorities in the years leading up to the financial crisis.[3] What was highlighted was the unprecedented reduction in policy rates, the substantial easing of monetary policy, and central banks' determination to maintain easy policies "as long as needed" while stressing a call for "credible exit strategies from the measures that need to be taken now." Ironically, the emphasis on credibility came at a time when it is very likely that central bank credibility had reached a low ebb (see Bordo and Siklos 2016a, 2016b).

In any case, the events of 2008 did result in a seemingly coordinated set of expansionary fiscal and monetary policies that put a floor under the rapid fall in output around the globe, a point made earlier (see chapter 1). This turn of events became clearer less than six months later, when the same G20 leaders met again, in September 2009, this time in Pittsburgh, to announce to the world that their crisis response strategy had, in their opinion, succeeded.[4]

---

[2] It is difficult to reach a definitive conclusion on the stance of fiscal policy both pre- and post-crisis. Different data sources clearly reveal that most G20 economies boosted government spending as a fraction of GDP during the 2007–10 period. Many economies retreated from the stimulus prompted by the onset of the GFC, but it is far from clear that, other than a one-time drop even before the crisis unofficially ended in 2009 or 2010, there was a return to pre-GFC levels of spending. Data from the World Bank, the IMF, and the OECD used to reach this conclusion are available in the online appendix.

[3] The leaders' statement, dated April 2, 2009, is available at www.imf.org/external/np/sec/pr/2009/pdf/g20_040209.pdf.

[4] In the United States, at the epicenter of the crisis, the U.S. Congress did its level best to prevent the Fed from intervening, as Bernanke 2015 reminds us. However, rather than ensure that the Fed in the future would retain the ability to react with flexibility when the next financial crisis hit, the

On the institutional front, the financial crisis moved the profile of the G20 to center stage in political discussions about international economic policymaking, while the Financial Stability Board (FSB) would be designated as the international institution best suited to ensure the world's financial system would become more resilient in the face of as yet unknown future financial shocks. Once again, however, there was no mention of an enhanced role for any central bank. Nevertheless, the central banks would take on more responsibilities. Some of these responsibilities would eventually be enshrined in legislation, while in other cases the banks ended up adopting those roles by default. In still other cases, the central banks actively sought greater responsibilities in the area of regulation, supervision, and maintenance of financial system stability. Indeed, as former Bank of Canada Governor Mark Carney, on the eve of his departure to the United Kingdom to become governor of the Bank of England, put it: "Although it has not been the case in Canada where policy has remained conventional; globally, central banks are being asked to do more, in more ways, than ever before" (Carney 2013). Canada was, of course, one of many countries where monetary policy would remain more or less conventional throughout the GFC.

It is instructive that while the GFC produced such a reaction, the critical details of the new regime—wherein monetary policy would to be carried out alongside what is now called "macroprudential" policies—were left largely undefined and no explicit policy strategy was articulated. Figure 5.1 illustrates the brave new world that central bankers faced in the aftermath of the GFC. Bar chart (a) indicates, for a sample of forty-six economies surveyed, that virtually all central banks were given responsibility for the maintenance of financial stability, though this responsibility was not always legislated. However, in only a slight majority of cases—that is, twenty-seven—has there been published a formal definition of what financial stability means (b).[5] Matters become still worse when it is considered whether a definition of financial stability has been entered into statute; in only four cases has that responsibility been legislated (c). Perhaps this reflects politicians' natural tendency to avoid dealing with issues after the worst has passed and worries over financial stability have subsided. Alternatively, it could be the case that a widely accepted definition is elusive because, as discussed in chapter 3, financial crises come in different shapes and forms.

Dodd-Frank financial reforms shackled the central bank by heaping on a complex set of institutional arrangements that would ensure an inability to react swiftly when needed. As a result, the locus of accountability falls squarely on Congress. Indeed, history is full of attempts by politicians to limit the responses of certain institutions when, ideally, they would be called on in a time of crisis; for examples from central banking, see Siklos 2002. Usually, these attempts stem from politicians' inability to allocate responsibility for tasks best left to nonpoliticians.

[5] An appendix to Lombardi and Siklos 2016 provides extracts of the formal definitions used by several countries. Also, see Allen and Wood 2006.

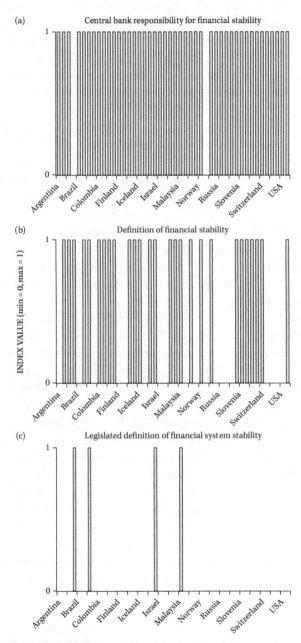

FIGURE 5.1 Cross-Country Evidence on the Main Responsibilities of Central Banks
(a) Central Bank Responsibility for Financial Stability
(b) Definition of Financial Stability
(c) Legislated Definition of Financial System Stability

Note: A 1 indicates that the characteristic at the top of each figure applies to the central bank in question. A 0 means the feature in question is not present. *Source:* Data are from Lombardi and Siklos 2016.

To be fair, when the debate about what is meant by price stability was raging over two decades ago, there was a comparable lack of consensus. In part this is because countries display well-known biases in their measurements of inflation. In addition, there have been lingering doubts about how much inflation is necessary to "grease the wheels" or, indeed, to what extent observed inflation represents a change in relative prices as opposed to a general rise in price level. Although in advanced economies the debate settled into a grudging acceptance that zero percent inflation is too low, while much more than 2% inflation is too high, the desire to relax restrictions against higher inflation has emerged from some important quarters.

This solution is seen by some as the easiest and possibly least painful way out of the current predicament the global economy finds itself in. Nevertheless, the strategy of using inflation to solve inherently different sets of economic problems ignores the impact it would have on the central banks. Indeed, attempting to generate considerably higher inflation risks burdens the central banks even more, especially when it comes time to taming inflation then deemed excessive; it also risks exacerbating the very distributional elements of monetary policy that central bankers are keen to avoid.

Wanted: A New Deal for Central Banks?

It took some time for central bankers to ask whether the "contract" between the bank and its country's government ought to be rewritten. In the speech by Mark Carney referred to earlier, the governor also suggested that "the contract between the central bank and the government was incomplete." Indeed, he went on to add that the crisis raises "a fundamental question about the appropriate constraints on central banks' delegated authority." In a government that places price stability at the center of its mandate, the belief was widely accepted that the central bank should use its authority in a flexible manner. However, the governor did not ask about the limits of the central bank's accountability. Indeed, flexibility post-GFC amounted to keeping interest rates lower for longer, a strategy adopted by a large number of central banks around the world.

The difficulty is that, even if it has been known for centuries that central banks play a natural role in the financial stability sphere,[6] many banks have sought to distance themselves from too actively taking on this role. This is partly because of the possibility of a conflict of interest with the institutions

---

[6] Consider Henry Thornton (1802:188) writing about the role of the Bank of England: ". . . , in future seasons of alarm, should be disposed to extend its discounts in a greater degree than heretofore, then the threatened calamity may be averted through the generosity of that institution." Thornton also well understood both contagion in finance as well as the problem of moral hazard.

that may lead to financial instability thanks also to the spread of shadow banking. Shadow banks sit uncomfortably outside the remit of central bank authority, but also because taking on too many risks poses threats to its balance sheet particularly, but not exclusively, from the sovereign. Given the challenges, the standard of accountability is more difficult to define.

Recall that a price stability objective, particularly when expressed in numerical terms, is relatively easily assessed against outcomes.[7] As argued in earlier chapters, it is precisely this feature, as well as the intensively researched connection between monetary policy and inflation, that allows for setting a standard of accountability in monetary policy. Moreover, accountability for setting clear objectives narrows the ability to share responsibility for any failure to meet those stated objectives, as well as placing the onus on the monetary authority to explain itself to the public.

When the central banks take on more responsibilities, the standards by which those banks are judged become less clear. Since there has been no definitive assessment of responsibility for the conditions that produced the GFC, one has to ask whether any new relationship between the central banks and their sovereign governments can be written that incorporates what has been learned. Otherwise, we may well be left with institutions that succumb to "mission creep."[8] In such an environment, the monetary authorities are able to become more intrusive, while the goals of monetary policy shift as the political authorities absolve themselves of their responsibility for setting goals to be met. Of course, this comes with a loss of democratic accountability, as more and more responsibility for aggregate demand management shifts to unelected officials. The extant historical experience suggests that an expansion of ambitions by an institution will end badly, especially if there is another financial crisis on a global scale. The central banks will then no longer be able to hide behind the explanation that they lacked the authority to intervene.[9]

Arguably, the most famous example of this is the U.S. Federal Reserve's effectively ceding control of monetary policy to the U.S. Treasury from 1942 to 1951. As told masterfully by Meltzer (2003), this resulted from a combination of benign neglect and serial errors in the conduct of monetary policy beginning late in the 1920s, continuing through the low point of the Great Depression, and lasting until well into the 1930s. Decades later, in a time of

---

[7] Less straightforward, as noted earlier, is whether the inflation metric against which monetary policy is judged is adequate. (I return to this question in the final chapter.)

[8] Also, see Orphanides 2013 who also expresses reservations about the added responsibilities central banks are faced with post-crisis. One potential implication of mission creep is that of policy inertia as different and competing objectives lead decision-making committees to favor the status quo over action. For the case of monetary policy, see, for example, Favoretto and Masciandaro 2016.

[9] Matters are, in fact, potentially worse if limits are placed on responding to a crisis in one area while responsibilities are increased in other areas without recognition of the spillover effects across areas of responsibility.

renewed crisis, political forces wanting to reverse the scope of the Fed's authority remain active. These range from the "End the Fed" movement in 2009 led by then Congressman Ron Paul and others, to the current legislative proposals by several senators to limit the Fed's authority and increase political oversight of the institution. No doubt these developments were partly spurred by the Financial Crisis Inquiry Commission (2011), which concluded that the Federal Reserve neglected its mission "to ensure the safety and soundness of the nations' banking and financial system and to protect the credit rights of consumers." In other words, the Fed already possessed responsibility for financial stability, but it was apparently not enough. It is not immediately obvious, however, that in the face of such a failure, the proper reaction was to burden the central bank with greater responsibilities.

Other threats come from the conduct of monetary policy, which after all remains the core function of the central banks. In 2012, the Federal Reserve's Monetary Policy Report began to publish its first "dot plot," so named because dots are used to show what target for the Fed funds rate members of the FOMC feel might be appropriate in the future. This device was intended to convey to financial markets and the public the timing of the U.S. central bank's policy rate "liftoff" from the ZLB, where it had remained from the end of 2008 to the end 2015. Figure 5.2 provides an alternative view of the same information so as to highlight the fact that, after only three years, the overwhelming majority of FOMC members significantly pushed back a tightening of U.S. monetary policy (also, see chapter 3). Indeed, these same members substantially reduced their view of what the "longer run" normal level of the policy rate would be. One has to ask what such a delay says about the public's interpretation of the role and ability of monetary policy to enable a return to "normal" economic conditions.

There are both domestic and international elements influencing the foregoing developments. Domestically, the central banks risked taking on too many responsibilities with objectives such as inflation put on hold while new and less clearly delineated concerns over financial stability remained a work in progress. At the international level, the central banks were opening themselves up to accusations that global concerns, not ordinarily falling within the mandate of a central bank, were taking on an importance hitherto not foreseen. Not only does this development risk a watering down of accountability, but it also risks opening up accusations that the central banks are taking on responsibilities that were not adequately debated at the political level.

It seems fairly clear that there exists greater room for policy mistakes when the environment in which the central bank operates—namely, the search and maintenance of financial stability—lacks clear objectives and is clouded with expressions and policies that have different meanings to different audiences. This element of the debate will become more apparent in the discussion that follows.

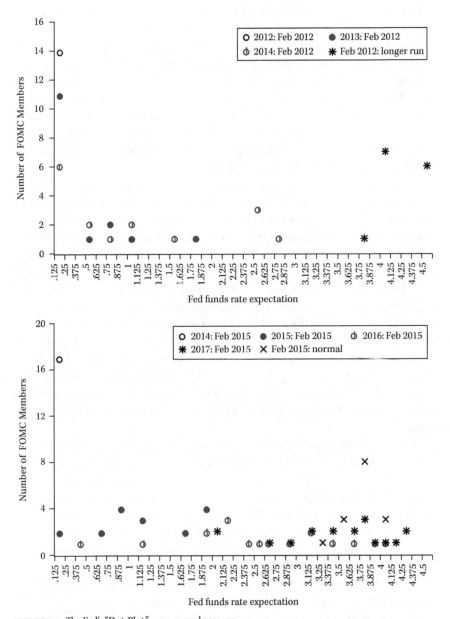

FIGURE 5.2 The Fed's "Dot-Plot," 2012–14 and 2014–17

Note: Expectations are for the dates shown in each dot-plot. Longer-run or normal refers to expectations once the U.S. economy reaches some equilibrium or long-run macroeconomic conditions. *Source:* Monetary Policy Reports, various issues, Summary of Economic Projections.

More fundamentally, one is reminded that a large measure of a central bank's success is in avoiding a centralization of authority over all matters financial. There is no better way of ensuring an accountability standard than through an appropriate division of powers. Since at least James Madison, who wrote in one of the Federalist Papers (1788:313), that "the accumulation of all powers, . . . may justly be pronounced the very definition of tyranny," the surest protection against authority's overreach is to not give too much responsibility to any one institution. This should include central banks.

It is important to keep in mind that there is a potential distinction between asking central banks to take on additional responsibilities and the impression that these same institutions can become overburdened. First, this assumes that the existing responsibilities of the central banks are in some sense optimal or ideal; clearly, the appropriate space occupied by a central bank among public institutions can and has changed over time. Second, there is an assumption that to ask the central banks to take on more responsibilities is somehow inappropriate. It is worth recalling that the Federal Reserve Bank was created to tame the U.S. financial system's tendency to experience crises after crises (e.g., see Meltzer 2013 and Lowenstein 2015). As a result, the function as the lender of last resort defines the origins of many central banks (e.g., see Siklos 2002). The fact that the central banks, post-World War II, evolved into institutions that maintained control over inflation reflects the improvements in our understanding of the link between monetary policy and inflation.

It is today's expectation that monetary authorities can implement a strategy capable of preempting future financial crises, as contrasted to their historic mission of acting as a bulwark against the fallout of financial crises. It is this expectation that sees the danger in central banks' becoming overburdened. Indeed, that expectation is not only bound to disappoint but is also very likely to produce a backlash against any attempts by central banks to simultaneously prevent the worst excesses of the financial markets and encourage the credit growth required to return the economy to something resembling pre-GFC growth rates. Again, quoting from the U.S. Financial Crisis Inquiry Report, "the Commission concludes that the Federal Reserve . . . created conditions in which a housing bubble could develop" (FCIC2011: 4064). The conditions necessary to create the next bubble are far more likely to occur if the institution is overburdened with responsibilities.

A risk that an institution will become overburdened stems from the possibility that it is tasked with responsibilities it is not equipped to handle or for which it is poorly understood. As we have seen, monetary policy helped create the financial conditions that led to the GFC, but it cannot by itself explain the whole story. It is a tall order to then expect the central banks to have the ability to identify financial conditions that might lead to an outright crisis, as opposed to monitoring the normal cyclical behavior of the real and financial sectors of the economy. We have had very few instances of crises on the scale of the GFC, let alone in a world where the financial markets are increasingly sophisticated and interconnected.

Whither Central Bank Autonomy?

At first, the GFC triggered alarms among observers of central bank policies. If imminent inflation was not enough of a threat (e.g., Greenspan 2010, Meltzer 2009b), there was political pressure building to limit the authority of central banks to intervene in financial markets. In any event, the strong consensus among policymakers, academics, and public officials about the desirability of the central bank's independence that had taken over two decades to form was now showing signs of disintegrating. Exactly which events or series of events is to blame is unclear, since the precise origins of the GFC remain in question (never mind whether the crisis has ended). As retrospective timelines and chronologies of the crisis have made clear, the specific event or events that may have triggered the GFC can be in the eye of the beholder. For example, the St. Louis Fed's timeline of the financial crisis[10] begins in early 2007 with Freddie Mac's[11] decision to withdraw from the market for subprime mortgages. This would soon be followed by downgrades of certain bonds, problems with Bear Stearns, and the liquidation of hedge funds even before BNP Paribas came into the picture. In contrast, the Federal Reserve Bank of New York's own timeline of the "market events" and the "policy response" to the financial turmoil does not begin until late June 2007.[12] The ECB is even more ambitious in its own "key dates of the financial crisis,"[13] which makes no distinction between events that originated in the United States and those that started in Europe,[14] begins in December 2005 with a warning on "financial imbalances."

Just as the "black swan" appeared in the money markets, there was a comparable development that led academics and policymakers astray concerning the sources and significance of central bank autonomy. When Alex Cukierman (1992) first developed an indicator of central bank autonomy, he understood

---

[10] See www.stlouisfed.org/financial-crisis/full-timeline.

[11] This is the name given to the Federal Home Loan Mortgage Corporation, a quasi-governmental organization in the United States.

[12] See www.ny.frb.org/research/global_economy/Crisis_Timeline.pdf . The New York Fed treats separately the international response, which began in earnest in 2008; see http://newyorkfed.org/research/global_economy/IRCTimelinePublic.pdf. I return to this issue later.

[13] www.ecb.europa.eu/ecb/html/crisis.en.html; accessed April 30, 2015, but the chronology was subsequently removed.

[14] This is interesting only because, as the crisis was unfolding, European officials were quite vocal about the fact that this was a "North American crisis," forgetting that Canada was spared the financial market turmoil even if the economic spillovers could not be avoided entirely. The message would begin to change by 2009, when Europe's own sovereign debt crisis was beginning to stir the world's financial markets.

that there was a difference between de jure and de facto forms of independence. Nevertheless, it seemed relatively easier at the time to devise an index that placed emphasis primarily on the contents of the legislation governing the role and functions of the monetary authority. For the time being, the discussion will center on statutory aspects of central bank autonomy. (The evolution of central bank independence around the world was first addressed in chapter 1.)

By the time Cukierman's volume (1992:349) was published, even he claimed that "a widespread feeling among economists" existed in favor of a link between central bank autonomy and inflation. To be sure, there were skeptics, but by the early 2000s, when the advanced economies were well into the Great Moderation, the topic would attract less attention. Indeed, Woodford's seminal work *Interest and Prices* (2003) effectively assumes that central banks need not be fettered by pressure from political authorities. The built-in inflation bias that plagued monetary policy, and found its theoretical justification in Kydland and Prescott's (1977) time-inconsistency argument, became something to be aware of, though it was no longer felt to be existential. Of course, not all central banks were equally autonomous. Nevertheless, by the time of the GFC, central banks that were as statutorily independent as a Cukierman-style index would allow could be found in any part of the globe. Figure 5.3 provides a visual confirmation of these stylized facts; it clearly reveals that average levels of (statutory) autonomy of central banks from their governments rose sharply throughout the 1990s. Even the least independent central banks were better off on the eve of the GFC, at least relative to their status in 1990.

One important problem with measures of the kind pioneered by Cukierman is that it does little good for a central bank to be autonomous in legal terms if the society it operates in has a poor record with respect to the rule of law. As shown in figure 5.4, there are large variations in the respect of the rule of law, even within the group of advanced economies (a), as defined by the IMF. Matters are even worse for a selection of emerging market economies (b), many of which contributed to the global rise in central bank independence apparent in figure 5.3. Even when the data are aggregated, there is considerable variation in changes to the rule of law. While average levels have risen in the 2000s, there have been reversals, especially since the GFC (not shown).[15]

What is less frequently discussed, however, would become another arguably more important form of independence—namely, the distance between the central banks and the financial markets. Blinder (1999) reminded us of the importance of this potential link over fifteen years ago. Yet, one is hard pressed to find serious discussion of this form of relationship, whose

---

[15] Taylor 2012 also bemoans the fact that economics has not stressed enough the principles of the rule of law and policy predictability. The latter was considered in greater details in chapter 4.

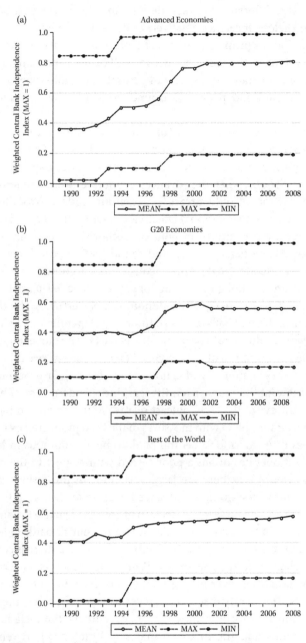

FIGURE 5.3 Varieties of Central Bank Independence
(a) Advanced Economies
(b) G20 Economies
(c) Rest of the World's Economies

Note: Central bank independence ranges from lowest (0) to highest (1). Mean refers to the average value of the index for a particular group of economies shown; MAX is the highest value recorded; MIN is the lowest value recorded. *Source:* Cukierman 1992, and Siklos 2002.

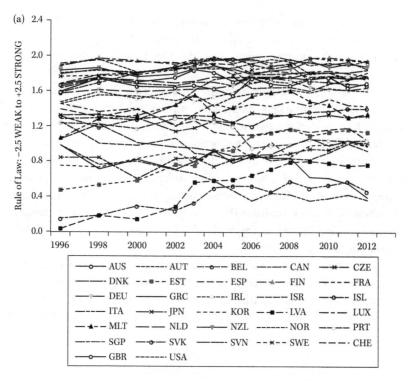

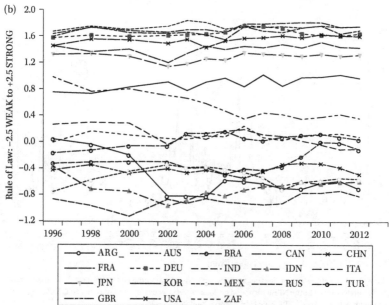

FIGURE 5.4 Central Bank Governance and the Rule of Law, 1996–2011
(a) Advanced Economies
(b) Emerging Market Economies

Note: World Bank Governance Indicators, www.govindicators.org. See the list of abbreviations for the individual country names.

independence emerges when the monetary authority is seen as delivering a policy-rate path that markets expect, as opposed to the central bank's own assessment of the future course of yields. The danger, as Blinder warns us, is that "if the central bank strives too hard to please markets, it is likely to adopt the markets' extremely short horizon as its own" (1999:61–62). Beyond the influence that markets might have on central bank policy-rate levels, the GFC has created a new avenue along which markets can influence the monetary authority—namely, their impact on central bank attempts to mitigate the prospects of future financial instability. The "taper tantrum" of 2013, prompted by then Fed Chair Ben Bernanke's musings about the gradual ending of the Federal Reserve's bond-buying program, is one such example. Nevertheless, market volatility beginning in May 2013 hardly dented the "fear index," also known as the VIX, which remained at pre-crisis levels, as shown in figure 5.5.[16]

The upshot is that the concept of central bank independence has become distorted, and the crisis has served to amplify these distortions. Instead of a clearer recognition that financial markets are just as likely to restrict a central bank's maneuverability as would political pressure on that central bank, the focus in

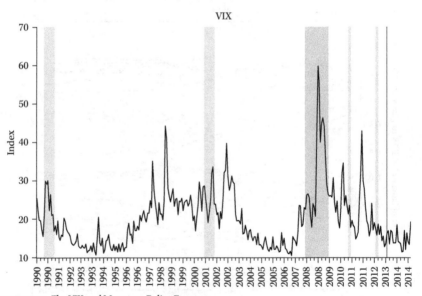

FIGURE 5.5 The VIX and Monetary Policy Events

Note: the vertical line at 2013 identifies the month when Bernanke announced the "tapering" of Treasury purchases. The shaded areas represent the NBER recession periods (www.nber.org/cycles.html), the GFC (2008–9), QE2 (2010), and QE3 (2012). *Source:* FRED, Federal Reserve Bank of St. Louis.

---

[16] The potential difficulties and challenges in relying on an indicator such as the VIX to divine the relationship between monetary policy and financial stability were considered in chapters 2 and 4.

the academic literature has almost entirely been on the threat from government. There is further irony, in that while there has been considerable activism, especially in the late 1990s, to reform central bank legislation, the effort nowadays is on the margins, with little zeal to reform the central bank's role, revisit its mandate, or even debate what autonomy implies in a world of bloated central bank balance sheets, quasi-fiscal activities, and expanded responsibilities.

Other than for Dincer and Eichengreen (2014), it is frequently forgotten that one half of Cukierman's index of central bank independence was devoted to the impact of limitations on lending primarily, but not exclusively, to government. Similarly, an indicator of the economic independence of central banks,[17] owing to Grilli et al. (1991), also stresses the latitude the sovereign has in relying on the monetary authority to finance deficits.[18]

One of the consequences of the wave of legislative changes to central bank autonomy that swept the globe was the addition of severe restrictions on governments and the private sector to tap the central bank for financial support. It comes as no surprise, then, that criticisms are leveled at central banks when the wall that separates the institution and the rest of the financial system is seen as being breached. But this wall was never intended to prevent all attempts at central bank financing. The Great Moderation simply exaggerated the confidence policymakers had in not needing government or private-sector support from the monetary authorities. It is no wonder, then, that central banks are seen as overburdened, as their inflated balance sheets (also see chapter 1) give the mistaken impression they are performing tasks for which they were not designed. The flaw here is not in the level of burden imposed on the central banks. Instead, the problem is a failure to build in the correct contingencies for defining the relationships between the central bank, the government, and the rest of the financial system.

Ambiguity Makes a Comeback

Central banks have made great strides in transparency over the past two decades. In particular, monetary authorities in the industrialized world have placed greater emphasis on what is now commonly referred to as forward guidance and showing how future monetary policy decisions are likely to be conditioned by the economic outlook (also see chapter 4). Whereas greater transparency sheds more light on why a central bank acts the way it does, forward guidance is an explicit attempt to influence market and public inflation

---

[17] As opposed to the political independence that underscores Bade and Parkin's (1982) original index of central bank independence (also see Alesina and Summers 1993).

[18] Freytag 2001 correctly points out that central bank autonomy also consists of external commitments (e.g., the exchange rate regime). He is not the first one to emphasize this point. See, for example, Siklos 1994 and references therein.

expectations by providing insights into the possible *future* direction of monetary policy.

Since the future is unknown, and with central bank policy rates in several economies currently near or at the effective lower bound, there is a premium on how central banks communicate their actions. Jaime Caruana, general manager of the BIS, expressed this view while being careful to add an important cautionary note: "At the current juncture, there is also a premium on central bank communication. Central banks need to clearly communicate the limits of monetary policy" (Caruana 2013). The statement not only reflects an environment in which there are growing concerns about the implications of historically low interest rates for an extended period of time; in addition, it meets the added burden of providing guidance with clarity. For central banks that are worried about a potential loss of credibility, this guidance cannot be accomplished unless communication is somewhat ambiguous.

While the role and potential benefits of forward guidance are not questioned, is it possible that central banks are taking it too far? If so, there is the potential for the central banks to hint at steps they are unable to carry out or to engage in interventions that are outside their remit, with the consequence that monetary authorities end up taking on burdens beyond their normal role. Worse still, in the event of a major failure to achieve stated objectives, all the progress made by the central banks and the governments pre-crisis to define the limits of their authority and set standards of performance can be quickly wiped out legislatively.

Originally, the promise of forward guidance was that it would be seen as a natural extension of autonomous central banks' wanting to be more transparent and, by implication, more accountable. In addition, there was the thorny problem of communicating flexibility as a counterweight to the potential of a knee-jerk reaction to perceived excessively loose or tight monetary policies, as interpreted from the application of policy rules (see chapter 4).

Of course, even as some central banks have become more explicit about the future course of the economy—that is, the likely evolution of interest rates, inflation, and real economic activity—they have always been careful to underscore the point that as facts change, so would the outlook for key macroeconomic aggregates. The mantra of the typical central bank, as we have seen, is transparency, which is also understood to mean an attempt at clarity. Clarity, however, does not entail a commitment to promises made today, regardless of the consequences, or to ignoring new information that might call for a different stance of monetary policy. Instead, any forward guidance is understood to be conditional. Much has been made, of course, of Alan Greenspan's remark, "If I've made myself too clear, you must have misunderstood me";[19] but this may have been as much about not

---

[19] The precise source of the quote is unclear, as some claim it was made before a business audience and others before Congress; the latter is more likely. See Eijffinger, Hoeberichts, and Schaling 2000.

wanting to be tying his, or the FOMC's, hands as it was of giving the appearance of the Delphic Oracle, who is seen, *ex post*, to be fallible.

Nevertheless, it is the case that central banks have greatly increased and enhanced their efforts at providing guidance. Policymakers would also come to refer to forward guidance as a policy designed to influence the markets' expectations when economic recovery seemed to stall but conditions were not in place to allow a rise in central bank policy rates.

However, at this point, forward guidance can easily lose the appearance of being informative about *possible* future changes in the policy stance and instead of becoming a device that reveals to the public how incapable a central bank is of relying on monetary policy to increase economic growth (or reduce unemployment) or individually to prevent the emergence of financial instability. This is especially true of forward-guidance policies that stipulate some threshold to be crossed before any action is taken. Pushing back or changing the threshold is no longer guidance that can be seen as helpful in influencing expectations; rather, it becomes a sign of a central bank's failure to meet an objective it has set on its own, without a proper airing of views to the contrary. Hence, forward guidance can be seen as a central bank's overburdening itself with false promises or actions that are put off because data-dependent decisions require it.

The Curious Case of Japan

Observers of central bank policies naturally tend to think of the much publicized forward guidance offered in the United States, beginning in 2013, as representative of this forward-looking policy strategy. Yet, it is arguably Japan where the notion of forward guidance originated in the late 1990s and where, after others adopted it in various alternatives, was revived when Haruhiko Kuroda became governor of the BoJ in 2013.

The BoJ's policy rate hit the ZLB in early 1999. Around the same time, Japan began to experience sustained periods of mild deflation. Fears of a deflationary spiral, however, were always overblown—rates of deflation rarely exceeded 2%. Also exaggerated was the magnitude of the economic "slump" Japan was supposedly in.[20] Why, then, worry about deflation? Part of the concern is that deflation is synonymous with poor economic performance and generates the wrong incentives to invest and purchase durable goods. The story goes

---

[20] See, for example, Fingleton 2012. The negative views about Japan were no doubt prompted by Krugman's 1998 views about Japanese monetary policy. In revisiting the subject (Krugman 2015b), he found that many of his comments still held and suggested that a higher inflation target would help, as would more aggressive demand management. Krugman, however, failed to consider that if previous attempts, also labeled "aggressive," failed, then why should the public believe another try will be successful?

something as follows: companies and households are likely to postpone some forms of spending if they believe that prices will be lower in future.

Figure 5.6 shows the contrast between price level behavior in Japan (a) and Canada (b). Whereas prices in Canada have been rising remarkably close to the Bank of Canada's inflation target of 2%, the Bank of Japan's record comes closest to a 0% inflation target. Yet, Japan's inflation record is nowhere near as dire as some seem to think, and there is little evidence of deflation spiraling out of control. Equally important is that Japan's population is aging and economists are still grappling with the effects of demographic changes on consumption, investment, and economic growth.

Although ambitious, and far from being implemented as this is written, what is apparent is the pressure applied to the BoJ to raise its inflation objective to 2% (from a 1% goal). The minutes of the January 2013 meeting of BoJ's policymaking committee reflect that: "most members expressed the view that it was desirable to designate the specific numerical expression for price stability as 2% in terms of the year-on-year rate of change in the CPI." The decision by the BoJ to acquiesce to those setting the newly installed prime minister's economic strategy naturally made news around the world, and more than a few observers wrote approvingly of the change.[21] Nevertheless, before reaching the conclusion that a mere declaration of a higher inflation target is enough, there are several reasons to question such an action, especially if other elements of "Abenomics" are not put into place.[22]

First, the decision by the BoJ to raise the inflation target was made quite reluctantly; it is unclear from the minutes of the BoJ's January 2013 meeting whether the board was enthusiastic about the change. Consider some additional comments in the minutes: "The Bank of Japan Act stipulated that the Bank should conduct monetary policy based on the principle that monetary policy was aimed at 'achieving price stability, thereby contributing to the sound development of the national economy.' According to the Bank's Opinion Survey on the General Public's Views and Behavior, approximately 80% of the respondents—irrespective of sex or age—consistently viewed a price rise as 'rather unfavorable.'" The gist of this statement is that inflation for its own sake is not desirable and the public does not appear to equate it with better economic performance.

Second, the BoJ's decision to raise the inflation objective came after many months of political pressure and its concerns about the loss of autonomy. As

---

[21] See, for example, Pilling 2013 for an initial overview of the "three arrows" strategy. A year later the reviews were less than glowing. The easy part apparently was quickly enacted; see, for example, Davies 2013 and Soble 2013. More than three years later, there is little evidence that the promised inflation is being delivered.

[22] This is the "three arrows" policy introduced by the prime minister when he returned to office in 2013.

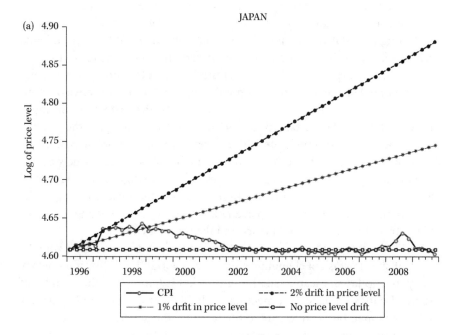

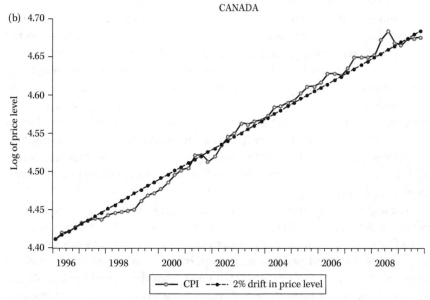

FIGURE 5.6 Drifts in the Price level and Inflation Targets
(a) Japan
(b) Canada

Note: The straight lines show what the price level would be under different scenarios for inflation.
Source: Siklos 2014b.

I pointed out earlier, economists view the autonomy of the central bank to mean an unfettered ability to carry out day-to-day policy, absent political pressure. Independence does not mean that the government should not change—say, through legislative actions—the principal objectives of the central bank, such as setting an inflation target. And, it certainly does not mean that the central bank is expected to bear the entire burden of attaining a particular inflation rate. For these reasons, economists prefer that the objective of monetary policy be set *jointly* with the government, as is the custom, for example, in several other inflation-targeting economies. Instead, in Japan, the government appeared to communicate with the central bank via public opinion in lieu of having a substantive discussion with the BoJ about setting a new course for monetary policy. This strategy becomes even more difficult to understand when, unlike many other central banks in the rest of the advanced economies, government representatives in Japan attend the BoJ's policy meeting (i.e., individuals from the Ministry of Finance and the Cabinet Office).

It is difficult to see how this kind of behavior, even if politically desirable, accomplishes the task of changing expectations about the ability of monetary policy to help Japan escape deflation. Indeed, it is telling that the minutes of the BoJ Board's January 2013 meeting explicitly warn elected policymakers that "Many members—referring to the fact that the government had shown its intention to aggressively pursue steps for strengthening the competitiveness and growth potential of Japan's economy—expressed the opinion that, as such steps made progress, the actual rate of inflation would be expected to rise and, accordingly, the inflation rate at which the general public perceived price stability would be likely to rise as well." Stated differently, the BoJ's board was arguing that inflation would rise *after* structural reforms have had a chance to impact the economy. Hence, it is easy enough to see why the mere declaration of a 2% (or higher) inflation objective ended up in early 2016 as sounding like empty words. Declarations such as these result in sounding like certain forms of forward guidance, and like other forms that failed, it is difficult to see how this kind of policy can prevent loss of central bank credibility.

The mere announcement of an inflation target is, however, insufficient. It is worth remembering that IT came into being for at least two reasons: the failure of alternative monetary policy strategies, such as exchange rate or money supply targeting; and perhaps more important, inflation previously was too high and the only way to convince the public that the central bank could deliver low and stable inflation was through a joint commitment with government to deliver lower inflation. The circumstances in Japan, however, are different. There, the goal is to *raise* inflation, which IT was arguably not designed to do. Whereas generating *lower* inflation through tight monetary policy is easy enough—albeit potentially economically costly—there is relatively less room to deliver an easier monetary policy once interest rates have reached the

ELB and vast amounts of various private and public assets are booked on the central bank's balance sheets.

Is Overwhelming Force the Answer?

The experience of Japan since 2013 is, sadly, not the first time the Bank of Japan has undertaken interventions of the kind now called unconventional monetary policy, or UMP. It is worth briefly reviewing the Japanese experience since 1999 as a cautionary tale, not because of the inability of UMP to have some economic impact but, rather, because of the added burden taken on by monetary policy when a broader set of economic problems need to be tackled.

In April 1999, the BoJ committed to maintaining a zero interest rate policy (ZIRP) "until deflationary concerns are dispelled" (Baba et al. 2005). After a period of economic improvement, ZIRP was lifted in August 2000; however, the 2001 recession led the BoJ to reinstate ZIRP in March 2001 and to adopt a quantitative easing (QE) program. After another period of improvement, the BoJ ended its QE program in March 2006 and began to downsize its balance sheet;[23] however, the 2008 recession forced the BoJ to expand its balance sheet, leading to a comprehensive monetary easing in October 2010.

Often, researchers employ an event study to capture the effects of monetary policy announcements and asset purchases in the financial markets. For example, Kuttner and Posen (2004) analyzed the behavior of long-term Japanese government bond (JGB) rates before and after a major policy announcement.[24] They conclude that there is no evidence various quantitative measures and expansions of eligible assets for open-market operations had an impact on long-term bond rates. Whether the policy announcements were poorly communicated or the markets felt that the BoJ would be tempted to prematurely withdraw loose monetary policies is unclear. Nevertheless, the evolution of inflation in Japan (see chapter 1) reveals frequent reversals around the time various QE measures were ceased. No doubt the track record of the BoJ (and the Finance Ministry) in the aftermath of burst housing bubble in the 1990s and the failure to properly address the weak banking system, likely also made observers' question the efficacy of monetary policy.

Bernanke, Reinhart, and Sack (2004) also conducted an event study to analyze the effectiveness of BoJ policy announcements in influencing short- to

---

[23] Koo (2015:103) suggests that the BoJ was "forced" to tighten "sooner than it would normally do because of QE." Exactly how the BoJ was strong-armed is not clear. A reference is made to foreigners' holding Japanese stocks and wanting to see more leverage; however, it simply appears that the exit from UMP was premature. Of course, as in many other instances, hindsight is 100% perfect.

[24] They analyze changes in long-term JGB rates during periods where short-term interest rates were stable in order to capture the influence of changes in expectations on interest rates.

long-term interest rates, as well as asset prices from 1998 (when the BoJ gained independence) to 2004. They defined four factors as candidates that affect interest rate changes after BoJ policy announcements: (1) the unexpected component of an announcement; (2) changes in the year-ahead euroyen futures rates; (3) changes in the five-year JGB coupon yields; and (4) changes in the Nikkei 500 stock index.[25] Their findings suggest that announcements by the BoJ influence interest rates by being unexpected and through innovation to long-term policy expectations; however, the BoJ's ability to influence year-ahead policy expectations is weak relative to a similar analysis using U.S. data.

To establish whether any type of surprise announcement has a stronger influence on interest rates, the authors examined the responsiveness of BoJ announcements to monetary policy decisions and macroeconomic surprises on each of the four candidate factors.[26] Surprise announcements regarding the path of interest rates affect the first factor (current rates), but surprise announcements have no effect on the second factor (one-year-ahead rates). In addition, surprise easing announcements regarding the path of interest rates (i.e., ZIRP) actually increase long-term rates, likely because of an increase in future inflation expectations, while surprise easing announcements concerning JGB purchases decrease long-term rates. Finally, all types of surprise announcements (interest-rate path, JGB purchases, and current account-balance targets) had a positive influence on asset prices. It should be noted that while the results suggest that BoJ had little ability to influence one-year-ahead interest rates, the analysis was based on a small sample size.[27]

Lam (2011) used data from December 2008 to August 2011 to capture the effects of the comprehensive monetary easing (CME) program introduced in October 2010. Announcements were found to have had a positive impact on JGB rates, corporate bond yields and issuance, stock prices, and consumer and business confidence. Moreover, expansion and exit announcements had little impact, while the introduction of new measures had the largest impact on these markets. Importantly, announcements and asset purchases did not have an impact on inflation expectations or exchange rates.

Yamaoka and Syed (2010) provide an account of the effectiveness of BoJ's exit from monetary easing in 2006. They suggest that by purchasing short-term assets, placing a cap on JGB holdings, and limiting the purchase of private assets, as well as including termination clauses, the BoJ was able to carry out a "natural" downsizing of its balance sheet. These actions were successful at avoiding inflation, an economic slump, and instability in the financial

---

[25] The authors were, of course, careful to remove elements in each factor that are likely to be related to each other.

[26] Surprise announcements were determined based on media response to the announcement.

[27] The sample included nineteen announcements, ten of which were categorized as surprise announcements.

markets. Yet, it would be difficult to find many who see the ending of QE as a success; otherwise, there would have been no need for unleashing the massive policy easing begun in 2013.

Ultimately, most of the literature concludes that ZIRP and QE were successful at changing expectations regarding future short-term interest rates and thereby also medium- and long-term rates. Moreover, there is evidence that QE provided liquidity where it was needed through credit channels, and there is evidence that QE had a positive impact on the equity markets. Nevertheless, there is little empirical evidence that either ZIRP or QE had an influence on expected inflation rates and there is little evidence of an effect on exchange rates. Does Japan, then, serve as a cautionary tale for other advanced economies that rely so heavily on monetary policy to restore pre-crisis economic growth levels? Is perseverance in executing forward guidance, combined perhaps with active forms of intervention in financial markets, essential? If so, is it a matter of doing whatever it takes, as well as not reversing course prematurely? A retrospective on the Japanese experience suggests that half-hearted attempts to intervene will simply not do. Forward guidance, Japanese style, was not blunt enough to have more than a temporary effect. Moreover, the accompanying interventions were on a sufficiently small scale to ensure that financial markets would not believe that, with the BoJ's help, a new regime, let alone a new era, had begun. Perhaps what is necessary, beyond an timely reversal, is the application of "overwhelming force," as former U.S. Treasury Secretary Geithner put it (Geithner 2014).

The lesson learned from Japan's experience is that a central bank can easily become overburdened, not because of taking on additional tasks (e.g., UMP, responsibility for maintaining financial system stability) but because the added responsibilities are inadequately supported by fiscal, structural, or institutional responses,[28] in addition to the central bank's own ambivalence about how committed it should be to a particular policy strategy and for how long.

Is Japan Special?

Much has been written about Japan and its apparent failure to exit from the ZLB and its mild bouts of deflation for over a decade. By the time the GFC ended, many other advanced economies were well under way toward repeating at least parts of the Japanese experience. Naturally, once QE policies were tried, the central banks continued to experiment on the interest-rate front by driving them below zero, as discussed in chapter 4.

---

[28] Koo (2015:168) would not likely disagree with this prescription, although the motivation for his study differs from mine. However, I do sympathize with his remark that "the term *structural reforms* [italics in original] has been used to mean a depressingly wide range of things over the years."

Presumably, if Japan's experience gave any indications of the likely success of such steps, then fewer central banks might have followed the Japanese route. Arguably, however, circumstances were different elsewhere, and the monetary authorities—notably in the United States, the United Kingdom, Switzerland, and Japan, to give some prototype examples—could make the claim that they were both more aggressive and more talkative about their attempts to steer interest rates lower along the entire term structure.

It is, therefore, not surprising that research has been undertaken to investigate how sensitive yields are to various sources of news, good or bad, as investors recalculate the effective return on their investments conditional on actions taken by central banks, as well as changes in the economic outlook (to name just two sources of news investors might respond to). But when the central bank's policy rate is at zero or the effective lower bound, and this is combined with forward guidance that, if credible, leads investors to believe the monetary authority will seek to keep yields low for a longer period, it is reasonable to think that yields will be less "data dependent" (e.g., Feroli et al. 2016). Hence, the sensitivity of interest rates to news will be dampened, as investors become convinced that policymakers will do whatever it takes to maintain an ultra-easy monetary policy stance.[29]

What if we assume it is possible to estimate the sensitivity of yield changes to news, and we define this sensitivity in such a way that a response to yields of 1 is deemed "normal"? Of course, we need to define this response to some benchmark established when yields were in fact normal and markets did not concern themselves with central bank interventions or the ZLB. It is natural to assume that the pre-crisis era—that is, pre-2007— can serve as the example of what is "normal."[30] On this basis, if the measured sensitivity of yields to various sources of news is below 1, there is less data dependence so that the ZLB is indeed a constraint on monetary policy.

Figure 5.7 shows a set of estimates of yield sensitivity to news announcements for the United States, the United Kingdom, Canada, and Switzerland. Additionally, the upper and lower bounds for these estimates—that is, the confidence intervals—are also shown. Of the four economies shown, only Switzerland introduced negative interest rates in late 2014. Canada's policy rate reached the ZLB briefly for less than a year in 2009, before the BoC removed the conditionality of its forward guidance and raised the policy

---

[29] There are multiple sources of news, such as the release of some data (e.g., inflation, unemployment, trade figures, wages, etc.), including central bank announcements of policy interventions (e.g., QE) or the content of central bank statements (i.e., policy rate statements). Since markets presumably form expectations from all of these releases, the differences between outturns and expectations, or a change in the tone or content of central bank statements, are sources of news that will impact bond yields.

[30] This is the approach taken by Swanson and Williams (2014a, 2014b) and Lombardi, Siklos, and St. Amand 2017 forthcoming.

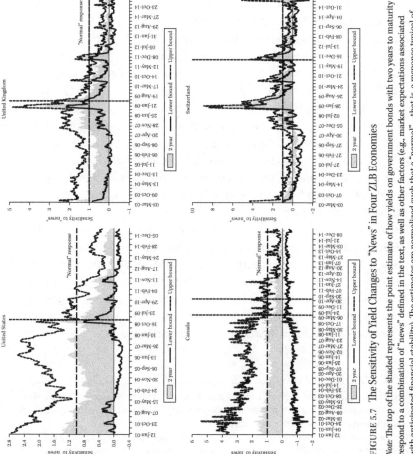

FIGURE 5.7 The Sensitivity of Yield Changes to "News" in Four ZLB Economies

Note: The top of the shaded represents the point estimate of how yields on government bonds with two years to maturity respond to a combination of "news" defined in the text, as well as other factors (e.g., market expectations associated with anticipated financial stability). The estimates are normalized such that a "normal"—that is, a response typical of pre-crisis periods—is set to 1. Estimates less than 1 imply relatively less sensitivity while values greater than 1 mean a relatively more sensitive response than might be observed in "normal" or pre-crisis times. The crisis here refers to the GFC. More details about the estimation technique are found in Lombardi, Siklos, and St. Amand 2017 forthcoming.

Source: Data are from Lombardi, Siklos, and St. Amand 2017 forthcoming.

rate. The BoE's policy rate remains at the ZLB as this is written, and while the Fed began to lift the Fed funds rate at the end of 2015, it stood at ZLB throughout the period shown in the figure. The role of news on yield changes is examined for the case of government bonds that mature in two years only.[31]

Beginning with the United States, we observe a noticeable decline in sensitivity of two-year yields to news, and this is a reflection of the lower-for-longer policy of the Fed, combined with the decline in both the speed of liftoff from the ZLB and the pushing back of the level of the Fed funds rate that would be consistent with a return to "normal" financial conditions.[32]

The United Kingdom's experience parallels the U.S. case, even if the nature and precise details of forward guidance and QE measures practiced by the BoE differed considerably from ones implemented by the Fed. Even the BoC, in spite of the calendar-based attempt at forward guidance with no QE, is not immune to a loss of responsiveness to news. Finally, the case of Switzerland, where the SNB did not practice the forward guidance strategy adopted by the other three central banks shown in the figure, also sees a reduction in yield sensitivity to incoming news. The brief but sharp rise in data dependence, in December 2014 to February 2015, reflects the breach of the ZLB into negative territory, combined with the surprise abandonment of the ceiling on the Swiss Franc (also see chapter 1).

Taken together, the results, at least for short-term yields, suggests that the ZLB does constrain yield sensitivity to news. However, if history is any guide, escape from the zero or effective lower bound—if it brings about more "normal" responsiveness of interest rate movements to economic news, including announcements and statements by central bank officials—increases the burden on monetary authorities to manage the return to higher yields, but also the possibility that the path will be a more volatile one.[33]

---

[31] The results are drawn from Lombardi, Siklos, and St. Amand 2017 forthcoming. They consider not only more economies and the impact of news on longer-term bond yields but also the sensitivity of estimates to different ways of measuring news effects.

[32] Williams 2016 updates some of the estimates from Swanson and Williams (2014a, 2014b), and these show greater sensitivity to news announcements at the 2-year term to maturity, though when combined with the confidence interval estimates, the differences do not appear to be statistically different. The differences have to do with the fact that the estimates shown in the figure also condition the interest rate response to the content of Fed announcements. See Lombardi, Siklos, and St. Amand 2017 forthcoming.

[33] Some have pointed out that an earlier episode, when bond prices became very volatile (the bond market crash of 1994) is instructive. Based on the results of Borio and McCauley 1994 one might conclude otherwise, as neither fiscal nor monetary policy was found to be to blame for that event. Crockett 2001, however, argues that unstable financial markets need not emerge exogenously, but their appearance contains an important endogenous element, and this presumably includes how monetary policy is conducted. Finally, it is important to remember that there was no forward guidance of the kind we observed in the 1990s, and the ZLB was not really contemplated as likely—certainly not as an event that would persist for years.

Vanishing Faith in Central Banks?

In chapter 1, it was pointed out that the principal remit of central banks is a focus on price stability. Hence, a natural expression of the trust and credibility invested in the monetary authority is how well it is able to match its expectations of inflation with actual outcomes. On this score, central banks in general have not always fared well. If the burden on the central banks is increased, then it is reasonable to presume that conventional indicators are inappropriate. While theoretical considerations guide us in associating credibility with a central bank's ability to meet an inflation objective, there is less help when the remit of central banks is broader.[34]

Figure 5.8 is an attempt to construct such an indicator based on seven variables that can conceivably be linked to the credibility of and trust in the monetary authority. The variables are, in addition to how far away observed inflation is from the target, forecast errors in real GDP growth, the spread between long-term and short-term interest rates on government financial instrument (i.e., bonds, Treasury bills),[35] the VIX, the size of the central bank's balance sheet in relation to GDP, credit growth,[36] and the degree of optimism expressed in central bank press releases over time.

All these variables have, in one way or another, been mentioned in this context in earlier chapters.[37] In most cases, the contribution of each component is of the expected sign. This means, for example, that faith in the central bank declines when it misses the target, or when its balance sheet rises relative to the size of the overall economy, or when the long–short spread falls.

What is striking about the results shown in figure 5.8 is not so much the finding that all central banks took a sizable hit to their reputations during the GFC, as the shaded areas make clear; we would expect as much if only because

---

[34] Parts of this section are inspired by research I have conducted jointly with Michael Bordo over the past few years (Bordo and Siklos 2017, 2016a, 2016b). In that research, central bank credibility was largely explained as a function of deviations between expected or forecasted inflation and observed inflation.

[35] As Blinder 2013:237–38, points out, "aficionados used spreads as a handy market measure of the severity of the crisis." Presumably, a crisis serves to cut the reputation of many institutions, central banks included.

[36] From Cooper 2008:87, "Financial stability requires limiting credit expansion while demand management requires maintaining credit expansion—the two roles do not sit well together, especially if the central bank is of a mindset to prevent any and all credit contractions." Clearly, when a central bank acts, this could be seen as a means to enhance the trust that the public has in its ability to manage monetary policy. Unfortunately, it is equally true that if too little is done too late, then the central bank's reputation will be hurt. That's all the more reason to treat the measure depicted in Figure 5.7 as illustrative and tentative; considerably more theoretical and empirical progress are needed to come up with a more sophisticated indicator of credibility and trust in the monetary authority.

[37] The online appendix provides the technical details about how these variables are (linearly) combined to create an indicator.

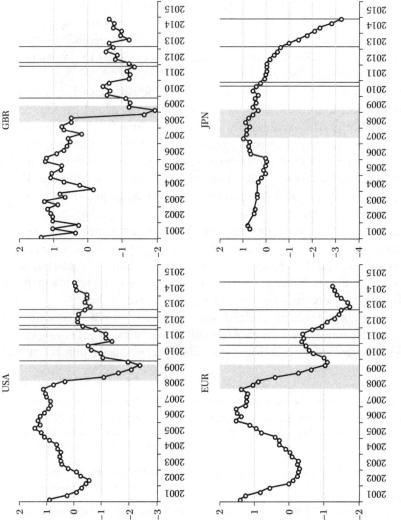

FIGURE 5.8 Quantifying the Evolving Trust in Central Banks

Note: See figure 5.5 note for an explanation of the shaded areas and the vertical lines. The estimates are based on the first principal component consisting of the inflation and real GDP growth forecast errors, the long-short interest rate spread, the VIX, the share of central bank assets to GDP, indicators of credit growth and the optimism content in central bank press releases. The online appendix contains more details. GBR is the United Kingdom, EUR is the Eurozone, JPN is Japan and USA is the United States.

of the behavior of most of the variables that make up the indicator during the GFC. More important, it is that more than five years after the GFC, the central banks have not come close to recovering their reputation. Other than the Fed, which after some fits and starts has come near to reaching its pre-crisis reputation, and saw a decline in its reputation during the GFC even larger in reputation than when the dot.com bubble burst of the early 2000s, the other cases shown show a very slow recovery, if at all. Indeed, the reputation of the BoJ shows a continuing significant decline. It is likely that this is partly driven by the extraordinary increase in its balance sheet. Clearly, it is reasonable to ask whether an increase in a central bank's balance sheet is seen as unambiguously contributing to a loss of trust. Yet, it is the central banks themselves, not just the outside analysts, who insist that the "new normal" cannot consist of balance sheets much inflated relative to levels reached pre-2008. If this is no longer the case, then the central banks' optimism in this regard is misplaced and will need to change, a topic to be taken up in the final chapter.

Conclusions

The chapter began by noting that doubts about the effectiveness of fiscal policy, combined with the perceived political costs of relying on debt to escape an economic slump, even when nominal interest rates are at historic lows, left the impression that central banks could fill the breach made by a noncommittal fiscal partner. Hence, it is an exaggeration to suggest that the behavior of governments through the years did not contribute to some extent to the loss of credibility experienced by several central banks. The environment that favors cooperation among central bankers is only very superficially felt by their respective governments, as earlier chapters have demonstrated.[38] This is another form of the overburdening of central banks that has received little attention.

It is no exaggeration to suggest that the years since 2007 have been anything but extraordinary in central banking. In much of the world, but especially in the advanced economies, the range of responsibilities held by many monetary authorities has expanded. Central bankers, to borrow from Irwin's 2013 journalistic account of the three central bankers at the center of the GFC—Trichet of the ECB, Bernanke of the Fed, and King from the BoE—succeeded in extending their alchemy, even if as "weary and frustrated modern-day alchemists" they knew that monetary policy could not operate as it had in the past. In particular, "neutral" forms of policymaking became a relic of the past

---

[38] Bordo and Schenk 2016 conclude, in a historical survey of central bank cooperation over the past few decades, that rules matter not only in explaining central bank credibility but also in fostering necessary cooperation among central bankers.

and were no longer defensible, however unpopular the resulting actions were politically.

These changes took place in spite of the fact that many believe a significant portion of the blame for the GFC rests with the central banks. Equally a problem is that, just as several institutions were accused of failing to properly supervise the financial sector, or to recognize the growing threats from shadow banking, the legislation governing the central banks artificially relegated to a bygone era the conditions under which those central banks can provide indirect support to the real economy. As a result, the important central banks systematically improvised and large discarded their carefully constructed rules-like behavior.

Whereas central banks were quite vocal prior to 2007 about the limits of monetary policy and the desirability of narrowing the scope of their responsibilities—encapsulated in inflation objectives defined with varying degrees of precision—post-crisis we now find these same institutions carrying out financial stability objectives they sometimes had been mandated to achieve even if they lacked the instruments to do so. Yet, the survey of central banks described earlier (see, for example, chapter 1), conducted almost five years after the height of the financial crisis, suggests that their thinking about monetary policy has changed little.

The absence of a clear understanding of what financial stability objectives ought to be, and even less clarity about how this goal can be shared or managed on a global scale, is problematic. It is troubling that politicians have largely failed, albeit with some notable exceptions, to keep up with the need to properly legislate the brave new world we find ourselves in. We are left with the very ambiguity that academics and policymakers used to decry. The paradox in this erosion of accountability and the return of ambiguity is not lost on a generation of scholars who have strived to convince policymakers that understanding the limited scope of monetary policy, combined with projections of forward-looking thinking, contributed to the environment that produced The Great Moderation. Instead, politicians have heaped more and more responsibilities on a single institution that has yet to convince the public this is best practice for going forward.

There is some irony in this development. After all, central banks such as the Fed were created to deal with problems of financial instability.[39] As central banks, governments, and the public viewed inflation control as a more serious challenge, especially after the late 1960s, the mandate of many central banks shifted toward an inflation target, occasionally stated in numerical terms and otherwise as the implicit goal of monetary policy. Now, financial stability is seen as an additional goal. Hence, central banks are being asked to do what

---

[39] A point also made, for example, by Reinhart and Rogoff 2012 about the Fed's creation.

they were always expected to do, and they should not, perhaps, be seen as overburdened.

Although price stability was indeed an objective, this was often couched as operating in tandem with a desire to tame the business cycle or to support government policies.[40] Now, when the expectation of inflation control remaining essential, as is the maintenance of financial stability, the question of whether the monetary authorities can indeed be overburdened is a valid one. After all, we know that the two objectives need not operate in parallel at all times; there will sometimes be conflicts between the two objectives and we lose the simplicity of viewing monetary policy through the operation of a single instrument. As a consequence, central banks will be required to place one goal ahead of the other. To pretend otherwise is to place expectations on the central banks that are too great to meet. Hence, the potential exists for the monetary authority to be overburdened.

To be sure, when it comes to the proper design of institutions, the same model is not suitable for all countries and at all times. Nevertheless, in economies where there is an important global element influencing behavior, the risks of asking too much from one institution and thereby endowing it with excessive authority, are real.

---

[40] A possible exception is the Bundesbank. See Siklos 2002.

6 }

Disquiet on All Fronts?

Sources of Disquiet

The title of this chapter suggests the possibility that there is widespread anxiety nowadays about central banks and their performance. Earlier chapters explained the sources of such concern for the direction taken by several central banks.

After the crisis events that began unfolding in 2007, the economic and financial landscape changed rather dramatically worldwide. Add the concerns of unsatisfactory economic growth globally, whether of the secular stagnation variety or not, and there are many reasons to feel unhappy about the current state of economic policies. Indeed, more generally, there are additional sources of disquiet. Not in any particular order of importance, we can point to the following: the shift from a fear of too high inflation rates to a fear of too low, concerns about whether financial instability can be contained, worries over the concentration of responsibilities vested in the central banks and a concurrent potential loss of democratic accountability, and fears of the next crisis to come.

Central banks did a fine job of convincing politicians and the public that price stability, however it is defined, requires that the central bank be sufficiently autonomous to meet such an objective with minimum political pressure. This territory has been covered far and wide by academics and nonacademics alike. What is less appreciated is that the central banks, thanks in large part to their convincing theoretical and empirical work, were able to secure their influence by demonstrating the feasibility of price stability. If financial stability, which few doubt is desirable, irrespective of one's preferred definition, is also a natural responsibility of the central banks, then the same question needs to be asked: Is financial stability feasible as well? Even if the answer is in the affirmative, this chapter demonstrates that the tactics and actions taken by the central banks and other authorities in this direction leave a lot to be desired.

Elsewhere in this book I have discussed the changing global macroeconomic landscape. As this is written, even the large emerging market economies (e.g., China and Brazil) are slowing or have slowed considerably while the debate rages on: Is a return to pre-crisis growth rates even possible in the advanced economies? Similarly, the central banks that led the way in reducing the high inflation rates of the 1970s and early 1980s, whether through numerical inflation objectives or a less explicit commitment, found themselves then fighting inflation rates that seemed uncomfortably close to the bottom range of their objectives, if not outright deflation. This situation appears to have turned on its head the age-old concern that inflation rates tend to be too high. In any event, these problems lie squarely within the technical realm of monetary policy, although, unsurprisingly, there are political overtones to these challenges faced by the central banks.

The last decade has raised the profile of an idea that many economists believed was complementary to best practices in monetary policy—namely, that low and stable inflation is necessarily associated with financial stability. Actually, two matters emerge from the presumed connection between monetary policy and financial stability. First, there is the nature and channels through which one task is related to the other. Second, if low and stable inflation is not enough for financial stability (setting aside the question of whether this state of affairs is desirable in its own right), then under what conditions is it appropriate for a single institution to be responsible for both tasks?

Next, and not entirely divorced from the problem of mixing monetary policy with the maintenance of financial stability, are the questions that arise when governments decide how much responsibility is to be vested in the central banks regulating the business cycle while simultaneously taming the financial cycle. It goes without saying that there are benefits to and of too much centralization, and that the choice must also depend on an economy's capacity to operate with several institutions coordinating their activities. Some economies—in particular, the ones at the core of the last global financial crisis—are systemically important, yet the responsibilities of their central banks are restricted to the domestic implications of their activities. Even if the central bank's responsibilities are largely domestic, some recognize that global concerns matter. How does an institution reconcile the pressures emanating from the likely spillovers of their policies? Is cooperation enough, or is a form of coordination necessary? Indeed, one is led to revisit a question raised a half century ago by Sir John Hicks, when he asked whether it makes sense to refer to central banks as "central" in the first place.[1]

---

[1] "Only in a national economy that is largely self-contained can a national central bank be a true central bank; with the development of world . . . (especially) financial markets, national central banks take a step down" (Hicks 1967:60).

Beyond these concerns are two other questions not sufficiently considered in relevant policy circles. First, does the centralization of authority raise the likelihood that the personalities of the central bankers will matter more than might be deemed desirable? Second, does endowing unelected officials with responsibilities that cover a wide scope of economic and financial activities overstep the bounds of what is considered sensible under principles of democratic accountability? Also relevant are fears that the correct mix of accountability and transparency is maintained.

Finally, although the last crisis had global repercussions (unlike the frequent financial crises that preceded it), most policymakers, including some central bankers, admit that future crises are almost inevitable. How far, then, should central bankers use their powers of oversight, or err in mixing monetary policy with fiscal policy, in preventing another crisis? Moreover, if the recent crisis has led to an overburdening of the central banks, is there a consequence, or knock-on effect, for the private sector, which ends up being constrained by both monetary policy and policies aimed at reducing the likelihood of another crisis? A related question is whether the changes put into place end up creating a structure that, in essence, is fighting the last war rather than creating a resilient environment prepared for the inevitable macroeconomic and financial shocks that will come?

Those with a somewhat different perspective might ask whether the GFC has shone light on the multitude of pressures felt by the central banks and whether this amounts to asking them to square a circle. Jaime Caruana, general manager of the BIS, suggested that the concept of central bank independence "beyond insulation from political pressure, including 'fiscal dominance,' should also include insulation from pressures from financial markets and indebted agents ('financial dominance') and against unrealistic expectations of what central banks can do ('expectations dominance')" (Caruana 2013). These are, to put it mildly, exacting demands. Moreover, it is not clear that they are achievable simultaneously. Finally, it is far from evident that such a state of affairs is all that desirable.[2]

The remainder of this chapter is a start at addressing many of these questions.

Confidence Gaps

Although the central banks have a primary responsibility for the maintenance of price stability, looking for trust in these monetary authorities as institutions

---

[2] Borrowing from the political science literature, we can frame the issues as asking what a typical central bank should look like so as to achieve both "input" and "output" legitimacy. The "input" refers to an assessment of the performance of a central bank; the "output" represents our understanding of how policy decisions are taken and the authority is exercised. Eichengreen and Woods 2015 apply these principles in proposing reforms of the IMF.

is likely to require more than an assessment of how well they perform in delivering a particular inflation rate (also see chapter 5). Indeed, the tendency to evaluate their performance based on this seemingly narrow concept is attractive because changes in the purchasing power of money are measurable. (I return to this metric later.)

Unfortunately, even if we broaden our view of what constitutes quality in a particular monetary policy strategy, it is unclear whether the public's trust in the institution is as narrowly defined as it is by economists. Indeed, it is not easy to define what generates confidence, especially in an institution like a central bank, which is seen as either remote or responsible for technical and difficult matters, or both. At the root of confidence building is a belief that the central bank will do what it says it plans to do. Therefore, there needs to be a good understanding of the central bank's aims and responsibilities, together with a clear outline of how its objectives or goals are to be attained. After all, a central bank can achieve an objective through sheer luck, rather than foresight and skill. Indeed, a small but notable literature (largely confined to the U.S. experience) suggests that good fortune—in the form of small macroeconomic shocks for an extended period of time— goes a long way toward explaining the low and steady inflation rates associated with the Great Moderation.[3] Indeed, luck may also have played a role in how the global economy, with the help of the central banks, responded in the aftermath of the financial shocks of 2007–8.[4]

Setbacks and failures are facts of life. Hence, confidence is likely also built or destroyed by how institutions respond to shocks and whether they are able to persuade the public not only to adapt to unusual circumstances but, perhaps more important, to objectively reflect on where things went wrong and how they can be made right again. This last point is arguably one of the least acknowledged ingredients in building confidence.

Confidence, credibility, trust, and *reputation* are all words that have been used to define or evaluate the central banks over time. Nevertheless, it has been difficult to agree on a common standard by which to operationalize these concepts in economic terms. Indeed, to paraphrase Churchill, the terminology has the feel of "a riddle wrapped in a mystery inside and enigma."[5] Yet, Churchill's quote ends with a sentiment expressed less often—namely, "but perhaps there is a key." In the case of the central banks, the key is that these institutions are ultimately guided by self-interest to preserve their reputations and their autonomy within the structure of government. Beyond self-interest is the acknowledgment that a loss of credibility or reputation may be permanent. But self-interest also dictates that credibility is easily obtained and

---

[3] Stock and Watson 2003. Also, see Bernanke 2004a and chapter 1.
[4] Cecchetti, King, and Yetman 2011.
[5] From Churchill's broadcast "The Russian Enigma," October 1, 1939.

maintained if built upon a feasible strategy. If that's not the case, carrying out that strategy will surely disappoint.

There is still the matter of some kind of operational definition of credibility. In previous research,[6] in the main theoretical, actions are contrasted with results. Of course, credibility is also a matter of trust, as the *New Oxford Dictionary* makes clear.[7] Theoretical models assume that a central bank is always competent, possibly has an informational advantage, and has only the most honorable of intentions. In view of these challenges, the approach that follows provides some evidence, from the broadest to the narrowest forms, of what factors might explain confidence or credibility in regard to the central banks.

It is helpful to begin with an assumption of sorts. In the spirit of "This Time is Different," it does appear that central bankers themselves, though reluctant to raise questions about confidence in central banks,[8] nevertheless have recently emphasized the uniqueness of the GFC. Instead, at the height of the crisis, the emphasis in their speeches was on how these institutions coped, managed, or otherwise tried to explain the crisis—as if the GFC was an exogenous event they had no hand in creating.

To be sure, there were some unique features of the GFC. As a result, some central bankers claimed that the impact of the crisis on the public's confidence is what made the GFC unique: "This crisis is different from the others because it affects confidence, which is at the root of a market economy" (Bini Smaghi 2008). Others have referred to the "unprecedented" nature of the crisis, suggesting that not only eroded confidence should be placed squarely on the doorstep of the central banks—clearly, there is plenty of blame to go around. Nevertheless, based on the assumption that price stability and financial stability tend to operate in parallel, there is added scrutiny of the role played by the monetary authorities. Moreover, that the crisis "did not come out of the blue" (Gieve 2008) suggests not only that a loss of confidence is at stake but, since financial crises are rarely unique, also that this is hardly a distinguishing characteristic of the GFC.[9]

---

[6] Bordo and Siklos 2016a, 2016b). Also, see chapter 5. Some of the definitions of credibility that guided previous research include: "extent to which the public believes that a shift in policy has taken place when, indeed, such a shift has actually occurred" (Cukierman 1986:6). Blinder 1999:64–65 offers a more prosaic definition: "that your pronouncements are believed – even though you are bound by no rule and may have an incentive to renege"; Blinder adds: "it is . . . built up by a history of matching deeds to words." More generally, Brunner 1983:36 makes the connection between credibility and the performance of the institutions mandated to carry out policies: "Credibility depends . . . on the history of policy making and the behavior of the policy institution."

[7] "the quality of being trusted and believed in."

[8] Based on the titles of central bank speeches at the height of the crisis—say, between October 2008 and March 2009.

[9] Never mind that *confidence*, or any of the other words mentioned earlier, is rarely explicitly defined in central bank speeches.

Confidence Hangs on a Thread

It is not difficult to find examples of a loss of confidence in central banks. A recent and arguably spectacular example comes from the Swiss National Bank's (SNB) decision to discontinue maintenance of a floor for the Swiss franc–euro exchange rate. The decision was taken a few days after the vice-chair of the SNB declared, on January 12, 2015, that "We took stock of the situation less than a month ago, we looked again at all the parameters and we are all convinced that the minimum exchange rate must remain the cornerstone of our monetary policy."[10] A mere ten days later, the SNB abandoned the policy. As with similar examples of changes in direction, the issue is the extent to which announcements such as these can be deemed a "surprise." Policy reversals seem to come out of the blue. Yet, with full knowledge that the ECB was launching a large QE program—the policy was signaled ahead of time—on the same day as the SNB abandoned its effective peg, one has to wonder why a senior SNB official made such an emphatic statement only a few days earlier. Obviously, establishing the element of surprise or its magnitude is not as straightforward as one might think.

Other examples from history can easily be marshaled to make the same point.[11] Consider, for example, the FOMC's decision on the policy rate (Fed funds) in August 2008, a mere month before the Lehman Brothers and AIG failures, when it suggested that, even if all was not well, there were few indications that much worse was to come. In its anodyne statement, the FOMC declared that "although downside risks to growth remain, the upside risks to inflation are also of significant concern to the Committee. The Committee will continue to monitor economic and financial developments and will act as needed to promote sustainable economic growth and price stability."[12] Later, when the committee's minutes were released, there was plenty of evidence that most members failed to recognize the severity of what was to come only a few weeks later.[13] Nevertheless, many in the meeting did worry about the potential credibility and reputation costs, as well as the need to be aware of the worst-case scenario. As departing governor Rick Mishkin pointed out, "If

---

[10] www.reuters.com/article/2015/01/12/swiss-snb-idUSL6N0UR3LW20150112.

[11] A recounting of additional examples can be found in the narratives section of Bordo and Siklos 2016a.

[12] www.federalreserve.gov/newsevents/press/monetary/20080805a.htm.

[13] The transcript of August 5, 2008, does, however, show that the Fed may have been preparing for the worst when, in response to questions from Charles Evans, president of the Federal Reserve Bank of Chicago, Bernanke indicates in passing to Vice-Chair William Dudley, "It is my understanding that the Chairman has asked you to look at unusual and exigent circumstances." The reference is to section 13(3) of the Federal Reserve Act, which defines the circumstances under which the Fed can engage in emergency lending by private borrowers. The Dodd-Frank Act of 2010 led to a narrowing of the Fed's ability to invoke this section of the Act. This was doubtlessly a politically motivated reaction to the Fed's bulging balance sheet. It took almost five years for the Fed to announce the procedures that would be triggered if another crisis took place. See www.federalreserve.gov/newsevents/press/bcreg/20151130a.htm.

the institution is damaged in terms of the confidence that the public and the politicians have in us, it will hurt us deeply. It will hurt us in terms of policy because it will weaken our credibility, which actually will make it harder to control inflation. So I consider this a very serious cost."[14]

Arguably, there is always the fear that, in sounding too alarmist, policy-makers can unwittingly trigger a panic. This, of course, is a valid concern. Nevertheless, pretending that a storm is not coming, when there are obvious indications of one brewing, helps to make the outcome that much worse; far better would be to simply inform the public that the central bank is casting a wary eye on financial conditions.

The Constituents of Institutional Trust

Taking a few steps back, we have at our disposal a rich set of observations to draw upon in assessing how institutions in general, and central banks in particular, have been viewed over time. Figure 6.1 shows two instances from the World Bank's governance indicators: (a) voice and accountability (VA) and (b) regulatory quality (RQ). While not aimed in particular at measuring the state of affairs in central banking, the data ought to reflect to some extent perceptions of the capacity of government to implement sound policies. Moreover, it seems reasonable to assume that freedom of expression ought to be related to the capacity of institutions to be sufficiently transparent. (Central bank transparency is considered separately.) To conserve space, the experience of the critical economies at the center of the crisis is highlighted— namely, the United Kingdom and the United States. Japan is also examined separately be-cause it has been labeled as an economy in crisis for several years, while China is highlighted because of its economic importance. To provide a basis for com-parison, the median score for the G20 economies is also plotted.

Japan is effectively the only economy that has displayed a steady increase in VA (a). Other economies, most notably the United Kingdom and the United States, have experienced a decline that precedes the onset of the GFC by sev-eral years. The drop in the United Kingdom is more noticeable than for the United States, which has remained approximately stable since 2006. China has also shown a recovery in VA over the past several years, but this is from a low level and, by 2013, is lower that it was in the early 2000s.[15]

---

[14] Janet Yellen, then an alternate on the FOMC and future chair of the FOMC upon Ben Bernanke's departure, tried to convince the committee to insert the following language in the FOMC's announce-ment: "Both downside risks to growth and upside risks to inflation are of significant concern to the Committee." The eventual language (see above) broadly reflects this sentiment. See www.federalre-serve.gov/monetarypolicy/files/FOMC20080805meeting.pdf.

[15] China is the only case measured on the right-hand axis. The negative numbers indicate that VA is seen as always weak overall.

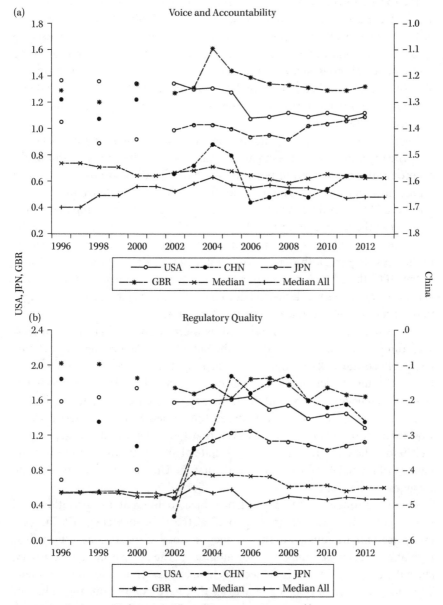

FIGURE 6.1 Governance Indicators in Selected Economies, 1996–2013 (I)
(a) Voice and Accountability
(b) Regulatory Quality

Note: USA is the United States, CHN is China, JPN is Japan, GBR is the United Kingdom; median and median all. are two different estimates of a median for the entire sample (G20 and all available economies in the dataset). The governance indicators range from -2.5 (worst) to +2.5 (best). *Source:* World Bank Governance Indicators (http://info.worldbank.org/governance/wgi/index.aspx#home) and author's calculations.

Turning to regulatory quality (b), the news is even less favorable for most of the cases shown. In spite of the promise of reform, RQ has also shown a steady decline in both the United Kingdom and the United States, at the center of the GFC. Indeed, even the G20, nominally the group that is supposed to spearhead reforms and ensure international cooperation aimed at preventing future financial crises, achieves a RQ index value by 2013 that is only modestly above the levels reached when the data were first collected in the second half of the 1990s. Only Japan seemingly goes against the grain by displaying steady increases in RQ over time.

Figure 6.2 essentially presents the same data but from a different perspective. The top and bottom lines in both figures indicate the strongest and weakest economies considered in terms of VA and RQ. All economies in the data set are now considered.[16] The next two lines indicate the relative positions of the United States and China over time. It is perhaps not surprising that China ranks near the bottom in terms of VA (a) while the United States is near the top. Notice a small increase in the gap between the best and worst performers in the VA category. In the case of the United States, a country at the epicenter of the GFC, the relative decline in a broad indicator of transparency does not appear to square with a desire to educate the public, which presumably ought to be part of any effort to learn from past mistakes.

In China's case, whose central bank is more "central" than most, at least according to our earlier description, the failure to make progress in this area likely reflects the lack of progress in reforming its institutions on a scale comparable to median let alone best international practices. The situation is not much different for RQ (b), although the gap between China and the United States is smaller while the gap between the United States and best practice worldwide also widens. Note, however, that the widening of this gap begins well before the GFC. It is surprising, in spite of all the fanfare surrounding the passage of financial reform legislation,[17] that the United States lags behind the strongest performers.

Regulatory quality (RQ) may well be subject to different interpretations and lead to trade-offs that are often ignored at the policymaker's peril. RQ certainly need not be equated to the number or scope of regulations, especially if regulation is seen as a substitute for judgment. The latter is always necessary, since the shape of finance is subject to changes that render old rules obsolete. The sheer number of books and articles that have pointed out the failure of regulation and supervision in the years prior to the GFC attests to this. Indeed, a multiplicity of rules, not to mention inaction by some of the authorities in

---

[16] The World Bank's indicators range from a maximum of +2.5 (best practice) and a minimum of -2.5 (worst practice).

[17] The Dodd-Frank Act of 2010 ushered in major financial sector reforms in the United States, as well as some changes in the Fed's role, as described earlier.

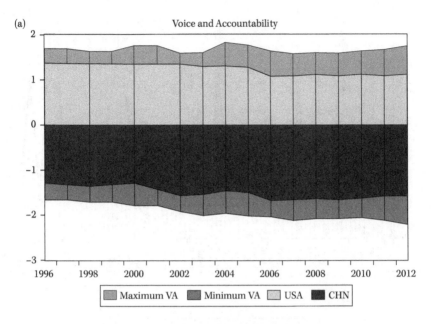

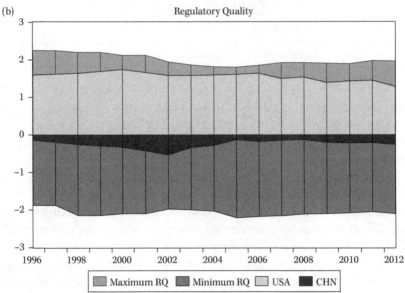

FIGURE 6.2 Governance Indicators in Selected Economies, 1996–2013 (II)
(a) Voice and Accountability
(b) Regulatory Quality

Note: RQ is regulatory quality, USA is the United States, CHN is China. Maximum and minimum are the largest and smallest estimates, respectively, in the sample. As in figure 6.1, the range is from -2.5 to +2.5. *Source:* World Bank Governance Indicators (http://info.worldbank.org/governance/wgi/index.aspx#home) and author's calculations.

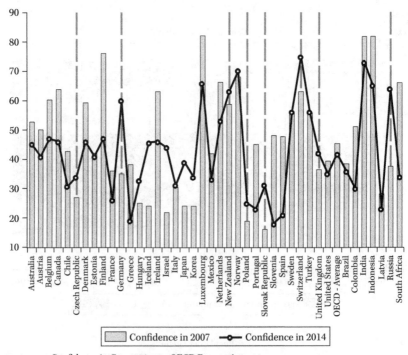

FIGURE 6.3 Confidence in Governments, OECD Economies, 2007–2014

Note: The vertical axis represents the percentage of survey responders who answered YES to "`Do you have confidence in the . . . national government?" The dashed vertical lines identify EU member economies. *Source:* OECD and author's calculations.

the years leading up to a crisis that could well have been foreseen, supports such an interpretation.[18] Hence, even if the data in figure 6.2 are instructive, they seem to underestimate the size of the failure of financial regulation prior to 2007.

A somewhat more mixed picture is obtained when, instead of attempting to evaluate confidence in government institutions by aggregating a variety of characteristics, a public poll is conducted that asks, without specifying a precise definition, about levels of trust in government. Figure 6.3 shows the results for OECD economies between 2007, arguably just before the GFC, and 2014, the latest available data as this is written. There is very little change, on average, in the fraction of the public that trusts government. Indeed, the U.S. results are quite similar to those for the average of OECD economies. Approximately 40% of countries sampled actually showed improvements, and there is no obvious link to the kind of monetary policy strategy or independence of the central bank. Indeed, there are large declines in trust in countries that were indirectly

---

[18] Kay 2015 reminds us about the dangers of excessive reliance on regulations to guarantee financial stability.

impacted by the crisis (e.g., Canada, South Africa), or impacted in different ways by the eurozone's sovereign debt crisis (i.e., Finland and Greece). Others, also affected by financial crises, such as Germany and Iceland, experienced noticeable increases in the level of trust of its citizens, including Japan, in spite of the "lost decades" label.

Obviously, it will be noted that trust in government is not the same as trust in the central bank. Strictly speaking, of course, this is true. However, even central bankers have repeatedly stressed that they operate within government. Therefore, it is legitimate to think that changes in trust in government may spill over into changes in the reputation of the monetary authorities. Some indication that such a link exists is obtained when we examine the members of the eurozone and the EU members that are not eurozone members. In the former case, all experience a decline in trust in government, with the notable exception of Germany. For the EU non-euro countries, the level of trust actually rises or remains approximately the same, with Latvia the only exception.[19]

This naturally leads to the next piece of evidence concerning institutional trust. Figure 6.4 plots levels of trust and distrust in the ECB, based on the Eurobarometer Survey that has been conducted twice a year since 1999 in the EU.[20] As with all surveys of this kind, it is not clear how much respondents actually know about the ECB or whether there is a common understanding about how trust is interpreted by the participants.

The data are plotted in four parts. The top left graph (a) indicates levels of trust and mistrust in the ECB for the European Union as a whole.[21] Although there is some volatility over time, an actual decline in trust and the concomitant rise in mistrust in the ECB at the EU level actually began with the global financial crisis. Indeed, it was during 2008 that the European Commission released its Report on EMU@10, which both celebrated the achievements of the single currency[22] and noted some of the trouble spots ahead, though nothing approaching the warning of the sovereign debt crisis to come. No doubt the sequence of events especially beginning in 2010 hastened the decline in

---

[19] Latvia, of course, has sometimes been referred to as the poster child for a successful austerity program. Readers will also see that Iceland, another economy hard hit by a financial crisis, earned a boost in levels of trust.

[20] http://ec.europa.eu/public_opinion/index_en.htm.

[21] The question is whether respondents "tend to trust" and "tend not to trust." Also, the number of economies included in the European Union has changed, notably in 2004, with the accession of ten countries from Central Europe.

[22] "The first decade of the euro shows that EMU is a resounding success. It has helped to deliver macroeconomic stability through a sound single monetary policy and much improved fiscal behaviour in member countries. It has ushered in an unprecedented period of price stability and low interest rates, bringing substantial savings for consumers and business. The single currency has also supported trade and investment and deepened financial integration. Economies in the euro area have become more integrated, better synchronised, better managed and more flexible in the last 10 years" (European Commission 2008:3) These are the introductory words of Klaus Regling, then its director general.

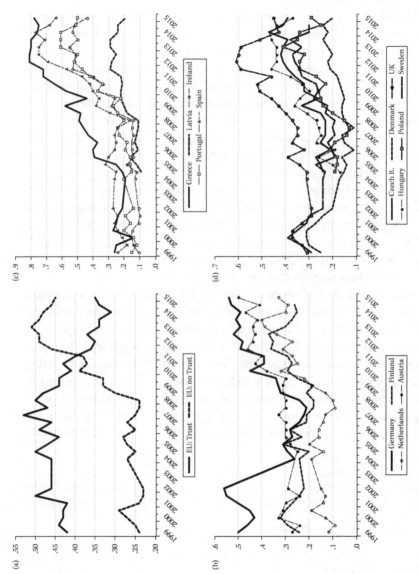

FIGURE 6.4 Trust in the ECB: The EU Barometer, 1999–2015

Note: The data represent the fraction of respondents who answered in the affirmative about whether they trust or tend to trust the ECB. For the EU as a whole, both the trust and the tend to trust, as well as the do not trust, figures are plotted. *Source:* Eurobarometer Survey.

confidence about the ECB as an institution. It is also worth noting, however, that 2013 brought about a reversal of fortunes.

A review of the ECB's interventions reveals perhaps why this may have happened. ECB President Mario Draghi was steadfast in promising to respond to a series of threats with stimulus measures. In a speech at De Nederlandsche Bank (the Dutch central bank) in April 2014, Draghi outlined circumstances that would generate a policy response and the policy tools that would be deployed to address them. The ECB was forced to confront each of the negative scenarios Draghi envisioned in 2014; and the central bank showed little hesitation as it responded just as Draghi said it would. There is also evidence that there was a growing consensus among Governing Council members, though Germany would more often than not stand apart from the others, and that UMP introduced elsewhere, including the United States and the U.K, was imminent.[23]

During the introductory statement to the press conference of the ECB Governing Council, following the April 2014 meeting, Draghi began explicitly stating "The Governing Council is unanimous in its commitment to using also unconventional instruments within its mandate in order to cope effectively with risks of a too prolonged period of low inflation." By May 2015, Draghi reflected on the events of the previous months when he suggested that it was the exchange rate appreciation that prompted the ECB to respond. In response, the ECB reduced the policy rate, introduced a negative deposit rate, and extended the fixed rate/full allotment (FRFA) tender procedures.[24] The intent of the change was to guarantee that liquidity needs in financial markets would not be arbitrarily determined by the ECB; rather, liquidity would always be at the disposal of financial institutions. In a Washington speech in May 2015, Draghi stated that policymakers "were not facing merely a downward shock to prices, but also a downward shock to inflation dynamics—a sustained adverse development." Indeed, during the third quarter of 2014, the Governing Council introduced two outright asset-purchase programs: the ABSPP and the CBPP3.[25] As conditions continued to deteriorate, the asset purchase program was expanded in January 2015 to include purchases of public-sector securities.

---

[23] Also see, for example, Coeuré 2014 and Constâncio 2014.

[24] The FRFA was introduced in 2008 as a mechanism to ensure that banks have access to liquidity from the ECB when it is in short supply in financial markets. Indeed, Gonzáles-Páramo, then a member of the Executive Board of the ECB, declared in 2011 that the "[F]ixed rate full allotment policy is possibly the most significant non-standard measure the ECB is implementing" Gonzáles-Páramo 2011. As is the case elsewhere when central banks invoke such facilities, "adequate" collateral is required. Also, see Cour-Thimann and Winkler 2013.

[25] ABSPP is the Asset Backed Securities Purchase Programme and CBPP3 is the third round of the Covered Bond Purchase Program. These are both balance sheet operations that seek to stimulate specific asset markets important for access to finance for banks.

If we now examine selected results from the Eurobarometer Survey, we see what might be viewed as some startling results. Consider the bottom left graph (b). The German public's mistrust in the ECB exhibited a sharp decline around the time of EU expansion into Central Europe and began to rise once again as the GFC erupted. Broadly speaking, for Austria, the Netherlands, and Finland, three countries that are seen to share the German economic position, the survey reveals a comparable pattern. Yet, it is striking that levels of mistrust were highest in Germany and lowest in Finland, followed closely by the Netherlands. It is worth keeping in mind that inflation rates do not differ much between these countries, but economic growth is lowest in Finland and the Netherlands.

The top right graph (c) is perhaps the least surprising at all. Four of the countries hardest hit by the sovereign crisis—that is, Greece, Spain, Portugal, and Ireland—exhibited sizable levels of mistrust in the ECB. Moreover, in these instances, the drop in reputation is clearly seen as sharply exacerbated by the event of 2010 and thereafter. Nevertheless, as elsewhere in the EU, levels of mistrust showed a steady albeit gentle rise since the Eurobarometer Survey was initiated.

Finally, the bottom right graph (d) reveals the findings for EU economies nominally expected to join the eurozone one day, as well as two EU member states, the United Kingdom and Denmark, that are permitted to opt out of the single-currency area. The steady deterioration in trust seen in Germany and other similarly inclined economies was replicated here. Indeed, levels of mistrust were actually lower by 2015 in the United Kingdom than in Germany.[26]

The broad lessons, whether measured in terms of inflation (see Bordo and Siklos 2016a, 2016b) or from a broader perspective, are that trust or confidence, once lost, is not quickly regained. Moreover, even if central banks underscore their autonomy vis-à-vis their governments, they cannot easily disassociate themselves from levels of confidence in public institutions more generally. To assume otherwise is effectively to pretend that central banks can have it both ways—that is, criticize governments for their inaction while extoling their performance as essential for a sustained economic recovery.

Words Matter

As noted previously, it is plausible to think that the central banks put their "money where their mouth is" by publishing their own forecasts. Moreover, we would expect that a central bank that is effective and seeks to build trust

---

[26] What accounted for the sharp rise in trust (or decline in mistrust) in the United Kingdom beginning in 2013 is unclear. A similar pattern is seen elsewhere, including Sweden, but was not as dramatic.

in the public sphere will want to engage in a regular evaluation of its record at meeting its operational target(s). Two specific questions address this issue in a survey mentioned in chapter 1. While the responses did not directly indicate confidence in the central bank, it is reasonable to assume that central banks that are willing to be open about their outlook and acknowledge the desirability of a review of their ability to meet certain goals are likely to boost public confidence in those institutions.[27]

Figure 6.5 shows the median response for a selection of inflation-targeting (IT) and non-inflation-targeting (NIT) economies since the late 1990s.[28] It is clear from figure 6.5a that, by the time the GFC erupted, the median IT central banks in the sample published forecasts on a regular basis. The same was not true of the median NIT central banks. Note, however, that in both groups the range of central banks includes both the least and most open types of central banks. Perhaps more intriguing is the issue of self-evaluation,[29] which is considered in figure 6.5b. There, both IT and NIT central banks have made significant strides in evaluating their performance. Indeed, the median NIT central bank was more open than its median IT counterpart. While this result could be due to the collection of economies included in the sample, all the systemically important and major adopters of IT are included.[30] If the response is even only partly explained by the reaction to the GFC, then this suggests that central banks became more responsive to the need for additional information about the outlook. This is certainly a commendable reaction.

Central banks, particularly since the 1990s, have placed far greater emphasis on announcements of their policy stance following regularly scheduled meetings of their policymaking body. A much smaller number of central banks have gone further by releasing the minutes of meetings of the monetary policy committee (MPC). Contrary to press releases that accompany policy rate or policy stance announcements, often representing the consensus or decisive

---

[27] More precisely, the question posed in the survey is: "Does the central bank publish its own forecast?" The answers are YES (= 1), meaning that at least quarterly 1- to 2-year forecasts are published, or NO (= 0), in which case no forecast is published. A value of ½ means that infrequent forecasts are published (i.e., at less than the quarterly frequency). The other question is: "Does the central bank regularly evaluate the extent to which its main policy operating targets have been achieved?" Results also are 0, which signifies infrequent assessments, or 1 (regular evaluation with an explanation of how monetary policy actions contributed to the outcome), with a value of ½ implying that evaluations are conducted but in a superficial manner.

[28] Most, but not all, central banks had explicit numerical targets at the beginning of the sample. Similarly, some of the non-inflation-targeting (NIT) economies eventually established some numerical targets, but these did not have the same legal authority perhaps as for the inflation-targeting (IT) central banks because they were not legislated or agreed to jointly with governments. Sixteen IT and thirteen NIT economies are included.

[29] Unfortunately, the question does not make a distinction between internally generated and external evaluations of the central bank's effectiveness. I return to this question later.

[30] The choice of countries was dictated by the participants in the BIS Survey discussed in chapter 1.

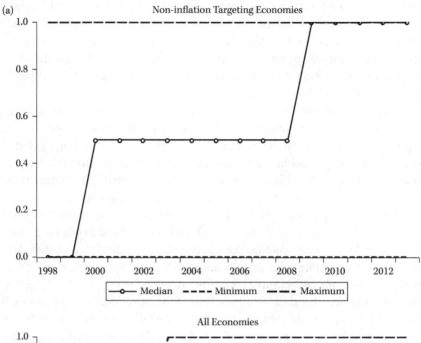

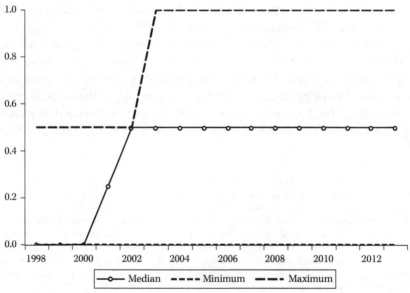

FIGURE 6.5 Central Bank Transparency (a) The Publication of Forecasts

Note: The question posed was: "Does the central bank regularly publish its own macroeconomic forecasts?"` IT economies include AUS, BRA, CAN, CHL, COL, CZE, HUN, KOR, MEX, NZL, NOR, POL, PHI, ZAR, SWE, GBR. Also, see online appendix and the list of country abbreviations. Median, maximum and minimum values are based on the values obtained across each group of economies examined. *Source:* Survey conducted with the BIS and Siklos (2016a). (b) The Evaluation of Achievement Note: The question posed in the survey was "Does the central bank regularly evaluate to what extent its main policy operating targets (if any) have been achieved?"` *Source:* Siklos 2016a.

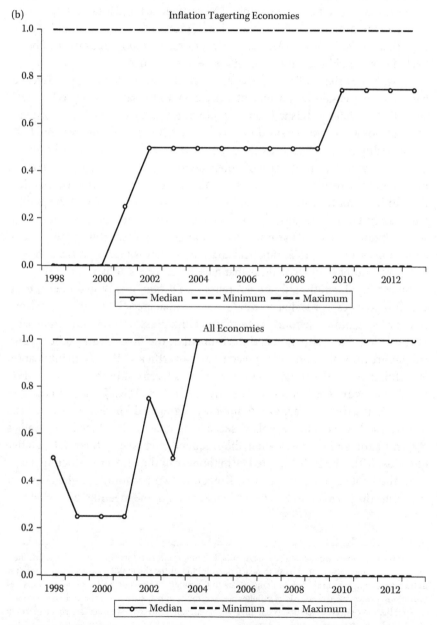

FIGURE 6.5 (*Continued*)

views of the MPC, minutes may represent a less constrained environment in which decision makers can more freely express their opinions. Of course, knowing that minutes will be released may temper the enthusiasm of MPC members to reveal their true feelings.[31] Nevertheless, there is no hiding the fact that if an institution is to be trusted, then minutes of meetings should capture the discussions that took place and, perhaps more important, ought to be reflected in any public announcements subsequently made.

As with the other indicators of confidence in a central bank, any differences between what is said in advance of a decision and what is expressed in decisions that are later published can only provide a glimpse into the consistency of inputs for a decision versus the decision itself. Moreover, minutes tend to be considerably lengthier records than the press releases announcing the stance of monetary policy. In the case of policy announcements, there is a premium placed on brevity and, we hope, clarity. Yet, if the content of the two publications differs over time in a persistent fashion, it is also possible that the public's trust can be eroded, because the central bank may end looking like an institution that does not say what it means.[32] In any event, quantifying the sense of a meeting as an input to a statistical analysis is a hazardous exercise, although there are a number of algorithms that have been successfully used.

By way of illustration, figure 6.6 relies on *Diction*, mentioned in chapter 1, which aggregates words that convey "stress," "imbalances," "unstable," and "contraction" to capture the tone of the central bank press releases and minutes reporting the current situation and the immediate outlook. Clearly, other aggregations are possible (and were considered). Nevertheless, if such quantification is useful, then the data ought to capture what is foremost in the minds of MPC members. Figure 6.6 considers the evidence for U.S., U.K., Japan, and Sweden central banks. The data are also temporally aggregated, since minutes are usually released weeks after a policy decision is taken.[33] The higher the values shown in the graphs, the greater the frequency, relative to the total number of words, with which the selected terms appear in the respective documents.[34]

In the United States and United Kingdom, two economies at the center of the crisis, the correlation between what was said in the meetings and what was

---

[31] Many academics argue that the release of Fed minutes influences its content. Perhaps, but their release does compel the central bank to reveal the thinking inside the FOMC. Equally important, it is in the interests of a central bank to demonstrate to the public the breadth and seriousness of its deliberations, however finely edited the minutes are. See, for example, Auerbach 2008 and Siklos 2016b.

[32] Of the 106 central banks surveyed in the transparency index described earlier (see chapter 1), only 29 released some form of minutes of meetings.

[33] The raw data are daily and are averaged to generate quarterly observations. Aggregation minimizes the time deformation, as it were, because the timing of minutes does not quite match the timing of policy stance announcements.

[34] As previously discussed, there are other metrics to measure the intensity of or focus on certain types of content.

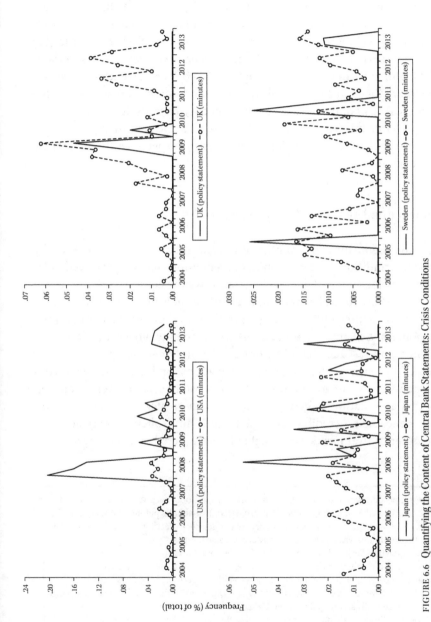

FIGURE 6.6 Quantifying the Content of Central Bank Statements: Crisis Conditions

Note: The data refer to the tone of central bank releases consistent with a "crisis." A crisis tone is the aggregation of words that convey "imbalances," "stress," "instability," and "contraction" in policy statements and minutes of policy committee meetings. *Source:* Author's calculations based on the content of press releases and minutes of central banks.

subsequently announced is fairly high.[35] The same is not true for the other two examples shown in the figure, where they remained significant, at least in statistical terms, but considerably smaller.[36] Perhaps unsurprisingly, on the basis that central bankers do not want to create undue alarm about any negative situation, it is more likely that negative sentiment emerges in policy meetings than in press releases.[37] This phenomenon is particularly evident for the United States, where there was a spike in the negative content of press releases beginning in 2007 and running through 2008, a brief recurrence in 2009, followed by another surge in 2010, likely stemming from the eurozone sovereign debt crisis. A temporary rise also appeared in 2013, perhaps due to fallout from the "taper tantrum." The example of Japan reflects the continuing struggle of the central bank to revive inflation, while Sweden's experience also reflects the fallout from the eurozone crisis.[38]

Confidence and Monetary Policy Objectives[39]

I conclude the analysis of confidence in central banks by returning to the narrow but traditional interpretation of credibility—namely, how well inflation expectations are matched with an objective the central bank has set out to achieve. Many central bankers have relied on such an interpretation of the metric by which the public can have confidence in the effectiveness of central bank policies. As Lars Svensson (2009), former deputy governor of Sweden's Riksbank, puts it, "The credibility of an inflation targeting regime is usually measured by to what extent inflation expectations for different time horizons correspond to the inflation target." Strictly speaking, such a definition suggests that an inflation-targeting regime bears a greater burden of accountability, hence being credible, because there is an explicit numerical target, while other central banks are arguably less hampered by such a restriction.

---

[35] The simple correlation between the two series is 0.770 (.000) for the United States, and 0.608 (.000) for the United Kingdom (*p*-values in parenthesis). It should be pointed out that in the United Kingdom, MPC members are individually accountable for their decisions, whereas at the Federal Reserve, the committee as a whole is ultimately accountable for its actions.

[36] The correlation for Japan is 0.358 (.025) and for Sweden is 0.325 (.043).

[37] Since there are only thirty-nine quarterly observations in total, one is reluctant to draw conclusions that are too strong. For what it is worth, however, the correlation disappears statistically for both Japan and Sweden for the "crisis" period (2008Q4–2013Q4), remains the same for the United Kingdom (0.601 [.004]), and falls substantially for the United States (0.501 [.021]).

[38] Recall that Sweden's exchange rate is allowed to float against the euro. It is unclear what explains the rise in negative sentiment in the early years of the sample, most notably in 2006. A change in government or rapidly rising housing prices, with the last point highlighted by the OECD's 2007 Economic Survey of Sweden, could be explanatory factors.

[39] As mentioned previously, some of what follows draws from joint research with Michael Bordo. See Bordo and Siklos 2016a, 2016b.

It is the same Lars Svensson, when he was an academic, who popularized the concept of flexible inflation targeting.[40] Based on this observation, one is hard-pressed to find a meaningful distinction between IT and NIT central banks. First, any inflation target is unlikely to be treated as a numerical value that should be expected to hold every period.[41] Second, inflation is ordinarily measured in terms of a headline measure. The "noise" around headline inflation, owing to volatile food and energy prices, and the occasional tax changes, are likely to be downplayed by central banks unless they are seen as influencing expectations.[42] Third, even if central bankers repeat the mantra of the desirability of low and stable inflation, they are equally fond of repeating ad nauseam the virtues of flexibility, since by definition "shocks" are unexpected. Nevertheless, even the most ardent advocates of flexibility must come to terms with the need to see the future with a reasonable amount of accuracy. To do so is not only a sign of competence but also an obvious and fairly objective means of generating confidence in the institutional capacity of the central bank to carry out its monetary policy effectively.

To create a benchmark, I use key characteristics that Svensson (2009) considers as signaling central bank credibility. It is likely that the requirements laid out here are ones not only shared by central bankers with numerical inflation targets but also equally germane to any modern central bank with responsibility for maintaining low and stable inflation rates. Svensson (2009) goes on to add: "How well inflation expectations are anchored also has a direct impact on how well the central bank succeeds in meeting the target." Finally, he suggests that "if the economic agents share the central bank's view of how inflation will approach the target, inflation expectations at different time horizons should be close to the central bank's forecasts. The degree of correspondence between inflation expectations and the central bank's inflation forecast then becomes a measure of how credible the central bank's inflation forecasts and analyses are."[43]

---

[40] The expression goes back to at least 1999, when the first set of evaluations of IT regimes, most notably in New Zealand, were under way. Also, see Svensson 2011.

[41] Typically, inflation data are published monthly.

[42] This requires the application, of course, of judgment. Even at the high-water mark of The Great Moderation, with less volatile economic growth accompanied by low and stable inflation, Bernanke pointed out that "even today inflation expectations may not be anchored as well as we would like" (Bernanke 2004a).

[43] He also suggests, prior to this statement, "as the central bank's inflation forecasts in the short and medium terms may deliberately deviate from the target." Svensson does not elaborate. Why the deviations would be deliberate—do central banks know something markets or the public does not?—or for how long is never spelled out. Clearly, this ought to have implications for central bank credibility. Moreover, this kind of obfuscation would have implications for central banks' ability to anchor expectations to a target, let alone allow the central banks to effectively communicate their outlook in a convincing manner.

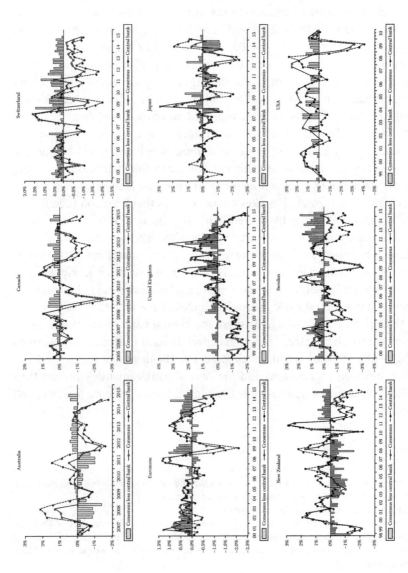

FIGURE 6.7 Professional versus Central Bank Forecasts

Source: Author's calculations and *Consensus Forecasts*. Also, see Siklos 2013b, 2017 (forthcoming).

Consider, first, a central bank's inflation forecasts and the inflation target. Figure 6.7 shows the difference between inflation forecasts published by nine central banks and a 2% target. The target is typical of the explicit target many inflation-targeting central banks are expected to meet. Central banks in Australia, Canada, the United Kingdom, New Zealand, and Sweden are all held to account according to this metric. The other central banks shown in the figure are not, but they are widely believed to act as if they follow a similar monetary policy strategy.[44]

It is clear from the figure that the ECB, the Reserve Bank of Australia, Sweden's Riksbank, and the SNB have permitted their forecasts to drift away from a 2% objective. Discrepancies observed for the other central banks are visibly smaller. Keeping in mind that inflation targets usually incorporate a ±1% tolerance level, none of these central banks appears to want to forecast inflation rates that consistently exceed the normally allowable tolerance range. In this respect, the GFC has not changed the inflation outlook for these central banks. Nor is the result peculiar to central banks with a formal inflation target. Indeed, to the extent that there is some "deliberate" departure from the 2% objective, this may simply reflect the underlying economic conditions—in particular, the deflationary pressures in some economies (e.g., the eurozone and Switzerland)—rather than some alternative policy strategy.

Next, I examine various ways in which the accuracy and, by implication, the credibility of central bank forecasts can be evaluated. In figure 6.7, the bars indicate the differences between consensus forecasts and central bank forecasts of inflation in nine economies, with Japan added to the central banks.[45] Consensus forecasts represent a large group of private-sector forecasters on an international scale. Guided by the well-known finding that averages of forecasts tend to outperform individual forecasts,[46] and the observation that central bank forecasts typically represent a mix of formal model-based forecasts and the application of judgment, the results shown in the figure ought to be representative of likely discrepancies between the thinking of the central banks and the private sector's outlook for inflation.

There is at least one striking common feature for almost all the economies considered. Differences in the inflation outlook between consensus forecasters and the central banks tend to be positive, and persistently so. In other words,

---

[44] But not the same. Whether this translates into a relatively more flexible inflation control regime is open to question. Nevertheless, the distinction just alluded to should be kept in mind.

[45] It would be difficult to justify a 2% inflation target for Japan in the period investigated. A 0% target seems more reasonable.

[46] This finding is occasionally referred to as the "forecast combination puzzle" (e.g., see Graefe et al. 2014 and Smith and Wallis 2009). The puzzle stems from partly from the fact that a simple linear combination of forecasts tends to outperform more complex attempts to exploit the accuracy of some forecasts over others. The finding that combining forecasts improves upon individual forecasts goes back to Bates and Granger 1969.

private-sector forecasters tend to be relatively more pessimistic about inflation than the published forecasts of their own monetary authorities. While there is some evidence that, over time, consensus and central bank forecasts tend to converge, the duration of these deviations tends to be on the order of eight to ten quarters. That is, if central banks are producing credible forecasts, then private forecasters tend not adjust theirs quickly. This could reflect an absence of credibility or that the central banks are attempting to convey a different message with their forecasts. It could also reflect a degree of inattention to other information about the outlook.[47] In any event, this is likely not conducive to generating credibility on a consistent basis. Japan is perhaps one exception to these findings, since the sign of the differences between consensus and Bank of Japan forecasts tends to change more frequently. Nevertheless, persistent differences remain evident. Broadly, the same conclusion can be drawn from eurozone inflation forecasts.

In spite of the apparent differences between private-sector and central bank forecasts, forecasting errors via-à-vis observed inflation are remarkably correlated in both cases. One possibility is that the private sector coordinates its forecasts with those of the central bank.[48] If so, and central bank forecasts contain a deliberate attempt to "miss a target," then the consensus forecasters are duped into viewing the outlook through the eyes of the central bank, as opposed to simply agreeing on the future. Alternatively, one can interpret the phenomena presented in the previous two figures by examining the graphs shown in figure 6.8. Here, it seems clear that private forecasts of inflation respond strongly to changes in a central bank's policy rate. Most notably, a decline in the policy rate sparks a rise in consensus forecasts relative to ones published by central banks. In addition, the link seemed amplified or became more sensitive following the GFC.

In Sweden, for example, the gap between the two types of forecasts became wider following a period when the Riksbank first raised and then began a series of reductions in the policy rate. The post-crisis peak of 1.5% in the repo rate reached in September 2012 eventually reached -0.35% when the sample ended in mid-2015. Australia represents another illustration of this phenomenon. Prior to 2011, consensus forecasts of inflation in Australia were below the RBA's expectations. Like the Riksbank, and unlike most central banks in advanced economies, the RBA went against the tide of looser monetary

---

[47] Economists continue to struggle to explain what drives changes in inflation expectations. Popular explanations include (rational) inattention of the kind alluded to here, as well as impediments in revising one's expectations because of the costs of doing so, or even to the difficulty posed by data that are "noisy" and hence can be uninformative, thereby preventing a potential revision to an inflation forecast. See, for example, Siklos 2017, forthcoming and references therein.

[48] See Morris and Shin 2002. Their theoretical model implies that, contrary to earlier intuition, the publication of central bank forecasts—a sign of greater transparency—can be harmful. It is important to keep in mind, however, that the authors assume perfect central bank credibility.

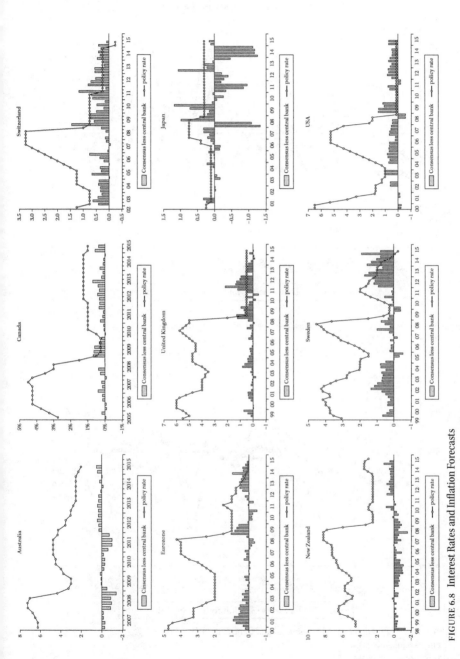

FIGURE 6.8 Interest Rates and Inflation Forecasts

Note: The policy rate is the central bank's policy instrument interest rate. *Source:* Author's calculations and *Consensus Forecasts*. Also, see Siklos 2013b, 2017 (forthcoming).

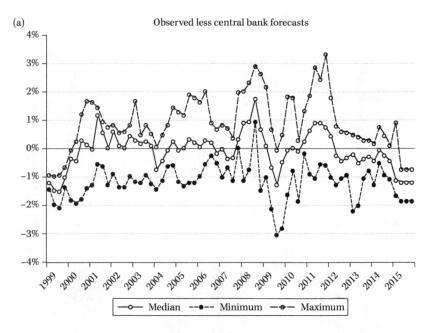

(a)

Observed less central bank forecasts

(b)

Observed less professional forecasts

FIGURE 6.9 The Spread Between Professional and Central Bank Forecasts
(a) Central Bank Forecasts
(b) Professional Forecasts

Source: Author's calculations and *Consensus Forecasts*. Also, see Siklos 2013b, 2017 (forthcoming).

policy, until it changed course and reduced policy rates. The experience of New Zealand's Reserve Bank is also comparable. Between early 2011 and March 2014, the RBNZ's cash rate remained at 2.5%, rising for a time to 3.5% by April 2015, before beginning a sharp retreat subsequently. Even Japan, at least for a time, reflects the same response to changes in the policy rate. Note, however, that the BoJ's discount rate, unchanged for several years, ceases in effect to provide signals about the direction of the stance of monetary policy. Indeed, by 2013, when Governor Kuroda replaced Governor Shirakawa at the helm of the BoJ, consensus forecasts resumed their tendency of remaining below the inflation forecasts of the majority of the policy board.

It is difficult to determine the extent to which private-sector forecasts seemingly coordinate their forecasts with those published by the central banks. Nevertheless, figure 6.9, which pools the forecasts for all nine economies considered in figure 6.7, shows the median inflation forecasts across all nine economies, as well as the highest and lowest inflation forecasts over time separately for consensus and central bank forecasts. In other words, the median, largest, and smallest forecast errors across all nine economies is evaluated separately for central bank (a) and professional forecasts (b).

The gaps between the largest and smallest forecasts are small. Nevertheless, at various times the most optimistic and pessimistic sets of forecasts tended to be quite different between the two groups of forecasters. Hence, if there is any evidence of forecast coordination, it is neither constant nor persistent through time.

The bottom line, then, is that at least two features of the forecast data, with implications for central bank credibility, are clear. First, differences persist between central bank forecasts and ones issued by private-sector counterparts. Hence, as Bernanke pointed out in 2004a, when the Great Moderation was still in full swing, central banks even in economies with already low and stable inflation rates had some way to go in demonstrating that expectations were well anchored. Second, in economies with low and stable inflation rates, both central banks and private-sector forecasts do not frequently deviate from a numerically announced or implicit inflation target of 2%, the only exception being Japan, a country long mired in a very low inflation environment.[49]

A Failure of Responsibility or Curiosity?

Svensson (2009) states: "In a democratic society, it is natural that the activities of the central bank are monitored and evaluated and that its independent

---

[49] Not shown here is the same set of exercises for real GDP growth, which largely reveal fealties similar to ones observed for inflation. One possible difference is that, post-GFC, differences between private-sector and central bank forecasts tend to be smaller in absolute value.

management can be called to account. . . . [D]etailed evaluations of monetary policy are becoming increasingly common." That monetary policy ought to be evaluated from time to time seems sensible, whether or not the central bank is "independent." Whether independence, as traditionally defined,[50] promotes accountability of the kind Svensson refers to is questionable. Whether such evaluations are, in fact, detailed and concern the conduct of monetary policy more generally speaking is normally very much in doubt.[51]

Nevertheless, it is worth looking at the facts, for they suggest a few important changes have occurred since the GFC, as well as a wide variety of mechanisms instituted to oversee a central bank's operations. Owing to the origins and development of the GFC, the focus here is on a few central banks in the advanced economies. Perhaps the most obvious question, assuming that some regular form of evaluation of monetary policy is desirable, is: To what effect and by whom?

As noted previously, in spite of the principle of independence, central banks remain an institution within a government. It appears, however, that the concept of independence is fragile, at least based on economists' interpretations of the legal frameworks governing the central banks. As shown in table 6.1, economies that obtained greater autonomy during the 1990s—most notably New Zealand, the United Kingdom, and the ECB—via significant changes in legislation are clearly identifiable. Setting aside possible differences in interpretation, it is striking, however, that Australia, New Zealand, the United Kingdom, and the Fed—three of which are known as IT central banks—earned far lower independence scores by 2010, arguably shortly after the apex of the crisis and when the European sovereign debt crisis was about to get under way. Only the Riksbank and the Norges Bank rose substantially in the rankings, both also IT central banks.[52] If central bank autonomy is indeed fragile, then establishing accountability or responsibility for the conduct of monetary policy, let alone assessing the record on financial stability, becomes paramount. In a world where central banks also compete to maintain their reputation internationally, changes in their autonomy over time may also signal deeper difficulties with the policy regime that may well have been triggered by the GFC.

In countries with parliamentary democracies (e.g., Australia, Canada, New Zealand, Norway, Sweden, United Kingdom), there are typically committees that formally review monetary policy and occasionally write reports on their views. While staff, some with the appropriate expertise, may provide input, these reviews tend to be written at a very general level; it is unclear whether such regular reporting has any demonstrable effect on the conduct of monetary

---

[50] For example, see Cukierman 1992 and chapter 5 this volume.

[51] Like Svensson, I have participated in evaluations of central bank research and policy. See Siklos and Vredin 2013. One exception to this observation is the report on the Riksbank by Goodfriend and King 2015. See later.

[52] To the extent possible, the same ranking methodology is used. However, the ranking for 2010 is unchanged when Dincer and Eichengreen's (2014) preferred score (CBIU) is used (results not shown).

TABLE 6.1 } Changing Independence of Central Banks in Selected Advanced Economies

Rank Order: Most to Least Independent	Cukierman 1992: app.A (1980s)	Siklos 2002: table 2.7 (1990s)	Dincer and Eichengreen 2014: table 8 (2010)
	Central Bank Rank		
1	Swiss National Bank	ECB	ECB
2	Bundesbank	RBNZ	Sveriges Riksbank
3	U.S. Federal Reserve	Swiss National Bank	n.d.
4	Bank of Canada/Reserve Bank of Australia	Bank of England	Norges Bank
5		U.S. Federal Reserve	Bank of Canada
6	Reserve Bank of new Zealand/Riksbank	Sveriges Riksbank	Bank of Japan
7		Bank of Canada	RBNZ
8		Bank of Japan	Bank of England
9	Bank of Japan	Reserve Bank of Australia	U.S. Federal Reserve
10	Norges Bank	Norges Bank	Reserve Bank of Australia

Sources: Cukierman 1992; Siklos 2002; and Dincer and Eichengreen 2014.

policy. After all, even if the central bank is a creature within a government, it is the relationship between the executive level of decision making in government and that in the central banks that is decisive. Indeed, many agreements, such as inflation targets, are typically negotiated between the Ministry of Finance or the Treasury and the central bank governor.

Next, at the level of the central bank, there may well be reviews of the bank's research function. These tend to be occasional, but they rarely involve asking how the research is supposed to improve monetary policy decision making. Instead, they often represent attempts to assess the quality of the output being produced, the skills of the research staff, and how well the research compares with the work carried out by academics or their peers.[53] A few evaluations of this type focus on the forecasting function of the central bank. As has been discussed earlier, the central banks, especially in the 2000s, distinguished themselves by deploying considerable resources to the forward-looking elements of their policy strategy. Forecasts represent the front line of this effort.

At other central banks, there are mechanisms that lead to a regular review of the work past, present, and future of monetary policy. Two different examples of this are the BoC and the RBNZ. In Canada, after abandoning the search for an operational definition of price stability, the Bank of Canada undertook to develop a strategy that relied on past performance, as it saw it, to inform the areas

[53] Freedman et al. 2011; Eijffinger et al. 2002; Meyer et al. 2008; Independent Evaluation Office 2011; Caballero, et al. 2012; Goodfriend, Lucrezia, and Gregory 2011 and Siklos and Vredin 2013 are examples of reviews of central bank research.

where the bank would conduct research to improve the conduct and performance of monetary policy. This was done with an eye toward preparing for the renewal of the inflation target. The implied assumption was that the target would be renewed, though the specifics would eventually have to be agreed to by the governor and the finance minister. The Bank of Canada Act does not stipulate an inflation target. The choice of policy strategy is not legislated. No overall outside evaluation of monetary policy has been conducted, though the occasional Royal Commission, which typically has a much broader mandate than just evaluating monetary policy, has in the past examined the conduct of the BoC.[54]

The RBNZ is also required to negotiate its objectives each time an election is called. The policy targets agreement, or PTA, also effectively amounts to a renewal of the inflation target without an indication of how research or the prospect of alternative policy strategies might play a role. Instead, the RBNZ has on a few occasions called for an external evaluation of either its entire monetary policy strategy or one important element of it. Externally conducted analyses of the overall conduct and performance of monetary policy are actually uncommon. The ECB conducted such a review in 2003. There have been none published by the Fed, the BoJ, or the Reserve Bank of Australia. In the United Kingdom, the Treasury conducted a review of this kind in 2013. Of course, at these central banks there are regular parliamentary or governmental committee evaluations, and all these central banks provide regular reports on monetary policy to government officials and the public, and testify in front of the appropriate committees.

The Riksbank comes closest to providing an overall review of the conduct of monetary policy. Three reports have been published so far, with the latest one covering the 2010–2015 period.[55] Unlike other reports, the Riksbank model is refreshingly blunt in its criticism that largely centers, as is the case elsewhere, on the central bank's forecasting record and forward guidance. Indeed, the problem of tunnel vision in the conduct of monetary policy, discussed in chapter 2, becomes clear when addressing the forward-guidance character of the future interest path for the policy rate. "There is something surreal about the precision of the guidance provided by individual board members as to the future path of the repo rate [the policy rate] when contrasted with the . . . fact that markets take too little notice of the published path in determining their own expectations" (Goodfriend and King 2015:7). The report also considers the behavior of the policymaking committee and highlights that just because a central bank publishes information about its deliberations and is therefore being more transparent, this need not translate into greater clarity. "It was not helpful that minutes and interviews by Board members displayed brusqueness

---

[54] The last Royal Commission that is relevant in this context is the McDonald Commission on the Economic Union and Development Prospects for Canada of 1985. See http://publications.gc.ca/site/eng/472251/publication.html.

[55] See Giavazzi and Mishkin 2006; Goodhart and Rochet 2011.

uncharacteristic of normal public debate in Sweden. . . . The minutes no longer represented to-and-from between different viewpoints on the Board, and did not reflect the balance of discussion" (Goodfriend and King 2015:9).

Two other variants of these models have been in place for some time in Norway and, more recently, in the United Kingdom. In Norway, the Ministry of Finance, with the tacit support of the Norges Bank, annually publishes the *Norges Bank Watch*. The report is meant as a review of the work of the Norges Bank for the past year, although in some cases longer-term matters are also examined. The report is also intended as a kind of second guessing of the policy decisions made by the central bank. Nevertheless, there is little indication that the report is meant to reconsider the chosen monetary policy strategy. The Bank of England, in 2014, created an independent evaluation office, loosely modeled on the organization that exists to oversee the work of the International Monetary Fund. As such, the intention is not only to conduct assessments of the short-term performance of the central bank but also to do "one-off" examinations that pertain to the BoE's policy strategy.

Arguably, most of the foregoing models are motivated not by a reaction to a major financial crisis but, rather, in response to a desire to update and understand what constitutes best practice in monetary policy. Then there is the reaction a systemic failure, as emerged in the United States in 2007. Eight years later, the U.S. Congress, which modified the Federal Reserve Act,[56] established a Centennial Monetary Commission to revisit the work of the Fed since its establishment over a century ago and to reconsider the appropriate policy regime the Fed should be mandated to follow.[57] The work of the commission extends to an evaluation of macroprudential supervision, as well as whether the central bank ought to continue as a lender of last resort. Curiously, no review of the microprudential framework was called for, even if the Federal Reserve Act now mentions the "unusual and exigent circumstances" to be triggered by events "that pose a threat to the financial stability of the United States." The decisions of the Congress even a decade since the start of the GFC reflect its continued unhappiness with the central bank, but more importantly, capture a festering absence of confidence in the monetary authority.[58]

---

[56] H.R. 3189, the Fed Oversight Reform and Modernization Act (FORM), of November 2015.

[57] The choices available to the commission range from complete discretion to the gold standard, via policy rules, price level and inflation targeting, to nominal GDP targeting.

[58] This is especially clear from the proposed Federal Reserve Accountability and Transparency Act (2014) and the Financial Regulatory Improvement Act (2015) in the United States. In essence, the legislation would require the Fed to set a benchmark based on a Taylor-type rule (see chapter 4), and the proposed legislation mandates that deviations or changes in some benchmark be explained to Congress on a regular basis. Whether this is a step too far, especially when politicians are also known to suffer from inattention to the details of monetary policy other than in the aftermath of a crisis, remains to be seen. For an interesting analysis of the consequences of the proposed legislation, see Nikolsko-Rzhevskyy, Papell, and Prodan 2016.

What should we make of the large variety of approaches to central bank accountability? Perhaps the most striking feature of all these arrangements is that they most frequently tend to be initiated by the central bank. This could reflect recognition by the monetary authorities that independence implies responsibility, hence they are simply demonstrating a desire to remain publicly accountable. Another interpretation is that all these developments highlight the sharp asymmetry in the (technical) ability of central banks versus the governments to which they are held accountable in providing independent assessments of strategies and the conduct of monetary policy.

This has all the hallmarks of an unhealthy relationship, especially since it is when things go wrong that governments confront the central bank and promote a change of course. Even if this asymmetry is considered acceptable, one has to ask how the remit of a regular assessment of monetary policy ought to be designed such that it is neither too onerous nor focuses too closely on individual decisions taken several times a year. Finally, there is the matter of how frequently such assessments ought to be conducted and how these should be designed for maximum effect—that is, whether to prompt a change of course when clear improvements are seen as necessary, and inform the government and the public when policy is conducted according to best available practices.[59]

The diversity of approaches to evaluating monetary policy suggests at least two factors at play. First, there may well be a statutory element, possibly related to the degree of autonomy a central bank enjoys, that dictates the precise manner and scope under which a review of monetary policy takes place. Second, as discussed in chapters 1 and 4 (also see Siklos 2002), there is a natural tension between central banks, which are the agents of monetary policy, and governments, which ostensibly represent the best interests of their publics and aim to maximize social welfare. Some broad conclusions and criticisms of how central banks have dealt with the problem do emerge. First, monetary policy decisions are well known to affect the economy with long (and variable) lags.[60] Hence, it is unlikely that annual reviews will provide the necessary insights that can translate into improvements in a particular monetary policy strategy. Reviews that address a particular feature of a central bank's operations (e.g., transparency), while useful in bringing attention to a potential weakness in how monetary policy is delivered, are of limited import; it is highly unlikely that even reforms in one area of policy or governance will leave the other areas untouched. More often than not, major reforms or changes in central bank legislation come about because several areas that pertain to monetary policy require rethinking. Finally, the one-off reviews that only a

---

[59] It is presumed that the individuals chosen to render reviews of monetary policy operations are beyond reproach.

[60] There is little indication that the GFC has changed the long and variable lags thesis. Indeed, if anything, at the ZLB the lags may indeed be longer, and possibly more variable as well.

few central banks have published are a snapshot of the accumulated ills and other irritants that prompted the review in the first place. They are rarely accompanied by the impact that the historical context may have had in arriving at the recommendations.

Clearly, navigating the sometimes opposing forces that might lead to an assessment of the quality and effectiveness of a central bank's operations is going to be difficult. This is not only because the structure of such reviews is determined by the form of government but also because there is a need to temper any assessment with the political motives that might well underlie criticisms or proposals for change. Ultimately, the irony is that central banks, which are always concerned with their credibility, and perhaps governments as well, have devoted considerable effort toward generating reports that review their performance but have spent little time asking whether these reviews have proved to be credible.

As discussed previously, the drop in trust for the central banks, most keenly felt in the eurozone and to a lesser extent elsewhere, reflects in part the difficulty in separating the central bank from other agencies of government.[61] The issue is an important one, especially as the conduct of monetary policy has become intertwined with the aim of maintaining financial stability. In the final chapter, I return to this question with some suggestions for how the credibility of this process could be improved.

The New Frontier: Combining Financial Stability and Monetary Policy

The GFC had altered the emphasis in major central banks around the world to having a greater focus on financial stability concerns. Contrary to some who believe that monetary authorities, especially in the advanced economies, have chosen to ignore inflation or have become more willing to let inflation drift away from an inflation target, the events of recent years have actually enhanced the role of inflation expectations. This is in part because the tendency for inflation to fall close to zero, if not produce outright deflation, has been forefront for the MPCs of central banks directly affected or impacted since 2007. Indeed, navigating the links between economic activity and financial stability continues to occupy the central banks and concerns about how they are to be managed has not abated since the GFC.

These developments have found expression in a new or, rather, a revival of an older question—namely, whether central banks should be entrusted not

---

[61] Of course, this also possibly reflects a general lack of understanding about what monetary policy is supposed to accomplish. See, for example, van der Cruijsen, Jansen, and de Haan 2015.

only with the conventional requirements of meeting certain macroeconomic objectives, especially on the inflation front, but also should evince some responsibility for administering what are now referred to as macroprudential instruments. Even if usage of the term is relatively recent, the GFC laid bare a problem that was thought to sort itself out when the time came. As Barwell (2013:12) points out, "no single body was given both the resources to monitor the ebb and flow of risk within the financial system as a whole *and* the responsibility to manage systemic risk *and* adequate tools to deliver on that financial stability mandate." Indeed, a role for financial stability was part of the central banking landscape, particularly in OECD economies, for decades. In Siklos (2002: table 3.6), I point out that financial stability became increasingly part of the statutory regimes of central banks by the 1990s. This marked a substantial change in the state of affairs relative to the 1960s through the 1980s. The difficulty then, as now, was that it was never entirely clear what financial stability represents. In OECD economies that made up the sample, it was generally meant to refer to the level of systemic risks, although it was not usually clear whether a distinction should be made between homegrown and international sources of risks.[62] Moreover, it was also generally the case that the resulting risks to monetary policy from these risks were treated as second order, behind ones that might threaten the conventional indictors of policy success in monetary policy circles.

Table 6.2 reprises a version of that table published in 2002. Most countries or economies do not have precise legislative language that defines financial stability. Nevertheless, there are at least four different terms that recur in the legislation: "confidence in the financial system," "resilience to shocks," "preventing disruption of the financial system," and "prevention of adverse financial shocks spilling over into the real economy."

If we view the financial sector's primary function as involving the efficient allocation of funds, moving them from holders of surplus funds to those operating with a deficit, while managing the risks thereof, one obvious indicator of these systemic risks resides in the limitations on access to credit. Figures 6.10 illustrate that what are called financial "frictions" can both get in the way of allocating those funds efficiently and trigger broader economic spillovers when the credit flows seize up.

These four figures show changes in lending standards applied by financial institutions in various regions of the world or according to the type of loans made. Put simply, when senior loan officers raise lending standards, lending becomes more difficult. This can have consequences for the entire macroeconomy. Figure 6.10 illustrates changes in expected lending standards across

---

[62] The risk that a financial disruption (e.g., as in a crisis) in one sector or economy can have repercussions in other sectors or economies. Also, see Siklos (2002:121).

TABLE 6.2 } The Meaning of Financial Stability: A Selection of Definitions

Australia
"A stable financial system is one in which financial intermediaries, markets and market infrastructure facilitate the smooth flow of funds between savers and investors and, by doing so, help promote growth in economic activity. Conversely, financial instability is a material disruption to this intermediation process with potentially damaging implications for the real economy"; www.rba.gov.au/fin-stability/about.html.

Austria
"Financial stability means that the financial system—financial intermediaries, financial markets and financial infrastructures—is capable of ensuring the efficient allocation of financial resources and fulfilling its key macroeconomic functions even if financial imbalances and shocks occur. Under conditions of financial stability, economic agents have confidence in the banking system and have ready access to financial services, such as payments, lending, deposits and hedging"; www.oenb.at/en/Financial-Stability.html.

Belgium (translation from CB Legislation)
"Stability of the financial system means a situation where the probability discontinuity or disruption of the functioning of the financial system slight or, if such disturbances would occur, where the impact on the economy would be limited"; www.nbb.be/fr/la-banque-nationale/administration-et-controle/cadre-juridique.

Canada
"Financial stability is defined as the resilience of the financial system to unanticipated adverse shocks, which enables the continued smooth functioning of the financial intermediation process"; Financial System Review, Bank of Canada, www.bankofcanada.ca/publications/fsr/.

Colombia
"Maintaining financial stability . . . is understood as a situation in which the financial system is able to broker financial flows effectively"; www.banrep.gov.co/docum/Lectura_finanzas/pdf/afsr_mar_2012.pdf.

Czech Republic
"The CNB defines financial stability as a situation where the financial system operates with no serious failures or undesirable impacts on the present and future development of the economy as a whole, while showing a high degree of resilience to shocks. The CNB's definition is based on the fact that financial stability may be disturbed both by processes inside the financial sector that lead to the emergence of weak spots, and by strong shocks, which may arise from the external environment, domestic macroeconomic developments, large debtors and creditors, economic policies or changes in the institutional environment"; www.cnb.cz/en/financial_stability/.

Estonia
"Financial stability means the smooth functioning of financial intermediation under both normal and unexpectedly adverse circumstances.

Safeguarding the stability of the financial system is one of the key functions of Eesti Pank under the Eesti Pank Act. The central bank oversees the functioning of the financial system as a whole, while individual financial institutions and markets are supervised by the Estonian Financial Supervision Authority"; www.eestipank.ee/en/eesti-panks-role-safeguarding-financial-stability.

Finland
"A stable financial system is capable of operating beyond reproach, of handling its basic tasks, such as the undisturbed transmission of finance and payments, pricing of financial instruments and efficient distribution of risk. Furthermore, the risk-bearing capacity of the financial market agents and public confidence in financial institutions and the financial markets must be sufficient to endure even larger disruptions in the operating environment"; www.suomenpankki.fi/en/rahoitusjarjestelman_vakaus/Pages/default.aspx

Malaysia (CB Legislation)
" '[R]isk to financial stability' means a risk which in the opinion of the Bank disrupts, or is likely to disrupt, the financial intermediation process including the orderly functioning of the money market and foreign exchange market, or affects, or is likely to affect, public confidence in the financial system or the stability of the financial system"; www.bnm.gov.my/index.php?ch=en_legislation&pg=en_legislation_act&ac=858&lang=en.

(Cont.)

TABLE 6.2 } *(continued)*

Norway
"Financial stability implies a financial system that is resilient to shocks and thus capable of channelling funds, executing payments and distributing risk efficiently"; www.norges-bank.no/en/Published/Publications/Financial-Stability-report/.

Slovakia
"The financial sector is deemed to be stable when it is able to smoothly fulfil its core functions, even amidst substantial adverse shocks in the external or domestic economic and financial environment. At the same time, financial sector stability is perceived as a necessary condition for sound functioning of the real economy"; www.nbs.sk/en/publications-issued-by-the-nbs/financial-stability-report.

Euro Area
"A condition in which the financial system—intermediaries, markets and market infrastructures—can withstand shocks without major disruption in financial intermediation and in the effective allocation of savings to productive investment"; www.ecb.europa.eu/pub/fsr/html/index.en.html.

United States
"[S]ystemic risk arising from financial markets and institutions and from the emergence of new products; studying financial market functioning and the interconnectedness of financial institutions; and understanding the roles of leverage and maturity transformation"; www.federalreserve.gov/econresdata/fspr-fsa-staff.htm.

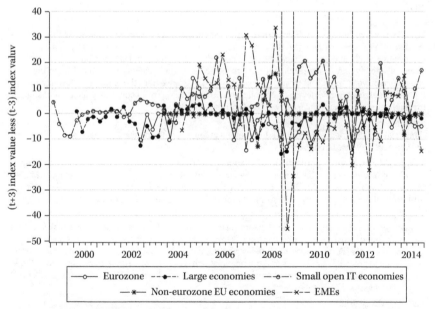

FIGURE 6.10 Lending Standards Expectations in Various Parts of the World

Note: Eurozone. Large economies consist of the U.S., Eurozone, Japan, and the U.K. Small open IT economies include Canada, New Zealand, Sweden, Australia, and Norway. Lending standards are based on a survey of senior loan officers. The differential between the index for the three-month-ahead versus three-month-lagged value is shown. A positive value implies that an expected tightening of lending standards is expected. A negative value implies an easing of standards. *Source:* Author's calculations and Filardo and Siklos 2016.

various country groupings. One can clearly see the anticipated tightening of standards in the emerging market economies in the years before the crisis, when the advanced economies were growing strongly, followed by the sharp loosening of standards from 2008 to 2010. Expectations of standards remained relatively loose thereafter, and this helps explain why emerging markets were resilient to the GFC shock.

The expected loosening of standards is far less noticeable in large econo-mies, which includes three of the four economies most directly impacted by the GFC. It is also interesting to observe how standards were expected to tighten in economies that target inflation. For the most part, these economies survived the financial disruption and did not have to implement QE-type poli-cies. Nevertheless, as the ripple effects of the GFC did not dissipate as quickly as expected, and as coupled with the onset of the euro area crisis, standards began to show signs of loosening fairly quickly thereafter, at least for a time.

A broader grouping of economies is considered in figure 6.11. Although the data only begin in 2009, we can see more signs of the extent to which lending standards were likely affected by the events taking place in some of the advanced economies. The experience of the Latin and South American regions, together with the emerging Europe, resulted in a considerable loosening of lending stan-dards. The impact of the GFC was barely noticeable in Africa, while emerging Asia seemed decoupled from the rest of the world, with the tightening of stan-dards evident through the end of 2014. Indeed, at least in terms of lending stan-dards, all these economies showed signs of recovery as standards were tightened in both absolute terms and as compared to levels attained in 2009.

Figure 6.12 delves more deeply into the experience of the large economies that were directly impacted by the GFC and where the data are more ample. Here, there is a distinction by type of loan. Another feature is an estimate of perceptions from the perspective of the same senior loan officers of the demand for lending aggregated across all types of loans. Not surprisingly, the demand for loans was sensitive to the state of the business cycle. Hence, we see a direct indication of the connection between the financial and real sectors. Also worth noting is that demand for loans and the tightening or loosening of lending standards, while generally inversely related, did not change in a synchronous manner. Perhaps the only notable exception was seen during the height of the GFC in 2008. It is also interesting to notice that standards did differ according to the type of loan made. Once again, however, the GFC stands out, with a general tightening of standards in 2007 when the GFC was under way, followed by a dramatic loosening of lend-ing conditions in 2008. Otherwise, standards for housing and consumer credit show relatively few signs of moving together. It should therefore come as no sur-prise that the GFC had such a dramatic impact in the large economies shown in the figure.

Finally, figure 6.13 illustrates that, while much of the focus in the eurozone has been on the sovereign debt crisis of 2010–11, the actual dramatic downturn

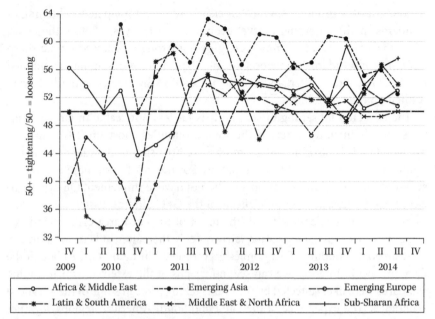

FIGURE 6.11 Evolution of Lending Standards Around the Globe

Note: Values above 50 are equivalent to a tightening of lending standards; below 50, lending standards are looser.
Source: Author's calculations and Filardo and Siklos 2016.

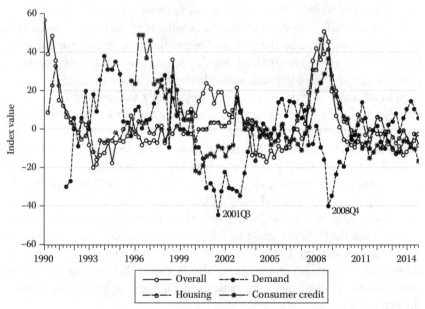

FIGURE 6.12 Lending Standards by Type of Loan—Median for Large Economies

Note: Positive values indicate a tightening of lending standards; negative values mean lending standards are looser. *Source:* Author's calculations and Filardo and Siklos 2016.

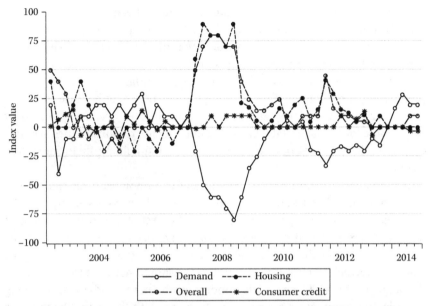

FIGURE 6.13 Lending Standards by Type of Loan—Median for Eurozone Periphery Economies

Note: Eurozone periphery economies listed earlier. *Source:* Author's calculations and Filardo, and Siklos 2016.

in loan demand, coupled with an equally dramatic tightening of standards beginning in 2007, are clearly visible. It is only the lending standards for consumer credit that remained largely unchanged throughout the period. Again, as a proxy for the degree to which financial frictions may have macroeconomic effects, figure 6.13 is yet another illustration that signs of trouble in the periphery of the eurozone were in evidence well before the events that transpired later at the level of the sovereign.[63]

Another indicator that reflects the tensions between macroprudential concerns and monetary policy more generally is conflict in the form of uncertainties, complications, and other problems with regard to the various other agencies responsible for maintaining financial stability.

The magnitude of the challenge facing monetary authorities as they grapple simultaneously with guaranteeing a form of price stability and maintaining financial system stability is daunting.[64] Twenty-seven economies around the world (all are G20 members) were surveyed about the governance and scope of their macroprudential policies, as well as their central banks' understanding

[63] An important consideration in the threat of an admittedly qualitative element in the transmission of monetary policy is the relative importance of bank intermediated lending versus other sources of credit (e.g., bonds, equity, shadow financial institutions).

[64] The discussion below draws from one small part of a much wider survey of macroprudential policies and instruments. See Lombardi and Siklos (2016).

of the connection between macroprudential and monetary policies. Note that not all economies in the sample experienced a banking crisis.

It is perhaps both a relief and a worry that there exists such variety of responses to the events that transpired since 2007. It is a relief because it highlights that a unique strategy to blend macroprudential policy with monetary policy has yet to emerge, if one ever will. It is worrisome because there is a considerable lack of clarity about how the various agencies in government responsible for financial stability (this would include responsibilities over microprudential policies) devote their efforts to maintaining financial system stability.

Nevertheless, it comes as no surprise that the economies at the epicenter of the serial financial crises since 2007 are far more advanced in dealing with the complexities of administering financial stability. Yet, it is also curious that so much of the responsibility in these economies has been put in the hands of the same central banks that, according to their fiercest critics, were asleep at the wheel. Nevertheless, even if the central banks should not have to shoulder all the blame for the GFC, one is left wondering whether it is advisable, let along sensible, that we now have a pyramid structure, with the central bank at the apex of a group of institutions responsible for using the most important stabilization tools in the macroeconomy.

Recall, as discussed in chapter 1, that central banks during the 1990s and early 2000s were fond of emphasizing how a focus on price stability avoided the kind of discretion that had previously ended in tears for policymakers. Even if policy rules were to be obeyed in a flexible manner, the notion of a fundamentally sound and reasonably straightforward link between price stability and macroeconomic stability (but not necessarily financial stability) made the accountability for policy failures clearer, at least in principle. Instead, we have a concentration of authority in areas that are, as yet, not clearly defined, using a multiplicity of tools that may or may not require approval by other authorities. This goes against making it practical to definitely allocate responsibility for economic and financial stabilization.

Even more troubling is that a global crisis elicited so few formal attempts at international cooperation. Policymakers are fooling themselves if they believe they know what they have gotten into. Central bankers especially are fond of repeating that there are always trade-offs. Yet, when it comes to financial stability, they give few indications about where these trade-offs are to be found and what the consequences are of action or inaction. The development and use of macroprudential tools was driven in large part by the desire to protect financial systems from their worst excesses. However, if we are still unable to define financial stability in a meaningful manner, then it becomes unclear what we are protecting.

Equally important is the question of who is being protected through these macroprudential policy actions. In the case of monetary policy, the protection against losses in purchasing power is universal. However, if financial stability needs to be protected by favoring one sector or one group over another, whether through ultra-low interest rates or outright subsidies, then redistribution is involved.

Finally, why is the effort to expand the scope of central banking deemed desirable? If the aim is to reduce the likelihood of panic in the financial markets, then this goal should have generated more effort at international cooperation, if not coordination. Moreover, if even the least cynical observer is convinced that financial crises are not a thing of the past, then all this effort has the look of window dressing. Of course, the next crisis will be the true test of whether a new regime is capable of appropriately taming the financial markets with the same degree of success as monetary policy in the 1990s and 2000s helped tame inflation. This sounds like something that, like the much maligned QE experiments, works in theory but not so much, or for so long, in practice.

Research efforts covering the topic of macroprudential policy has experienced what can only be called a surge.[65] While the term apparently dates back to the 1970s (e.g., see Barwell 2013), the GFC of 2008–9 spurred a tremendous increase in the frequency with which the term is employed. Yet, a decade after the crisis, agreement on the meaning of the concept eludes policymakers,[66] its objectives remain unclear,[67] and its effectiveness is mixed, at best.[68]

Several difficulties confront researchers and policymakers alike when the topic of macroprudential policy comes up. Unlike monetary policy, which can be explained via instrument rules as in the Taylor Rule (see chapter 4), nothing of the kind exists to explain macroprudential policies. Indeed, macroprudential policy appears to be the antithesis of rules-like policies, especially as its effects are specifically designed to be asymmetric.[69] The financial crisis produced a plethora of financial interventions (and acronyms) around the world (e.g., TARP, LSAP, OMT, FFL),[70] reflecting the fact that central banks were determined to do whatever necessary to prevent a financial collapse.[71]

If we take seriously Reinhart and Rogoff's (2009) conclusion that policymakers easily fall into the self-deluding trap of "this time is different," then burdening the central banks with macroprudential responsibilities will end up contradicting the theoretical idea worked out long ago[72] that one ought

---

[65] Some of what follows draws upon Lombardi and Siklos 2016.

[66] Barwell 2013:33.

[67] See, for example, Claessens 2014.

[68] See, for example, Galati and Moessner 2014.

[69] See McDonald 2015.

[70] TARP, or Troubled Asset Relief Program; LSAP, or Large Scale Asset Purchases, both from the U.S. Fed and Treasury. Also, OMT, or Outright Monetary Transactions, from the European Central Bank; and FFL, or Funding for Lending, from the Bank of England.

[71] See, for example, Wessel 2009.

[72] See Brainard 1967.

to be conservative in deploying new policy instruments with uncertain outcomes. Clearly, monetary and financial stability are related, but they have different goals.

Moreover, proposed reforms by multilateral agencies such as the FSB to limit the financial system's tendency of being crisis prone instead will generate complexity, limiting policymakers' ability to communicate how they will keep the world's financial system safe. If the goals are unclear and the instruments through which they are to be attained are not well understood, then communication becomes a challenge.

Conclusions

Superficially, central banks have a lot to be happy about. They remain arguably the most critical partner in stabilization policy. Rather than being held back, they have, since the GFC, intervened frequently and heavily to prevent deflation, maintain financial stability, and create conditions that promote economic growth.

Nevertheless, scratching beneath the surface reveals a far more fragile state of affairs. Part of the explanation is in the number of years that have elapsed since the crisis yielded other crises, with little optimism for a return to the average economic growth rates that prevailed before 2007. Then there is the ever-present threat of financial instability, coupled with a continuation of what several central banks believe are excessively low inflation rates.

There is considerable evidence for a loss of confidence and trust in the institution of central banking. One source of this loss of confidence is the inability of monetary authorities to match deeds with words, or poor communication skills. A second source is the impression that accountability, so proudly promoted by the central banks pre-GFC, is being eroded, as is the autonomy of several central banks in question. Finally, there is a feeling that the hard-fought battle to equate central banking strictly with monetary policy, which yielded a coherent framework and policy strategy, has been lost, or at the very least is weakened by policy responses collectively referred to as unconventional monetary policies (UMP). In an era in which political, financial, and public pressures seem to be conspiring to undermine their ability to function with adequate flexibility, the central banks find that the lines of authority remain insufficiently articulated. This does not imply that there is a single model that ensures the legitimacy of a central bank. But it does require that the responsibilities of certain institutions be distributed appropriately.

L'art est difficile, et combien la critique est aisée[73] is a natural response to the criticisms that have been leveled at the central banks and at central banking more generally. Consequently, the final chapter attempts to bring some order to the various issues raised so far and suggest some ways forward. One of the guiding principles of this book is that not everything is broken, but there exist alternative strategies to repair what needs mending.

---

[73] From Diderot (1818:568), loosely translated, means that it is easy to criticize but more difficult to create art.

7 }

Trust, But Verify: The Road Ahead

Where We Have Been and Where We Are Now

The last decade or so in central banking has been an eventful one, to say the least. It is difficult, of course, to separate broader geopolitical and economic events from purely monetary policy ones. Nevertheless, as 2016 comes to a close, there are at least two remarkable features about central banks, and monetary policy more generally, that stand out.

First, in spite of complaints from several quarters, the desirability of a monetary policy strategy to maintain some inflation control has not diminished. Even if the number of countries adopting a formal inflation target has slowed, the idea that the remit of central banks ought to include low and stable inflation has not been successfully challenged. Certainly, there are prominent voices (see following, but also chapter 1) advocating for higher inflation, but the case for doing so has faltered, for several reasons. Perhaps that is because critics of the current regime cannot convincingly explain why a faster loss of purchasing power can be credible, effective, or, more important, guarantee a return to pre-crisis levels of economic growth. Instead, advocates for higher inflation appear primarily to want to reduce the likelihood of hitting the ELB in future.[1]

Ultimately, critics of low inflation cannot explain why, when there is persistent undershooting of current targets, they can be confident that the policies to prevent a future overshooting of some higher inflation target can be avoided. Political economy considerations alone, not to mention the history of inflation, suggest that future central bank governors will respond to excessively

---

[1] Strangely, there is little acknowledgment that the combination of low inflation and low interest rates of the 1950s and early 1960s did not prompt a similar reaction among policymakers. Clearly, the financial system today is vastly different from how it was a decade ago, but the desirability of protecting the purchasing power of money ought to be timeless.

high inflation by saying that it will fall in the future, just not yet, and will keep repeating such a statement as long as necessary.[2]

Second, many central banks have inherited or, rather, rediscovered a role in the prevention of financial instability of the kind that gripped the global economy in 2007–9, and again in the aftermath of the 2010 eurozone sovereign debt crisis. Unlike the goal of inflation control, ensuring—let alone communicating—financial stability remains a work in progress and does not seem amenable to the application of simple principles. Nevertheless, central banks are in the uncomfortable position of resuming a role many of them were originally meant to play—that is, until the post-World War II shift toward preserving purchasing power, once the "golden fetters" of the Gold and Gold Exchange standards were no longer viable. However, unlike the late nineteenth or early twentieth centuries, central banks now share at least part of the responsibility for maintaining financial stability, with some institutions vying for a similar role while others are happy to share it. Also, it is unclear how to resolve the conflict of interest between the central banks' regulation or supervision (or both) of the financial markets and their suppression of risk as the principal mechanism to maintain stability and prevent another financial crisis.

Having shown such success at devising a policy regime that was more or less successful in anchoring inflation expectations to some publicly stated, if not government mandated, inflation objective, the central banks gave the impression that once inflation control was achieved, financial stability must surely follow; so, it is ironic that now they are at a loss to explain the persistence of a low growth–low inflation environment. As a result, some central bankers have called for a "new contract"; others have requested clarity in their assignment of responsibility for ensuring macroeconomic stabilization; and yet still others have taken on the responsibility for doing whatever is needed within their mandate. The latter is sometimes loosely interpreted, along with the occasional court case (e.g., as in Europe) or political pressure (e.g., as in the United States), to determine what is or is not permissible in the realm of monetary policy. Unfortunately, in the absence of a full discussion of the differences between governing in crisis times and under normal conditions, we are already witnessing an effective—if not statutorily mandated— narrowing of the scope for action (e.g., the U.S. Fed) and the consequent loss of a central bank's flexibility for responding in crisis conditions. It is as if one can legislate away the likelihood of a future financial crisis by limiting the central bank's capacity to respond to such events (also, see chapter 3).

---

[2] For example, a cynic might interpret the regular letters from the governor of the Bank of England to the chancellor of the Exchequer (three in 2016 at this writing, four in 2015, and twelve between 2008 and 2011) as a reflection of the problem. Of course, central banks cannot control every wiggle in the inflation rate, nor is the policy horizon only one month ahead. For an earlier example of the challenges of high inflation, Arthur Burns's (1979) *Anguish of Central Banking* is worth reading.

A decade after the first financial tremors started spreading around much of the globe, there are few indications that we have settled into a "new normal," or some version of the "old normal," as far as macroeconomic conditions are concerned. Central bankers worry about what some feel are excessively low rates of inflation and weak economic growth, even if the GFC is receding into history. Simultaneously, governments have been unwilling or unable to take advantage of these low nominal interest rates to implement policies that only they are capable of implementing. Even if many economists are incredulous at the lost opportunity to exploit the current ultra-loose monetary policy environment, much of the fiscal response is a reflection of battles won many years ago over the importance of fiscal responsibility in any economic environment. This governmental response is partly reflected in the sharp rise in the number of countries with fiscal councils and rules, and a lengthening of their budgetary horizons akin to the medium-term horizon that has long governed monetary policy (e.g., International Monetary Fund 2013b). However, just as with monetary policy, less thought is given to what kind of allowance should be made for "unusual and exigent" conditions, not to mention at what point fiscal rules overstep the bounds of democratic accountability by removing the discretion that is the essence of political action. Finally, as the ongoing saga of Europe's Stability and Growth Pact illustrates (also, see chapter 3), what is or what is not considered responsible is an elastic concept.

Central banks continue to argue that even looser monetary policies are the answer, thought in the systemically important advanced economies it might be unclear how to weigh the macroeconomic benefits of ultra-low interest rates against the costs of losing an institutional reputation for managing stabilization. More interestingly, there has been a reluctance to articulate a strategy that recognizes the need for monetary and fiscal policies to act in tandem. It is as if the legitimacy of the central banks might be threatened if monetary authorities are not seen as supporting the stance of fiscal policy that has been adopted by elected officials.

We can obtain some impression of the macroeconomic dilemma faced by policymakers, especially in the advanced economies, by examining figures 7.1 and 7.2. In both figures, the real GDP growth rates are shown for the ten advanced economies I have from time to time considered in this book. Similar data were discussed earlier, but the emphasis here is on the broader historical dimensions of economic growth. Moreover, since data for over a century are available, we can also ask in very general terms what experience offers by examining past growth experiences in selected economies. To enhance the legibility of the figures, I have averaged the growth rates for the ten economies, as well as shown the range of growth experienced through time from the highest to the lowest.

Figure 7.1 is subdivided into two parts, (a) and (b). Graph (a) considers the record of economic growth in the post-World War II era; the pre-Great

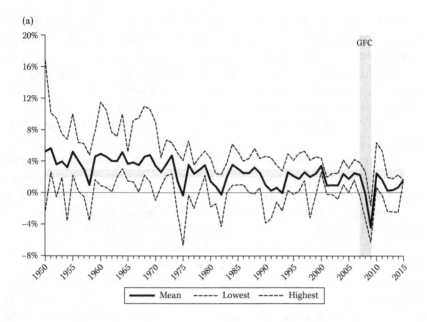

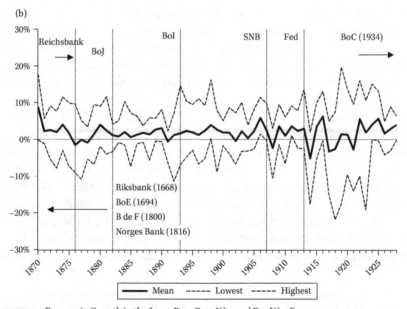

FIGURE 7.1 Economic Growth in the Long-Run: Post-War and Pre-War Era
(a) Post World War II
(b) Pre World War II

Note: All data are annual. Growth is the percent change in real GDP. The data show the arithmetic mean, highest, and lowest growth rates for ten economies: Canada (CAN), Switzerland (CHE), Germany (DEU), France (FRA), United Kingdom (GBR), Italy (ITA), Japan (JPN), Norway (NOR), Sweden (SWE), United States (USA). The vertical lines in (b) indicate the year central banks were created when in sample. Otherwise, the years are shown separately. *Source:* Data since 1955 are from the July 2016 edition of the IMF *International Financial Statistics* CD-ROM. Pre-World War II data are from Bordo and Siklos (2016a).

Depression growth record is shown in graph (b). Estimates of average growth rates over these (and other samples) suggest that 2 to 3% growth rates seem "normal" over extended periods of time (results not shown), although there were growth spurts that exceeded these values and large slumps (e.g., as in the Great Depression of the late 1920s and early 1930s) are also part of the longer-run growth experience. To provide an indication of what "normal" economic growth might look like, I've used a band to highlight the 2 to 3% range in both graphs of figure 7.1.

There are at least three features in figure 7.1 relevant to the discussion of the current state of monetary policy. First, the 2008–9 slump stands out because it appears so synchronized in the advanced economies shown and also by virtue of its severity. Previous recessions are visible, of course, but are not associated with any financial crisis of the global variety.[3] Second, the V-shaped recovery at the end of the sample appears to be undone by a sharp return to lower growth rates that are again somewhat synchronous. Nevertheless, it is also the case that divergences in growth rates across the ten economies have grown sharply. It is more difficult to observe anything approaching the experience of the past decade, at least since the 1950s. Finally, if the Great Moderation is the "normal" we are aiming for, it emerges more because of the reduced volatility of business cycle movements than because of the average performance of real GDP growth rates. Indeed, growth during the 1960s alone exceeds the 2 to 3% corridor far more often than at most other times during the 1984–2006 period. Perhaps it is some combination of these observations that gives rise to the unhappiness in policy circles about real economic performance in the post-GFC era.[4]

Presumably, we do not wish to return to the experience of the 1870–1928 era, as shown in graph (b) of figure 7.1, where the 2 to 3% average corridor for economic growth is barely visible. Instead, what is striking about this period is the volatility of business cycles, partly enhanced by World War I (1914–18), though not all economies shown were equally impacted by that conflict.[5] Also notice that as more and more central banks are created, there is no obvious decline in the volatility of business cycle movements. If we see to the data in graph (b) as representing global business cycle movements, then it becomes clear that central banks did not originally play a role in facilitating stable economic growth.

---

[3] Bordo and Landon-Lane 2010 identify five global financial crises: 1880, 1890–1, 1907–8, 1913–14, 2007–8. They conclude that the recent crisis most resembles the 1907–8 crisis in terms of overall economic performance.

[4] Breaking down economic performance by decade, or some other combination based on historical events, does not change the interpretation of the foregoing results in any meaningful fashion.

[5] The vertical lines in figure 7.1b, where appropriate, show when some central banks were created. Their creation had more to do with enhancing financial stability, partly via the lender of last resort function, or in the U.S. case the elimination of seasonal fluctuations in interest rates, than with implementing monetary policy as it is understood today.

Figure 7.2 illustrates the post-1950 growth record from a different perspective. Individual growth rates are now indicated by dots of various shapes and sizes. This permits highlighting the historical experience as one where recessions are not uncommon but are typically followed by sharp expansions. Indeed, generally speaking evidence shows that the sharper the recession, the sharper the expansion.[6] However, as discussed earlier in chapter 1, the most recent recovery appears more muted than previous ones, and it may well have reversed this course. Especially if one draws a line to capture the "long-run" growth experience across the ten economies since the 1950s (see the dashed line ending with an arrow), the impression is that growth rates have been declining slowly for some time. There is little doubt that this observation contributes to the present dissatisfaction with aggregate economic performance.

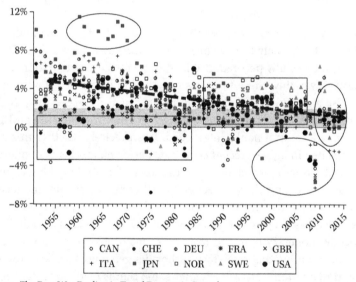

FIGURE 7.2 The Post War Decline in Trend Economic Growth

Note: Countries are the same as in figure 7.1.The boxes and ellipses highlight periods of unusually high or low growth rates, and the period of the Great Moderation. The dashed downward sloping line is an approximation of the trend growth rate across all countries. The shaded area identifies annual growth rates of 2 to 3%.
Source: Annual data are from the July 2016 edition of the IMF *International Financial Statistics* CD-ROM.

---

[6] This notion is not a new one. Friedman (1964, 1993) observed that recessions seem "plucked" from the steady growth in output toward potential. This gave rise to the so-called plucking model of economic growth, which unsurprisingly has produced mixed evidence. See, for example, De Simone and Clarke 2007. Friedman felt that output could not exceed potential, whereas the economic theory and analysis that underlies the application of policy rules (e.g., see chapter 4) clearly admits that output can exceed potential. Indeed, this is what, at least in theory, produces a rise in inflation unless monetary policy is tightened.

Figure 7.3 perhaps also captures today's unhappiness with overall economic performance since the GFC. It focuses on the three economies at the center of the GFC and Japan, arguably a country in crisis since the 1990s. Current and one-year-ahead real GDP growth forecasts are shown for the period since 2000.[7] A crude interpretation of the optimism or pessimism of forecasters is the difference between these two sets of forecasts. After all, forecasts are revised monthly; hence, if next year's real GDP growth forecast rises relative to this year's forecast, it is reasonable to suppose that the forecast is optimistic about the near future. With the exception of Japan, which has long been mired in low or negative inflation, optimism tends to persist throughout the GFC and post-GFC periods. Indeed, if optimistic and pessimistic waves or runs are expected to be distributed randomly through time, and the post-GFC period is defined as starting in 2010 (that is, the last third of the sample), the data suggest that forecasters were excessively optimistic about next year's real GDP growth performance. In rank order, eurozone forecasts are most optimistic, followed by the U.K. and U.S. forecasts. Only the Japanese forecasts appear just as optimistic before as after the GFC.[8]

One cannot be certain whether the excessive optimism is due to the promise of QE, but it is likely to have been one of the key factors at play. If so, QE has, so far, successfully persuaded at least some forecasters that higher growth lies ahead. Invariably, these forecasts have had to be revised downward. But there is also a cautionary tale here, because it can also be seen that, in all four economies shown in figure 7.3, pessimism in 2008 rose quickly and persistently until the central banks intervened. It is precisely whether this success can be repeated in light of recent economic performance that is in question.

Even if there are many elements in the story of central banking during the past decade or so, and there is recognition that monetary and financial policies cannot on their own solve all the ills of the global economy, we can ask whether what has been accomplished to date has improved the credibility and resilience of monetary policy to respond to major economic shocks. Equally important, assuming that monetary authorities generally have lost some credibility and reputation, is to ask whether some claims made for recent reforms and policies have contributed to restoring economies to better health and, perhaps more critically, whether the role of monetary policy for financial stabilization is as reliable as it was once claimed to be. As pointed out in earlier chapters (e.g., see chapters 4 and 6), this questioning may translate into a return to

---

[7] These are from *The Economist*. Other professional forecasters (e.g., Consensus Economics) produce a similar interpretation as the one described here.

[8] For the eurozone, the crude calculation would have led to 35 months of optimistic forecasts but optimism reigned for 50 months; the same figures for the United Kingdom are 31 versus 43; for the United States, 31 versus 42; and 26 versus 28 for Japan.

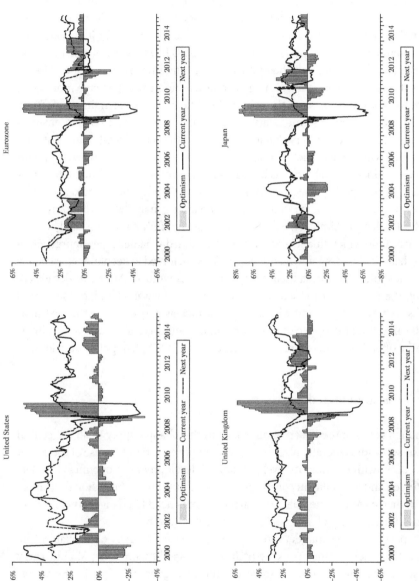

FIGURE 7.3 Optimism and Pessimism in Real GDP Growth Forecasts

Note: Current and next year calendar year forecasts for real GDP growth in the four countries are shown. The difference between next year's forecast and this year's forecast is a measure of optimism (positive) or pessimism (negative). *Source:* Author's calculations.

an era when there was a less clear division of responsibility between monetary policy, financial stability, and fiscal policy.

One notable exception here is the ECB. Relative to many of the other central banks considered in this book, it is both still in its infancy and the only central bank that, curiously, was designed to be the only game in town. Yet, in the event of an unforeseen financial crisis, its response would be statutorily limited in the support it could provide to the sovereign states it is nominally accountable to. Instead, policymakers at the ECB have chosen innovation and experimentation to stretch the ECB's mandate and increase the scope of its interventions. How far such a strategy can be extended and, perhaps more critically, whether it can sustain the required political support remain in question.

It is precisely because monetary policy could no longer on its own ensure a complete economic recovery that at least some of the central banks have lost their way. Conveying what monetary policy can or cannot do, especially when the maintenance of financial stability has become paramount, is accomplished rather tentatively, in part perhaps because to do communicate effectively would also shine a light on the other *sine qua non* of central banking, namely its autonomy from political influence. Similarly, policy decisions are not fully communicated because the manner in which financial stability is maintained—namely, the suppression of risk—has felt like a trap in which policymakers are forced to keep monetary policy looser for longer to forestall another economic downturn. After two decades of telling the public that monetary policy should be forward looking, the central banks are now in a position where the past is increasingly dictating the next steps to take in setting the stance of monetary policy. This is certainly one way to interpret the often-repeated resort to "data dependence" to explain policy decisions.

A Few Essential Ingredients

Although some of the observations made in this chapter apply to all the central banks, some idiosyncratic responses will be required, either because of the size of the economy in question, its level of financial development or openness to external forces, and any political constraints, to name but three factors. Equally important is that, even if some policies or arrangements need to change, others should remain unchanged. What is not broken does not need fixing.

In particular, the mandate for low and stable inflation is unassailable. The desire to achieve some measure of financial stability, however, should carry the same flexibility as proved so successful for monetary policy in the 2000s. Similarly, having clear rules is inherently desirable; nevertheless, this situation has to be coupled with contingencies covering when those rules are no longer appropriate for meeting the central bank's mandate. Lastly, there needs to be more clarity concerning how decisions are made and the conditions under which actions are taken.

The notion of "data dependence" has been taken too far and, as just noted, moves us significantly away from the central banks' avowed attempts to convince policymakers and the public that best practice dictates looking ahead when assessing the impact of current decisions. Arguably, data dependence as it is commonly understood—that is, a wait-and-see attitude—poses the greatest danger in that central banks might repeat the Japanese experience of the 1990s and 2000s.[9] A particularly egregious example is the BoJ's attempt to explain the inability to achieve its 2% inflation target (also, see chapter 6). In a report assessing the results to date of the 2013 shift in policy strategy, the BoJ argues that expectations are more anchored to past inflation performance than they are in other advanced economies.[10] Of course, the BoJ's leap from an effective zero percent inflation target to 2% was, as pointed out earlier, neither credible nor justified. The failure is the BoJ's, which has been unable to convincingly explain why 2% is the new price stability metric, when previously zero percent was thought to fulfill the definition.

In addition, the central banks have perhaps unwittingly become too imperial in their stabilization policy role. The ideal of a more modest institution, certainly critical to ensuring adequate economic conditions, is not in question. What is in question, however, is whether the scope of their authority in delivering monetary policy and financial stability oversteps the bounds of acceptable democratic accountability and best practice.

Finally, the central banks can and should advocate for greater international cooperation, but not coordination other than at crisis times. They cannot effectively do so, however, unless they convince politicians that this will bring about improved macroeconomic outcomes. This greater cooperation will also require a rethink of the remit of many central banks. Unless a truly global central bank is envisioned, which is a very low probability event, the central banks remain symbols of sovereignty.

Should the Unconventional Become Conventional?

In principle, there is little that is unconventional about a central bank policy that relies on the balance sheet as a major instrument in its monetary policy toolkit. The notion that monetary policy has become unconventional owes as

---

[9] Geithner 2014:323 recalls that Larry Summers, himself a former Treasury secretary, defined Japanese policy as "watchful waiting." This is also reminiscent of the debate inside the FOMC about whether the Fed would watch financial developments "closely" or "carefully" (Federal Reserve 2008:79–85).

[10] See Bank of Japan 2016: app. chart 3. In other words, expectations in Japan are more adaptive than elsewhere, with the implication that the Japanese place much more weight on past inflation performance (by a factor of almost seven times the U.S. estimate) than on expected future inflation outcomes. The Japanese, however, appear far less backward-looking when core inflation is used.

much to a desire to return to the status quo ante as to the observation that certain assets or liabilities don't belong on the balance sheet of a public institution (e.g., publicly traded shares, private assets). Both notions underscore the unusual nature of actions recently taken by several central banks. Had these actions lasted only a short time, the extraordinary aspects of events that took place in 2008–9 might have been overlooked and would now be the subject of historical reflections rather than the subject of continuing debate and controversy. In any event, it did not take long for analysts would begin to question what the central banks were trying to accomplish.

For example, "What other central banks have been doing must be reversed. I am very sceptical about the extent of the Fed's actions and the way the Bank of England has carved its own little line in Europe," and "We must return to independent and sensible monetary policies, otherwise we will be back to where we are now in 10 years' time" (Benoit and Atkins 2009). "The world needs central bankers who avoid problems, not those who specialize in post-damage control. For that reason, alone, he should not be reappointed" (Roach 2009). The last comment reflects the period when Fed Chair Ben Bernanke's reappointment in 2009 and 2010 was being debated. Even if one agrees with some of these sentiments, the complaints fail to acknowledge the need for a crisis management strategy when things go wrong, as they occasionally do. It is possible to praise the central banks' responses following the GFC while simultaneously criticizing their failure to prevent a crisis in the first place.

Doubts about what monetary policy can accomplish at the ZLB partly reflect a lack of comfort with the fallout from this new environment the central banks were facing, as the following comment makes clear:

> [T]he Fed chairman outlined how policy could evolve once short-term interest rates get to near zero. A key focus in such an environment will be to bring down long-term interest rates, which help determine the rates of mortgages and other debt instruments. This would likely involve in practice the Fed buying longer-term Treasury bonds. . . . Such actions will not solve the problem but will merely compound it, by adding debt to debt. (Wood 2008)

Yet, the state of affairs that some central bankers found themselves in originated in (post-crisis) a hesitation to breach the ZLB, led by Japan's example starting in the 1990s, as well as in an unwillingness to convey to the public the idea that the era of a single instrument (i.e., the policy rate) to meet a single objective (i.e., low and stable inflation) was coming to an end. It is, therefore, not surprising that central banks such as the Fed were planning an exit from balance sheet policies even as the financial crisis was still raging.

Indeed, it was not long after forward guidance was reintroduced into the language of central banking, beginning in 2009, when the Bank of Canada (for example) pledged to keep the policy rate at the then ZLB for a year, that several voices inside the FOMC were becoming uncomfortable with the tension between historically low policy rates for an indefinite future and the potential ineffectiveness of monetary policy. Unfortunately, as we have seen (see chapter 6), forward guidance, which was intended to shape expectations about the scope and duration of the unconventional policy, was undermined by resorting to a dogma that seemed out of place under the circumstances.[11]

Nevertheless, the impression is that what could not be done explicitly, because policy rates were near or already at the ZLB, could be done at least partially through conditional promises to act. As discussed in chapter 5 (also see chapter 1), after a time, this was seen an illusion. The crux of the problem lay in the inability to articulate how forward guidance could affect expectations, even if the central bank were credible. Having successfully persuaded policymakers and many academics that monetary policy could only eventually be neutral, there was no persuasive narrative about how the financial environment engineered by the central banks could trigger the other nonmonetary changes that lay at the heart of the current weak economic environment. Now that the ZLB has been overcome, it seems more like a sign of desperation or a confidence trick, rather than a well-articulated policy to generate economic growth via favorable policy conditions.[12]

Even before QE1 was launched by the Fed in 2008, many in the FOMC thought that monetary policy was sufficiently accommodative. Members were also aware of the risks of not appearing forward looking enough to remain credible in the face of mounting criticisms for past failures. Indeed, the transcript of the meeting that preceded the introduction of QE1, on September 16, 2008, finds Fed Chair Bernanke echoing the sentiment of many on the FOMC when he indicated that:

> I also agree with those who say that, when the time comes, we do need to be prompt at removing accommodation. It is just as much a mistake to move too late and allow inflation, and perhaps even financial imbalances, to grow as it is to move too early and be premature in terms of assuming a recovery. I think that is a very difficult challenge for us going forward, and I acknowledge the importance of that. (Federal Reserve Board of Governors 2008 [Bernanke]:76)

---

[11] For example, Fischer 2015, vice-chair of the FOMC, would not acknowledge that the link between inflation and unemployment, such as the one hypothesized by the Phillips Curve, was broken, but he admitted that it was never strong. As we shall see, this could well represent an understatement of the relationship between aggregate real activity and price movements.

[12] As discussed earlier, in the academic literature several years before the GFC, negative interest rates were seen as a viable alternative under certain conditions. It was not the feasibility of negative rates that was in question but, rather, the unknown consequences for the banking system in particular, for the financial system more generally, and for the need to implement other potentially far reaching reforms (e.g., eliminating cash, changing the ability to exchange certain deposits to cash or vice-versa on a par basis) that are problematic or currently not feasible.

Consider also the following passage, almost two years later, from the August 10, 2010, FOMC meeting transcript. At the time, the Fed's balance sheet reached its apogee and the committee was seeking ways to reverse course as the economic recovery, albeit seemingly unsatisfactory, was taking hold. The ZLB had been in place for only a little over a year and a half.

> A key problem that we face is that conventional interest rate policies could become passive. Under current policy, when a negative shock is encountered, we cannot react by lowering the policy rate, and we can only react by altering the length of time financial markets expect that we will remain with a near-zero rate policy. This tool has some theoretical backing, but it is suspect from a practical perspective. We are talking about extending promises to stay at zero many quarters or years in the future, depending on how the economy performs. The effectiveness of such a tool depends on the foresight of the private sector, our own credibility, and the length of the horizon. I submit that the effectiveness of this tool is questionable at this point. It's okay with me to try to manipulate these expectations, but I think we should supplement that policy with a more tangible policy. The policy to stay at near-zero rates for a long time can also be counterproductive. That policy is also consistent with a mildly deflationary steady state like Japan's. Escape from that type of outcome is problematic. (Federal Reserve Board of Governors 2010 [Bullard]:29)

Of course, as previously discussed (see chapters 5 and 6), the "counterproductive" elements of Japan's original policies to fight deflation and falling economic growth stem from a combination of their small size, the unwillingness or inability of policymakers to convey their importance, and the excessive reliance on "data dependence" as the trigger for their removal.

As this is written, we are entering the seventh year since the sentiments just expressed, or comparable ones, were written. Either policymakers have become more comfortable with the actions they have taken or they cannot bring themselves to see a return to interest rates that appear more normal relative to historical norms. It bears asking why, during the same 2010 FOMC meeting, then vice-chair Donald Kohn argued:

> A key question over the past year is why the economy hasn't responded more vigorously to the very accommodative monetary policy and fiscal policy. Our answer has been that spenders have faced a number of restraining forces—headwinds—that are expected to abate gradually, producing faster economic growth down the road when the effects of those really low interest rates begin to take over. (Federal Reserve Board of Governors 2010 [Kohn]:62)

Unfortunately, over six years later, "headwinds" apparently continue to hamper the return to a pre-crisis type of economic growth.

Changing the Message and Improving the Strategy

Policymakers in the central banks understood that they could create an environment for faster economic growth, but not the conditions that convince financial markets and the public that a pre-GFC state of the world has resumed. Yet, this message was often conflated with fears of the consequences of taking action, such as depressing economic activity, promoting excessive inflation, or both. Regrettably, the international community, almost a decade after the first indications of the magnitude of the GFC were becoming apparent, still advocates what can only be considered "unfinished business," as the following recommendations from the IMF to the G20, published in the summer of 2016, highlight:

> Where demand is still falling short, this requires a broad-based approach that exploits policy synergies by combining structural and balance sheet reforms with continued monetary support and growth-friendly fiscal policies—including using available fiscal space, anchored by strong policy frameworks. Stronger domestic demand support, especially in creditor countries with policy space, would also help reduce external imbalances. (IMF 2016:1)

Unfortunately (see chapter 1), sentiments such as these could also be found soon after the GFC erupted.

But there are other reasons why monetary policy appears not to be as effective as in the past, including an impairment of the monetary transmission mechanism. This is partly apparent from the earlier discussion about the state of lending standards, which does not appear to reflect in a convincing manner the desire of the monetary authorities to encourage the necessary borrowing that would bring about stronger economic growth. To be sure, the degree of impairment is unevenly distributed, with some economies and sectors affected more than others. Nor can the situation be divorced from attempts to redefine the regulatory space within which financial institutions operate. Nevertheless, there is a sense that the conditions created by several central banks are decoupling from what might be expected, as a result of the borrowing activities in some sectors of many economies.

The current state of affairs also reflects the tension between a wish to keep monetary policy loose, allowing the aggregate economy to heal sufficiently, and the tendency of households, among others, to pile up debt that will become much more difficult to service if and when interest rates rise substantially higher, even if those interest rates continue to be lower than the historical norm. No doubt more than one central banker sympathizes with the governor of the Swedish Riksbank, who on the eve of launching its own experiment with QE, in January 2015, commented in the minutes of the December 2014 meeting, "Another central problem is that housing prices and household indebtedness are increasing rapidly. Mr. Ingves pointed out, as he has done on many previous occasions, that we really would need two policy rates—one for companies and another, higher rate for households" (Riksbank 2014:6).

The comment, of course, brings to mind the role of macroprudential policies, but as we have also seen, these involve decisions that are more often political, adding to the central banks' discomfort at being unable to differentiate financial stability elements of policy from monetary policy proper. No wonder, then, that over a quarter of a century ago, Paul Volcker, the former Fed chair credited with taming the high inflation of the late 1970s, expressed the tension between price and financial stability as follows: "We need to return to a more stable financial system partly so that monetary policy itself can be free to act more in response to concerns about inflation and the stability of the currency instead of in defense of the financial system itself" (Volcker 1991:179).

In addition, central banks, especially in the industrial world, must now confront a problem of their own making: the contradiction between a belief that they are autonomous from government and a sense that they are unable to exit until "data dependent" conditions permit. Yet, a reading of MPC minutes from the last few years suggests a concern about losing credibility. Consider, for example, the following scenarios laid out by the former secretary to the FOMC when, during the 2008 meeting that preceded the QE1 in the United States, he summarized the existing policy environment as follows:

> The discussion at your last meeting suggested that you generally saw the next move in policy as likely to be a firming, a point that was explicit in the minutes of the meeting. Even though market volatility and financial strains have increased notably in recent weeks, you might view those developments as having only limited implications for the economic outlook and hence see economic fundamentals as continuing to suggest that policy should soon be firmed. Inflation has been well above the rates that Committee members judge as appropriate for the longer run, and despite lower oil prices and greater slack in labor markets, there remains considerable uncertainty about how soon and how much core inflation will slow. In these circumstances, you may believe that a firming of policy is appropriate. . . .
>
> But at the same time, you may want . . . to let the dust settle a bit before concluding that these developments warrant an adjustment in your policy stance. In particular, you may think there is a good chance that the latest enhancements to the Federal Reserve's special liquidity facilities will help keep markets functioning and mitigate the risks to growth. (FOMC transcript, September, 16, 2008:25–26)

Hesitation is partly a reflection of "data dependence" but can also be thought of representing a loss of faith in the Fed's policy strategy. In other words, such a reaction represents a desire to avoid being "time inconsistent." The fact that a Presidential election was looming may also have played a role.

Nevertheless, there are echoes of the same problem at other central banks. For example, the minutes of the Bank of England's MPC meeting in January 2009, the month before the United Kingdom's version of QE would be introduced, recorded the following impression about views circulating at the meeting:

> The Committee discussed whether, amidst all the news about the outlook for growth, there remained any substantial upside risks to inflation over the next few years. These could arise, for example, from a sharp fall in the exchange rate, beyond that warranted by economic fundamentals; a renewed surge in commodity prices; or a quicker than expected rebound in the real economy. But, on balance, the weakening prospects for output growth, at home and abroad, suggested that the balance of risks to the medium-term inflation outlook remained to the downside. (Bank of England 2009:7–8)

These words appear to suggest that the committee felt it was on the cusp of further monetary stimulus, but was not yet ready to announce such a move. Hence, it was less a matter of data dependence, since the data clearly pointed to a need for additional monetary easing, and more that the time was not yet ripe to take the next step. There are other things to consider besides simply acting on the messages contained in the "data."

A final illustration is from the ECB's own foray into QE beginning in 2015. Unlike other central banks, we had to wait until 2015 for the ECB to publish an "account" of the Governing Council's (GC) meeting. A press conference follows each Governing Council decision, and in the December 2014 edition, ECB President Mario Draghi summarized the opinion of the GC as follows:

> [E]arly next year the Governing Council will reassess the monetary stimulus achieved, the expansion of the balance sheet and the outlook for price developments. . . .. The Governing Council will continue to closely monitor the risks to the outlook for price developments over the medium term. In this context, we will focus in particular on the possible repercussions of dampened growth dynamics, geopolitical developments, exchange rate and energy price developments, and the pass-through of our monetary policy measures. We will be particularly vigilant as regards the broader impact of recent oil price developments on medium-term inflation trends in the euro area. (European Central Bank 2014; Press Conference, December)[13]

---

[13] The link is https://www.ecb.europa.eu/press/pressconf/2014/html/is141204.en.html.

The GC had or would very soon reach a tipping point at which it would introduce a European-style QE. Indeed, the account of the January 2015 meeting suggests they were building up to a decision, rather than using "data dependence," as in the following:

> Taking into account both the weakened medium-term outlook for price stability and the smaller than envisaged monetary stimulus introduced by the policy measures adopted in June and September 2014, the prevailing degree of monetary policy accommodation was seen to fall short of sufficiently countering the heightened risks to the ECB's medium-term price stability objective. (European Central Bank 2015)

The ECB clearly was unsure about the impact of its policies or the way ahead, but was also unwilling to be seen as doing nothing.

The upshot of this is that central banks have fallen into the trap of insisting that their policies are unconventional, which while true to a point cannot be interpreted in this manner so many years after they were labeled as such. In fact, MPC members infrequently employed this terminology, simply insisting that resorting to such policies is necessary under the circumstances. To whit, the September 2008 FOMC transcripts, just referred to, record commentary of the following tenor:

> I am fully supportive of the actions that we take in terms of liquidity—the TAF[14] and the other efforts to provide liquidity into the market. These are tools that we can and should use for these kinds of shocks in a short-term context. On the other hand, I would encourage the Committee to resist the impulse to ease policy in a sense of doing something. The issue is not the level of our policy rate at this time. It is the dysfunction of the markets that we hope our liquidity efforts will help address. To begin to talk about easing or even to put language in there that suggests easing is to cause people, on the expectation that we might ease at some point even if we hold off now, to delay decisions that they would otherwise make that would benefit the economy. I also encourage us to look beyond the immediate crisis, which I recognize is serious. (Federal Reserve Board of Governors 2008 [Hoenig]:31)

Perhaps it would have been better for the central banks to emphasize the unusual nature of their policies, suggesting that these will some day be reversed,

---

[14] This refers to the Term Auction Facility. In 2007, when short-term liquidity was beginning to dry up, the Fed provided access to short-term funds even to financial institutions that were not stressed. However, to avoid the stigma of borrowing from the lender of last resort, the Fed effectively designed a program wherein it would act as a facilitator to prevent the diminution of liquidity without their seeming to be borrowing directly from the Fed. The program ended in 2010. See www.federalreserve.gov/newsevents/reform_taf.htm.

but they would be available in the future under certain well-specified conditions. Instead, as Yellen (2016), among other central bankers, have claimed, it is the increased number of tools that can be used in implementing monetary policy that has been advertised. The difficulty is that many if not most of these tools blur the line between monetary and fiscal policies that the central banks have sought for so long to ingrain in the public's mind. Almost a decade later, instead of inspiring confidence, this blurring invites a further erosion in the credibility of the central banks.

If, as some of the discussion in chapter 6 and chapter 1 suggests, words matter, then these policies should be emphasized as appropriate under the circumstances, introduced and withdrawn when the time is ripe; that communication should also encourage having considerable patience for them to work. However, this is not sufficient, since the lines of accountability remain unclear. Because central banks are institutions within, and not separate from, government, there is a need for directives to be in place to determine for determining which of these policies is deemed temporary, and that there are in place assessments of their maintenance subject to review at regular intervals. And precisely because these policies can easily extend beyond the normal time horizon of the political cycle, any policies deemed unconventional or unusual ought to be portrayed as a joint decision of government and the central bank, even if the latter has the responsibility to enact them. Moreover, to minimize the possibility that the burden of stabilization policy should fall mostly, if not entirely, on the central bank, some accountability should rest with government to ensure that its fiscal policy is compatible with monetary policy and remains so over time. Clearly, there is room to tailor these arrangements to fit the specific political and other considerations that dictate how these institutional arrangements are set up.[15]

A place to start might be the formal separation of balance sheet activities with the potential for fiscal spillovers. Some examples already exist (e.g., at the Bank of England). Alternatively, some form of consolidation of fiscal and monetary authorities' balance sheets might be preferable in some jurisdictions. Ultimately, since preservation of the separation principle between central banks and government is deemed best practice, a clear and precise policy indemnifying the central banks for policies that may have fiscal implications is yet another option. The Fed, the Bank of Canada, and the Bank of England offer models for this kind of arrangement. The Fed's is in the form of

---

[15] This means that there needs to be serious attention paid to some of the ideas in the fiscal theory of the price level. Sims 2016 is a recent and readable account, as well as a good source for main references on the topic. It should be noted, however, that the fiscal theory does not square well with the Japanese experience, dismissed by Sims for other reasons, nor does the Brazilian case he also refers to ring true. Sims might also have relied on Canada's experience during the 1980s, when the discussion of the interest cost of government debt was publicly debated.

a requirement that the government direct the central bank to change policies, with the onus for the decision resting on government. In this case, there is an understanding between the Fed and the U.S. Treasury that broadly defines their respective roles. Nevertheless, it is imperative that all such models be revisited from time to time. It should be presumed that statutory solutions meant to forestall some unanticipated scenario are never timeless; they are usually creatures of past crises.

Central banks have apparently taken only partially to heart Franklin Roosevelt's advice: "It is common sense to take a method and try it. If it fails, admit it frankly, and try another. But above all try something" (Roosevelt 1932). However, where the monetary authorities have gone wrong is in not admitting failure or a lack of success as they continue to experiment. Equally important, they have failed to remember the lesson learned long ago that monetary policy must consistently act in concert with fiscal policy. This means giving it space to work when monetary conditions allow and reducing its scope when it is economically inappropriate. The heavy lifting in matters of stabilization policy, it seems, is still largely left to monetary policy.

So far, these ideas rest exclusively on the domestic dimension of monetary policy. The international dimension requires a different approach, as we shall see.

The Inflation Solution and Deflation Mongering

Although the continued disappointment with the overall state of the economy has many sources, monetary policy is only one of them. QE and interest rates low for longer, if not negative interest rates, have so far proved to be the instruments that have prevented even worse outcomes, and they are to have contributed to economic recovery. Nevertheless, a distinction needs to be made between QE as a means of ensuring smooth functioning of the financial markets within a loose monetary policy and UE's role in helping economies recover. There is likely little disagreement about monetary policy's success concerning the smooth functioning (e.g., see Gagnon 2016; Lombardi, Siklos, and St. Amand 2017 forthcoming), but considerably more skepticism about economic recovery. Indeed, the evidence presented in this book gives credence to the anxiety concerning the objectives of QE, if not its duration. Even if the net result is positive, we are still evaluating the potential costs of asset price inflation.

Beyond any other improvements via the application of fiscal policy or providing a list of "structural" reforms, both of which are beyond the scope of this book, is there anything else that monetary policy can do? Are there policies that central banks should avoid implementing? Is there a risk that past interventions represent a slippery slope that portends permanently harming the institution of central banking?

Assuming the problem is that the stance of policy is still not loose enough to remove some of the impediments to stronger and more persistent economic growth, then is higher inflation part of the solution? After all, higher inflation would reduce the debt burden to the sovereign and other debt holders, whereas if both short-term and long-term interest rates are kept low for longer, the future burden of current borrowing is reduced. Unfortunately, as is often the case, this is only one side of the argument. More recent suggestions to raise inflation modestly from the 2% goal, which is part of the remit of many central banks in the advanced economies, to 4% often rest on the belief that this would give the central banks more room, in the future, should they face the constraint of the ZLB. However, this assumes that the entire burden of reaching the ZLB rests with monetary policy. Policymakers themselves admit that there are other reasons for inflation seemingly being too low and the blame does not have to rest entirely with a 2% inflation objective, nor do central banks have to rush to the ZLB with impunity when inflation rates underperform relative to the target. This is the point of using a central bank's balance sheet as an additional source of policy easing.

Indeed, if inflation is part of the solution, one has to ask why the policy has not been adopted earlier. After all, Ken Rogoff (2008) suggests: "Fortunately, creating inflation is not rocket science. . . . [T]he main fear is that inflation could overshoot. . . . [F]ear of overshooting paralyzed the Bank of Japan for a decade. But this problem is easily negotiated. With good communication policy, inflation expectations can be contained, and inflation can be brought down as quickly as necessary." Were it so simple.

I have earlier discussed the persistence of inflation, which in spite of better communication however one wishes to defines this, makes a quick decline once inflation has risen to what is believed to be an acceptable level a difficult feat to achieve (e.g., see chapter 1). Indeed, the central bankers' favorite word in recent years—the ever-present "headwinds"—testifies to this persistence in making the central bank's best-laid plans go awry. Three years after "better communication" and a 2% inflation target, the Bank of Japan is nowhere near reaching its inflation objective. Equally important is that inflation has, on many occasions, not only been prone to overshooting some objective but has, more than once, led central banks astray because it was not at all clear to whether the source of the problem was demand or supply factors. Perhaps more important, the reference to the Japanese experience is misleading, since during the 2000s the inflation objective, largely supported by the public, was closer to 0%, not the 2% goal adopted elsewhere.

Consider also Janet Yellen's comment in the transcript from the August 10, 2010, FOMC meeting when the Fed funds rate had been at ZLB for over a year and a half and the Fed's balance sheet stood at its peak. Yellen reflected the views of several others on the committee when she stated, "[t]he accommodative stance of monetary policy is providing considerable support to private sector spending. Nonetheless, that stimulus may ultimately prove insufficient to overcome a daunting list of headwinds, including tight credit, impaired household balance sheets, a housing overhang, state and local budget crises, and heightened uncertainty" (Federal Reserve Board of Governors 2010 [Yellen]:43). It is doubtful that monetary policy, let alone higher inflation, represents a viable solution to all of these problems.

Other claims we have considered earlier point to doubts about the presumed low costs of permitting an extra 2% inflation. While such estimates may well be plausible, they are for the most part based on models—often the same flawed models as have been used to criticize the profession—and not on the historical experience. A flaw in such arguments is that we simply do not know with any precision at what point the marginal benefits of an extra 1% inflation exceed the marginal costs. The profession has devoted considerable effort to answering this question, and the only agreement is that the state of economic and institutional development likely warrants a considerably lower inflation for more highly developed economies than those that are in earlier stages of economic development.[16]

The belief that declarations are enough, that inflation expectations can be manipulated relatively easily, and that a spurt of inflation will sufficiently grease the wheels to generate strong economic growth is tantamount to rejecting some fairly clear empirical and historical facts, as discussed in chapters 1, 4, and 6. I have already mentioned the difficulty of finding support for the first two claims. The third claim rests in part on the inability of our most cherished macroeconomic models to show that a connection exists between inflation and economic growth at all times. Hall (2013:3) bluntly summarizes many of these difficulties as follows:

> Since the birth of the Phillips curve of the 1950s, the idea has dazzled macroeconomists that inflation depends on tightness or slack. Yet extreme slack has done little to reduce inflation over the past five years (fortunately) and extreme tightness in the late 1990s did not result in much inflation. . . . But the model has yet to appear that embodies anchoring in a persuasive way. The New Keynesian model has a major role for expectations, but only because of a mechanical feature preventing businesses from responding to shifts in demand except with a substantial lag.

To illustrate, consider figure 7.4, which consists of six parts (a–f). Each part illustrates the relationship between inflation, measured on the horizontal axis,

---

[16] There is a rich literature on the welfare costs if inflation. McCallum 1989: sec. 6.7 has a comprehensive discussion of the literature until the late 1980s. Estimates of the costs of inflation are based on abstract models, from which one can conclude that, say, the costs of a rise from 2% to 4% in inflation may well be small. A more recent analysis that also highlights the sensitivity of these kinds of calculations to model assumptions is Gorodnichenko 2010. However, these calculations ignore the costs incurred from the loss of reputation or trust in the central banks.

and real economic growth, measured on the vertical axis for the United States, the United Kingdom, the eurozone, Japan, Canada, and Sweden. Economic growth is evaluated at four critical moments in time, as earlier analysis demonstrated not only the importance of assessing information in real time but also so as to understand what policymakers saw at the time the decisions were made. The top left graph in each figure shows growth as known in January 2015— that is, well after the recovery began and the GFC had passed. The lower left graph has data as known in December 2006—that is, on the eve of the GFC. The top right graph reveals what was known about economic growth around the height of QE in May 2010, while the lower right graph shows what was known in December 2008, when the Fed reduced the policy rate to the ZLB, near the high point of the GFC.

Other than the fact that the three IT economies shown—the United Kingdom, Canada, and Sweden—appear to generate inflation rates within the target ranges set for their central banks, Hall's (2013) diagnosis of the situation rings true. It is simply not always the case that higher inflation results in higher economic growth, and there is certainly no evidence that any sustained higher inflation produces persistently better aggregate economic performance.[17]

Though the foregoing suggestive evidence, together with other support marshaled for the view against adopting a higher inflation strategy, is sufficiently persuasive, there is possibly one more reason for preferring higher inflation—namely the desire to avoid very low inflation or even deflation at all costs. The evidence against the destructive nature of deflation was discussed previously. Nevertheless, that such a condition is to be avoided is one of the principal arguments that both the Fed, and more recently the ECB, has voiced for higher inflation and the inability to exit from the ELB and QE.[18] For example, the

---

[17] Given the length of the sample, real GDP growth rates are shown instead of the more commonly used output gaps. In a real-time context (also see chapter 4), resorting to a more theoretically pleasing measure of economic tightness or slack would not produce a better outcome (results not shown). Moreover, especially for the GFC and QE vintages (top right and bottom right graphs), there is considerable uncertainty about the estimates of potential output. Nevertheless, it does remain true that if the economics profession were ever to arrive at a broad consensus on how to measure economic slack, the results such as that shown in figure 7.4 might well look different. It is interesting to note a growing preference, in U.S. policy circles, in using the unemployment rate gap instead of the output gap. Unfortunately, even if such a proxy for economic slack is believed to be more reliable, it is unlikely to be the case when cross-country data are considered. Not only are classifications of the unemployed different across economies, but international structural differences in labor markets are also bound to make international comparisons difficult. The OECD does, however, publish unemployment data that attempt to be internationally comparable.

[18] The Bank of England and more recently the Riksbank have not faced inflation rates that were too low at the time QE was introduced in either economy. Indeed, in the BoE's case, as the frequent letters to the chancellor testify, inflation was too high.

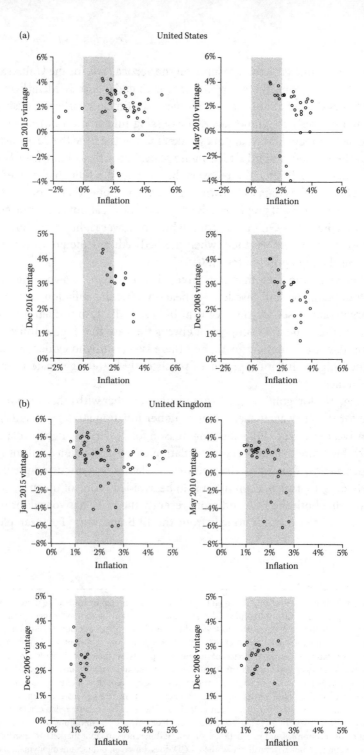

FIGURE 7.4 Economic Slack and Inflation in Real Time
(a) United States; (b) United Kingdom; (c) Eurozone; (d) Japan; (e) Canada; (f) Sweden
Note: The sampling frequency is quarterly. Inflation is the annual rate of change in the CPI. The shaded areas highlight the 1 to 3% inflation range commonly used as the target range for inflation, except for Japan, the Eurozone (less than 2% but positive), and the U.S. (medium-term range of 2% but positive). *Source:* Data are from the July 2016 edition of the IMF *International Financial Statistics* CD-ROM. Data for real GDP vintages are from the OECD Original Release data and Revisions Database http://stats.oecd.org/mei/default.asp?rev=1).

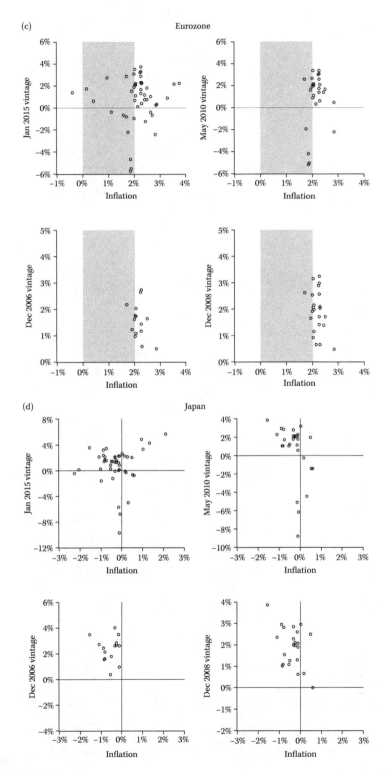

FIGURE 7.4 *(Continued)*

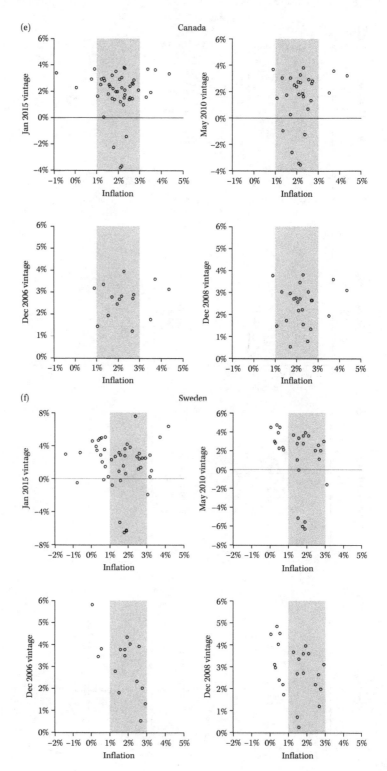

FIGURE 7.4 *(Continued)*

first published account of the ECB's GC's meeting in January 2015 set up and backed the argument in favor of QE in the following manner:

> Taking all arguments into account, the risk of an un-anchoring of inflation expectations was generally perceived as a matter of concern for the euro area and it was crucial to avoid any potential impact of the currently very low inflation rates on medium-term wage and price-setting behavior. The potential adverse impact of lower inflation expectations and low or negative inflation on real GDP growth also continued to be a matter of concern. (ECB 2015)

Evaluating the Unobserved: The Natural Rate Question

There is little evidence, based on historical experience, either that expectations are unanchored or that such departures indicate the size or nature of inflation's adverse impact on the real economy. However, even if some of the evidence is discounted, there is another reason for questioning the ECB's strategy—namely, an excessive concern about inflation performance. Also, it would appear that there is relatively less weight placed on the role of global conditions. In contrast, although much was made of how the Fed raised the profile of global factors beginning in 2016 (viz., China and later, Brexit), global worries were already on the minds of more than a few FOMC members before QE1 was launched, as made clear in these remarks in 2008 by former Fed Governor Randall Kroszner:

> As a lot of people have mentioned, the rest of the world is seeing a very significant slowdown. I think the elevated commodity prices had helped to mask a lot of the underlying fiscal and structural problems in these economies, actually much like rising housing prices in the United States had masked the problems in underwriting standards and what was going on in the mortgage market. So I think there are going to be significant challenges in a lot of countries around the world. (Federal Reserve Board of Governors 2008 [Kroszner]:65–66)

These considerations point to perhaps a key reason why QE, at least as far as supporting the real economy, appears to have been more successful in the United States than in the eurozone. Whereas the Fed emphasized the real effects of the ZLB combined with QE, the ECB was more firmly guided by the implications of such policies for inflation. Some will have drawn attention to the dual mandate of the Fed versus the price stability goal of the ECB, but it is doubtful this tells the whole story. The single-minded task of the ECB does not prevent its being concerned about the real economic motives behind its policies. Similarly, the desire for low and stable inflation has not been any less important at the Fed than at its counterpart in the eurozone.

Nevertheless, it is worth asking whether there is other evidence that can be marshaled for supporting the foregoing view. The important role of the real interest rate concept was discussed earlier (see chapters 1 and 4). While this concept is essential for understanding the degree to which monetary policy is loose or tight, an important complication arises because there are at least two real interest rate concepts involved. One concept is the real return on financial assets that is observed, ordinarily measured as the difference between the nominal asset return and some indicator of inflation. However, as economies evolve and change, and longer-term structural factors, including demographics, productivity, and financial development, evolve and so will the "natural" rate. This second concept is the real interest rate that would be sufficient to allow the economy to grow at capacity.[19] An estimate of the existing natural rate provides the clearest indication of the actual stance of monetary policy. As we have seen, estimates vary considerably, and there is as yet the unresolved matter of whether the "structural" factors alluded to earlier have led to a persistent decline in this real interest rate.

Equally interesting, and relevant in any assessment of the merits of current and past central bank decisions, is that models used by academics and central banks typically estimate these natural rates to be negative soon after the GFC erupted (e.g., Laubach and Williams 2016; Curdia et al. 2015; Barsky, Justiano, and Melosi 2014; Del Negro et al. 2015), primarily in the United States, but also elsewhere. Yet, policymakers, including the central banks and other agencies, as well as private-sector analysts, generally estimate the natural rate as remaining positive.[20] This suggests that there potentially exists a large discrepancy between policymakers' and private agents' views on the stance of monetary policy. However, this too is somewhat of an exaggeration.

For example, for each FOMC meeting, the staff prepares a large quantity of background information, including several estimates of the natural or equilibrium real rate. These are subsequently published in the Teal Books.[21] At the time of this writing, the 2010 editions were the latest published. Figure 7.5 has estimates based on the large-scale model used by the Fed (the FRB/US model) since 2002. These reveal the sharp turn to the negative in the model estimated real rate around the time of the GFC. Although current levels of the real rate are higher than when the GFC was in the most acute phase, they remained firmly negative as QE3 was launched. Nevertheless, as pointed out on several occasions

---

[19] For some, it is the real interest rate that allows the economy to grow at a trend level that can change over time. For others, it is the real interest rate that generates the aggregate level of output that is produced most efficiently. This is not the place to debate the finer, but important distinctions between various versions of the natural or "equilibrium" real interest rate. Nevertheless much of our understanding of the appropriateness of the current stance of monetary policy does hinge on some quantification of these concepts.

[20] Although all observers agree that the natural rate has fallen relative to pre-crisis samples.

[21] Previously, called the Blue Book.

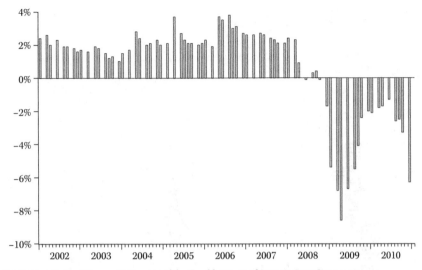

FIGURE 7.5   Federal Reserve Estimates of the Equilibrium Real Interest Rate Since 2002

Note: Prior to 2010, these books were referred to as the Blue Books. The equilibrium Fed funds rate is the observed Fed funds rate less the inflation rate in the CPI (not the PCE deflator), which produces similar results. The sampling frequency is monthly. *Source:* Based on calculations used the Federal Reserve's Teal Books (http://www.federalreserve.gov/monetarypolicy/fomc_historical.htm#tealbooks).

(e.g., see chapter 4), one must be wary of focusing too much on point estimates, particularly when a concept's numerical counterpart is not observed or cannot easily be quantified. Since various models are used by the Fed and communicated to members of the FOMC, and they can change over time, even the published estimates of confidence intervals are difficult to obtain. However, a look at the various editions of the Blue Book/Teal Book suggests that a ±3% confidence interval seems to capture the broad range of estimates of the natural rate.

Aside from the difficulties of providing a reliable estimate of the natural rate, what can we say about more recent estimates and their potential contributions to encouraging economic growth? To provide some indications, figure 7.6 shows, for seven of the advanced economies that have been considered in this chapter, estimates of the natural real rate as the difference in the policy rate less headline inflation and (other than for Switzerland) less core inflation.[22] Instead of estimating a confidence interval based on some model, an estimate of the range of natural rates is provided by using the real rate calculated from headline inflation ±3%. As noted earlier, this kind of approximate range would appear, based on historical experience, to capture the bulk of the distribution of potential values for the natural rate.

---

[22] There are two additional measures presented in the Teal Books. For the United States, inflation in the PCE headline and core indices is used. For the other economies shown, headline CPI inflation is used.

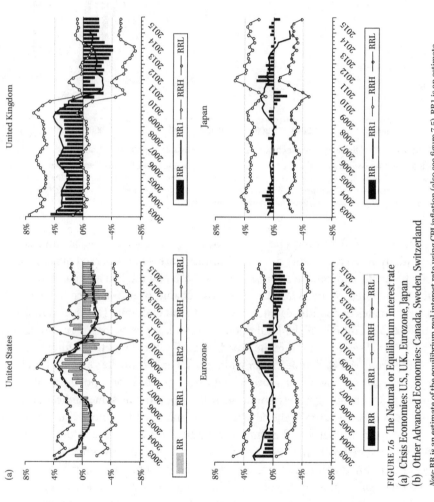

FIGURE 7.6 The Natural or Equilibrium Interest rate
(a) Crisis Economies: U.S., U.K., Eurozone, Japan
(b) Other Advanced Economies: Canada, Sweden, Switzerland

Note: RR is an estimate of the equilibrium real interest rate using CPI inflation (also see figure 7.5). RR1 is an estimate based on using core inflation (except Switzerland). RRH and RRL are proxies for the confidence interval (H means high, L means low), which assumes a ±3% variation around the mean estimates based on CPI inflation. Also, see the chapter 7 for additional definitions and details.

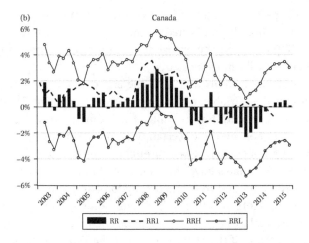

(b)

Canada

RR ---- RR1 —○— RRH —●— RRL

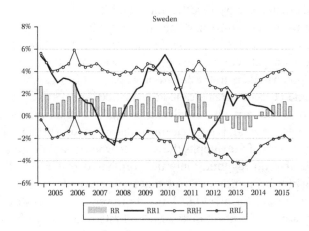

Sweden

RR —— RR1 —○— RRH —●— RRL

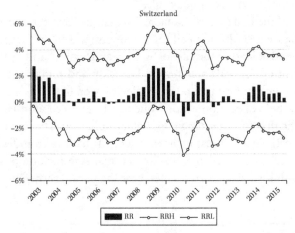

Switzerland

RR —○— RRH —●— RRL

FIGURE 7.6 (*Continued*)

As shown in part (a) of figure 7.6, the contrast in estimates among the three economies most directly implicated in the GFC—that is, the United States, the United Kingdom, and the eurozone—and the other economies is striking. Whether the real rate is measured by netting out the impact of headline or core inflation, we have to wait until the end of 2009 or early 2010 in the United States for this variable to remain persistently negative. This interpretation more or less also holds for the United Kingdom. It is true that the approximation applied to convey the uncertainty around point estimates still shows the possibility of a positive real rate throughout most of the sample. Even the most pessimistic estimates have the natural real interest rate at 1% or less in both the United States and the United Kingdom, and only beginning around mid- to late 2014. Note also that, other than Sweden, only the United States displays negative real rates over a two-year period on the eve of the GFC. This is another illustration of the charge leveled at the Fed that its policy was too loose to experience a sharp reversal until 2009.[23]

Turning to the eurozone and Japan, we see the noticeable contrast with the other two economies. In the eurozone, only the headline-based real rate measure turns negative, and only by 2012—well after the start of the GFC. Recall that policymakers in the eurozone were, for a time, smug in their belief that the single-currency area escaped the financial shocks of 2007–8. The core inflation–corrected real rate hardly turns negative at all during the period shown. The case of Japan is even clearer. Other than for a brief period in 2010, and at the very end of the sample, the real rate where headline inflation is used remains positive throughout. Only the core-based real rate indicator turns sharply negative beginning in 2013—that is, when the BoJ once again turned to a more aggressive form of QE. Notice, however, that when we allow for the uncertainty around point estimates, the real rate remains firmly positive and around or even above the 2% value that is often used in interpreting monetary policy through the prism of policy rules.

Estimates of the real rate for Canada, Sweden, and Switzerland are shown in part (b) of figure 7.6. Although all three economies were not impacted at first by the GFC, and at least in the case of Sweden and Switzerland by the eurozone sovereign debt crisis, real rates respond quickly and remain negative in the two IT economies, but remain positive, albeit lower, in the Swiss case. Clearly, even though the real economic consequences in these economies were not as acute as in the first four discussed, monetary policy does become looser fairly quickly. Nevertheless, it must be acknowledged that the confidence intervals around the headline-based measure of the real rate include positive values consistent with historical norms, at least for the period shown in the figure.

---

[23] By 2006, the Fed's Teal Book also revealed that its own models were showing negative equilibrium real rates.

Needless to say, apart from the fact that estimates of the real rate appear to broadly display the properties shown in figure 7.6, their relevance is also dependent on the concept's link to real economic growth. Normally, we would expect that if the economy's potential economic growth slows, for possible reasons first discussed in chapter 1, then the natural rate would also decline. Of course, it is worth emphasizing that the concept, at least in theory, refers to conditions prevailing when the economy is at potential, and the period considered so far is hardly conducive to this kind of interpretation. On the other hand, if it is due to the comingling of the end of the Great Moderation, the GFC, the eurozone sovereign debt crisis, and the subsequent recovery, the rates reflect the attempt of monetary policy to help stimulate economic activity; while the longer-run factors are more muted, the evidence on this score is, unfortunately, ambiguous. For the United States, Canada, Sweden, and to a lesser extent the eurozone, the simple correlation between the real rate adjusted by using headline inflation is negative (and significant).[24] For the remaining economies considered, the same correlations are not significant at all.[25]

Clearly, advocates of sharply negative policy rates can find solace in the considerable scope for easing policy. Unfortunately, the room to maneuver must be traded-off against its impact on the financial sector. There are few indications that central banks have a well-worked-out strategy to deal with this problem.[26]

The Uses and Abuses of Rules

We have seen that, even in the case of the standard Taylor Rule that summarizes how central banks are thought to conduct monetary policy in "normal" times, the inputs used by academics and policymakers are subject to a large number of choices, many of them hardly straightforward (see chapter 4). These choices include the appropriate natural or equilibrium real interest rate, how the inflation and output gaps are evaluated, how forward looking the central bank is thought to be, whether the coefficient of the response to inflation and output

---

[24] Simple correlations are: -0.6 (United States; -0.30 if using model-based estimates from the Fed; see figure 7.4); -0.51 (Canada); -0.63 (Switzerland); and -0.27 (eurozone).

[25] The simple correlations obtained are: -0.18 (United Kingdom); -0.04 (Japan); and 0.20 (Sweden).

[26] As an example, when the Bank of Japan introduced negative interest rates in 2016, the actual impact was subjected to a complex set of thresholds to blunt the anticipated effect on the banking system. Meanwhile, the Fed and the United Kingdom are reluctant to join in and allow negative policy rates (e.g., see Bernanke 2016). Even the Bank of Canada, another holdout when it comes to negative policy rates, has reluctantly accepted that, while feasible, negative interest rates need not be the most desirable option to further loosen monetary policy. Most recently, Goodfriend 2016 has advocated dismissing the ZLB altogether. Of course, the reforms needed to "unemcumber" interest rates at the ZLB are far from straightforward to implement (also, see n.10 this chapter). In particular, banks have some room to maintain profitability by increasing non-interest income, an element not examined by Goodfriend 2016. In this connection see, for example, Jobst and Lin 2016.

gap shocks ought to be predetermined or estimated at different times with the available data, and even the extent to which real-time data considerations can skew the picture for the appropriate setting of the policy rate, as the economic environment changes over time.[27]

Nevertheless, all such rules do have something in common—namely, an attempt to provide an objective assessment of where the central bank's policy rate ought to be. As is true with estimates of the natural or equilibrium rate of interest, this means that allowance should be made for the likely uncertainty of such estimates. This does not, however, contradict the desirability of relying on straightforward attempts to understand the stance of monetary policy, and more importantly, of providing a platform for policymakers and the public to understand the various pressures to change that stance of monetary policy.

A different perspective on relying on rules as a means of providing advice about the appropriate stance of monetary policy (as opposed to an automatic device to evaluate whether monetary policy is too loose or tight) is to consider the language of monetary policy. While helpful for and important in obtaining a sense of the various demands on policymakers, language is no substitute for formal indicators of the environment or the conditions that influence setting the policy rate relative to some outcome that would be predicted by a rule.[28] While statements from speeches given by the central bankers provide some examples, arguably a better way is to consider the choices available to policymakers at the time a change in policy stance is being considered. There is no better illustration of this than the U.S. Fed and the Teal Book/Blue Book mentioned earlier. The staff always provides alternative language in the press release that accompanies the Fed funds rate announcement. It is instructive to have some examples that illustrate why, assuming other central banks face the same dilemma (which is a likely scenario), the central bank's explanation of its policy response cannot substitute for more effective means of conveying what is being done and how far it may be from what others think it ought to be.

FOMC members are quite familiar with the language inherited from previous Fed funds rate announcements; while alternative language might be considered sometimes (perhaps more often than not) it is a sin of omission to not employ it at times. Hence, for example, in February 2005, the language finally adopted excluded changes in perceptions about the balancing inflation risks. The Fed was considering a range of options, from leaving the Fed funds rate unchanged to a rise of 50bp. Although alternatives included mention of "robust" economic growth, the actual press release was more subdued, with

---

[27] I have not even considered more complex rules that add financial asset prices or a real exchange rate, or more exotic versions of the rule that allow for even more flexibility (e.g., nonlinearity) to capture a wider variety of economic environments.

[28] A reminder (also see chapters 1 and 4) that a policy rate as predicted by any imposed or estimated policy rule need not be optimal, in the sense that it is occasionally used by economists when they treat the policymaking decision as if it were an optimal control problem.

moderate the word used to describe the pace of aggregate economic activity.[29] By 2006, a more optimistic tone was adopted, as opposed to expressing worries over real economic performance. By October of 2006, the Fed was no longer sitting on the fence when it came to a tightening of the stance of monetary policy, by insisting that the balance of risks was on the tightening side. One alternative, later rejected, was a rise in the Fed funds rate. However, this seemed inconsistent with the suggestion that economic growth was slowing "further," a word that does not appear in the Fed's press release.[30] Once the GFC was in full swing, the Fed changed its communication strategy in at least two ways. Initially, the concern was over how to portray the risks of inflation when commodity prices have risen sharply while there were signs of an economic slowdown. By 2010, the FOMC was zeroing in on a few words while decomposing the language of the press release into a larger number of categories, a reflection of the introduction of UMP together with the need to remind the public of the importance of its dual mandate in a ZLB environment. In debating the language to appear in the published statement in November, for example, the FOMC resorted to indicating that progress toward achieving the dual mandate was "disappointingly slow,"[31] instead of the "unacceptably low" wording that was one alternative considered in the Blue Book.[32]

The foregoing is not to suggest that the Fed, or for that matter any other central bank, is dissembling in its attempt to convey the stance its current monetary policy and its outlook. Rather, it is a reminder that language is considerably rich with words, together with a recognition that what is not said (which then limits the information that can be usefully extracted from, say, press releases) may be just as important as what is said. Actions can and do speak louder than words. To be sure, communication that is clear and fairly conveys the views of the committee is an essential ingredient of best practice in monetary policy. However, unless the public is expected to apply an algorithm of some kind to translate the content of these press releases and other forms of central bank communications, language can never substitute for action when the circumstances are ripe.

Leaving the Status Quo Ante Behind

In the preface to the 1982 edition of his *Capitalism and Freedom* (2002: xiv), Milton Friedman argued: "Only a crisis—actual or perceived—produces real change. When that crisis occurs, the actions that are taken depend on the ideas

---

[29] See table 1, at www.federalreserve.gov/monetarypolicy/files/FOMC20050202bluebook20050127.pdf and www.federalreserve.gov/boarddocs/press/monetary/2005/20050202/default.htm.

[30] See www.federalreserve.gov/newsevents/press/monetary/20061025a.htm and table 1 at www.federalreserve.gov/monetarypolicy/files/FOMC20061025bluebook20061019.pdf.

[31] See www.federalreserve.gov/newsevents/press/monetary/20101103a.htm.

[32] See www.federalreserve.gov/monetarypolicy/files/FOMC20101214tealbookb20101209.pdf, table 1.

that are lying around. That, I believe, is our basic function: to develop alternatives to existing policies, to keep them alive and available until the politically impossible becomes politically inevitable." It is worth considering, therefore, what ideas were left "lying around" after 2007 and what alternatives, if any, might have been implemented. Friedman only contemplated the "good" ideas he felt would someday be ripe for adoption. Unfortunately, there is always the possibility that "bad" ideas are also waiting to be adopted.

In the rush to judgment about the role of the central banks post-crisis, it is often forgotten that the most important currency of an institution that will always be part of government, but at arm's length, is its credibility and the trust the public has in its ability to ensure the welfare of the entire population is its most important concern. As explained earlier and in chapter 6, whether by association or otherwise, arguably the greatest damage central banking has experienced is the loss of reputation. As this is written, there are few signs of a reversal.[33]

The issue, then, is the extent to which current policy regimes ought to be modified or not. I have made the case that, when it comes to inflation control, low and stable inflation rates ought not to be taken off the table. The impression left by several policymakers is that inflation rates should be reconsidered even if the motivation for change is unclear and there is growing dissonance among central bankers regarding inflation objectives. This is hardly a recipe for restoring credibility.

At the root of the problem is an inability to square the circle when financial stability and monetary policy come into conflict—that is, the space occupied by macroprudential instruments. As explained earlier (see, for example, chapter 6), resorting to nonmonetary policy instruments to prevent a recurrence of financial instability will surely fail if the instruments are built on institutional foundations in need of reform. Ideally, this calls for an evaluation of the governance of institutions for financial stability prior to dividing up the responsibilities for those monetary and financial stability policies. And, as noted previously, different arrangements are suitable for different countries. Unfortunately, this kind of sequencing is no longer possible. Nevertheless, it remains desirable to assess the current state of play and for policymakers to agree on how much tolerance there ought to be for cross-country differences. After all, it is unlikely that unanimity is possible, nor is this goal especially attractive given the diversity of financial sector development. Figure 7.7 illustrates this challenge based on data for the G20 drawn from Lombardi and Siklos (2016).[34]

---

[33] Indeed, in the case of the Fed, the most recent data reveals the most precipitous drop relative to other agencies of the U.S. government. See Hilsenrath 2016.

[34] The authors examine the state of play in a wide variety of indicators of macroprudential capacity for 46 economies. Figure 7.7 is a modified version of their figure 2.

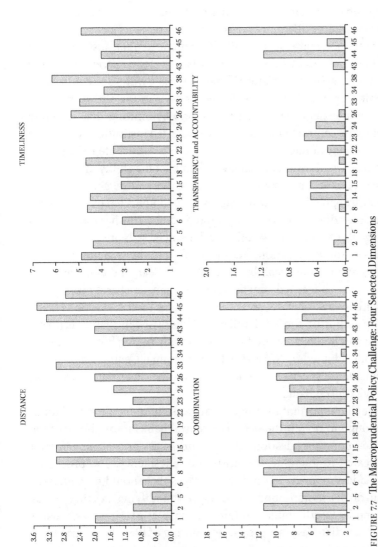

FIGURE 7.7 The Macroprudential Policy Challenge: Four Selected Dimensions

Note: DISTANCE represents a measure of improvements in macroprudential regulations based on a 2013 survey; a higher signals greater improvements. TIMELINESS is an estimate of the response time to FSB recommendations based on an FSB survey of national progress; a higher number indicates a slower response time. COORDINATION refers the number of bodies involved in macroprudential policies, central bank involvement, among other factors; the higher the number, the more complex the arrangement. TRANSPARENCY AND ACCOUNTABILITY refers to the role of public outreach, explanations of macroprudential policies, and clarity in the central banks role in macroprudential policies; the higher the number, the more transparent and accountable the central bank. *Source:* Based on data in Lombardi and Siklos 2016.

The data in figure 7.7 show that when it comes to how far economies have gone in reforming their financial sectors to meet FSB standards, the speed with which reforms are being implemented, the levels of accountability and transparency in conveying what has so far been accomplished, and the degree to which institutions that share responsibility for carrying out a macroprudential strategy, diversity remains the order of the day. Indeed, merely trying to quantify cross-country differences in this domain remains a big challenge.

Beyond governance matters, the GFC has taught us that, just as flexible inflation targeting is a successful monetary policy strategy, success in taming the risks of a future systemic or global financial crisis will also require flexibility for existing or new institutions to respond when the situation arises. Unfortunately, politicians have tended to respond by limiting this flexibility and encouraging the central banks and other interested institutions to narrow the scope of the financial markets' ability to absorb or distribute risk. The resulting distortions, well documented, may well impact the ability of monetary policy to influence expectations and economic activity more generally. As a result, the pass-through effects of monetary policy, complicated by macroprudential policies, may diminish or become unpredictable. This has the potential to damage the goals of both price stability and financial stability.

Needless to say, some distortions are inevitable and the trade-off between monetary policy and financial stability will never be clear. Therefore, as far as the central banks are concerned, any flexibility to "do whatever it takes" must be combined with regular outside assessments of all the tasks and actions taken by the monetary authority. The Riksbank model, discussed in chapter 6, serves the goal of ensuring public accountability. An equally useful, but incomplete, strategy is the one adopted in Norway, where an annual *Central Bank Watch* provides an outside perspective on selected issues that bear on the role and work of Norway's central bank.

Since it is equally important for the central banks to remain forward looking, it is not enough to review the past. The central banks must also have the freedom to raise important questions about future issues or problems in their never-ending search to guarantee the institution's resilience. The procedure adopted in Canada— namely, to outline the issues that should be addressed in anticipation of discussion about retaining or modifying existing policy strategy—is a model worth emulating (also see chapter 6). However, what is missing in the Canadian case is a precise accounting of how the central bank chooses the topics to investigate and, more important, what issues were not considered and the reasons for not pursuing them.

In designing a governance structure that permits information and ideas to flow so that differences are aired and good policies are likely implemented, it is ironic that the U.S. Federal Reserve System is well placed to provide such independent advice to the Board of Governors; it had been thought by some that the Fed was a historical anachronism, owing to the role and influence of its member banks. This proves to be, in fact, a useful alternative to approaches adopted elsewhere.[35]

While these arrangements are likely portable in one form or another globally, the eurozone requires additional attention to restore trust. It is fair to say that no central bank mandate, no guarantee of central bank autonomy, no amount of flexibility to react as needed in a crisis can survive a fiscal policy that is at cross-purposes. For the single-currency area, this likely means greater shared responsibility between the ECB and its member governments for the welfare of the eurozone. Whether this can be accomplished within the limits imposed by the Maastricht Treaty is unclear, but reforms along these lines are essential.

Alternatively, symbols of the interdependence between fiscal and monetary policy could be improved by creating a market for commonly issued debt. In addition, to avoid speculation about entry or exit from the single-currency area, whether legally sanctioned or not, the realistic possibility of exiting from the eurozone needs to be accepted. To ensure that this is a last resort—that is, when all other attempts to prevent exit have failed—the conditions for exiting need to be clear and jointly agreed upon on a case by case basis. Artificial rules, such as various vintages of the Stability and Growth Pact, are unlikely to be credible, nor will they adequately capture the seriousness of the decision to leave the eurozone. The reason is perhaps best expressed in the following quote from the great American jurist Oliver Wendell Holmes (1904:400–401): "Great cases like hard cases make bad law. For great cases are called great, not by reason of their importance ... but because of some accident of immediate overwhelming interest which appeals to the feelings and distorts judgment."[36]

Therefore, to redress the imbalance in responsibilities between the ECB as a whole and sovereign preferences of the member states, eurozone member should be subjected to a "stress test." This test would be a means of judging the state of each member's economy and the likelihood of its requiring some form of financial assistance in the future. Any requests for financial assistance would then have to be sanctioned by the member states before turning to the ECB for action. Of course, the devil is in the details; but if such tests can be carried out independently,[37] and member states agree a priori that though assistance is a last resort it may be necessary at times and be in the interests of preserving the

---

[35] The creation of the reserve banks system is the result of political maneuvering that allowed the Federal Reserve to be created. The original Act specified anywhere from eight to twelve reserve banks. In any event, twelve were created by then Treasury Secretary William McAdoo in 1914. See Lowenstein's (2015) entertaining account of the creation of the Fed.

[36] Oliver Wendell Holmes (1904) *Northern Securities Co. v. United States*, 193 U.S. 197, 400–401– Judicial opinions.

[37] Preferably not by the ECB. Whether a new agency is required is debatable, but it is highly likely that a new treaty would be required to carry out this strategy. Needless to say, the current environment makes this unlikely, but this does not diminish its necessity.

currency union, then there is at least a chance that the blame game will cease in time, replaced by a preference for collective action.

Bretton Woods Reimagined?

There was a time when, in both textbooks and policy discussions, the focus of concern was on the role of the exchange rate regime. This is perhaps best epitomized by Stan Fischer's (2001) argument that intermediate regimes between the fixed and pure floating can and do persist, because they reflect sovereign concerns about how external shocks can impact domestic monetary policy. As the Great Moderation reached maturity, however, emphasis on the inflationary effects of exchange rate movements faced contradictions from two sources: the globalization of finance and the apparent reduction in pass-through effects, the latter perhaps owing to global efforts at taming inflation rates.

Old ideas, however, are slow to disappear. Indeed, the exchange rate as a policy tool, largely abandoned or deemed unnecessary by the central banks, has reappeared but in a different form—as the collateral damage arising from the race to the bottom and beyond for policy rates. As Mervyn King, former governor of the Bank of England, argues, "there is a sense of desperation in going to negative interest rates. . . . The hope is that the announcement will lower the exchange rate and that's the main transmission mechanism that seems to be in operation."[38]

Elsewhere, policymakers became interested in various "imbalances" that emerged in capital flows and current accounts. Interest transcended the type of exchange rate regime in place. The eurozone crisis revealed the extent of imbalances within the single-currency area. Meanwhile, the imbalances between the United States and, most notably, China took place in the context of a floating exchange rate regime in one case and an exchange rate regime with limited flexibility in the other. The G20, in particular, captured the flavor of the problem by agreeing on a program of "mutual assessments" of the state of imbalances. These were to be compared to a set of "indicative" guidelines discussed in 2010 and agreed to in 2011. These guidelines include debt, savings, and external account balances.[39]

The indicative nature of the imbalances, the pivot toward higher (though unsatisfactory) economic growth, and the inability even in the eurozone to rely

---

[38] Quote is from a March 25, 2016 interview in the *Wall Street Journal*'s *MoneyBeat* webpage when discussing his book *The End of Alchemy*. Interestingly, while Goodfriend 2016 makes the case for breaching the ZLB the same way as the case for freeing the exchange rate from its "golden (or other) fetters" was made in the past, the resort to negative interest rates as a device to move the exchange rate in a desired direction is not addressed in his paper.

[39] See, for example, www.imf.org/external/np/exr/facts/g20map.htm.

on "name and shame" to influence policies designed to mitigate imbalances[40] put to rest arguments that solutions to these intractable problems were at hand. Of course, an evaluation of imbalances shares a problem with the search for financial stability—that is, an inability to arrive at a common understanding, on the global level, of what is or is not excessive.[41] Perhaps equally important, the connection with monetary policy remains unclear. To be sure, there is a connection between exchange rates, capital flows, and monetary conditions. Similarly, there exists a link between current account imbalances and overall economic activity and inflation. Nevertheless, untangling the components to be shouldered by monetary policy or to ensure financial system stability is difficult, and is likely to be country- and time-dependent. Even Wolf's (2008:195) detailed examination of global imbalances leaves little or no room for monetary policy to play a decisive influence with the "performance of the financial system" playing the leading role.

In view of this state of affairs, and given the role of central banks in preventing financial instability, it is best to shift as much of the burden of explanation as possible to the politicians. After all, the choice of exchange rate regimes has traditionally been a political decision, even if there is likely to be input from the central bank in, for example, managing foreign exchange reserves. Since central banks in the future will be called upon again to fill the breach when the next crisis arrives, there is little point now in assigning responsibility to the monetary authority; little is known about the ultimate aims in diagnosing the state of imbalances, even if policymakers can agree on the precise indicators. Indeed, this option underscores the sovereign nature of the central banking institution.

One is reminded of Hayek's (2008:104) warning about the dangers of not knowing where to go from here: "The effect of the people's agreeing that there must be central planning, without agreeing on the ends, will be rather as if a group of people were to commit to take a journey together without agreeing where they want to go; with the result that they may well have to take a journey which most of them do not want at all."

Conclusions: Use as Directed

It is hoped that economic historians will some day be able to sort out whether the aftermath of the GFC reflected primarily the unhappy coincidence of secular forces outside the normal purview of monetary policy or it demonstrated

---

[40] Reflected in the macroeconomic imbalance procedure of the European Commission. See http://ec.europa.eu/economy_finance/economic_governance/macroeconomic_imbalance_procedure/index_en.htm. In the 2015 review, 12 of 18 countries examined were found to have imbalances.

[41] The G20 program focuses on three broad indicators, while the EC relies on a list of 14 indicators.

the limits of monetary policy while putting a floor on the size and duration of a severe economic downturn. To be sure, the behavior of policymakers, including the central banks, prior to the GFC will no doubt prove to be the disrobing that exposed the weaknesses of a critical institution of government, evidenced in the series of financial crises that hit the advanced economies beginning in 2007.

Central bankers, and many others including politicians and academics, were lulled into the fiction of simplicity in explaining and delivering policy. They thought it could mask the complexities inherent in a monetary transmission mechanism in which financial shocks are transmitted in ways that are occasionally poorly understood. Therein lay the appeal of a clear monetary policy framework that focuses on limiting the loss of purchasing power via inflation, with the full knowledge that any predictable and stable trade-off with real economic outcomes is subject to change and cannot be taken for granted. Indeed, this is what adds to the appeal of an autonomous monetary authority. The inability to exploit such trade-offs in a consistent fashion suggests that the focus on inflation control is a valid one, and the temptation to exploit it never really disappears. Modern observers of monetary policy tend to forget how deeply rooted is the desire for a policy to maintain stable prices. The version of the Federal Reserve Act of 1913 passed by the House (and later modified only slightly by the Senate) directed the new central bank to observe a mandate "with a view to accommodating the commerce of the country and promoting a stable price level."[42] The language used in creating other central banks may differ, but the desire for a stable unit of account is ever present. Clearly, there is a debate about what level of inflation is consistent with price stability. Merely changing the rate, even temporarily, does not enhance a central bank's reputation and credibility.

The original responsibility of the central banks—namely, the financing of wars and the management of public debt as lender of last resort (now a device to mitigate financial instability and the primary economic stabilization tool)— has evolved. Neither is it the case that the relationship between the sovereignty and central banking is as symbiotic as one might be tempted to claim. As shown in figure 7.8, there is often a large gap (in years) between statehood (as it is understood in modern terms) and the creation of a central bank. And from its creation, a central bank evolves (e.g., see Siklos 2002; Roberds and Velde 2016), so that even if monetary policy remains primarily a domestic concern, financial instability, which is an outcome enhanced by financial globalization, can be mitigated via supra-national institutional devices.[43]

---

[42] See https://fraser.stlouisfed.org/scribd/?title_id=967&filepath=/docs/historical/federal%20reserve%20history/bog_publications/legman_bog_19390419.pdf.

[43] The growing importance and influence of the Financial Stability Board (FSB) is one example. However, there is still a long way to go before the reforms proposed by the FSB are implemented (as shown in figure 7.7), and only time will tell the extent to which the jurisdictions (essentially the G20, with some additional member countries) will abide and enforce global rules.

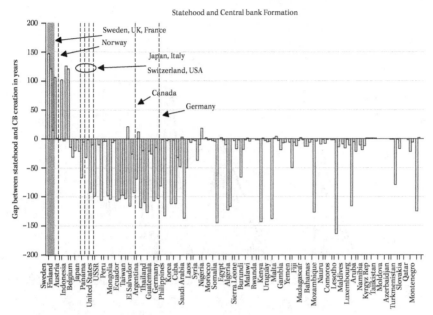

FIGURE 7.8 Gap Between Statehood and Creation of Central Bank

Note: The bars show the difference, measured in years, between the formation of a central bank and the creation of a state. A positive number indicates that a central bank came first; a negative value means that the central bank was created after statehood. *Source:* Data are from various issues of *Central Bank Directory* and author's calculations.

As Geithner (2014) rightly points out, "overwhelming" force is helpful in a crisis, as are anchors. The contrast between Japan and the United States is frequently mentioned, a point also discussed in chapter 5. Of course, establishing the size of a program needed to convince the financial markets is the real difficulty. As has often been said, inflation expectations lie at the core of monetary policy. Forecasters can still disagree quite strongly about the near-term outlook, even if they agree that inflation will move only slowly over time. Hence, central banks can be left thinking that all is well on the inflation front, even when disagreement about the outlook actually conveys a different message. Whether it is uncertainty about economic policy or uncertainty in the environment more broadly, the dispersion of views about the future are certainly a signal that forecasters at least are unhappy about the current stance of monetary policy.

Consider figure 7.9, which traces disagreements in inflation forecasts for the United States and Japan since 1999.[44] Forecast disagreement, and a statistical evaluation of the range in estimates of inflation forecasts over time, is shown.

---

[44] The measurement of forecast disagreement, and the confidence intervals for the estimates, is detailed in Siklos 2017 forthcoming. Figure 7.9 adapts some of the results presented in that study. The forecasters in the study included not only professional forecasters but also households, public agencies, and even central banks.

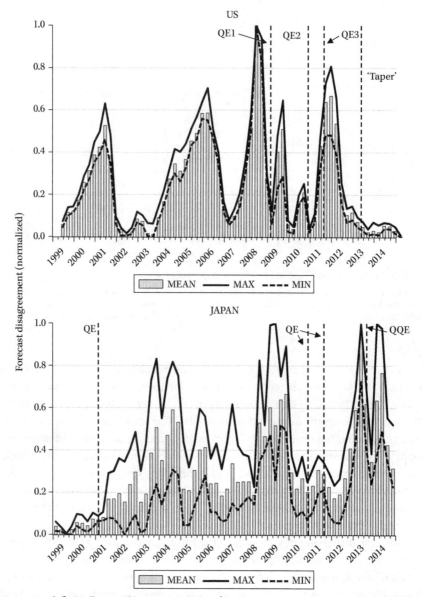

FIGURE 7.9 Inflation Forecast Disagreement: U.S. and Japan

Note: Forecast disagreement is essentially an indicator of the level of dispersion in inflation forecasts. MAX and MIN lines represent a quasi-confidence interval for MEAN forecast disagreement levels. The vertical dashed lines indicate when quantitative easing (QE) interventions took place. The data are quarterly. *Source:* Estimates based on Siklos 2017, 2013b.

The estimates are presented in such a way that a value of 0 implies no forecast disagreement, while maximum disagreement translates into a value of 1.

It is worth noting that a financial crisis need not be the only source of forecast disagreement. Forecast disagreement in the United States rose during the relatively small financial crisis associated with dot.com bubble burst after 2000, whereas the gradual tightening of monetary policy in the dying quarters of the Great Moderation was characterized by greater forecast disagreement. Matters are more difficult to assess in Japan's case, arguably because policy has been in crisis since before 1999.

The complexity involved in dealing with financial crises on the scale experienced after 2007 and the mixed reaction of forecasters does, however, indicate that disagreement has been more volatile since the GFC in both countries. However, note also that, other than the Economic Stimulus Act of 2008, the rapid decline in the Fed funds rate in early 2008, and the Troubled Asset Relief Program (TARP) later in the year, only QE1 and QE3 influenced the dispersion of inflation forecasts. However, these programs affected the uncertainty concerning mean estimates of forecast disagreement that rose, especially following QE2 and QE3. Turning to the Japanese case, there are two additional differences to note vis-à-vis the U.S. experience. First, uncertainty about the mean estimate of forecast disagreement has been a persistent fact of life since the beginning of the sample. This likely reflects the lack of policy certainty over a period of more than a decade and a half. Second, even the much-heralded QQE policy begun in 2013 could only temporarily reverse a steady rise in forecast dispersion that continued to reach near maximum levels by 2015.

One of the lessons learned is that, just as central bankers meeting in Jackson Hole in 2005 were later accused of turning a blind eye to the financial crisis to come (e.g., see Irwin 2013:107–8), they are also turning a blind eye to the loss of faith in the central banks. Central banks are once again lost in an ideology that confuses an understandable desire to experiment with and assess the efficacy of different tools with the belief that an autonomous central bank is defensible under the circumstances.

Historically, successful central banks have understood that an appropriate separation between politics and economics requires clarity in the directives governing the monetary authority to intervene when necessary. Such directives need to be enshrined in legislation, even more critically when the central bank is dealing with the maintenance of financial stability. These good ideas already exist in the form of crisis management rules (e.g., as in the case of the Bank of England). No doubt these rules will need to be revisited when the next financial crisis arrives.

No one knows how the current state of affairs will play out. However, as far as monetary policy and financial system stability are concerned, there is a sense that the central banks are incapable of smoothing the way for better days ahead. Even if their efforts are anything but motivated by the right reasons, they are incapable of escaping notions that their autonomy is their only salvation. Which kind of autonomy? The discussion centers on independence from government influence. Yet, while it is true that politicians have threatened central bank autonomy, they have generally not acted on their threats, in part because central banks have convinced them that their policies can set the stage for a satisfactory recovery. This has conveniently allowed fiscal policy to remain more passive. However, there is another form of independence—autonomy from the financial markets. Here, the central banks have been less persuasive that their policies are conducive to a satisfactory economic recovery.

The institution of central banking is not fundamentally broken, but it is certainly in need of some mending. Establishing how and when the central banks act in a future crisis is one place to start. Making clear that business as usual means that the contract between the central bank and its government is a conditional one, reflective of an economic environment each nation faces. At the present time, the concern is for a fiscal policy out of tune with monetary policy, when it is thought that there is a need to revitalize the infrastructure in several economies. Even if this position is wholeheartedly accepted, one must anticipate the day when the same divergence between fiscal and monetary policies could return us to a fiscal dominance that results in excessive inflation. Unlike the GFC, this is no black swan; there is plenty of historical evidence to back up this possibility (e.g., Bordo and Orphanides 2013; Bremner 2004).

It is essential to recognize that financial stability is part of central banking, but that central banks need not be the only institution with a stake in achieving that stability. An argument frequently used is that the central banks already have the skills and human capital to manage the complex problems posed by the twin objectives of price and financial stability; hence, they should simply be assigned greater responsibilities in these areas. This may be merely a temporary palliative. Central banks did step into the breach by doing some of the work other institutions could not or did not want to do. However, this is no substitute for revisiting the division responsibilities for governing monetary policy and financial system stability.

Instead, the emphasis should be on building similar institutional capacity elsewhere in government. It is unclear how the lopsided assignment of skills and responsibilities can better serve the transparency and accountability that is required to restore the public's confidence and trust in the central banks.

Accordingly, a new regime of accountability must be implemented that calls for proper accounting of past successes and failures, and that is less self-serving than has been the case. Central banks cannot continue to hide behind their superior technical skills and their capacity to analyze data. Their data dependence has not produced an overwhelmingly superior ability to predict the outlook or understand past failures. As long as judgment plays a critical role in policy, as it must, there is a place for outsiders to look inside the conduct of monetary policy. Trust, once lost, is difficult to regain, but not impossible; the central banks can at least count on some past successes to counter their notable failures. But time seems to be running out for institutions more interested in maintaining the status quo ante than in devising a strategy to deal with the challenges that lie ahead.

Epilogue

THE TWILIGHT ZONE?

The manuscript for this book was largely written during 2015 and 2016. It was completed approximately two months before the last U.S. elections, but shortly after the referendum in the United Kingdom to exit the EU ended with a decision in favor of Brexit. As this is written, early in 2017, monetary policy conditions have changed little, with the Fed the only major central bank that has raised interest rates and only the third time since the end of 2008. Many other central banks, especially in small open economies (e.g., Canada, New Zealand, Australia), are either leaving monetary policy conditions unchanged or show a bias toward further easing if this in their best interests. At the more systemically important central banks, the talk has also shifted away from the necessity of additional loosening and in the direction of standing pat, with the hope that the future will perhaps bring about a long-awaited, but very gradual, raising of policy rates.

If the drive to reduce policy rates to the zero lower bound, or beyond, combined with the occasional dose of quantitative easing in various manifestations had defined monetary policy until around the end of 2015, the possibility that monetary policies across countries will diverge, largely because the economic environment in different economies is also diverging, has gained ground. Other than perhaps in China, whose exchange rates continue to attract attention from U.S. authorities, discussions about exchange-rate behavior have been surprisingly muted. Yet, if the euro–dollar exchange rate serves as an example, the single currency's exchange rate has depreciated over 30% beginning in the second half of 2014, with more modest changes in 2016. A similar fate befell the British pound, though the Brexit referendum accelerated the currency's depreciation during the second half of 2016. The situation is less dramatic for the renminbi–dollar exchange rate, with a gradual depreciation of a little over 10% since the end of 2014. These are large movements in exchange rates—not by historical standards, but in an environment of heightened concerns about the cross-border spillovers in economic policies.

The year 2017 represents one decade since the start of the global financial crisis.[1] There is no longer much talk about whether monetary conditions might return to anything resembling pre-crisis conditions. Instead, central bankers are more vocal than at any time during the past ten years about when policy rates might resume a return to levels not seen since the early 2000s.

Central bankers still worry that inflation rates are too low, with a good deal of the blame placed on sluggish economic growth. Ironically, while some observers claim that we should accept a still largely undefined "new normal," politicians certainly yearn for pre-crisis growth while worrying considerably less about whether this can be achieved alongside pre-crisis inflation rates. Yet, if central banks are happy with inflation overshooting their stated or implicit targets for some undefined period of time, and are successful in attaining this objective before pre-crisis growth is restored, there is little acknowledgment that the resulting stagflation, even if it happens to be short-lived, will simply add insult to injury to real incomes that either have been sluggish or have declined in most advanced economies over the past decade or more. In the meantime, there are few indications that the often-publicized benefits of historically low interest rates are being taken advantage of in the fiscal realm.

Unlike the past, when unsustainable fiscal policies eventually promoted a correction, which was often economically costly, and thereby facilitated the institutionalization of central bank autonomy and the provision of a clearer mandate was provided, we now have a monetary policy that is deemed ultimately unsustainable while fiscal policy strains to prove that it is responsible, while not fully taking advantage of the ultra-loose monetary conditions.

If the crisis was unexpected, we are still waiting for its end and for the moral of the story to be written with the benefit of sober second-guessing. It is tempting, of course, to say that the rise of populism is an aftershock. In the realm of monetary policy and central banking, which is the subject of this book, we have yet to reach firm conclusions about the proper role and responsibilities of the monetary authorities. And we have yet to come to a decision on how to balance the desire to emphasize sovereignty in economic affairs—seemingly one of today's rallying cries from politicians around the world—with a definition of the limits and tasks of monetary policy that are entrusted with the one institution, namely the central bank. From its creation, it has always been an important symbol of sovereignty. Unfortunately, relying on sovereignty, like

---

[1] The Federal Reserve Bank of St. Louis timeline begins on February 27, 2007, with a press release from the Federal Home Loan Mortgage Corporation suspending the purchase of the "riskiest" mortgage-related securities. See www.stlouisfed.org/financial-crisis/full-timeline. Needless to say, other timelines disagree with this start date, but almost all I have looked at have a start date sometime during 2007, often beginning with BNP Paribas's announcement that they were no longer able to value the collateralized debt obligations of subprime loans.

trade agreements or institutional mechanisms that seek to bind countries by economic or political means, is often done selectively. The concept is touted for its benefits, while responsibilities vis-à-vis other countries are seen as something akin to a cafeteria table where one can select some items but not others. The resulting tensions can persist for a time, but if they build, as they appear to be doing these days, the possibility of a breaking point cannot be dismissed.

A good place to understand the source of these tensions is with the role of exchange rates. For a long time, floating exchange rates were viewed as enough to insulate the domestic economy against foreign shocks. The crisis of 2007 and beyond was a reminder that, since financial and business cycles are asynchronous, and are both hostage not just to domestic developments but also to an increasingly important global factor, floating exchange rates cannot serve two masters simultaneously. As a consequence, the realization that international factors may require managing has led to a revival of steps, since called "macroprudential," that are seen as the obvious response to a need to short-circuit some of the negative externalities that are the by-product of the exchange-rate channel. However, like unconventional monetary policy, prudential responses such as limits on capital movements (e.g., capital control measures) have historically proved to be a slippery slope in a race to the bottom that ends up defeating the original purpose to maintain financial system stability without unduly impairing real economic growth. Unfortunately, we know all too well that there is always the danger that some new orthodoxy will be defended until well past the time it is useful.[2]

If we are to accept the view of a permanently lower neutral real interest rate, whether it is because of global demographic factors or all the low-hanging fruits from technological improvements have largely been exhausted, the discussion about the future of monetary policy must go beyond the platitude that simply adopting multiple instruments must become conventional, with central bank policy rates taking a back seat—at least so long as we cannot see a return to "normal" economic growth and inflation rates. After all, the question of how multiple instruments improve the delivery of monetary policy, while the latter still aims to achieve one or, at most, dual objectives, remains very much debated, with no immediate prospect of a new consensus being formed. The irony is that some central banks, notably the Fed, likely have far less space to maneuver in case of a future crisis than they used to. One simply has to look at Geithner's (2016) list of post-reform limitations on the Fed's financial crisis tool kit described in his Per Jacobsson Lecture.

Of course, the central banks are becoming more than just an institution that primarily aims for a single objective—namely, a low and stable inflation rate. The challenge of incorporating a role for financial stability; indeed, how

---

[2] As Ahamed 2009 and Eichengreen (2015a) remind us vividly.

we should define it continues to be unsettled. The current stance of monetary policy seems more akin to being a tool to repress almost any form of financial instability, rather than a device to jointly manage two separate goals that inevitably come into conflict with each other. As a result, the central banks end up looking as if they ignore the distributive and distortionary consequences of monetary policy used in the service of mitigating excessive volatility in some parts of the financial system.

A microcosm of the consequences of the foregoing pressures on central banks can be seen from the announcement, in January 2017, of December 2016 inflation in Germany and the eurozone. While eurozone inflation remained low, and well below the ECB's own inflation objective, inflation in Germany was seen as having "soared" to 1.7%, still below the ECB's objective. Core inflation remains low throughout the single-currency area and, as has often been true in the past, headline inflation merely reflects short-term changes to volatile food and energy prices; but that fact took a back seat to angry reactions suggesting that German citizens' savings were being "expropriated."[3] One can only imagine the frustration of the ECB's President Mario Draghi who, like other central bankers have been saying for years now, can only call for patience.[4]

If we have largely abandoned the fiction that exchange-rate systems are well described by the corner solutions of fixed and flexible exchange rates, it seems odd that the current discussion is about either raising interest rates or using macro-prudential measures to deal with the current macroeconomic environment, but much less so both in some measure.[5]

The previous chapters have argued that international cooperation is inherently necessary, if not desirable, and that clearer and more realistic governance structures that define the relationship between the central bank and its government ought to be sought. However, if the current political mood is here to stay, at least for some time, and seeks to undermine these goals, then the global imbalances that were discussed in earlier chapters are set to be taken over by a new set of imbalances. These may largely be political in nature, but they will

---

[3] This is not a new charge leveled at the ECB. The ECB previously attempted to respond to the concerns. See www.ecb.europa.eu/pub/pdf/scpops/ecbop161.en.pdf?2524a4eb09681b63470d7e645a1e5 aod. The accusation that savings are being deliberately eroded is also one that was made some years ago with some assistance from the Bundesbank president's own uncomfortable response to the issues; see www.ecb.europa.eu/pub/pdf/scpops/ecbop161.en.pdf?2524a4eb09681b63470d7e645a1e5aod. He could only promise that interest rates would eventually rise again. Almost four years later, there are few indications that this will happen anytime soon, at least in the eurozone.

[4] See www.bloomberg.com/news/articles/2017-01-19/draghi-says-ecb-unconvinced-on-inflation-driven-mainly-by-oil and www.ecb.europa.eu/press/tvservices/webcast/html/webcast_pc_youtube.en.html.

[5] This is the so-called leaning against the wind debate.

draw in the central banks in a manner that has yet to be properly considered. What then?

Should the central banks, as one central banker has alluded to, become more like weather forecasters? Should monetary policy appear less techno-cratic, since this may well partly explain why the last global financial crisis was unexpected? Should monetary policy be conducted with a view that relegates external factors to be essentially ignored, with domestic objectives the only ones that matter?

The weather forecasting analogy is misleading on several counts. First, weather forecasters are not required to meet a certain economic objective. Even if weather forecasting has improved in recent years, the horizon over which individuals make decisions conditional on the weather is typically far shorter than the one a central bank generally employs. Moreover, monetary policy is not exclusively reliant on the predictions of a single model, or even a multiplic-ity of models; rather, it includes an important role for judgment. Models serve as a disciplining device. Otherwise, the alternative is for monetary policy deci-sions to be made on the basis of instinct alone. This might work from time to time, but it is not a recipe for delivering consistently good monetary policy.[6]

Obviously, judgment cannot easily be quantified and its effects are difficult to observe, but it is an aspect of policymaking at central banks that has, sur-prisingly, been downplayed. Good judgment is a critical ingredient in deliver-ing good monetary policy and is as essential as all the technical background employed to carry out monetary policy in 2017. Moreover, if the nexus be-tween real and financial factors is seen as complex, then central bankers will be the first to point out that models can only serve as benchmarks and must be supplemented by judgment. Nevertheless, central bankers can be accused of excessively highlighting the importance of the technical aspects in the conduct of monetary policy, instead of underscoring the subtleties and human element of decision making.[7]

It is, of course, early in this apparently new political environment, but it has the feel of the twilight zone, where we are unsure how long we should per-sist with some policies while abandoning others. Until such time, there is the distinct impression that another surprise is in store. The optimist, of course, hopes for a good outcome. The pessimist is convinced that the past ten years are

---

[6] If the criticism is leveled at the manner in which central banks present forecasts, and perhaps their record, then the criticism is fair as discussed earlier in this book. Central banks still overwhelm-ingly focus on point forecasts. In contrast, a weather forecast is always couched in probabilistic terms. Attempts to show confidence bands (e.g., as in the Bank of England's "rivers of blood") may be helpful to those well versed in the technical aspects surrounding point forecasts, but they do not clearly convey to markets and the public the probabilistic nature of point forecasts.

[7] Indeed, the same is true for weather forecasters, who are at pains to point out that predictions from many models are "weighed" (i.e., judgment enters the picture) into an "ensemble" to improve forecast accuracy.

simply a dress rehearsal for the next global financial crisis. The reality is likely somewhere in between, but the speed with which news and information travel also increases the scope for smaller and bigger mistakes to have deleterious effects on the global economy. Individuals who hold either of these expectations, however, seem prone to forgetting that history fairly quickly. A reminder, for example, comes in the form of the release of the 2011 Fed transcripts in early January 2017.[8] With so much of the focus on the events of 2007–2008, a reading of the 2011 transcripts reveals that the Fed that year had to deal with the debt ceiling crisis, prompted by a political conflict between the U.S. administration and the Congress, that led to a downgrade of U.S. government debt; at the same time, there was a worsening of the eurozone sovereign debt crisis, resulting in a joint intervention by several major central banks later in the year to forestall a possible liquidity crisis. Those were just two significant events that preoccupied the monetary authorities. Therefore, we should perhaps focus less on anniversaries that have little meaning and instead ensure that the central bank as an institution and its policy strategies are adjusted to meet a constant stream of stresses and challenges. Asking why we are not back to normal ten years after a major shock that can be likened to a major earthquake thus downplays the succession of shocks, akin to aftershocks, that followed these events.

There is one other irony in the state of affairs we currently find ourselves in. Economic policies are being implemented largely in the name of sovereignty, in part because the existing rules of the game are seen as inadequate or as not serving the best interests of the majority of the electorate. However, when no alternative or coherent strategy is proposed, we are left with few or no rules at all. In the case of monetary policy, we are finding that when policy rules are set aside and no adequate narrative is developed to explain why, for how long, and whether existing rules should be modified or a new set of rules be adopted, then the anchor that allows the public to readily evaluate how well policy is carried out is also discarded. Policy is then seen as rudderless, and the task of convincing the public that policy is rigorous and fact-driven becomes far more difficult. Asking the central bank to carry out additional tasks and meet new objectives only serves to further weaken the resilience of the institution and opens it up to accusations that it is serving the wrong interests.

If there is any time for slow thinking to take more precedence, it is now. In particular, central bankers ought to use their bully pulpit to underscore not the desirability of caution but the importance of clear and realistic goals, and to insist that their political masters should shoulder their responsibilities and accept the accountability that central bankers now treat as second nature. Until this happens, however, fast thinking is likely to influence how central banking is carried out.

---

[8] See www.federalreserve.gov/monetarypolicy/fomchistorical2011.htm.

REFERENCES

Ahmed, Shagil, Andrew Levin, and Beth Ann Wilson. 2004. "Recent U.S. Macroeconomic Stability: Good Policies, Good Practices and Good Luck." *Review of Economics and Statistics* 86(3): 824–32.

Aizenman, Joshua, Menzie D. Chinn, and Hiro Ito. 2016. "Monetary Policy Spillovers and the Trilemma in the New Normal: Periphery Country Sensitivity to Core Country Conditions." *Journal of International Money and Finance* 68 (November): 298–330.

Aizenman, Joshua, Menzie D. Chinn, and Hiro Ito. 2008. "Assessing the Emerging Global Financial Architecture: Measuring the Trilemma's Configurations over Time." NBER Working Paper 14533.

Alesina, Alberto, and Lawrence H. Summers. 1993. "Central Bank Independence and Macroeconomic Performance: Some Comparative Evidence." *Journal of Money, Credit and Banking* 25 (May): 151–62.

Allen, William, and Geoffrey Wood. 2006. "Defining and Achieving Financial Stability." *Journal of Financial Stability* 2 (June): 152–72.

Alterlind, Jan, Hanna Armelius, David Forsman, Björn Jönsson, and Anna-Lena Wretman. 2015. "How Far Can the Repo Rate Be Cut?" *Economic Commentaries*, Sveriges Riksbank, November 11.

Angell, Norman. 1911. The Great Illusion: A Study of the Relation of Military Power in Nations to Their Economic and Social Advantage. New York and London: G.P. Putnam.

Appelbaum, Binyamin. 2014. "By Its Own Yardstick, the Fed is Falling Short." *New York Times*, April 30.

Archer, David, and Paul Moser-Boehm. 2013. "Central Bank Finances." BIS Paper 71, April.

Auerbach, Robert D. 2008. *Deception and Abuse at the Fed: Henry B. Gonzales Battles Alan Greenspan's Bank*. Austin: University of Texas Press.

Baba, Naohiko, Shinichi Nisihoka, Nobuyuki Oda, Masaaki Shirakawa, Zajuo Ueda, and Hiroshi Ugai. 2005. "Japan's Deflation: Problems in the Financial System and Monetary Policy." BIS Working Paper 181, November.

Bade, R., and M. Parkin. 1982. "Central Bank Laws and Monetary Policy." Manuscript, University of Western Ontario.

Bailliu, Jeannine, Wei Dong, and John Murray. 2010. "Has Exchange Rate Pass-Through Really Declined? Some Recent Insights From the Literature." *Bank of Canada Review* (Autumn): 1–8.

Baker, Scott R., Nicholas Bloom, and Steven J. Davis. 2016. "Measuring Economic Policy Uncertainty." *Quarterly Journal of Economics* 131 (July): 1593–636.

Ball, Laurence. 2014. "The Case for a Long-Run Inflation Target of Four Percent." IMF Working Paper 14/92, June.

Ball, Laurence, Daniel Leigh, and Prakash Loungani. 2013. "Okun's Law: Fit at 50?" IMF Working Paper 13/10, January.

Bank for International Settlements [BIS]. 2013a. *83rd Annual Report*. Basel: BIS.

Bank for International Settlements [BIS]. 2013b. "Basel III: The Liquidity Coverage Ratio and Liquidity Monitoring Tools." Basel Committee on Banking Supervision, January.

Bank for International Settlements [BIS]. 2005. *75th Annual Report*. Basel: BIS.

Bank of England. 2009. "Minutes of the Monetary Policy Committee Meeting 6 and 7 May." At www.bankofengland.co.uk/publications/minutes/Documents/mpc/pdf/2009/mpc0905.pdf.

Bank of Japan. 2016. "Comprehensive Assessment: Developments in Economic Activity and Prices as Well as Policy Effects Since the Introduction of Quantitative and Qualitative Monetary Easing (QQE)." September 21. At www.bo.or.jp.

Barth, James R., Gerard Caprio Jr., and Ross Levine. 2013. "Bank Regulation and Supervision in 180 Countries from 1999 to 2011." NBER Working Paper 18733, January.

Barsky, Robert, Alejandro Justiniano, and Leonardo Melosi. 2014. "The Natural Rate of Interest and Its Usefulness for Monetary Policy." *American Economic Review* 104 (May): 37–43.

Barwell, Richard. 2013. *Macroprudential Policy*. New York: Palgrave Macmillan.

Basu, Susanto, John Fernald, and Miles Kimball. 2006. "Are Technology Improvements Contractionary?" *American Economic Review* 96 (December): 1418–48.

Bates, J. M., and Clive W. J. Granger. 1969. "The Combination of Forecasts." *Operational Research Quarterly* 20: 451–68.

Bauer, Michael D., and Chris J. Neely. 2012. "International Channels of the Fed's Unconventional Monetary Policy." Federal Reserve Bank of St. Louis Working Paper Series, Working Paper 2012-028A.

Bean, C. 2013. "Note on Negative Interest Rates for Treasury Committee." Bank of England. At http://www.bankofengland.co.uk/publications/Documents/other/treasurycommittee/ir/tsc160513.pdf.

Benoit, Bertrand, and Ralph Atkins. 2009. "Merkel Mauls Central Banks." *Financial Times*, June 3.

Berger, Allen N., Robert DeYoung, Hesna Genay, and Gregory F. Udell. 2000. "Globalization of Financial Institutions: Evidence from Cross-Border Banking Performance." Brookings-Wharton Papers on Financial Services, 23–120.

Bergsten, C. Fred. 2013. "Currency Wars: The Economy of the United States and the Reform of the International Monetary System." Stavros Niarchos Foundation Lecture, Washington, DC, May 16.

Bernanke, Ben (2016), "What Tools Does the Fed Have Left? Part 1: Negative Interest Rates", www.brookings.edu/blog/ben-bernanke/2016/03/18/what-tools-does-the-fed-have-left-part-1-negative-interest-rates/

Bernanke, Ben S. 2015a. *The Courage to Act*. New York: W.W. Norton.

Bernanke, Ben S. 2013. *The Federal Reserve and the Financial Crisis*. Princeton, NJ: Princeton University Press.

Bernanke, Ben S. 2012a. "Monetary Policy Since the Onset of the Crisis." Speech delivered at the Federal Reserve Bank of Kansas City Economic Symposium, Jackson Hole, Wyoming, August 31.

Bernanke, Ben S. 2012b. "U.S. Monetary Policy and International Implications." Remarks at seminar on Challenges of the Global Financial System: Risks and Governance Under Evolving Globalization, Bank of Japan, International Monetary Fund High-Level Seminar, October 14.

Bernanke, Ben S. 2004a. "The Great Moderation." Speech at the Meeting of the Eastern Economic Association, Washington, DC, February 20.

Bernanke, Ben S. 2004b. "Central Bank Talk and Monetary Policy." Talk at the Japan Society Corporate Luncheon, October 7. At New York City, www.federalreserve.gov/boarddocs/speeches/2004/200410072/default.htm.

Bernanke, Ben S., and Mark Gertler. 1989. "Agency Costs, Net Worth, and Business Fluctuations." *American Economic Review* 79 (March): 14–31.

Bernanke, Ben S., Thomas Laubach, Frederic S. Mishkin, and Adam S. Posen. 1999. *Inflation Targeting*. Princeton, NJ: Princeton University Press.

Bernanke, Ben. S., V. Reinhart, and B. Sack. 2004. "Monetary Policy Alternatives at the Zero Lower Bound." *Brookings Paper on Economic Activity* 2: 1–100.

Bernholz, Peter. 2015. "The Swiss Experiment: From the Lower Bound to Flexible Exchange Rates." *Cato Journal* 35 (Spring/Summer): 403–10.

Bini Smaghi, Lorenzo. 2008. "Restoring Confidence." Talk as part of Panel on Society, State, Market: A European Answer. International Forum Economia e Società Aperta "Uscire della crisi," Madrid, November 25.

Black, Fisher. 1995. "Interest Rates as Options." *Journal of Finance* 50 (December): 1371–76.

Blanchard, Olivier, Giovanni Dell'Ariccia, and Paolo Mauro. 2010. "Rethinking Macroeconomic Policy." IMF Staff Position Note, February 12.

Blanchard, Olivier, and John Simon. 2001. "The Long and Large Decline in U.S. Output Volatility." *Brookings Papers on Economic Activity* 1: 135–64.

Blinder, Alan S. 2013. *After the Music Stopped*. New York: Penguin.

Blinder, Alan S. 2004. *The Quiet Revolution*. New Haven, CT: Yale University Press.

Blinder, Alan S. 1999. *Central Banking in Theory and Practice*. Cambridge, MA: Cambridge University Press.

Blinder, Alan S., and J. B. Rudd. 2013. "The Supply-Shock Explanation of the Great Stagflation Revisited." In *The Great Inflation*, ed. M. D. Bordo and A. Orphanides, 119–75. Chicago: University of Chicago Press.

Blinder, A. S., M. Ehrmann, M. Fratzsche, J. De Haan, and D-J. Jansen. 2008. "Central Bank Communication and Monetary Policy: A Survey of Theory and Evidence." *Journal of Economic Literature* 46 (December): 910–45.

Bloom, Nicholas. 2009. "The Impact of Uncertainty Shocks." *Econometrics* 77(3): 623–85.

Bordo, Michael, and Barry Eichengreen, eds. 1993. *A Retrospective on the Bretton Woods System*. Chicago: University of Chicago Press.

Bordo, Michael D., Barry Eichengreen, Daniela Klingebiel, and Maria Martinez-Peria. 2001. "Is the Crisis Problem Growing More Severe?" *Economic Policy*, April.

Bordo, Michael D., and Thomas F. Helbling. 2010. "International Business Cycle Synchronization in Historical Perspective." NBER Working Paper 16103, June.

Bordo, Michael D., Owen F. Humpage, and Anna J. Schwartz. 2015. *Strained Relations: U.S. Foreign-Exchange Operations and Monetary Policy in the Twentieth Century*. Chicago: University of Chicago Press.

Bordo, Michael D., and John S. Landon-Lane. 2010. "The Global Financial Crisis of 2007-08: Is It Unprecedented?" NBER Working Paper 16589, December.

Bordo, Michael D., and Olivier Jeanne. 2002. "Boom-Busts in Asset Prices, Economic Instability, and Monetary Policy." NBER Working Paper 8966, June.

Bordo, Michael D., and Athanasios Orphanides, eds. 2013. *The Great Inflation*. Chicago: University of Chicago Press for NEBR.

Bordo, Michael, and Catherine Schenk. 2016. "Monetary Policy Cooperation and Coordination: An Historical Perspective on the Importance of Rules." Economics Working Paper 16112, Hoover Institution, May.

Bordo, Michael D., and Pierre L. Siklos. 2017. "Central Banks: Evolution and Innovation in Historical Perspective. Unpublished manuscript.

Bordo, Michael D., and Pierre L. Siklos. 2016a. "Central Bank Credibility: An Historical and Quantitative Exploration." In *Central Banks at a Crossroads*, ed. M. D. Bordo, Ø. Eitrheim, M. Flandreau, and Jan Qvigstad, 62–144. Cambridge: Cambridge University Press.

Bordo, Michael D., and Pierre L. Siklos. 2016b. "Central Bank Credibility Before and After the Crisis." *Open Economies Review* 27 (August): 1–27.

Bordo, Michael D., and David C. Wheelock. 1998. "Price Stability and Financial Stability: The Historical Record." *Review of the Federal Reserve Bank of St. Louis* (September/October): 41–62.

Borio, Claudio. 2012. "The Financial Cycle and Macroeconomics: What Have We Learnt?" BIS Working Paper 395, December.

Borio, Claudio, Magdalena Erdem, Andrew Filardo, and Boris Hosmann. 2015. "The Costs of Deflations: A Historical Perspective." *BIS Quarterly Review* (March): 31–54.

Borio, Claudio, and Robert N. McCauley. 1994. "The Anatomy of the Bond Market Turbulence of 1994." BIS Working Paper 32, December.

Brainard, William. 1967. "Uncertainty and the Effectiveness of Policy." *American Economic Review* 57 (May): 411–25.

Bremner, Robert P. 2004. *Chairman of the Fed*. New Haven, CT: Yale University Press.

Broner, Fernando, Tatiana Didier, Aitor Erce, and Sergio L. Schmukler. 2013. "Gross Capital Flows: Dynamics and Crises." *Journal of Monetary Economics* 60: 113–33.

Brown, E. Cary. 1956. "Fiscal Policy in the Thirties: A Reappraisal." *American Economic Review* 46 (December): 857–79.

Bruner, Robert F., and Sean D. Carr. 2007. *The Panic of 1907*. New York: John Wiley.

Brunner, Karl. 1983. "The Pragmatic and Intellectual Tradition of Monetary Policy-making." In *Lessons of Monetary experiences from the 1970s*, ed. K. Brunner, 97–141. Berlin: Springer.

Brunnermeier, Markus K., and Yuliy Sannikov. 2012. "Redistributive Monetary Policy." In *The Changing Landscape*, 331–84. Kansas City: Federal Reserve Bank of Kansas City.

Buiter, Willem, Ebrahim Rahbari, and Juergen Michels. 2011. "Making Sense of Target Imbalance." *VOX*, September 6. At www.voxeu.org.

Bullard, James. 2013. "Perspectives on the Current Stance of Monetary Policy." Speech at the NYU-Stern Center for Global Economy and Business, February 21.

Burdekin, Richard, and Pierre L. Siklos. 2008. "What Has Driven Chinese Monetary Policy Since 1990? Investigating the People's Bank' s Policy Rule." *Journal of International Money and Finance* 27: 847–59.

Burdekin, Richard C. K., and Pierre L. Siklos. 2004. *Deflation*. Cambridge: Cambridge University Press.

Burke, Chris, Spence Hilton, Ruth Judson, Kurt Lewis, and David Skeie. 2010. "Reducing the IOER Rate: An Analysis of Options." Board of Governors of the Federal Reserve System, August 5. At www.federalreserve.gov/monetarypolicy/files/FOMC20100805memo05.pdf.

Burns, Arthur F. 1979. *The Anguish of Central Banking*, Per Jacobsson Lecture, Belgrade.

Burns, Arthur F. 1972. "Some Essentials of International Monetary Reform." Speech before the 1972 International Banking Conference, Montreal, May.

Caballero, R., J. Galí, L. Reichlin, and L. Servén. 2012. "Research at the Bank of Spain: An Evaluation." January. At www.bde.es/investigador/report_eval.pdf.

Campbell, John, and Robert Shiller. 1991. "Yield Spreads and Interest Rate Movements: A Bird's Eye View." *Review of Economic Studies* 58: 495–514.

Caprio, Gerry Jr., Daniela Klingebiel, Luc Laeven, and G. Noguera. 2005. "Banking Crisis Database." In *Systemic Financial Crises*, ed. P. Honohan and L. Laeven, 307–40. Cambridge: Cambridge University Press.

Cargill, Thomas, Michael Hutchison, and Takatoshi Ito. 2003. *The Political Economy of Japanese Monetary Policy*. Cambridge, MA: MIT Press.

Carney, M. 2013. "Monetary Policy After the Fall." Speech delivered at the Eric J. Hanson Memorial Lecture, University of Alberta, Edmonton, May 1.

Caruana, Jaime. 2013. "Making the Most of Borrowed Time." Speech on the occasion of the Bank's Annual General Meeting, Basel, June 23.

Cecchetti, Stephen, Michael R. King, and James Yetman. 2011. "Weathering the Financial Crisis: Good Policy or Good Luck?" BIS Working Paper 351, August.

Chernow, Ron. 2004. *Alexander Hamilton*. New York: Penguin.

Claessens, S. 2014. "An Overview of Macroprudential Policy Tools." IMF Working Paper 14/2014.

Clarida, Richard. 2012. "What Has – and Has Not – Been Learned About Monetary Policy is a Low-Inflation Environment? A Review of the 2000s." *Journal of Money, Credit and Banking* 44: 123–40.

Clarida, Richard, and Daniel Waldman. 2009. "Is Bad News About Inflation Good for the Exchange Rate?" In *Asset Prices and Monetary Policy*, ed. John Campbell, 371–96. Chicago: University of Chicago Press.

Coeuré, Benoît. 2014. "The Internationalisation of Monetary Policy." Keynote address at the ECB-IMF Conference on the International Dimension of Conventional and Unconventional Monetary Policy, Frankfurt, April 30.

Constâncio, Vítor. 2014. "Recent Challenges to Monetary Policy in the Euro Area." Speech at the Athens Symposium on Banking Union, Monetary Policy and Economic Growth, Athens, June 19.

Cooper, George. 2008. *The Origins of Financial Crises*. New York: Vintage.

Cour-Thimann, Philippine, and Bernhard Winkler. 2013. "The ECB's Non-Standard Monetary Policy Measures: The Role of Institutional Factors and Financial Structure." ECB Working Paper 1528, April.

Coval, Joshua, and Tobias Moskowitz. 1999. "Home Bias: Local Equity Preferences in Domestic Portfolios." *Journal of Finance* 54 (December): 2045–73.

Cowen, Tyler. 2013. *The Great Stagnation: How America Ate All The Low-Hanging Fruit of Modern History, Got Sick, and Will (Eventually) Feel Better*. New York: Penguin.

Crockett, Andrew. 2001. "Financial Market Distress: Causes, Consequences and Policy Options." Speech given at the 26th Annual Conference of the International Organization of Securities Commissions (IOSCO), Stockholm, June 23–29.

Crockett, Andrew. 1997. "Why Is Financial Stability a Goal of Public Policy?" *In Maintaining Financial Stability in a Global Economy*, 7–36. Kansas City: Economic Symposium of the Federal Reserve Bank of Kansas City.

Cross, Philip, and Philippe Bergevin. 2012. "Turning Points: Business Cycles in Canada Since 1926." *Commentary* 366 (October).

Cukierman, Alex. 2015. "US Banks' Behavior Since Lehman's Collapse, Bailout Uncertainty and the Choice of Exit Strategies." Unpublished manuscript.

Cukierman, Alex. 1992. *Central Bank Strategy, Credibility, and Independence.* Cambridge, MA: MIT Press.

Cukierman, Alex. 1986. "Central bank behavior and Credibility: Some Recent Theoretical Developments." *Review of the Federal Reserve Bank of St. Louis* (May): 5–17.

Cukierman, Alex, and Yehuda Izakhian. 2015. "Bailout Uncertainty in a Microfounded General Equilibrium Model of the Financial System." *Journal of Banking and Finance* 52: 160–79.

Curdia, Vasco, Andrea Ferrero, Ging Cee Ng, and Andre Tambalotti. 2015. "Has U.S. Monetary Policy Tracked the Efficient Interest Rate?" *Journal of Monetary Economics* 70 (March): 72–83.

Dalquist, Magnus, Lee Pinkowitz, René Stulz, and Rohan Williamson. 2003. "Corporate Governance and the Home Bias." *Journal of Financial and Quantitative Analysis* 38 (March): 87–110.

Davies, Gavyn. 2015. "The Swiss Currency Bombshell – Cause and Effect." *Financial Times,* January 18.

Davies, Gavyn. 2013. "Abenomics One Year On." *FT* blog, October 27. https://www.ft.com/content/0b26b0cd-fae1-373d-aca0-0680b1611302.

De Grauwe, Paul. 2009. "The Euro at Ten: Achievements and Challenges." *Empirical* 36(1): 5–20.

De Haan, Jakob. 2000. *The History of the Bundesbank.* London: Routledge.

Del Negro, Marco, Marc P. Giannoni, and Frank Schorfheide. 2015. "Inflation in the Great Recession and New Keynesian Models." *American Economic Journal: Macroeconomics* 7(January): 168–96.

De Simone, Francisco N., and S. Clarke. 2007. "Asymmetry in Business Fluctuations: International Evidence on Friedman's Plucking Model." *Journal of International Money and Finance* 26: 64–85.

Diderot, Denis. 1818. *Oeuvres de Denis Diderot, tome quatrième.* Paris: A. Belain.

Dincer, N. Nergiz, and Barry Eichengreen. 2014. "Central Bank Transparency and Independence: Updates and New Measures." *International Journal of Central Banking* 10 (March): 189–253.

Dotsey, Michael. 2016. "Monetary Policy and the New Normal." *Economic Insights,* Federal Reserve Bank of Philadelphia, First Quarter, 1–4.

Economist, The. 2014. "How Long Will the Expansion Last? Weighing the Evidence." December 7.

Eichengreen, Barry. 2015a. *Hall of Mirrors.* New York: Oxford University Press.

Eichengreen, Barry. 2015b. "Secular Stagnation: The Long View." NBER Working Paper 20836, January.

Eichengreen, Barry. 1992. *Golden Fetters.* Oxford: Oxford University Press.

Eichengreen, Barry, and Andrew Rose. 2014. "Capital Controls in the 21st Century." CEPR Policy Insights 72, June.

Eichengreen, Barry, and Ngaire Woods. 2015. "The IMF's Unmet Challenges." *Journal of Economic Perspectives* 30 (Winter): 29–52.

Eijffinger, Sylvester, Jakob de Haan, and Kees Koedjik. 2002. "Small Is Beautiful: Measuring the Research Input of the European Central Bank." *European Journal of Political Economy* 18(2): 365–74.

El-Arian, Mohamed. 2016. *The Only Game in Town.* New York: Random House.

Engle, Robert. 2002. "Dynamic Conditional Correlation: A Simple Class of Multivariate Generalized Autoregressive Conditional Heteroskedasticity Models." *Journal of Business and Economic Statistics* 20 (July): 339–50. [fig]

European Central Bank [ECB]. 2015. "Account of the Monetary Policy Meeting, January 14. At www.ecb.europa.eu/press/accounts/2016/html/mg160114.en.html.

European Central Bank [ECB]. 2008. "The New Euro Area Yield Curves." *ECB Monthly Bulletin,* February: 95–103.

European Commission. 2008. "EMU@10: Successes and Challenges After Ten Years of Economic and Monetary Union." *European Economy* 2.

Fama, Eugene, and Robert Bliss. 1987. "The Information in Long Maturity Forward Rates." *American Economic Review* 77 (September): 680–92.

Favoretto, Federico, and Donato Masciandaro. 2016. "Too Little, Too Late? Monetary Policymaking Inertia and Psychology: A Behavioral Model." Unpublished manuscript.

Federal Open Market Committee [FOMC]. 2010a. "Meeting Transcript." Bluebook, Washington, DC, August 10.

Federal Open Market Committee [FOMC]. 2010b. "Report to the FOMC on Economic Conditions and Monetary Policy." Book B, Monetary Policy: Strategies and Alternatives. Bluebook, Washington, DC, August 5.

Federal Reserve Board of Governors. 2010. Transcripts of Federal Open Market Committee Meetings (various issues). At www.federalreserve.gov/monetarypolicy/fomchistorical2010.htm.

Federal Reserve Board of Governors. 2008. Transcripts of Federal Open Market Committee Meetings (various issues). At www.federalreserve.gov/monetarypolicy/fomchistorical2008.htm.

Federal Reserve Bank of New York. 2016. "Financial Turmoil Timeline." At www.newyorkfed.org/research/global_economy/policyresponses.html.

Federalist Papers. 1788. Alexander Hamilton, John Jay, and James Madison. At www.gutenberg.org/files/1404/1404-h/1404-h.htm.

Feldstein, Martin, ed. 1991. *The risk of Economic Crisis.* Chicago: University of Chicago Press.

Ferguson, Roger W. 2006. "Economic Outlook for the United States." Remarks at the Howard University Economics Forum, Washington, DC, March 3.

Fernandez, A., M. W. Klein, A. Rebucci, M. Schindler, and M. Uribe. 2015. "Capital Control Measures: A New Dataset." IMF Working Paper 15/80, April.

Feroli, Michael, David Greenlaw, Peter Hooper, Frederic Mishkin, and Amir Sufi. 2016. "Language after Liftoff: Fed Communication Away from the Zero Lower Bound." Paper prepared for the 2016 U.S. Monetary Policy Forum, February 26.

Filardo, Andrew J. 2000. "Monetary Policy and Asset Prices." *Economic Review,* Federal Reserve Bank of Kansas City, Third Quarter: 12–36.

Filardo, Andrew J., and Diwa Guinigundo. 2008. "Transparency and Communication in Monetary Policy: A Survey of Asian Central Banks." BIS Working Paper.

Filardo, A., and B. Hofmann. 2014. "Forward Guidance at the Zero Lower Bound." *BIS Quarterly Review*, March: 37–54.

Filardo, Andrew J., and Pierre L. Siklos. 2016. "The Cross-Border Lending Channel and Lending Standards Surveys: Implications for the Effectiveness of Unconventional Monetary Policies." Working Paper.

Financial Crisis Inquiry Commission [FCIC]. 2011. *The Financial Crisis Inquiry Report.* Washington, DC: U.S. Government Printing Office.

Fingleton, Eamonn. 2012. "The Myth of Japan's Failure." *New York Times*, January 6.

Fischer, Stanley. 2015. "Monetary Policy Lessons and the Way Ahead." Talk at the Economic Club of New York, March 23.

Fischer, Stanley. 2001. "Exchange Rate Regimes: Is the Bipolar View Correct?" *Journal of Economic Perspectives* 15 (Spring): 3–24.

Fischer, Stanley. 1998. "The Asian Crisis and the Changing Role of the IMF." *Finance and Development* 35 (June): 2–5.

Forbes, Kristin, Ida Hjortsoe, and Tsvetelina Nenova. 2015. "The Shocks Matter: Improving Our Estimates of Exchange Rate Pass-Through." External MPC Unit, Discussion Paper 43, November.

Forder, James. 2000. "Central Bank Independence: Is There a Shred of Evidence? Review." *International Finance* 3(1): 167–85.

Frankel, Jeffrey. 1998. "No Single Currency Regime is Right for All Countries or at All Times." *Essays in International Finance* 215 (December).

Freedman, Charles, Philip R. Lane, Rafael Repullo, and Klaus Schmidt-Hebbel. 2011. "External Evaluation of the Directorate General Research of the European Central Bank." At www.ecb.int/pub/pdf/other/ecbresearchevaluationfinalen.pdf.

Freedman, Lawrence. 2014. *Strategy: A History.* Oxford: Oxford University Press.

Freytag, Andreas. 2001. "Does Central Bank Independence Reflect Monetary Commitment Properly? Methodical Considerations." *Banca Nazionale del Lavoro Quarterly Review* 217 (June): 181–208.

Friedman, Milton. 2002. *Capitalism and Freedom*, 40th ed. Chicago: University of Chicago Press.

Friedman, Milton. 1993. "The Plucking Model of Business Cycle Fluctuations Revisited." *Economic Inquiry* 31 (April): 171–77.

Friedman, Milton. 1992. *Money Mischief.* New York: Houghton Mifflin Harcourt.

Friedman, Milton. 1977. "Nobel Lecture: Inflation and unemployment." *Journal of Political Economy* 85: 451–72.

Friedman, Milton. 1972."Have Monetary Policies Failed?" *American Economic Review* 62(2): 11–18.

Friedman, Milton. 1964. "Monetary Studies of the National Bureau: The National Bureau Enters its 45th Year." 44th Annual Report. Cambridge, MA: National Bureau of Economic Research.

Gagnon, Joseph. 2016. "Quantitative Easing: An Underappreciated Success." Peterson Institute for International Economics policy Brief, PB16-4, April.

Galati, Gabriele, and Richhild Moessner. 2014. "What Do We Know About the Effects of Macroprudential Policy?" DNB working paper 440, Netherlands Central Bank.

GAO. 1996. "Mexico's Financial Crisis: Origins, Assistance, and Initial Efforts to Recover." GAO/GGD-95-96, February 23.

Geithner, Timothy. 2014. *Stress Test.* New York: Broadway Books.

Geithner, T. F. 2016. "Are We Safer? The Case for Strengthening the Bagehot Arsenal." Per Jacobsson Lecture, Annual Meeting of the International Monetary Fund and World bank Group, October 8, 2016.

Giannone, Domenico, Lucrezia Reichlin, and David Small. 2008. "Nowcasting: The Real-Time Informational Content of Macroeconomic Data." *Journal of Monetary Economics* 55: 665–76.

Giavazzi, Francseco, and Frederic S. Mishkin. 2006. "An Evaluation of Swedish Monetary Policy Between 1995 and 2005." Reports from the Riksdag 2006/07:RFR1, Committee on Finance, November 28.

Gieve, Sir John. 2008. "Learning from the Financial Crisis." Speech at the European Business School London, Europe in the World Lecture Panel, November 19.

Gilchrist, Simon, and John V. Leahy. 2002. "Monetary Policy and Asset Prices." *Journal of Monetary Economics* 49: 75–97.

Gilovich, Thomas, and Lee Ross. 2015. *The Wisest One in the Room*. New York: Free Press.

Gonzáles-Páramo, José Manuel. 2011. "The ECB's Monetary Policy During the Crisis." Closing speech at the Tenth Economic Policy Conference, Málaga, October 21.

Goodfriend, Marvin. 2016. "The Case for Unencumbering Interest Rate Policy at the Zero Bound." In *Designing Resilient Monetary Policy Frameworks for the Future*, Symposium of the Federal Reserve Bank of Kansas City, August 26.

Goodfriend, Martin, and Mervyn King. 2015. "Review of the Riksbank's Monetary Policy." Riksbank, Stockholm, January.

Goodhart, Charles, and Jean-Charles Rocher. 2011. "Evaluation of the Riksbank's Monetary Policy and Work with Financial Stability, 2005-2010." Reports from the Riksdag 2010/11:RFR5, Committee on Finance, August 30.

Gordon, Robert J. 2012. "Is U.S. Economic Growth Over? Faltering Innovation Confronts the Six Headwinds." NBER Working Paper 18315, August.

Gorodnichenko, Yuriy. 2010. "Endogenous Information, Menu Costs and Inflation Persistence." Working Paper, University of California, Berkeley, November.

Graefe, Andreas, J. Scott Armstrong, Randall J. Jones Jr., and Alfred G. Cuzáne. 2014. "Combining Forecasts: An Application to Elections." *International Journal of Forecasting* 30: 43–54.

Greenspan, Alan. 2010. "The Crisis." Tall given at Brookings Institution Conference, March 9.

Greenspan, Alan. 2005. Testimony. Federal Reserve Board, Semiannual Monetary Policy Report to the Congress before the Committee on Banking, Housing, and Urban Affairs. U.S. Senate, February 16.

Greenspan, Alan. 1999. "Currency, International Reserves and Debt." World Bank Conference on Recent Trends in International Reserves Management, 29 April.

Grilli, Vittorio, Donato Masciandaro, Guido Tabellini, Edmond Malinvaud, and Marco Pagano. 1991. "Political and Monetary Institutions and Public Financial Policies in the Industrial Countries." *Economic Policy* 6 (October): 241–392.

Guidotti, P., F. Sturzenegger, and A. Villar. 2004. "On the Consequences of Sudden Stops." *Economia* 4 (2): 171–203.

Gurley, John G., and Edward S. Shaw. 1960. *Money in a Theory of Finance*. Ann Arbor: University of Michigan Press.

Hall, Robert E. 2013. "The Routes In and Out of the Zero Lower Bound." In *The Global Dimensions of Monetary Policy*, Federal Reserve Bank of Kansas City Economic Policy Symposium, Kansas City Federal Reserve, 1–36.

Hamilton, James. 2010. "Macroeconomics and ARCH." In *Festschrift in Honor of Robert Engle*, ed. T. Bollerslev, J. Russell, and M. Watson, 79–96. Oxford: Oxford University Press.

Hannoun, Hervé. 2012. "Monetary Policy in the Crisis: Testing the Limits of Monetary Policy." Speech at the 47th SEACEN Governors' Conference, February 12–14.

Hansen, A. H. 1941. *Fiscal Policy and Business Cycles*. London: Allen and Unwin.

Havranek, Tomas, and Marek Rusnak. 2013. "Meta-Analysis of Monetary Policy Lags." *International Journal of Central Banking* 9 (December): 39–75.

Hayek, Friedrich. 2008. *The Road to Serfdom*. London and New York. (First published in 1944 by George Routledge & Sons.)

He, Zhongfang. 2010. "Evaluating the Effect of the Bank of Canada's Conditional Commitment Policy." Bank of Canada (Ottawa). Discussion Paper 2010-11.

Herndon, Thomas, Michael Ash, and Robert Pollin. 2013. "Does High Public Debt Consistently Stifle Economic Growth? A Critique of Reinhart and Rogoff." *Cambridge Journal of Economics* 46 (December): 1–23.

Hicks, John. 1967. *Critical Essays on Monetary Theory*. Oxford: Oxford University Press.

Hilsenrath, Jon. 2016. "Years of Fed Missteps Fueled Disillusion with the Economy and Washington." *Wall Street Journal*, August 26.

Ho, Corrinne. 2010. "Implementing Monetary Policy in the 2000s: Operating Procedures in Asia and Beyond." In *Challenges in Central Banking*, ed. P. L. Siklos, M. T. Bohl, and M. E. Wohar, 83–117. Cambridge, MA: Cambridge University Press.

Holmes, Douglas R. 2014. *Economy of Words*. Chicago: Chicago University Press.

Independent Evaluation Office. 2011. *Research at the IMF: Relevance and Utilization*. Washington, DC: International Monetary Fund.

International Monetary Fund [IMF]. 2016. *World Economic Outlook: Subdued Demand: Symptoms and Remedies*. Washington, DC: IMF.

International Monetary Fund [IFM]. 2013a. *Unconventional Monetary Policies – Recent Experience and Prospects*. Washington, DC: IMF.

International Monetary Fund [IMF]. 2013b. "The Functions and Impact of Fiscal Councils." Policy Paper, July 16.

International Monetary Fund [IMF]. 2006. "Ireland: Financial System Stability Assessment Update." Country Report 06/292, August.

International Monetary Fund [IMF]. 2002. *World Economic Outlook*. Washington, DC: IMF.

Irwin, Neil. 2013. *The Alchemists*. New York: Penguin.

Issing, Otmar. 2008. *The Birth of the Euro*. Cambridge: Cambridge University Press.

Issing, Otmar. 2005. "Communication, Transparency, Accountability: Monetary Policy in the Twenty-First Century." *Review of the Federal Reserve Bank of St. Louis*, (March/April): 65–83.

Issing, Otmar. 2003. "Monetary and Financial Stability: Is There a Trade-off?" Speech at the European Central Bank Conference on Monetary Stability and the Business Cycle, March 28–29. At www.ecb.europa.eu/press/key/date/2003/html/sp030329.en.html.

Ito, Tatsuo, and Takashi Nakamichi. 2015. "Bank of Japan Delays Timing of Hitting Price Target." *Wall Street Journal*, December 1.

James, Harold. 2012. *Making the European Monetary Union*. Cambridge, MA: Harvard University Press.

Jeanne, Olivier, and Romain Rancière. 2006. "The Optimal Level of International Reserves for Emerging Market Countries: Formulas and Applications." IMF Working Paper 06/229, October.

Jobst, Andreas, and Huidan Lin. 2016. "Negative Interest Rate Policy (NIRP): Implications for Monetary Transmission and Bank Profitability in the Euro Area." IMF Working Paper 16/172, August.

Johnson, M. H., and R. E. Keleher. 1996. *Monetary Policy, A Market Price Approach*. Westport, CT: Greenwood Publishing Group.

Joyce, Michael, David Miles, Andrew Scott, and Dimitri Vayanos. 2012. "Quantitative Easing and Unconventional Monetary Policy – An Introduction." *Economic Journal* 122 (November): F271–F288.

Kanaya, Akihiro, and David Woo. 2000. "The Japanese Banking Crisis of the 1990s: Sources and Lessons." IMF Working Paper 00/7, January.

Karagedikli, Özer, and Pierre L. Siklos. 2013. "A Bridge Too Far? RBNZ Communication, The Forward Interest Rate Track and the Exchange Rate." In *Central Bank Transparency, Decision-Making, and Governance: The Issues, Challenges, and Case Studies*, ed. P. L. Siklos and J.-E. Sturm, 273–309. Cambridge, MA: MIT Press.

Karni, Ed. 1979. "Review of 'The Theory of Money' by Jürg Niehans." *Journal of Political Economy* 87 (February): 217–20.

Kay, John. 2015. "Absurd Roots of Modern Regulatory Practice." *Financial Times*, December 22.

Kahneman, Daniel. 2011. *Thinking, Fast and Slow*. New York: Farrar, Straus and Giroux.

King, Mervyn. 1997. "Changes in UK Monetary Policy: Rules and Discretion in Practice." *Journal of Monetary Economics* 39: 81–97.

Kiyotaki, Nobuhiro, and John Moore. 1997. "Credit Cycles." *Journal of Political Economy* 105 (April): 211–48.

Koo, Richard C. 2015. *The Escape from Balance Sheet Recession and the QE Trap*. New York: John Wiley.

Koo, Richard C. 2008. *The Holy Grail of Macro Economics*. New York: John Wiley.

Korinek, Anton. 2011. "The New Economics of Prudential Controls." *IMF Economic Review* 59(3): 523–61.

Kose, M. Ayhan, Christopher Otrok, and Eswar Prasad. 2010. "Global Business Cycles: Convergence or Decoupling?" Working Paper, April.

Krippner, Leo. 2015. *Zero Lower Bound Term Structure Modelling*. London: Palgrave Macmillan.

Krugman, Paul. 2015a. "The Not-So-Bad Economy." *New York Times*, December 7.

Krugman, Paul. 2015b. "Rethinking Japan." *New York Times*, October 20.

Krugman, Paul. 2014. "Inflation Targets Reconsidered." Draft paper for the ECB Sintra Conference, May.

Krugman, Paul. 1998. "It's Baaack: Japan's Slump and the Return of the Liquidity Trap", Brookings Papers on Economic Activity 2: 137-187.

Kuttner, K., and A. Posen. 2004. "The Difficulty of Discerning What's Too Tight? Taylor Rules and Japanese Monetary Policy." *North American Journal of Economics and Finance* 15(1): 53–74.

Kydland, Finn, and Edward Prescott. 1977. "Rules Rather Than Discretion: The Inconsistency of Optimal Plans." *Journal of Political Economy* 85 (June): 473–92.

Lagos, Ricardo. 2006. "Inside and Outside Money." Federal Reserve Bank of Minneapolis, Staff Report 374.

Laidler, David. 2011. "The Monetary Economy and the Economic Crisis." Center for the History of Political Economy Working Paper 2011-04.

Lam, W. Raphael. 2011. "Bank of Japan's Monetary Easing Measures: Are They Powerful and Comprehensive." IMF Working Paper 11/264, November.

Laubach, Thomas, and John C. Williams. 2016. "Measuring the Natural Rate of Interest Redux." *Business Economics* 51: 257–67.

Laubach, Thomas, and John Williams. 2003. "Measuring the Natural Rate of Interest." *Review of Economics and Statistics* 85 (November): 1063–70.

Lewis, Michael. 2010. *The Big Short*. New York: W.W. Norton.

Lombardi, Domenico, and Pierre L. Siklos. 2016. "Benchmarking Macroprudential Policies: An Initial Assessment." *Journal of Financial Stability* 27 (December): 35–49.

Lombardi, Domenico, Pierre L. Siklos, and Samantha St. Amand. 2017. "Government Bond Yields At the Effective Lower Bound: International Evidence." Contemporary Economic Policy, forthcoming.

Lombardi, M., and F. Zhu. 2014. "A Shadow Policy Rate to Calibrate US Monetary Policy at the Zero Lower Bound." BIS Working Paper 452, June.

Lowenstein, Roger. 2015. *America's Bank*. New York: Penguin.

Marsh, David. 2009. *The Euro: The Politics of the New Global Currency*. New Haven, CT: Yale University Press.

Marsh, David. 1993. *The Most Powerful Bank: Inside Germany's Bundesbank*. New York: Random House.

Masson, Paul. 2013. "The Dangers of an Extended Period of Low Interest Rates: Why the Bank of Canada Should Start Raising Them Now." C.D. Howe Institute Commentary No. 381, May.

Mayer, Thomas. 2012. *Europe's Unfinished Currency*. London: Anthem Press.

McCallum, Bennett. 1989. *Monetary Economics: Theory and Policy*. New York: Macmillan.

McCallum, Bennett. 1999. "Issues in the Design of Monetary Policy Rules." In *Handbook of Macroeconomics*, vol. 1, ed. John Taylor and Michael Woodford, 1483–1530. Amsterdam: Elsevier.

McConnell, Margaret M., and Gabriel Perez-Quiros. 2000. "Output Fluctuations in the United States: What Has Changed Since the Early 1980's?" *American Economic Review* 90 (December): 1464–76.

McDonald, Chris. 2015. "When Is Macroprudential Policy Effective?" BIS Working Paper 496, March.

McKinnon, Ronald. 1973. *Money and Capital in Economic Development*. Washington, DC: Brookings Institution.

Mehrling, Perry. 1997. *The Money Interest and the Public Interest, American Monetary Thought 1920-1970*. Cambridge, MA: Harvard University Press.

Meltzer, Allan H. 2013. "What's Wrong With the Federal Reserve: What Would Restore Independence." *Business Economics* 48 (April): 96–103.

Meltzer, Allan H. 2009a. "Inflation Nation." *New York Times*, May 4.

Meltzer, Allan H. 2009b. *A History of the Federal Reserve*, vol. 2. Chicago: Chicago University Press.

Meltzer, Allan H. 2003. *A History of the Federal Reserve*, vol. 1. Chicago: Chicago University Press.

Meyer, L., M. Eichenbaum, D. Gale, A. Levin, and J. McAndrews. 2008. "External Review of Economic Research Activities at the Bank of Canada." At www.bankofcanada.ca/wp-content/uploads/2011/05/ext_review.pdf.

Milesi-Ferretti, Gian Maria, and Assaf Razin. 1996. "Persistent Current Account Deficits: A Warning Signal?" *International Journal of Finance & Economics* 1 (July): 61–81.

Miller, Brett. 2015. "Core Core Means No One Is Sure How to Measure Japan's Inflation." *Bloomberg*, June 7.

Milne, Richard. 2014. "Central Banks: Stockholm Syndrome." *Financial Times*, January 7.

Minsky, Hyman P. 1991. "Macroeconomic Consequences of Financial Crises." In *The Risk of Economic Crisis*, ed. M. Feldstein, 158–66. Chicago: University of Chicago Press.

Morgenson, Gretchen, and Joshua Rosner. 2011. *Reckless Endangerment*. New York: Times Books.

Morris, Stephen, and Hyun Song Shin. 2002. "Social Value of Public Information." *American Economic Review* 92 (December): 1521–34.

Mourlon-Druol, Emmanuel. 2012. *A Europe Made of Money*. Ithaca, NY: Cornell University Press.

Münchau, Wolfgang. 2010. *The Meltdown Years*. New York: McGraw-Hill.

Murray, John. 2013. "Transitioning to More Balanced and Sustainable Growth." Remarks at the Federal Reserve Bank of San Francisco, November 5.

Niehans, Jürg. 1978. *The Theory of Money*. Baltimore, MD: Johns Hopkins University Press.

Nikolsko-Rzhevskyy, Alex, David H. Papell, and Ruxandra Prodan. 2016. "Policy Rule Legislation in Practice." In *Central bank Governance and Oversight Reform*, ed. John Cochrane and John Taylor, 55–107. Stanford, CA: Hoover Institution Press.

Obstfeld, M., J. C. Shambaugh, and A. M. Taylor. 2005. "The Trilemma in History: Tradeoffs among Exchange Rates, Monetary Policies, and Capital Mobility." *Review of Economics and Statistics* 87 (August): 423–38.

Office of Strategic Services. 1944. "Simple Sabotage Field Manual Provisional." January 17.

Olson, Mancur. 1965. *The Logic of Collective Action: Public Goods and the Theory of Goods*. Cambridge, MA: Harvard University Press.

Orphanides, Athanasios. 2013. "Is Monetary Policy Overburdened?" BIS Working Paper 435, December.

Orphanides, Athanasios. 1997. "Monetary Policy Rules Based on Real-Time Data." *American Economc Review* 91(4): 964–85.

Ostrom, Elinor. 2009. "Beyond Markets and States: Polycentric Governance of Complex Economic Systems." Prize Lecture, Workshop in Political Theory and Policy Analysis, Indiana University, December 8.

Ostry, Jonathan D., Atish R. Ghosh, and Marcos Chamon. 2012. "Two Targets, Two Instruments: Monetary an Exchange Rate Policies in Emerging Market Economies." IMF Staff Discussion note, 12/01.

Padoa-Schioppa, Tommaso. 2004. *The Euro and its Central Bank*. Cambridge, MA: MIT Press.

Palmer, Randall, and Leah Schnurr. 2016. "Bank of Canada's Rate Cut Validated, But Market Still Wary of Stephen Poloz's Style." *National Post*, January 7.

Pang, Ke, and Pierre L. Siklos. 2016. "Macroeconomic Consequences of the Real-Financial Nexus: Imbalances and Spillovers Between China and the U.S." *Journal of International Money and Finance* 65 (July): 195–212.

Parkin, Michael. 1980. "Oil Push Inflation?" *Banca Nazionale del Lavoro Review* 133 (June): 163–85.

Pescatori, Andrea, Damiano Sandri, and John Simon. 2014. "Debt and Growth: Is There a Magic Threshold?" IMF Working Paper 14/34, February.

Pilling, David. 2013. "Three Arrows and Five Rings: Abe's Inflationary Quest." *Financial Times*, September 11.

Piris, Jean-Claude. 2012. *The Future of Europe*. Cambridge: Cambridge University Press.

Plosser, Charles. 2014. "Influencing Expectations in the Conduct of Monetary Policy." Speech at the 2014 Bank of Japan – Institute for Monetary and Economic Studies Conference on Monetary Policy in a Post-Financial Crisis Era, May 28.

Poloz, Stephen. 2016. "Life After Liftoff: Divergence and U.S. Monetary Policy Normalization." Speech at the Mayor's Breakfast Series, Ottawa, January 7.

Poloz, Stephen. 2015. "Central Bank Credibility and Policy Normalization." Remarks at the Canada-United Kingdom Chamber of Commerce, London, March 26.

Poloz, Stephen. 2014. "Float of the Loonine." Remarks at the Société de development économique de Drummodnville, September 16.

Posen, Adam. 1995. "Declarations Are Not Enough: Financial Sector Sources of Central Bank Independence." *NBER Macroeconomics Annual* 10: 253–74. Cambridge, MA: MIT Press.

Rawdanowicz, Lukasz, Romain Bouis, and Shingo Watanabe. 2013. "The Benefits and Costs of Highly Expansionary Monetary Policy." Economics Department Working Paper 1082, OECD, Paris.

Redelmeier, Donald A., and Daniel Kahneman. 1996. "Patients' Memories of Painful Medical Treatments: Real-Time and Retrospective Evaluations of Two Minimally Invasive Procedures." *Pain* 66 (July): 3–8.

Reinhart, Carmen, and K. Rogoff (with Carmen M. Reinhart and Vincent R. Reinhart). 2012. "Public Debt Overhangs: Advanced-Economy Episodes Since 1800." *Journal of Economic Perspectives* 26 (3) (Summer): 69–86.

Reinhart, Carmen, and K. Rogoff. 2004. "The Modern History of Exchange Rate Arrange ments: A Reinterpretation." *Quarterly Journal of Economics* 119 (1): 1–48.

Reinhart, Carmen M., and Kenneth S. Rogoff. 2010. "Growth in a Time of Debt." *American Economic Review Papers and Proceedings* 100 (May): 573–78.

Reinhart, Carmen M., and Kenneth S. Rogoff. 2009. *This Time Is Different*. Princeton, NJ: Princeton University Press.

Reis, Ricardo. 2015. "QE in the Future: The Central Bank's Balance Sheet in a Fiscal Crisis." Paper presented at the 16th Jacques Polak Annual Research Conference, November 5–6.

Rey, Hélène. 2014. "Dilemma Not Trilemma: The Global Financial Cycle and Monetary Policy Independence." Speech on Global Dimensions of Unconventional Monetary Policy, Economic Symposium, Federal Reserve Bank of Kansas City, August, and General Discussion.

Riksbank. 2014. Minutes of the Monetary Policy Meeting, December 15. Sveriges Riksbank, Stockholm.

Roach, Stephen. 2009. "The Case Against Bernanke." *Financial Times*, August 25.

Roberds, William, and François Velde. 2016. "The Descent of Central Banks (1400-1815)." In *Central Banks at a Crossroads*, ed. M. D. Bordo, Ø. Eitrheim, M. Flandreau, and Jan Qvigstad, 18–61. Cambridge: Cambridge University Press.

Rogoff, Kenneth. 2008. "And the Lesser Evil is...Inflation." *Globe and Mail*, December 2.

Roosevelt, Franklin. 1932. Address at Oglethorpe University, May 22.

Roubini, Nouriel. 2008. "Warning: More Doom Ahead." *Foreign Policy* (October 2, /foreignpolicy.com/2009/10/02/warning/more-more-doom-ahead/).

Roubini, Nouriel, and Stephen Mihm. 2010. *Crisis Economics: A Crash Course in the Future of Finance*. New York: Penguin.

Rudebusch, Glenn. 2002. "Term Structure Evidence on Interest Rate Smoothing and Monetary Policy Inertia." *Journal of Monetary Economics* 49 (September): 1161–87.

Sack, Brian. 1998. "Uncertainty, Learning, and Gradual Monetary Policy." Finance and Economic Discussion paper 1998-34, July.

Samuelson, Paul. 1991. "Macroeconomic Consequences of Financial Crises." In *The Risk of Economic Crisis,* ed. M. Feldstein, 167–70. Chicago: University of Chicago Press.

Sandbu, Martin. 2015. *Europe's Orphan: The Future of the Euro and the Politics of Debt*. Princeton, NJ: Princeton University Press.

Schaechter, Andrea, Tidiane Kinda, Nina Budina, and Anke Weber. 2012. "Fiscal Rules in Response to the Crisis—Toward the 'Next-Generation' Rules. A New Dataset." IMF Working Paper, WP/12/187.

Schonhardt-Bailey, Cheryl. 2013. *Deliberating American Monetary Policy*. Cambridge, MA: MIT Press.

Schularick, Moritz, and Alan Taylor. 2012. "Credit Booms Gone Bust: Monetary Policy, Leverage Cycles and Financial Crises, 1870-2008." *American Economic Review* 102 (April): 1029–61.

Schwartz, Anna (1995), "Why Financial Stability Depends on Price Stability", *Economic Affairs*, vol. 15–16, 21–25.

Schwartz, Anna. 1988. "Financial Stability and the Federal Safety Net." In *Restructuring Banking and Financial Services in America*, ed. William S. Haraf and Rose Marie Kushneider, 34–62. Washington, DC: American Enterprise Institute.

Schwartz, Anna. 1995, "Why Financial Stability Depends on Price Stability." *Economic Affairs* 15–16: 21–5.

Shambaugh, David. 2013. *China Goes Global*. Oxford: Oxford University Press.

Shiller, Robert. 2000. *Irrational Exuberance*. Princeton, NJ: Princeton University Press.

Shirai, Sayuri. 2013. "Monetary Policy and Forward Guidance in Japan." Speech at the International Monetary Fund and the Board of Governors of the Federal Reserve System, Washington, DC, September 19 and 20, Bank of Japan.

Shirakawa, Masaaki. 2010. "Future of Central Banks and Central Banking." Speech at the International Conference, Institute for Monetary and Economic Studies, Bank of Japan, May 26.

Siklos, Pierre L. 2017 (forthcoming). "The Central Bank Versus Others: What Has the Publication of Inflation Forecasts Wrought?" In *The Handbook of Central Banking*, ed. D. G. Mayes, P. L. Siklos, and J.-E. Sturm. Oxford: Oxford University Press.

Siklos, Pierre L. 2016a. "Has Monetary Policy Changed? How the Crisis Shifted the Ground Under Central Banks." Unpublished manuscript.

Siklos, Pierre L. 2016b. "Sixty years of FOMC Minutes: Quantifying and Estimating Their Macroeconomic Consequences." Unpublished manuscript.

Siklos, Pierre L. 2014a. "The Global Financial Crisis and Central Bank Speak." In *Communication and Language Analysis in the Corporate World*, ed. R. P. Hart, 293–314. Hershey, PA: IGI Global.

Siklos, Pierre L. 2014b. "Communications Challenges for Multi-Tasking Central Banks: Evidence and Implications." *International Finance* 17 (Spring): 77–98.

Siklos, Pierre L. 2013a. "Another Fine Mess: Reporting the Governance of International Financial Regulation." CIGI Paper 12.

Siklos, Pierre L. 2013b. "No Coupling, No Decoupling, Only Mutual Interdependence: Business Cycles in Emerging Versus Mature Economies." In *Global Interdependence, Decoupling, and Recoupling*, ed. Yin-Wong Cheung and Frank Westermann, 55-86. Cambridge, MA: MIT Press.

Siklos, Pierre L. 2013c. "Sources of Disagreement in Inflation Forecasts: An International Empirical Investigation." *Journal of International Economics* 90(1): 218–31.

Siklos, Pierre L. 2011. "Central Bank Transparency: An Updated Look." *Applied Economics Letters* 18 (July): 929–33.

Siklos, Pierre L. 2010a. "Inflation Targeting: It's Not Broke, It Doesn't Need Fixing, But Can It Survive?" *Journal of International Commerce, Economics and Policy* 1 (April): 59–80.

Siklos, Pierre L. 2010b. "Revisiting the Coyne Affair: A Singular Event that Changed the Course of Canadian Monetary History." *Canadian Journal of Economics* 43 (August): 994–1015.

Siklos, Pierre L. 2008a. "No Single Definition of Central Bank Independence Is Right for All Countries." *European Journal of Political Economy* 24 (December): 802–16.

Siklos, Pierre L. 2008b, "Inflation Targeting Around the World." *Emerging Markets Finance and Trade* 44 (November-December): 17–37.

Siklos, Pierre L. 2002. *The Changing Face of Central Banking*. Cambridge: Cambridge University Press.

Siklos, Pierre L. 1999. "Pitfalls and Opportunities in the Conduct of Monetary Policy in a World of High Frequency Data", in Information in Asset Prices (Ottawa: Bank of Canada), pp. 361–369.

Siklos, Pierre L. 1997. "Charting a Future for the Bank of Canada: Inflation Targets and the Balance Between Autonomy and Accountability." In *Where We Go From Here: Inflation Targets in Canada's Monetary Policy Regime*, ed. D. E. W. Laidler, 101–84. Toronto: C.D. Howe Institute.

Siklos, Pierre L., ed. 1994. *Varieties of Monetary Reforms: Lessons and Experiences on the Road to Monetary Union*. Boston: Kluwer Academic.

Siklos, Pierre L., and Andrew Spence. 2010. "Faceoff: Should the Bank of Canada Release its Projections of the Interest Rate Path? – The Cases For and Against." C.D. Howe Institute Commentary, October.

Siklos, Pierre L., and Anders Vredin. 2013. *Evaluation of MNB Research: A Review of the Research Function at the National Bank of Hungary*. Budapest: National Bank of Hungary.

Siklos, Pierre L., and Mark E. Wohar. 2005. "Estimating Taylor Rules: An Unbalanced regression?" In *Advances in Econometrics: Econometric Analysis of Financial Time Series*, ed. T. Fomby and D. Terrell, 239–76. Amsterdam: Elsevier.

Sims, Christopher A. 2016. "Fiscal Policy, Monetary Policy and Central Bank Independence." In *Designing Resilient Monetary Policy Frameworks for the Future*, Symposium of the Federal Reserve Bank of Kansas City, 26 August.

Sims. Christopher A. 2015. "Rational Inattention and Monetary Economics." In *Handbook of Monetary Policy*. Amsterdam: Elsevier, forthcoming.

Sinn, Hans-Werner. 2014. *The Euro Trap*. Oxford: Oxford University Press.

Smethurst, R. 2009. *From Foot Soldier to Finance Minister: Takahashi Korekiyo, Japan's Keynes*. Cambridge, MA: Harvard University Press.

Smith, J., and K. F. Wallis. 2009. "A Simple Explanation of the Forecast Combination Puzzle." *Oxford Bulletin of Economics and Statistics* 71: 331–55.

Soble, Jonathan. 2013. "Reluctant BoJ Given Deflation-Beating Role." *Financial Times*, January 22.

Söderlind, Paul, and Lars Svensson. 1997. "New Techniques to Extract Market Expectations from Financial Instrument." *Journal of Monetary Economics* 40 (October): 383–429.

Sorkin, Andrew Ross. 2009. *Too Big to Fail*. New York: Viking.

Staiger, Douglas, James Stock, and Mark Watson. 1997. "How Precise Are Estimates of the Natural Rate of Unemployment?" In *Reducing Inflation: Motivation and Strategy*, ed. C. Romer and P. Romer, 195–246. Chicago: Chicago University Press.

Stein, Jeremy C. 2014. "Incorporating Financial Stability Considerations into a Monetary Policy Framework." Remarks at the International Forum on Monetary Policy, Washington, DC, March 21.

Stein, Jeremy C. 2013. "Overheating in Credit Markets: Origins, Measurement, and Policy Responses." Speech at the research symposium on Restoring Household Financial Stability After the Great Recession: Why Household Balance Sheet Matter, St. Louis, February 7.

Stein Jeremy C., and Adi Sunderam. 2016. "The Fed, the Bond Market, and Gradualism in Monetary Policy." Unpublished manuscript, Harvard University.

Stock, James H., and Mark W. Watson. 2003. "Has the Business Cycle Changed? Evidence and Explanations." In *Monetary Policy and Uncertainty*. Federal Reserve Bank of Kansas City Symposium, Jackson Hole, WY, August 28–30.

Stock, James H., and Mark W. Watson. 2001. "Vector Autoregressions." *Journal of Economic Perspectives* 15 (Fall): 101–15.

Summers, Lawrence H. 2015. "The Global Economy Is in Serious Danger." *New York Times*, October 7.

Summers, Lawrence H. 2014. "U.S. Economic Prospects: Secular Stagnation, Hysteresis, and the Zero Lower Bound." *Business Economics* 49(2): 65–73.

Summers, Lawrence H. 1991. "Macroeconomic Consequences of Financial Crises." In *The Risk of Economic Crisis*, ed. M. Feldstein, 135–82. Chicago: University of Chicago Press.

Svensson, Lars E. O. 2015. "Forward Guidance." *International Journal of Central Banking* (September): 19–64.

Svensson, Lars E. O. 2013. "Some Lessons from Six Years of Practical Inflation Targeting." CEPR Discussion Paper 9756.

Svensson, Lars E. O. 2011. "Inflation Targeting." In *Handbook of Monetary Economics*, vol. 3B, ed. B. M. Friedman and M. Woodford, pp. 1237–1302. Amsterdam: Elsevier.

Svensson, Lars E. O. 2009. "Inflation Targeting." In *The New Palgrave Dictionary of Economics*, 2nd ed., ed Stephen N. Durlauf and Lawrence E. Blume, 1237–1302. Palgrave Macmillan.

Svensson, Lars E. O. 2006. "Social Value of Public Information: Comment. Morris and Shin (2002) Is Actually Pro-Transparency, Not Con." *American Economic Review* 96 (March): 448–52.

Swanson, Eric, and John C. Williams. 2014a. "Measuring the Effect of the Zero Lower Bound on Yields and Exchange Rates in the U.K. and Germany." Federal Reserve Bank of San Francisco Working Paper 2013-21, August.

Swanson, Eric, and John C. Williams. 2014b. "Measuring the Effect of the Zero Lower Bound on Medium and Longer-Term Interest Rates." *American Economic Review* 104 (October): 3154–85.

Taleb Nassim. 2007. *The Black Swan*. New York: Random House.

Taylor, John B. 2012. "Why We Still Need to Read Hayek." The Hayek Lecture, May 31, New York.

Taylor, John B. 2011. "Macroeconomic Lessons from the Great Deviation." In *NBER Macroeconomics Annual 2010*, ed. D. Acemoglu and M. Woodford, 387–95. Cambridge, MA: MIT Press.

Taylor, John B. 2009a. "The Financial Crisis and the Policy Responses: An Empirical Analysis of What Went Wrong." NBER Working Paper 14631, January.

Taylor, John B. 2009b. *Getting Off Track*. Stanford, CA: Hoover Institution Press.

Taylor, John B. 1999. *Monetary Policy Rules*. Chicago: University of Chicago Press for NBER.

Taylor, John B. 1998. "Monetary Policy and the Long Boom." *Review of the Federal Reserve Bank of St. Louis* 80 (December): 3–12.

Taylor, John B. 1993. "Discretion Versus Policy Rules in Practice." In *Carnegie-Rochester Conference Series on Public Policy*, 39, 195–214. Amsterdam: North-Holland.

Tenbrunsel, Ann, and Jordan Thomas. 2015. "The Street, The Bull and the Crisis: A Survey of the U.S. and U.K. Financial Services Industry." Report by the University of Notre dame and Labaton Sucharow LLP, May.

Tetlock, Philip E., and Dan Gardner. 2015. *Superforecasting: The Art and Science of Prediction*. New York: Penguin Random House.

Teulings, Coen, and Richard Baldwin. 2014. *Secular Stagnation: Facts, Causes and Cures*. London: CEPR.

Thaler, Richard. 2013. *Misbehaving*. New York: W.W. Norton.

Thiessen, Gordon. 2001. The Thiessen Lectures: Lectures delivered by Gordon G. Thiessen, Governor of the Bank of Canada 1994 to 2001. At www.bankofcanada.ca/wp-content/uploads/2010/07/thiessen-eng-book.pdf.

Tinbergen, J. 1952. *On the Theory of Economic Policy*. Amsterdam: North-Holland.

Timberlake, Richard H. 1993. *Monetary Policy in the United States*. Chicago: University of Chicago Press.

Tucker, Paul. 2006. "Reflections on Operating Inflation Targeting." Speech at the Graduate school of Business, University of Chicago, May 25.

van der Cruijsen, Carin, David-Jan Jansen, and Jakob de Haan. 2015. "How Much Does the Public Know About the ECB's Monetary Policy? Evidence from a Survey of Dutch Consumers." *International Journal of Central Banking* 11(4): 169–218.

Velde, François. 2009. "The Recession of 1937 – A Cautionary Tale." Federal Reserve Bank of Chicago. *Economic Perspectives* 4: 16–37.

Volcker, Paul. 1991. "Financial Crises and the Macroeconomy." In *The Risk of Economic Crisis*, ed. M. Feldstein, 174–79. Chicago: University of Chicago Press.

Volcker, Paul. 1984. "Remarks" by Paul A. Volcker at the 78th Commencement of the American University, Washington, D.C., January 29. Available from /fraser.stlouisfed.org/files/docs/historical/volcker/Volcker_19840129.pdf

Volcker, Paul, and Toyoo Gyohten. 1992. *Changing Fortunes: The World's Money and the Threat to American Leadership*. New York: Times Books.

Weidmann, Jens. 2014. Dinner Speech at the German-British Chamber of Industry & Commerce Annual Dinner 2014. At www.bundesbank.de/Redaktion/EN/Reden/2014/2014_07_23_weidmann.html.

Wessel, David. 2009. *In Fed We Trust*. New York: Crown Business Books.

White, William. 2006. "Is Price Stability Enough?" BIS Working Paper 205, April.

Wiederholt, Mirko. 2010. "Rational Inattention." In *The New Palgrave Dictionary of Economics*, ed. Stephen N. Durlauf and Lawrence E. Blume, 1–6. Basingstoke, UK: Palgrave Macmillan.

Williams, John C. 2016. "Presentation at U.S. Monetary Policy Forum." New York, February 26. At www.frbsf.org/our-district/press/presidents-speeches/williams-speeches/2016/february/language-after-liftoff-fed-communication-away-from-the-zero-lower-bound/.

Williams, John C. 2013. "Lessons from the Financial Crisis for Unconventional Monetary Policy." Federal Reserve Bank of San Francisco, panel discussion at the NBER Conference, October 18.

Wilson, Woodrow. 1917. "Address of the President of the United States to the Senate." January 22.

Wolf, Martin. 2015. "The Challenges of Central Bank Divergence." *Financial Times*, December 8.

Wolf, Martin. 2008. *Fixing Global Finance*. Baltimore, MD: Johns Hopkins University Press.

Wood, Christopher. 2008. "The Fed Is Out of Ammunition." *Wall Street Journal*, November 24.

Woodford, Michael. 2012. "Methods of Policy Accommodation at the Interest-Rate Lower bound.", Federal Reserve Bank of Kansas City Economic Policy Symposium. *The Changing Policy Landscape*, 185–288. Kansas City: Federal Reserve Bank of Kansas City.

Woodford, Michael. 2003. *Interest & Prices*. Princeton, NJ: Princeton University Press.

Wu, Jing Cythia. and Fan Dora Xia. 2016. "Measuring the Macroeconomic Impact of Monetary Policy at the Zero Lower Bound." *Journal of Money, Credit and Banking* 48 (March-April): 253–91.

Xiaochuan, Zhou. 2009. "Reform the International Monetary System." People's Bank of China, March 23. At www.pbc.gov.cn/english/detail.asp?col=6500&id=178.

Yamaoka, H., and M. Syed. 2010. "Managing the Exit: Lessons from Japan's Reversal of Unconventional Monetary Policy." IMF Working Paper 10/114, May.

Yellen, Janet L. 2016. "The Federal Reserve's Monetary Policy Toolkit: Past, Present, and Future." Speech at symposium on Designing Resilient Monetary Policy Frameworks for the Future," sponsored by the Federal Reserve Bank of Kansas City, August 26, Jackson Hole, WY.

Yellen, Janet L. 2014a. "Monetary Policy and Financial Stability." Remarks at the 2014 Michel Camdessus Central Banking Lecture, Washington, DC, July 2.

Yellen, J. L. 2014b, "Monetary Policy and Economic Recovery." Speech at the Economic Club of New York, April 16.

Zarnowitz, Victor. 1992. "The Regularity of Business Cycles." In *Business Cycles: Theory, History, Indicators, and Forecasting*, ed. Victor Zarnowitz, 232–64. Chicago: University of Chicago Press.

INDEX